TECHNICAL CHANGE AND INDUSTRIAL TRANSFORMATION

The book can be read in two ways, either as a theoretical analysis of the patterns of technical change in modern economies with an illustrative case study on the semiconductor industry, or, conversely, as a reconstruction of the history of that industry, which is at the core of the microelectronics revolution, backed by detailed and unorthodox theoretical premises.

A general theoretical task is the explanation of the determinants, procedures and directions of technical change, and its effects on industrial performance, structural change and international trade. Despite powerful economic inducements, technology maintains rules and a momentum of its own which binds the direction of technological developments.

There are, it is suggested, *technological paradigms* which define clusters of *technological trajectories* of progress. Scientific advances together with various institutional factors contribute to determine the timing and the nature of new paradigms, while markets perform as important selection environments.

Innovative activities show varying degrees of private appropriability and determine the patterns of lags and leads between firms. Technological *asymmetries* between firms play a paramount role in explaining industrial performance, including prices, margins, profit rates. The assumptions of traditional industrial economics have to be reversed: instead of starting from an assumption of identity between all firms and then introduce oligopolies as a complication, one should begin from the opposite assumption. Technical change makes every firm different: a "competitive environment" is that particular case whereby the forces of technological diffusion are powerful enough to wither away innovation-based asymmetries.

The analysis can be extended to account for international trade and international investment. Technological asymmetries at the international level define what classical economists called absolute advantages (and disadvantages) and thus also the configuration of the universe within which cost-based and, first of all, wage-based adjustments take place.

This book undertakes a detailed analysis of the effects of technical change on the patterns of transformation of industries, in both a closed-economy and an open-economy context, and in many ways can be considered an exploration into the microfoundations of economic dynamics.

The case of the semiconductor industry is not only an illustration of the hypotheses and the methodology but is also of interest in its own right. The analysis of the process of birth of the specific semiconductor paradigm, with the contextual impact of American military and space policies, helps in explaining the American technological leadership. Innovation-based competition, cumulativeness of technological advantages, learning by doing, "technology-gap" patterns of trade and investment are factors which through time produced the American leadership over Europe. A different case is Japan; there, the book shows, important institutional and policy factors fostered a very rapid catching-up process ultimately leading to a joint Japanese–American leadership in the world semiconductor oligopoly which has been forming throughout the 1970s and early 1980s.

The semiconductor industry is the main engine of transformation of all the industries influenced by microelectronics. Its impact on the user sectors is not confined to ever-improving components at rapidly falling prices, but provides also (and is affected by) a set of untraded technological interdependencies, stimuli, information flows, etc., which shapes the overall pattern of transformation of the electronics industry.

Finally, the book provides a thorough statistical analysis of the semiconductor industry in the major European countries, the USA and Japan, with respect to output, productivity, prices, market shares, trade and investment flows.

———————

Giovanni Dosi is a Research Fellow at the Science Policy Research Unit (SPRU) of the University of Sussex. After graduating at the State University of Milan, he has specialized in economics at ISTAO (Ancona, Italy) and worked on a D.Phil at the University of Sussex. He has written several articles on technical change, the semiconductor industry and macroeconomic issues. He has been a consultant for the OECD, the EEC, and the Italian Energy Commission (ENEA).

His previous work includes a monograph, 'Technical Change and Survival: Europe's Semiconductor Industry'.

TECHNICAL CHANGE
AND INDUSTRIAL
TRANSFORMATION

Giovanni Dosi

St. Martin's Press   New York

All rights reserved. For information, write:
St. Martin's Press, Inc., 175 Fifth Avenue, New York, NY 10010
Printed in Hong Kong
Published in the United Kingdom by The Macmillan Press Ltd
First published in the United States of America in 1984

ISBN 0–312–78775–8

Library of Congress Cataloging in Publication Data

Dosi, Giovanni, 1953–
   Technical change and industrial transformation.
   Includes index.
   1. Technological innovations. 2. Semiconductor
industry—Technological innovations. I. Title.
HD45.D67   1984   338.4′562138152   83–16017
ISBN 0–312–78775–8

Contents

List of Illustrations

List of Tables

Foreword

Professor Christopher Freeman

A perennial problem in the social sciences is the tendency for theoretical models and generalisations to gain acceptance with inadequate empirical evidence or testing, and indeed occasionally with none at all. The difficulties of obtaining and analysing satisfactory evidence are very considerable, and it is often not feasible to conduct controlled experiments. Social scientists are sometimes driven by force of circumstances to use data which do not precisely correspond to their real needs, because of difficulties in classification, response rate, comparability, reliability, and so forth. This presents a continuous and complex challenge to anyone attempting research in this area of industrial economics.

The response to this challenge varies considerably. Some theorists act *as if* the evidence really did exist; some empiricists simply ignore most of the theories and confine themselves to the presentation of whatever published data are available; others substitute the elaboration of mathematical models for the understanding of the real world. Unfortunately these types of response are often encouraged by the pressures towards ideological conformity or a false concept of what constitutes academic 'respectability' and the pattern of a typical academic career.

This book is remarkable for many reasons, but most of all for the integrity, originality and determination with which it confronts this challenge. It is at one and the same time both a major and original contribution to economic theory and a substantial empirical survey of one of the most important and interesting branches of advanced economics – the semiconductor industry. Each part of the book enriches the other, and Giovanni Dosi is to be congratulated for his resistance to the temptation to segregate the two in separate books or papers, or to abandon one or the other field of enquiry.

He has made a root-and-branch attack on the orthodox neoclassical theory of the firm, and one which is in my view unanswerable within the terms of that paradigm. He argues that it is both empirically ridiculous and theoretically untenable to start from the assumption that all agents are equal in their access to technology in any branch of industry and in their capacity to innovate. On the contrary, any satisfactory model of firm behaviour must start from the contrary assumption of a manifestly high degree of inequality and variability, in addition to the uncertainty about the future already recognised in such models as that of Nelson and Winter. Within such a framework the issues of appropriability of new technology, of cumulative learning processes, of technological diffusion, imitation and overtaking can all be approached in a realistic manner as dynamic problems.

The semiconductor industry is an excellent example of this approach. It merits a great deal of attention in its own right as one of the fastest-growing branches of the economy and one which underpins the computer industry, the robot industry and many other industries which are vital to economic performance in the final decades of this century. Giovanni Dosi has been successful in assembling much new information on the development of the industry, which in several important respects takes us beyond the earlier primary work of Golding, Tilton and Sciberras. His work is particularly good in relating product and process innovations to the evolving structure of the industry (Chapters 3 and 4) and to the international environment (Chapter 5). In this respect it goes beyond the work of Nelson and Winter, which, although a massive contribution to economic theory, lacked any detailed empirical evidence.

The history of this industry also illuminates many wider problems of the nature of technical innovation in advanced capitalist economies, such as the role of 'science-push' and 'demand-pull'. Dosi's book is the best original assessment of this tangled controversy which I have ever come across. Finally, it is the best available discussion and comparison of government policies towards the semiconductor industry. These constitute a remarkable achievement and will amply reward the reader who makes the effort necessary to master all parts of a long, but very important book. After the combined onslaught from this book and the earlier work of Nelson and Winter, the theory of industrial economics must now undergo a paradigm change. It can never be the same again.

CHRISTOPHER FREEMAN

Preface

I am certainly not the only one who feels a dramatic uneasiness especially in the field of microeconomics, faced with the dilemma between empiricism without theory or, at best, sophisticated irrelevance. This book is an attempt to suggest some tentative theoretical propositions inherent in exploring how the economic world moves and changes, in the belief that the conflict between theory and evidence can only be resolved through the search for more powerful theoretical models.

The remote origin of some of the questions this book tries to address goes back to my first learning of economics and the feeling of intellectual irritation, facing an articulated construction full of erroneous abstractions and unacceptable ideological fantasies.

The project which inspired this book in the present form was started in 1978, at the University of Sussex, as a D.Phil. degree. It has grown out of research on public policies towards the semiconductor industry, undertaken at the Sussex European Research Centre (SERC) within the 'Industrial Adjustment Project', and has been completed at the Science Policy Research Unit (SPRU), both at the University of Sussex.

The research has been financed at different stages by Fondazione Einaudi, Turin; Ente Einaudi, Rome; Consiglio Nazionale delle Ricerche (CNR), Rome; the Nuffield Foundation, and the Innovation Group of the Science Policy Research Unit, sponsored by the Leverhulme Foundation.

It is impossible to acknowledge all contributors, stimuli and criticisms. Aware of making several injustices, I am forced to thank only a few.

First, I want to mention Michele Salvati, without whom this research would not have been possible, and who taught me, when I was still a philosophy student in Italy, that it is possible to couple rigour and relevance, maintaining the intellectual passion of discovery.

My supervisor at Sussex University, Tibor Barna, invested his trust in this research and has been a sometimes invisible but always very real intellectual challenge.

I want to thank François Dûchene and my previous colleagues at SERC, Geoffrey Shepherd, Daniel Jones and Jürgen Müller: the interchange of ideas within the 'Industrial Adjustment Project' has played an important part in the development of this book.

From the start I have been working in close contact with the Science Policy Research Unit (SPRU), which I later joined. Outside this environment it would have been much harder to grasp the 'state of the art' in the economics of technical change. The intellectual debt toward Chris Freeman emerges throughout this book and the contribution to the theory of technical change I hope to make here shows a clear continuity with his approach. Throughout the research I benefited from frequent discussions with Keith Pavitt and Luc Soete on a great number of theoretical issues. It has been a unique 'context condition' for the development of the ideas in this book. Ed Sciberras introduced me to the world of semiconductors, which, at the beginning, I did not know anything about.

Mick McLean, editor of *Electronics Times*, has been a continuous, valuable source of comments, contacts and criticisms. I used his magazine more than it is explicitly quoted, and – more important – I enjoyed long discussions on wide topics ranging from epistemology to system theory.

Richard Nelson has not only been a source of intellectual inspiration through his writings but also through a long correspondence: his comments contributed to improve and shape more precisely the hypotheses and gave me authoritative encouragement.

Jean-Louis Truel from the University of Paris XIII, in addition to providing information and analyses of the semiconductor industry, tried to prove the interpretative use of some of the hypotheses of this book and forced me to clarify them further. He has also been a very important link with the French economic tradition, which maintains a more 'classical' spirit than the dominant Anglo-Saxon approach and is unfortunately largely neglected in the English-speaking countries (and even in Italy).

A special mention is reserved for my friend Arthur Merin. Despite working in different spheres of social science, it has been surprising and stimulating to discover a similarity at the heart of certain problems. In many fields, undoubted achievements would come from a better general understanding of such topics as the inner dynamics of complex social systems and the relationship between structures and change.

Franco Momigliano, Franco Malerba, William Walker and Margherita Balconi read previous drafts or parts of this work. The final version takes into account their valuable comments. I benefited also from seminars on various aspects of this research held at the University of Sussex, the University of Modena, the University of Strasbourg, Bocconi University (Milan), and the Istituto Ricerche Sociali (Milan). A paper for OECD, partly based on the present work, has been discussed at length with the OECD Secretariat and especially with François Chesnais and Henry Ergas.

The trade model developed in this book has been thoroughly discussed and partly tested within a research project on 'Technology and Italian International Competitiveness', directed by Fabrizio Onida, at Istituto Ricerche Sociali (IRS), Milan, sponsored by the Italian Energy Agency (ENEA).

The final version of the book has been read and commented by my friend Gigi Orsenigo, with whom I shared part of my time in Sussex, in an atmosphere of high intellectual excitement.

Donald Kelly from the office of Technology Assessment and Forecast (OTAF) of the US Department of Commerce and Jerome Mark from the US Bureau of Labor Statistics have been extremely helpful in providing special reports on US patents in semiconductors and statistical information on US electronic sectors, respectively.

It is impossible to mention here all the company and government representatives and experts who were interviewed on the semiconductor industry. Their help has been essential to the empirical part of this research.

I want to express my deep gratitude to SPRU secretaries, especially Fiona Robertson Campbell and Hazel Hobards, who had to go through the typing and editing of endless manuscripts, written in an English which did not quite match Oxbridge standards.

Finally, I gratefully acknowledge the permission granted by Dr T. J. Gordon and Dr T. R. Munson to republish figures 2.2 to 2.4 and by Lexington Books to republish figure 3.7, from Wilson *et al.* (1980).

GIOVANNI DOSI

To Cesi

1 Introduction

This book can be read in two ways, either as a theoretical analysis of the patterns of technical change in modern economies with an illustrative case study on semiconductors, or, conversely, as an industry study with long (and unorthodox) theoretical premises. It has been written in a somewhat modular form so that both the theoretical parts and the empirical investigation are relatively self-contained. Both topics bear a major relevance. The semiconductor industry is at the core of the 'microelectronics revolution', whose impact on the structure of industry and the broader social environment can be compared to that of the fundamental technological innovations which marked an epoch of modern history such as the steam engine or electricity. Technical change, in general, is one of the fundamental engines of economic growth and structural transformation in modern societies.

Facing the task of analysing where technical change comes from and what are its determinants and its effects, one immediately realises the poverty of the theoretical instruments provided by the prevailing economic theory (that written in the textbooks which most economics students have to learn in universities). A random glance at most economic journals highlights how the dominant stream of economic thought is essentially concerned with a static problem of efficient allocation of given resources, and even that is dealt with by means of dubious theoretical hypotheses. The attempt to analyse industrial changes and transformation must confront the painstaking search for an adequate theoretical framework. We tried to analyse, step by step, the process of generation of technical progress, its procedures, its impact on changing industrial structures, the relationship between technical change and oligopoly and the effect of international technological differences on trade and investment flows. The exercise is in many respects an exploration of the microfoundations of economic dynamics. In other words, we address the following question: what are the technological factors and the microeconomic impulses underlying growth and transformation of modern economies? On the broad regularities in macroeconomic change we can find inspiration and methodological guidance in classical economics (that ranging, grosso modo, from the physiocratic thought to Ricardo and Marx, revived, under partly different perspectives, by the 'Keynesian revolution' and what is sometimes referred to as the 'Cambridge School'). One of the fundamental questions of classical economics concerns the long-run determinants of the patterns of growth and change in the macroeconomic environment. The problem of the technological and microeconomic foundations, however, is left relatively unexplored, in two respects. First, technical change is assumed, correctly, as one of the core stylised facts of modern development, without, however, specific investigation of its determinants and its procedures (a partial exception is Marx). Only a few recent contributions in the last two decades provide seminal insights into the question: we will have the chance of discussing the works by Freeman, Nelson, Rosenberg, Utterback and Abernathy, and Sahal. Second, the issue of company behaviour under conditions of technical change and the related issues of the patterns of change and the performance indicators of industrial structures are often neglected or, even when an attempt of analysis is made (such as, for example, in the 'managerial theories' of the firm), one is left with models which can hardly be linked with the broad regularities and patterns of change of the macroeconomic environment. In this field there is, of course, Schumpeter's pioneering analysis of the dynamics of innovation-based competition. In this respect, we shall study how the existence of Schumpeterian competition affects the performance variables of each industry (such as productivity, costs, prices, margins, concentration, market shares). The question is particularly relevant, because it allows us to link context variables such as the trends in technology with the mentioned structural variables which have a direct macroeconomic significance. The model put forward by Sylos-Labini – later discussed at length – attempts a similar linkage whenever technological conditions are primarily defined by size-related economies of scale. We will try to develop a model in more general conditions when there are continuous innovative processes occurring in an industry.

A theoretical crossroad concerns what firms actually do and how they interact with each other under conditions of technical change. We shall analyse the question in detail making extensive use of the seminal models suggested by Nelson and Winter and their 'evolutionary theory of the firm'.

These brief remarks may help to place the analysis about to be undertaken in the context of economic theory, its 'state-of-the-art' and, in our view, its unsolved or badly solved problems. The central question to be analysed can be illustrated by some examples from the natural sciences.

The economic system is a complex environment whereby change and transformation stems from the interaction of its constituent parts, and from partly exogenous variables. In our view there are two such variables of paramount importance: first the evolution of the 'technological system' and second, the system of, *lato sensu*, social relations. It is possible to discuss here only the former.

The environment changes also as a result of the inner interaction of its constituent parts. What is a given set of constraints, possibilities, incentives, from the point of view of an individual actor (say a firm), is also, with respect to the system as a whole, a moving thread of inter-relationships which define its stability and its dynamics. Using a biological metaphor we can consider the relationship between individuals, species and overall environment. At any time the environment can be considered as given for any one individual (and thus it is also a selector of mutations), while the relative patterns of growth of the species, together with the emergence of mutations within them, induce change and transformation in the environment. There are thus two fundamental problems. The first concerns how the environment is made at each point in time, i.e. what is the complex thread of inter-relations which defines that system. For the topics under discussion, this is the question concerning the microfoundations of macroeconomics: what are the regularities in firms' behaviour for given technological conditions which add up to a certain configuration of state variables? The question pertains to statics and accounts for the inner stability and order of the system. The second problem concerns the directions of change in the environment. This clearly relates to dynamics and must take into account the effects of technical change upon growth and transformation patterns.

Classical economics provides us with a powerful methodology to analyse such dynamic factors as the determinants of growth and such general static forces as the tendency towards profit equalisation, the relationship between prices and costs of production, etc. We do not yet have a complete microeconomics consistent with and underpinning macroeconomic regularities. Let us illustrate the question with yet another example. In physics the principles of thermodynamics were discovered well before the development of atomic theory and quantum mechanics. Thermodynamic laws could provide an accurate account of macrostates but were unable to explain what happened within the system to produce such a macrostate. The theory of Brownian motions bridges the micro and the macro, explaining why and how macrostates are in equilibrium or change. 'Classical' macroeconomics can be taken to be similar to 'classical' thermodynamics, in need of a Brownian theory. Note that in this respect the prevailing (neoclassical) economic thought appears to be scientifically regressive in that it is able to tell us only that each particle 'optimises its movements'. The theory is either trivial, whenever there is only one direction for the particle to take, or indeterminate, when the possible directions are numerous and we do not know exactly what each particle is optimising, when, how, etc. Physics obviously never took seriously the paradox of 'Maxwell's demon' allowing all molecules to go in only one definite direction. In economics, on the contrary, we are left with a similar 'theology of the invisible hand' which is taken very seriously indeed.

The economic system is, of course, complex. The patterns of relations between its constituent parts are structured and ordered. We are not so much interested in knowing the precise movements of each individual particle, to which we must grant some degrees of freedom, as in understanding what moves them and the regularities in these movements. In our analysis we shall argue that technical change is the moving force and that a finite and small number of functional relationships and behavioural regularities can be identified. In order to do that we ought to reverse some traditional assumptions of microeconomic analysis. The investigation conventionally starts with the twin hypotheses: (a) let us suppose the absence of technical change and (b) let us suppose that every firm is equal to each other. These hypotheses of traditional theory lead to the construction of the theorems of 'pure competition'. Only at a further stage, by complication, through an 'add-on *ad hoc* procedure' (we borrowed this expression from R. Nelson), differences, i.e. oligopolies, etc. are accounted for. The problem is that bad statics make dynamics impossible. If in physics we started with a gravitational theory ruling out ex-hypothesi that bodies can move and can have different inertial masses it would have become impossible, and even inconceivable, to develop a theory of changing reference systems.

Instead of an initial hypothesis of identity between firms, we shall make precisely the opposite assumption, namely: let us suppose that every firm is different because it is affected in different ways by technical change. The analysis will give a central role to the concept of *asymmetry*, between firms and between countries. From a static point of view we shall study how these asymmetries, related to different innovative and imitative capabilities, affect prices, margins, trade flows and patterns of investment. In other words, the configuration of the industrial system will be explained also by means of the asymmetric position of firms with respect to a 'technological frontier' that we shall define. In this respect free competitive conditions will emerge as a limit case – albeit a very important one. From a dynamic point of view, the analysis will concern how interfirm and international asymmetries change through time as a joint effect of technical change, in the forms of both innovation and imitation, and competitive interactions between firms. The distinctions between statics and dynamics and their reciprocal relationship may be easily illustrated by means of the foregoing physical analogy. Statics, in our case, concern the gravitational forces within a given reference system, i.e. for a given state of technology (more precisely, for a given position of the technological frontier). Dynamics focuses on the case of changing reference systems, which are represented in our case by technical change.

A pre-condition of the investigation of dynamics is a satisfactory account of the procedures and direction of technical change. Too often its interpretation swings between a totally endogenous idea of a ready-to-use black box (money will pay your way in any technological direction and at any rate you wish) or a totally exogenous image (the economic agents are stuck with what scientist and engineers give them). In dominant economic theory, we seem to have the worst of the two worlds, namely a technology which is endogenous in the short-run (via movement along production functions) and exogenous in the long-run (via movements of the production function itself). Even simple common sense would suggest the other way round. Of course, it is not a question of working out a middle-of-the-road compromise. The task of the theory is to study precisely the general conditions which affect exogenous and endogenous technical progress. We will attempt a few steps in this direction and suggest that (relatively) exogenous changes relate to the emergence of new 'technological paradigms', while endogenous change concerns technical progress along the 'trajectories' which these paradigms define.

The approach suggested here focuses on the twin questions of the ('static') configurations of complex economic systems characterised by technical change and their 'dynamic' patterns of transformation. A great number of theoretical elements and stylised facts are well known and established in economic literature. However, their interpretation and their role will often be redefined in the light of this approach.

In this respect, this brief introduction should serve to suggest the *gestalt* which underlies our work. Problems related to systems and system dynamics are certainly very complicated and this work cannot aim at any thorough introduction even to the sub-set of problems related to microanalysis of technical change. We hope, however, to have been able to move a few steps forward and, even more important, point at a theoretical task and at a methodology.

Each chapter is comprised of a first part which is theoretical and a second part analysing the semiconductor industry. The latter provides an excellent case study for methodology and hypotheses. It is a new and fast changing industry. Technical progress plays a major part in its dynamics. Industrial structures transform very quickly. Interfirm and international technological asymmetries are particularly pronounced, while the sources of oligopolistic positions may be seen clearly. In many respects, it is the nearest we can expect to get to the ideal experimental conditions natural scientists can create in their laboratories.

The semiconductor industry, however, maintains a deep interest of its own. The industrial case study will allow the anatomy of the main engine of the microelectronics revolution. After a brief introduction to semiconductor technology we shall discuss in turn how the patterns of technical change observed today came about in the first place, the factors which yielded to an American technological leadership, the Japanese 'catching-up' and the reasons for the European technological weakness (Chapter 2). Chapter 3 will examine the nature of the competitive patterns in the industry, the effects of technical change on industrial structures, pricing behaviours, price and margins levels, the factors affecting entries and concentration, the impact of technical change on productivity and demand. In Chapter 4 we shall extend the analysis to the international scene and account for the determinants of trade and investment flows throughout the history of the industry, which showed a progressive internationalisation and a tendency towards a world oligopoly. Finally, in Chapter 5, some observations on inter-industrial diffusion of semiconductors serve as an introduction to the broader issue of the microelectronics revolution which is affecting manufacturing industry and the entire economy.

The book maintains a somewhat modular nature, so that the theoretical and empirical parts can be read independently. The economist horrified by empirical evidence can read sections 2.1 and 2.2 of Chapter 2, 3.1 to 3.3 in Chapter 3, 4.1 and 4.2 in Chapter 4, while the rest of the chapters still make a relatively self-contained industry case study for these uninterested in any theoretical model. Either strategy, however, will imply a loss, for we believe – paraphrasing the old philosopher – any theory without empirical evidence is empty and any empirical evidence without theory is blind.

2 Trends in Innovation and its Determinants: The Ingredients of the Innovative Process

The history of the discovery of the first transistor and of the fast and far-reaching innovative dynamics in semiconductor products and processes have already been told several times.[1] Here we will just try to interpret the basic features of the patterns of innovation and its determinants.

First, we will suggest a model of the determinants and directions of technical change aiming at a wider generality than a simple interpretation of the technological trends in semiconductors. The semiconductor case, in this respect, may be considered a partial test for the model.[2]

In the light of our theoretical framework we will then discuss the patterns of development of the semiconductor industry and their economic impact. More precisely, we will analyse the establishment of the American technological lead and the factors which induced different technological capabilities in the USA, Europe and Japan.

2.1 THEORIES OF TECHNICAL CHANGE: DEMAND–PULL VS TECHNOLOGY–PUSH

Although everyone recognises that there can be – and generally are – different and contextual origins of inventive activity, in the economic literature there has been a substantial effort to define the common elements among a wide range of inventions and/or innovations,[2] together with the search for some kind of 'prime mover' of inventive activity. In the literature on the subject, one used to define two basic different approaches, the first pointing to market forces as the main determinants of technical change ('demand–pull' theories) and the

7

second defining technology as an autonomous or quasi-autonomous factor, at least in the short run ('technology–push' theories). Such a clear-cut distinction is, of course, hard to make in practice but remains useful for the sake of exposition: there is indeed a fundamental distinction between the two approaches and that is the role attributed to market signals in directing innovative activity and technical changes. It seems to us that this distinction (the role attributed to market signals), although overlapping a great deal with the distinction 'demand–pull' vs. 'technology–push' theories, is indeed the main core of the discussion.

A Critique of 'Demand–pull' Theories

Let us consider first a 'pure' demand–pull theory. As discussed exhaustively in a comprehensive and critical paper by Mowery and Rosenberg (1979), the causal prime mover in those theories is some supposed 'recognition of needs' by the productive units in the market, to which their efforts follow in order to fulfil those needs through their technological activities. This 'pure' market–pull theory would run more or less as follows (both causally and chronologically).

(1) There exist a set of consumption and intermediate goods, at a given time, on the market, embodying different 'needs' by the purchasers. In passing, one must notice – as we shall recall below – that the same definition of 'needs' is quite ambiguous: at the one extreme one may define them in very general 'anthropological' terms (the needs to eat, have shelter, communicate, etc.), but then they express a total indifference to the way they are satisfied and do not have any economic relevance; or, at the other extreme, 'needs' are expressed in relation to the specific means of their satisfaction, but then each 'need' cannot emerge before the basic invention to which it is related.[3]

(2) Consumers (or users) express their preferences about the features of the goods they desire (i.e. the features that fulfil their *needs* the most) through their patterns of demand. This is another way of saying that demand functions are determined by the existence and the forms of utility functions. We may assume now that the pattern of demand changes (i.e. that the demand function shifts upwards or downwards), or just that – which is basically the same – in a growing economy, given the relative prices of the considered commodities, the income elasticities of demand of the latter are different.

(3) The theory would argue that, with a growing income relaxing the budget constraint of the consumers/users, the latter demand propor-

tionally more of the goods which embodied some relatively preferred characteristics (i.e. those which more adequately satisfy their needs).

(4) At this point the producers enter into the picture, realising – through the movements in demand and prices – the revealed needs of the consumers/users: some 'utility dimensions' have a greater weight (there is more *need* for them).

(5) Here the proper innovative process begins, and the successful firms will in the end bring to the market their new/improved goods, allowing the 'market' (as defined above) to monitor their increased capability to fulfil consumers' needs.

Of course, not even the most extreme 'demand–pull' theorist would entirely support this crude view. The basic argument, however, maintains that there *generally exists* a *possibility* of *knowing a priori* (before the invention process takes place) the direction in which the market is 'pulling' the inventive activity of producers, and furthermore that an important part of the 'signalling process' operates through movements in relative prices and quantities. Thus, in this perspective, the innovative process can be placed – although with consistent difficulties – inside the neoclassical framework.[4] With respect to producers, this viewpoint implies that the 'choice sets are given and the outcomes of any choice known'.[5] The assumption of 'known outcomes' could perhaps be relaxed to introduce risk and stochastic variables, but the first assumption has to be maintained (i.e. a given and finite set of choices).

The viewpoints outlined above might be criticised on different levels, namely: (a) the general theory of prices as determined by supply and demand functions; (b) the difficulties of defining demand functions as determined by utility functions and the same feasibility of a 'utility' concept; and (c) the logical and practical difficulties in interpreting the innovative process through this approach.

The first question is undoubtedly the biggest one because it could undermine the entire theory on which this approach is based. This is not the place though to deal with that issue[6] and the discussion will be restricted to the third point.

With respect to this more circumscribed question, some significant problems throw doubts on the entire adequacy of demand-based theories of innovations.

(a) A theory of innovation is supposed to explain not only (and not even primarily) 'incremental' technical progress on the existing products/processes, but first of all it is meant to interpret major and minor technological breakthroughs. As far as the latter are concerned the range of 'potential needs' is nearly infinite and it is difficult to argue that these would-be demands can explain why, in a definite point in time, an invention/innovation occurs.[7]

(b) Even after allowing *a priori* recognition of a 'need', it is difficult to explain with this approach what happens between that recognition by producers and the final outcome of a new product. Either we have to assume a set of technological possibilities already in existence (but then we must wonder why those possibilities have not been exploited before)[8] or we must assume a limited time lag between research and the outcomes of that research. The concept of technology (and, at least indirectly, of science) underlying this approach is of a very versatile and 'responsive' mechanism which can be directed with limited effort and cost in one direction or another. To avoid a crude conception of technology as a 'freely available black-box', there have been some theoretical attempts to consider information as an expensive commodity.[9] Those attempts, while representing a big advance because they account for the micro-economic aspects of technological efforts (which has a cost and an expected return for each single firm), and also because they somehow account for the inter-relation of science–technology–production, do not seem to be able to consider the entire complexity of scientific and technological procedures.[10]

To summarise, there appear to be three basic weaknesses in the 'strong' version of demand–pull approaches: first, a concept of passive and mechanical 'reactiveness' to technological changes *vis-à-vis* market conditions; second, the incapability of defining the *why* and *when* of certain technological developments instead of others and of a certain timing instead of others; third, the neglect of changes over time in the inventive capability which do not bear any *direct* relationship with changing market conditions.

The theoretical ambiguities of demand–pull theories seem inevitably reflected in the empirical studies on the determinants of innovation.[11] Not surprisingly, most of the studies find that 'market is important in determining successful innovations'. We find ourselves in agreement with Mowery and Rosenberg, however, in that most of the studies with a demand–pull approach fail to produce sufficient evidence that 'needs expressed through market signalling' are the prime movers of innovative activity.[12]

This is precisely the question at stake. Those studies which tend to prove demand–pull theories appear actually incapable of explaining the timing of innovations and the existence of discontinuities in their patterns. Moreover, they provide a very crude account of the interaction between scientific progress, patterns of technical change and the evolution of economic variables: what these tests successfully demonstrate is that most enterprises and individual innovators undertaking innovative projects perceive the existence of a potential demand for their would-be product or process. This conclusion is hardly surprising. We would be quite impressed by the opposite, i.e. firms trying to produce innovations which, they believe, they will *not* be able to sell! The perception of a potential market generally belongs to the *necessary* conditions for innovation but it is *not* by any means the sufficient one.

'Technical Push' and the Importance of Economic Factors

The difficulties incurred by strong versions of 'technology–push' theories are in some respects opposite to those discussed above: there, it was the difficulty of taking into account the complexity, the relative autonomy and the uncertainty associated with technological change and innovation. Here, the problem arises in relation to the obvious fact that 'economic factors are important indeed' in shaping the direction of the innovative process. The process of growth and economic change, variations in distributive shares and in relative prices all affect the direction of the innovative activity and one feels rather uneasy in accepting a view of technical progress – paraphrasing Joan Robinson – as 'given by God, scientists and engineers'. The main theoretical task with respect to supply-side approaches is the avoidance of a one-directional conception 'science–technology–production' in which the first would represent a sort of exogenous and neutral *deus-ex-machina*. One realises that, in actual fact, there is a complex structure of feedbacks between the economic environment and the directions of technological changes. A tentative theory of technical change should define – in as general a form as possible – the nature of these interactive mechanisms. In different ways demand–pull and technology–push theories appear to fail to do so. In the former, technical change and innovation are basically a *reactive* mechanism which certainly shows some consistency with the traditional assumptions of neoclassical economics (consumer sovereignty, optimising behaviours, general equilibrium, etc.) but presents also unavoidable logical and empirical difficulties. On the other hand, if supply-side factors present some independence – at least in the short run – from market changes, it must be possible to show how they are affected in the long run by the economic transformation.

A Few Stylised Facts About the Innovative Process

Several empirical studies, at different levels of generality and inspired by different theoretical approaches, point at multi-variable explanations of innovative activity and to some kind of 'contextual determination' between science-related factors and economic variables.[13]

Some aspects of the innovative process can be considered – in our view – rather established. Among them:

1. The increasing role (at least in this century) of scientific inputs in the innovative process.
2. The increased complexity of R & D activities which makes the innovative process a matter of long-run planning for the firms (and not only for them) and witnesses against a hypothesis of prompt innovative answer by producers *vis-à-vis* changes in market conditions.
3. A significant correlation between R & D efforts (as proxy of the inputs in the innovative process) and innovative output (as measured by patent activity) in several industrial sectors[14] and the absence, in *cross-country* comparisons, of evident correlations between market and demand pattterns on the one hand, and innovative output on the other hand.
4. A significant amount of innovation and improvement is originated through 'learning-by-doing' and is generally embodied in people and organisations (primarily firms).
5. The increasing institutional formalisation of research notwithstanding, research and innovative activities maintain an intrinsic *uncertain nature*: this militates against any hypothesis of a set of technological choices which are known *ex-ante*.
6. Technical change does *not* occur at random, in two ways. First, the *directions* of technical change are often defined by the state-of-the-art of the technologies already in use. Second, it is often the case that the probability of firms and organisations achieving technological advances is, among other things, a function of the technological levels already achieved by them.[15]
7. The evolution of technologies through time presents some significant regularities and one is often able to define 'paths' of change in terms of some technological and economic characteristics of products and processes.

In the following section we shall try to define a model of the determinants and directions of technical change capable of accounting for the features of the innovative process which have just been outlined. The approach we will adopt may require a few introductory words. We began this work by stressing the fundamental inter-relationship between scientific progress, technical change and economic development. Their mutual influence has been one of the fundamental engines of social transformation, at least since the time of the industrial revolution (but most likely since long before then, even if in different forms). In industrial societies this inter-relationship is particularly strong, in many ways institutionalised and incorporated within the dynamics of the economic system: scientific and technological research is quite often directly undertaken by companies themselves or sponsored by them, while on the other hand scientific and technical developments are crucial factors in competitiveness and growth. Despite all this, however, it is fruitful to make a logical distinction between what we may name the 'scientific system', the 'technological system' and the 'economic system'. The tasks, the structures and the inner dynamics of these systems – as we shall argue – are different even when they are strongly overlapping. Take the example of the R & D activities within firms as one of the most obvious cases of strong interdependence between economic activities and 'technological activities': even in this case one can observe how the 'rules', the targets and the 'sociology' (e.g. the organisation and the *gestalt*) of R & D institutions might be significantly different from the rest of the firm. All this is going to sound quite evident to a managerial economist or an historian of technology. There have been relatively few attempts, however, to develop models of the interaction between these 'systems' at a sufficient degree of generality.

In the following section we shall examine precisely some features of the 'technology system' and its relationship with the economic variables.

2.2 A PROPOSED INTERPRETATION: TECHNOLOGICAL PARADIGMS AND TECHNOLOGICAL TRAJECTORIES

The Nature and Procedures of Technological Advances

Economic theory usually represents *technology* as a combination of a given set of factors, defined (qualitatively and quantitatively) in relation to certain outputs. Technical progress is generally defined in terms of a moving production possibilities curve, and/or in terms of the increasing number of producible goods. The definition we suggest here is, on the contrary, much broader. Let us define technology as a set of pieces of knowledge, both directly 'practical' (related to concrete problems and devices) and 'theoretical' (but practically applicable although not necessarily already applied), know-how, methods, procedures, experience of successes and failures and also, of course, physical devices and equipment. Existing physical devices embody the achievements in the development of a technology in a defined problem-solving activity.

At the same time, a 'disembodied' part of the technology consists of particular expertise, experience of past attempts and past technological solutions, together with the knowledge and the achievements of the state-of-the-art. Technology, in this view, includes the 'perception' of a limited set of possible technological alternatives and of notional future developments. This definition of technology is very impressionistic, but it seems useful to the exploration of the patterns of technical change. One can see that the conceptual distance between this definition and the attributes of 'science' – as suggested by modern epistemology – is not so great.

We shall push the parallel further and suggest that, in analogy with scientific paradigms (or scientific research programmes), there are 'technological paradigms' (or technological research programmes).[16]

A 'scientific paradigm' could be approximately defined as an 'outlook' which states the relevant problems, a 'model' and a 'pattern' of inquiry. 'The success of a paradigm . . . is at the start largely a promise of success discoverable in selected and still incomplete examples. Normal science consists in the actualisation of that promise, an actualisation achieved by extending the knowledge of those facts that the paradigm displays as particularly revealing, by increasing the extent of match between those facts and the paradigm's predictions, and by further articulation of the paradigm itself' (Kuhn, 1963, pp. 23–4). In broad analogy with the Kuhnian definition of a 'scientific paradigm', we shall define a 'technological paradigm' as a 'model' and a 'pattern' of solution of *selected* technological problems, based on *selected* principles derived from natural sciences and on *selected* material technologies.

First of all, the similarities relate to the mechanism and procedures of 'science', on the one hand, and those of technology on the other.[17] As a scientific paradigm determines the field of enquiry, the problems, the procedures and the tasks (the 'puzzles', in Kuhn's words), so does 'technology' in the sense defined above (it would be perhaps better to talk of 'cluster of technologies', e.g. nuclear technologies, semiconductor technologies, synthetic organic chemistry technologies, etc.).

As 'normal science' is the 'actualisation of a promise' contained in a scientific paradigm, so is 'technical progress' defined by a certain 'technological paradigm'. We will define a *technological trajectory* as the pattern of 'normal' problem solving activity (i.e. of 'progress') on the grounds of a technological paradigm.

More precisely, if the hypothesis of technological paradigm has to be of some use, one must be able to assess also in the field of technology the existence of something similar to a *positive heuristic* and a *negative heuristic*.[18] In other words, a technological paradigm (or research programme)[19] embodies strong prescriptions on the *directions* of technical change to pursue and those to neglect. Given some generic technological tasks (one could call them generic 'needs') such as, for example, those of transporting commodities and passengers, producing chemical compounds with certain properties or switching and amplifying electrical signals, certain specific technologies emerged, with their own 'solutions' to those problems at the exclusion of other notionally possible ones: in our three examples, historically these technologies were the internal combustion engine, petrochemical processes and semiconductors, respectively.

Technological paradigms have a powerful *exclusion effect*: the efforts and the technological imagination of engineers and of the organisations they are in are focused in rather precise directions while they are 'blind' with respect to other technological possibilities.

At the same time, technological paradigms also define some idea of 'progress'. Again in analogy with science, this can hardly be an absolute measure but has some precise meaning within a certain technology. The identification of a technological paradigm relates to the generic task to which it is applied (e.g. amplifying and switching electrical signals), to the material technology it selects (e.g. semiconductors and more specifically silicon), to the physical/chemical properties it exploits (e.g. the 'transistor effect' and 'field effect' of semiconductor materials), to the technological and economic dimensions and trade-offs it focuses upon (e.g. density of the circuits, speed, noise-immunity, dispersion, frequency range, unit costs, etc.). Once given these technological and economic dimensions, it is also possible to obtain, broadly speaking, an idea of 'progress' as the improvement of the trade-offs related to those dimensions.

The broad analogy between 'science' and 'technology' we have been drawing should not clearly be taken as an identity. In addition to the obvious difference related to the different nature of the problem-solving activity, technological 'knowledge' is much less well articulated than is scientific knowledge, much of it is not written down and is implicit in experience, skills, etc. This implies also that the definition of a 'technological paradigm' is bound to be much looser while the distinction between 'normal activity' and 'problem-shifts' is likely to be hard to make in practice. The same idea of a 'technological paradigm' should be taken as an approximation, adequate in some cases but less so in others. In our view, however, the analogy keeps its validity in that both ('scientific' and 'technological') activities represent strongly selective *gestalten* embodying powerful heuristics.

The Process of Selection of Technological Paradigms

A crucial question relates to how an established technological paradigm emerged in the first place and how it was 'preferred' to other possible ones. Let us consider 'downward' the sequence science-technology-production, remembering that it is meant to be just a *logical* simplification which neglects the crucial long-run influence of the economic and technological environments upon science itself.

Even within 'science', the problems and the 'puzzles' *actually* tackled (and those solved) are, of course, much more limited in number than the total number of problems and puzzles that the scientific theories potentially allow, and even more so the pieces of theory, puzzles, possibilities of development, 'passed-on' from scientific theory to 'applied sciences' and to technology (the last two, at least, being significantly overlapping). Leaving temporarily aside the problems of feedbacks, the hypothesis is that along the stream science-technology-production, the 'economic forces' (that we will define below) together with institutional and social factors, operate as a *selective device* (the 'focusing device' of Rosenberg (1976)). Within a large set of *possibilities* of directions of development, notionally allowed by 'science', a first level of selection (at least in the overwhelming majority of research activity in the enterprise sector) operates on the grounds of rather general questions like: Is any practical application conceivable?; Is there some possibility for the hypothesised application being marketable?, etc. Along the downstream from 'Big Science' to production (on a path which is much easier to conceive as a continuum instead of a strictly defined discrete set of steps), the *determinateness* of the selection increases: at one end we have the 'puzzle-solving activity'[20] defined by scientific paradigms *stricto sensu*; at the other end we have a technology totally embodied in devices and equipment. In between, in a field that we must already call technology because it is specifically ('economically') finalised, the activities aimed at 'technical progress' still have many procedures and features similar to 'science', namely the problem-solving activity along lines defined by the nature of the paradigm. The economic criteria acting as selectors define more and more precisely the *actual* paths followed inside a much bigger set of possible ones.

The Directions of Technical Progress

Once a path has been selected and established, it shows a momentum of its own,[21] which contributes to define the directions towards which the problem-solving activity moves: those are what Nelson and Winter (1977a) define as *natural trajectories* of technical progress.[22] A technological trajectory, i.e., to repeat, the 'normal' problem-solving activity determined by a paradigm, can be represented by the movement of multi-dimensional trade-offs among the technological variables which the paradigm defines as relevant. Progress can be defined as the improvement of these trade-offs.[23]

One could thus imagine the trajectory as a cylinder in the multi-dimensional space defined by these technological and economic variables. (Thus, a technological trajectory is a cluster of possible technological directions whose outer boundaries are defined by the nature of the paradigm itself). Some features of these technological trajectories, defined on the grounds of technological paradigms are worth considering:

1. There might be more general or more circumscribed as well as more powerful or less powerful[24] trajectories.
2. These are generally complementarities between different forms of knowledge, experience, skills, etc.[25] Furthermore, developments or lack of development in one technology might foster or prevent developments in other technologies.
3. In terms of our model one can define as the *technological frontier* the highest level reached upon a technological path with respect to the relevant technological and economic dimensions.[26]
4. 'Progress' on a technological trajectory is likely to retain some cumulative features: the probability of future advances is in this case related also to the position that one (a firm or a country) already occupies *vis-à-vis* the existing technological frontier. This is strictly consistent with Nelson and Winter's representation of technical progress at firm and industry levels, with Markovian chains.[27]
5. When a trajectory is very 'powerful', it might be difficult to switch to an alternative one. Moreover, when some comparability is possible between the two (i.e. when they have some 'dimensions' in common), the frontier on the alternative ('new') trajectory might be far behind that on the old one with respect to some or all the common

dimensions. In other words, whenever the technological paradigm changes, one has got to start (almost) from the beginning in the problem-solving activity.

6. It is doubtful whether it is possible to *a priori* compare and assess the superiority of one technological path over another. There might indeed be some objective criteria, once some indicators are chosen, but only *ex-post*.[28] This is one of the reasons behind the intimate uncertain nature of research activity (even leaving aside the market evaluations of the results, but just considering purely technological indicators).

Economics and Technology

The role of economic, institutional and social factors must be considered in greater detail. A first crucial role – as already mentioned – is the *selection* operated at each level, from research to production-related technological efforts, among the possible 'paths', on the grounds of some rather obvious and broad criteria such as feasibility, marketability, profitability.

On these very general grounds, there might still be many possible technological paradigms that could be chosen. Given the intrinsic uncertainty associated with their outcomes, in terms of both technological and economic success, it is hardly possible to compare and rank them *ex-ante*.[29] Other more specific variables are likely to come into play, such as (a) the economic interests of the organisations involved in R & D in these new technological areas; (b) their technological history, the fields of their expertise, etc.; (c) institutional variables *stricto sensu* such as public agencies, the military, etc. All these factors are likely to operate by focusing forces upon defined directions of technological development. In particular, one must stress the role often played in the establishment of a particular technological trajectory by public ('political') forces. As we shall see, clear examples of public intervention are semiconductors and computers during the first two decades of the post-war period. Military and space programmes operated then as a powerful focusing mechanism towards defined technological targets, while at the same time providing financial support to R & D and guaranteeing public procurement. Other similar cases can be found throughout the modern history of technology: for example, the emergence of synthetic chemistry in Germany bears a close relationship to the 'political' drive of that country towards self-sufficiency in the post-Bismarck period.[30]

These kinds of direct institutional effects upon the emergence of new technologies are not a general rule: the point we want to stress, however, is the general weakness of market mechanisms in the *ex-ante* selection of technological directions especially at the initial stage of the history of an industry. This is, incidentally, one of the reasons that militates for the existence of 'bridging institutions' between 'pure' science and applied R & D.[31] Even when a significant 'institutional focusing' occurs, there are likely to be different technological possibilities, an uncertain process of search, with different organisations, firms, individuals 'betting' on different technological solutions. Proceeding on our parallel with epistemology, this resembles a world *à la* Feyerabend (1975) with different competing technological paradigms: competition does not only occur between the 'new' technology and the 'old' ones which it tends to substitute, but also among alternative 'new' technological approaches.

We did not say very much about *positive ex-ante* criteria of selection among potential technological paradigms, apart from rather general ones such as marketability or potential profitability. Another powerful selecting criterion in capitalist economies is likely to be the cost-saving capability of the new technology and in particular its labour-saving potential: this is obviously consistent with Nelson and Winter's suggestion of 'natural trajectories' towards mechanisation and exploitation of economies of scale. Certainly in societies where industrial conflict and conflict over income distribution are structural features, substitution of machines for labour must be a powerful determinant in the search process for new technologies.

More generally, the patterns of industrial and social conflict are likely to operate, within the process of selection of new technological paradigms, both as negative criteria (which possible developments to exclude) and as positive criteria (which technologies to select). In this respect, one might be able to define some long-run relationship between patterns of social development and actually chosen technological paradigms (one quite clear example is the relationship between industrial relations at the turn of last century and the selection and development of 'Tayloristic' patterns of technical change in mechanical engineering).

Let us consider the final stage of this logical sequence from science to production, when – in cases of product innovations – a commodity is produced and sold: at this final stage markets operate again as selective environment.[32] It must be noted that this 'final selection' has a different nature from the previous stages. In the choices of the technological paths some kind of economic indicators were operating as *a priori* directing devices among a big number of possible technological choices. Here the market operates *ex-post* as a selecting device, generally among a range of products already determined by the broad technology patterns chosen *on the supply side*. To clarify the distinction further, let us take the following biological analogy. The final market selection may be equated with the environmental selection on mutations (Nelson and Winter models describe mainly this 'evolutionary' mechanism within the economic environment). The discussion above relates, on the contrary, to the selection of the 'mutation generating' mechanisms. Thus the economic and social environment affects technological development in two ways, first selecting the 'direction of mutation' (i.e. selecting the technological paradigm) and then selecting among mutations, in a more Darwinian fashion (i.e. the *ex-post* selection among Schumpeterian trials and errors). At times when new technologies are emerging, one can often observe new (Schumpeterian) companies trying to exploit different technological innovations. Markets perform as a system of rewards and penalties, thus checking and selecting among different alternatives. In this respect, the existence of a multiplicity of risk-taking actors, in non-planned economies, is crucial to the trial-and-error procedures associated with the search of new technological paths. These 'actors' take risks, of course, because there are markets which offer high rewards (i.e. profits) as a result of commercial success.

Incidentally, one must notice that if our interpretation of the process of technical change is correct, the emergence of new technological paradigms is *contextual* to the explicit emergence of economically defined 'needs'. In other words, the supply side determines the 'universe' of possible modalities through which generic 'needs' or productive requirements (which as such do not have any direct economic significance) are satisfied. In this, one can see the element of truth contained in those sociologically based theories suggesting needs 'induced' by corporate strategies.

A Look from the Opposite Side: How do Changes in the Environment affect Technical Change?

Changing economic conditions clearly interact with the process of selection of new technologies, with their development and finally with their obsolescence and substitution. One has, therefore, to analyse the feedback mechanisms 'upward', from the economic environment to the technology. One should also consider the long-term influence of economic and technological factors upon scientific change: this is, however, well beyond the scope of this work. Changing relative prices and distributive shares are bound to affect demand for the various commodities and the relative profitabilities in manufacturing them. Producers certainly react to these signals from the economic environment, trying to respond through technical advances. However, this often occurs *within the boundaries of a given technological trajectory*, which might either be conducive or place increasing constraints on any development consistent with the 'signals' the economic environment is delivering.[33] Difficulties and unsolved technological puzzles and problems, to use Kuhnian language again, operate upward as focusing devices, sometimes putting pressure on other technological fields to go further in their problem solving, and finally, facilitate or hinder the switch to other technological trajectories. It must be stressed, though, that unsolved technological difficulties do not imply automatically a change to another 'path'.[34] Of course, changes in market conditions and opportunities (among which changes in demand patterns, relative prices, distributive shares, costs of production, etc. are all very important) continuously bring pressures 'upward', at various levels, upon technological trajectories, and upon the same selection criteria on the grounds of which those trajectories are chosen. But this fact does not imply by any means an assumption of malleable 'ready-to-use' alternative technological paths, or, even more so, instantaneous technological responses to changes in market conditions. Furthermore, an implicit result is that the 'upward' impact of changing economic conditions on technological research patterns seems directly proportional to the *technological determinateness* of the economic stimuli themselves.[35] So one would generally expect this determinateness to increase coming from consumers' goods to investment goods and to other kinds of non properly market goods (such as military equipment).[36]

Note that changes in the economic environment are a permanent feature of the system: those changes often stimulate simple technical progress (as defined above) *along* one technological trajectory. Again in parallel with epistemology we can call it the 'normal' technological activity. 'Extraordinary' technological attempts (related to the search for new technological directions) emerge either in relation to new opportunities opened up by scientific developments, or to the increasing difficulty in going forward on a given technological direction (for technological or economic reasons), or both.[37]

In the next chapter we will examine the implications of this interpretation of the patterns of technical change and innovation with regard to industrial structures. First, however, we will consider the technological history of the semiconductor industry in the light of this model.

2.3 THE SEMICONDUCTOR INDUSTRY: DEFINITION AND TECHNOLOGICAL FEATURES[38]

The semiconductor industry is generally defined as that branch of the electronics industry which manufactures electronic components (almost entirely *active* components) utilising the properties of semiconductor materials, of which silicon is by far the most common.

Semiconductors are elements or compounds (such as silicon, germanium, selenium, gallium arsenide, etc.) which show a much lower conductive capability than conductors (whose conductivity is allowed by the movement of free electrons), but higher than insulators. More precisely, they can act in certain conditions as conductors and in others as insulators. This is due to their property of having in their atomic structure, either a 'hole' in their outer cluster of electrons (these are called p-type semiconductors) or just one electron (n-type semiconductors). To increase their n-type or p-type conductivity, the number of electrons or 'holes' can be increased, adding some impurities to the material: the process is called 'doping'. Thus, when a semiconductor device is defined as a p-n type this means that it is composed by a layer of p-type semiconductor and a layer of n-type semiconductor, etc. The conductive or insulating properties of semiconductors can be affected by the presence of an electrical current, electromagnetic fields, temperature, light or other electromagnetic waves exposures.[39]

These properties have been exploited in different ways and in different semiconductor devices. Due to their alternatively conductive or insulating properties, semiconductors can perform many tasks as active components in electric circuits and modulate, rectify and amplify electrical signals.

Moreover, this property of alternatively allowing or preventing the flow of electrical current may be exploited in electrical circuits associating these two states with two values of a given variable (i.e. zero and one, or – which is essentially the same – yes and no). Very loosely speaking, this is the basic principle of digital circuits, which manipulate information translated into electrical impulses, based on a binary logic.

In the history of electric components, the first semiconductor rectifier was built by Popow in 1895, but after the invention of the electron-tube (de Forest, 1906), thermoionic valves completely replaced solid-state devices as active components. Semiconductors were used merely as wave detectors in the early radar equipment around the time of the Second World War.[40]

Generally the date of birth of the semiconductor industry is placed in 1948 (more precisely 23 December 1947), when Shockley, Bardeen and Brattain announced the development of the first point-contact transistor (i.e. a semiconductor amplifier) at Bell Laboratories.[41]

Later in the history of semiconductors, the first *integrated circuit* was developed by Texas Instruments and Fairchild in 1961. An integrated circuit (IC) is a device performing more than one function on a single chip, i.e. it embodies more than one component, either active or passive (for example, several transistors connected through patterns 'written' on the chip).

Finally microprocessors (MPUs), developed in 1971, are, roughly speaking, a 'big' integrated circuit which incorporates on a single chip all the logical functions of a complete computer.

In the definition of the industry we include:

(a) *Discrete devices* such as diodes and rectifiers, transistors, special discrete devices like thyristors, zener diodes, and triacs.

(b) *Integrated Circuits*.[42] They can be subdivided, in terms of functions performed, between analog ICs, digital ICs and memories, or, on the grounds of their technological features between bipolar and MOS (metal oxide).[43]

The distinction between analog and digital circuits is based on whether they operate on elements of information expressed in binary logic (as in digital ICs) or whether, on the contrary, they process the inputs of informations as they are (in the analog case).[44]

Strictly speaking, memories are digital ICs which can store binary information, through storing electrical charges. Memories can either be 'ready-only' (ROM), whenever the bits of information are permanently written at the manufacturing stage, or RAM ('random access'), whenever the elements of information are volatile and each information can be written, read, cancelled.[45]

In terms of product technologies, bipolar ICs are based on 'electron action taking place within the body of semiconductors'[46] whereby, in a vague similarity with the previous valve technology, under certain conditions (i.e. a voltage applied in the middle junction of each transistor, often called 'base'), a flow of electrons and 'holes' occurs inside each transistor between its two extremes (often called 'emitter' and 'collector' – again in analogy with valve technology).

Metal oxide silicon (MOS) technology, on the other hand, operates

24

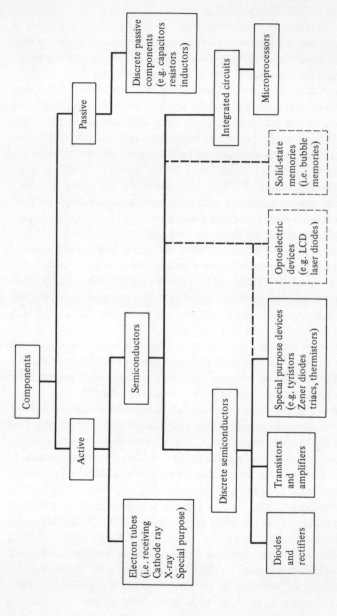

FIGURE 2.1 *An overview of electronic and electrical components*

SOURCE Elaboration on Tilton (1971, p. 8)

on electrical flows on the surface of each layer which compose the IC, exploiting the 'field effect': a voltage applied to the layer below the surface controls whether a flow occurs on the surface itself through the electrical field it creates.[47]

(c) *Microprocessors*, as already mentioned, may be considered a very complex integrated circuit which can undertake (in conjunction with an input–output device and with two or more memories) a complete processing of information according to a chosen programme (software) which can be instructed to the device.

(d) *Optoelectronic devices* such as light emitting diodes (LED) and liquid crystal displays (LCD).[48] This group of products is often considered together with the other discrete devices. We choose to keep them as a separate category for their relatively different characteristics and applications.

(e) *Solid-State Memories* (i.e. magnetic bubble memories – MBM).[49] Note that neither magnetic bubble memories nor some optoelectronic devices are *stricto sensu* semiconductors. However, they are often manufactured by semiconductor companies through production processes which bear some similarities with semiconductor manufacturing.

The process of production of semiconductors (following the stage of research and prototype development) can be subdivided into five phases:[50] (1) design, (2) mask-production, (3) fabrication, (4) assembly, (5) testing. At the design stage, the complete network of the circuit is drawn, at dimensions several hundred times bigger than the planned circuit. The design is, of course, a labour-intensive and technology-intensive procedure. Today, many steps towards the computerisation of design have been made, but it still relies heavily on technical knowledge and design capability. As we shall see, this stage is a critical one in defining the technological capabilities of companies and countries.

The design of the circuit is then photo-reduced to obtain masks which represent the patterns of the circuit. The proper production phase begins from slices of pure silicon.[51] Those crystals are then sliced to obtain 'wafers' (which used to be 2–3 inches in diameter and today are also 4 and 5 inches). These wafers are put in a furnace where some elements (for example, boron), at gaseous state, are *diffused* on them. Then, being exposed to oxygen, they develop an oxidated surface. Finally, wafers are coated with a photo-sensitive emulsion ('photoresist'). By means of aligning the wafer to the mask and exposing the latter to intense light, the pattern of the circuit is reproduced on the wafer, so that, after baking the wafer and 'etching' it in an acid solution, only the regions of the wafer which were not exposed to the light will remain covered by the layers of silicon dioxide. Now, some 'impurities' (e.g. phosphorous, arsenium, indium, depending on the desired p–type or n–type properties) are diffused – again at gaseous state – on the exposed circuit pattern on the wafer. The small 'doped' areas perform as microscopic parts of transistors (either of n– or p–type).

Depending on the complexity of the circuit, the operations of oxidation, light exposure through a mask, etching and diffusion are repeated several times until the complete integrated circuits are obtained. Finally, a metal layer (generally aluminium) is grown – through the same process of gaseous diffusion. The layer is again oxidated, covered with a photoresist, light exposed, and etched to form the pattern of electrical inter-connections of the ICs developed on the wafer. The wafers are then visually inspected and electronically tested and, if they pass the controls, cut to separate each IC: a 3-inch wafer might yield from some hundreds to several thousands integrated circuits. Whenever we refer to the 'yields' in manufacturing, it will mean the percentage of 'good' ICs – i.e. those working according to specifications – in the total number obtained from the wafer.

The IC is then bonded to a base and all the connecting wires are linked to the chip, in the case of manual or semi-automated assembly, with the use of a microscope. After being sealed in a protective package, ICs undergo a final testing, in order to separate the faulty ones and determine their electrical characteristic (frequency, dissipation, etc).

The functional features of semiconductor devices may be described in terms of density (number of components per chip), speed, energy consumption, frequency, dissipation, heat-immunity, electrical noise-immunity, maximum power charge, acceptable change in the supply voltage, etc.

2.4 THE DEVELOPMENT OF SEMICONDUCTOR TECHNOLOGY

From Valves to Semiconductors

Let us briefly consider the electronic technology which semiconductors were going to supercede.

Before the discovery of the transistor, the tasks of amplifying, rectifying and modulating electrical signals were performed by valves, except in a few applications for which valve technology was inappropriate (e.g. high frequency wave detectors). Thermoionic valves (known also as vacuum tubes or electronic tubes) were first developed in 1906.

Valves' basic scientific principles were well understood since the beginning of the century. On the contrary, although many semiconductor properties were known – as mentioned – since the previous century, the theoretical reasons for such physical behaviour was unknown until the emergence of quantum physics, and, even after that, quantum physics was providing a workable and powerful theoretical framework, but was not yet developed to explain all of the observed properties of semiconductors.

Since their first introduction, valves underwent an impressive improvement in performance and, on the basis of the same 'technological paradigm' and physical principles, new types of valves were developed. The technology itself, however, defined the extreme boundaries of technical possibilities and the inherent limitations. Among them there are:

—limited frequency range at which they could operate
—high energy consumption (the valve had to be heated before a flow of electrons could occur between the 'emitter' and the 'collector')
—high heat disperson
—limited reliability
—size unreduceable below certain dimensions
—limited average life

Technical progress along valves' technological trajectories pushed performances near the technical limits, while at the same time reducing unit costs.

On the other hand, solid-state physics was one of the least established fields of theoretical physics, even after the development of quantum physics. It is important to notice that solid-state theory was one of the areas where the new scientific paradigm could be tested.

From a technological point of view, some possible applications of semiconductor active components could be foreseen (substitution for, at least, some kinds of valves, other applications in high frequencies, etc.). In the thirties and forties, though, this was a mere possibility and not a practical target: the distance between theoretical state-of-the art, on the one hand, and practical applications on the other hand, was very high indeed.

The first discovery of the transistor occurred at Bell Laboratories (the research facility of American Telephone and Telegraph). In the USA, a consistent amount of research was under way also in various universities and big corporations (University of Pennsylvania, Purdue University, General Electric, Sylvania).[52] These researches were not generally undertaken with the main aim of producing a solid-state amplifier (transistor), but with the purpose of advancing the understanding of solid-state physics (the 'scientific puzzle-solving activity'), the construction of some semiconductor device being to a certain extent a by-product and a consequence of the possible success in explaining solid-state phenomena.[53]

The early development of transistor devices put pressure upon the extension of theoretical knowledge in several related fields and, on the other hand, was 'shaped' by the level of that knowledge itself and by the degree of development of other complementary technologies.[54] With respect to the first point, developments in transistor technology were not possible until the role of 'minority carriers' was understood.[55] Similarly, developments in field-effect transistors technology were made possible by its theoretical understanding[56] and contextual to it. It is worth noticing that one of the reasons for the early preference for germanium, first, and then silicon, in addition to technological and economic factors, was the better understanding of the physical properties of these elements. At least the first ten years of the history of the semiconductor industry are characterised by a crucial inter-relationship between 'science' and 'technology'. However, since the sixties the distance between the two has increased. Semiconductor basic technology had become established and its path of development no longer needed a direct 'coupling' with 'Big Science'.

This is reflected also in a declining trend of basic research undertaken by the firms in the sixties and seventies.[57]

Research and Innovation: The Role of Big Research Establishments in the Early Days of Semiconductors

After the discovery of transistors, research continued at Bell Laboratories as well as in big electrical corporations such as General Electric, RCA, Philco, Westinghouse, and Sylvania. In those days (until approximately the beginning of the 1960s) applied research activities were to a considerable extent connected with 'proper' scientific inquiry.[58]

A striking feature of the first decade of the history of semiconductors is the remarkable difference between those companies which originated the overwhelming majority of innovation, and those companies which successfully exploited these innovations in the market. In other words, successful innovators were not generally successful producers of the devices based on these innovations. We will try to give some explanations for this apparent paradox in the next chapter when discussing the dynamics of the industry and the changes in market structure. First of all, however, we must analyse the nature of the innovative process.

Let us define the main features of research activities on semiconductors in the fifties. Most of the research, in the USA as well as in Europe, was undertaken by big established companies, quite often valve producers (cf. also Tilton, 1971). Tables 2.1 and 2.2 provide an overview of the major innovations between 1950 (the date of the first commercial production of transistors) and 1978.[59] Table 2.3 attributes the innovation to the various types of companies. On the period 1950–61 established electrical companies accounted for 31 per cent of all major innovations (26 per cent by US companies and one innovation attributed to Siemens from Germany). Bell Laboratories[60] alone accounted for 33 per cent. Their share in process innovations is even bigger (33 per cent and 44 per cent, respectively).

In terms of R & D efforts, Bell Laboratories and big tube firms in 1959 were contributing for 57 per cent of total R & D expenditure.[61] Finally, in terms of patents over the same period (1952–61), Bell Laboratories were granted 24 per cent of the total and tube firms 42 per cent.[62]

If one looks at the first five years of the history of semiconductors the picture is even more impressive: between 1950 and 1955, Bell Laboratories and established electrical companies originated jointly 92 per cent of all major innovations.

Even after the 1960s, established electronic companies and public laboratories show a disproportionately high number of patents (see Table 2.4).

It is particularly important to stress the role played in those early days by Bell Laboratories as a decisive *bridging institution* between 'pure' and applied research. In more economic terms, we could define it as an institution ready to undertake research projects involving a very high uncertainty about possible future commercial outcomes. This has been important especially in a period in which technological patterns were not yet well established, the relevance of basic research was high, there were several directions of possible enquiry and the uncertainty associated with each of them was very high. Furthermore, part of those research efforts – even when *successful* – do not produce a *direct* profitable outcome, although they have, of course, a positive impact on the technological level of the innovator and of the industry. Consider

TABLE 2.1 *Major innovations in products and design in semiconductor industry*

Innovation	Firm	First Production
Point contact transistor	Western Electric[a]	1951
Grown junction transistor	Western Electric	1951
Alloy junction transistor	General Electric/RCA	1952
Surface barrier transistor	Philco	1954
Silicon junction transistor	Texas Instruments	1954
Diffused transistor	Western Electric/Texas Instruments	1956
Silicon controlled rectifier	General Electric	1956
Tunnel diode	Sony	1957
Planar transistor	Fairchild	1960
Diffused resistor	Fairchild	1960
Epitaxial transistor	Western Electric	1960
MOS capacitor	RCA	1960
Integrated circuit	Texas Instruments/Fairchild	1960–1
Resistor–transistor logic	Fairchild	1961
MOS transistor	Fairchild/RCA	1962
DTL integrated circuit	Signetics	1962
Substrate diffused collector transistor	Sylvania/Fairchild	1962
Gunn diode	IBM	1963
Emitter–coupled logic	Motorola	1963
Light-emitting diode	Texas Instruments	1964
TTL integrated circuit	TRW/Sylvania/TI	1964
MOS resistor	Fairchild/GMe	1965
MOS integrated circuit	General Microelectronics/General Instruments	1965
Deposited metal resistor	n.a.	1965
Magnetic bubble memory	Western Electric[b]	(1968–77)
MOSFET (MOS field-effect transistor)	Western Electric/Phillips	1968
CMOS integrated circuit	RCA	1968
Schottky TTL	Texas Instruments	1969–70
Depletion mode MOS resistor	Mostek	1969
CCD (charge coupled device)	Fairchild	1969

1–K MOS RAM	Intel/AMS	1969
Bipolar–junction field effect combination	National Semiconductor	1970
Silicon-on-sapphire (SOS)	RCA[c]	(1970–73)
P–MOS	n.a.	1971
3 transistor cell dynamic RAM (1K bits)	Intel	1971
Trapped charge storage	Intel	1972
Microprocessor	Intel	1971–2
Bipolar MOS combination	RCA	1972
Bipolar RAM	Fairchild	1972
I^2L integrated circuit	Philips	1973
1 Transistor cell dynamic RAM (1K bits)	Intel/Mostek/TI	1974
Isoplanar, Coplamos, etc.	Fairchild/Std. Microsystem	1975
VMOS integrated circuit	AMI	1975
C^2D integrated circuit	n.a.	1976
MNOS	n.a.	1976
16–K MOS RAM	Intel/Mostek	1976
Micro computer (8048)	Intel	1977
V–MOS	Mitsubishi/IBM/Siliconik	1977–8
64–K RAM	Fujitsu	1978

[a] Western Electric, being the manufacturing branch of AT & T, undertakes the proper production, while the product is first developed at Bell Laboratories.

[b] First prototype 1968 – commercial production begins around *ten* years later.

[c] Different sources suggest different dates. This is also due to some ambiguity on the definition of the boundaries between prototype developments and first commercial production.

n.a. = not available.

COMMENT:

(1) There is a significant ambiguity in the classification of some innovations between either processes, products or both. We chose the latter option whenever a process innovation is strictly contextual to new products (e.g. the cases of the Integrated Circuit, MOS or SOS).

(2) One of the major omissions of this list concerns Gate Arrays (which in Europe are better known as ULA – Uncommited Logic Arrays – introduced by Ferranti, UK, in 1973–4). The assessment of the importance of innovations requires a lot of hindsight and unfortunately their importance began to appear at the turn of the decade. Facing the uncertainty about the relative relevance of the various innovations in the field, we chose the easy option of excluding them.

SOURCES   Tilton (1971); Golding (1971); Finan (1975); Sciberras (1977 and 1980); Wilson *et al.* (1980, interviews).

TABLE 2.2 *Major process innovation in semiconductor industry*

Innovation	Firm	Date of introduction
Single crystal growing	Western Electric	1950
Zone refining	Western Electric	1950
Alloy process	General Electric	1952
3–5 compounds	Siemens	1952
Jet etching	Philco	1953
Oxide masking and diffusion	Western Electric	1955
Planar process	Fairchild	1960
Epitaxial process	Western Electric	1960
Resistive metal deposition	n.a.	1960
Ultrasonic bonding	Fairchild	1961
Plastic encapsulation	General Electric	1963
Beam lead	Western Electric	1964
Annealing for stress relief	Western Electric	1965
Dielectric isolation	Motorola	1965
Gettering processes	Western Electric	1965
Collector diffusion insolation	Western Electric	1969
Glass chemical vapor deposition	Western Electric	1969
Direct bonding – bump	IBM/Western Electric	1966
Nitride chemical vapor deposition	General Instruments	1968
Ion implantation	Mostek	1970

Schottky junction	TI	1970
Silicon-on-sapphire[a]	RCA	1970–3
Self-aligned silicon gate	Intel	1972
Sputtering	Veeco	1973
Integrated injection logic	Philips	1973
Polysilicon deposition	Intel	1973
Plasma etching	Standard Telecom Labs	1974
Vertically oriented transistor	AMI	1975
Ion milling	Veeco	1975
Double polysilicon process	Mostek	1976
E–beam	TI/IBM	1976
Photolithography projection alignment	Perkin–Elmer	1976
Plasma nitride processing	n.a.	1976
Automatic bonding on 'exotic' (35 mm film) substrate	Sharp	1977
Deep ultra-violet photolithography	Perkin–Elmer	1977
Vertical injection logic	Mitsubishi	1978

[a] See note (c) from Table 2.1.
See also comment on Table 2.1.
n.a. = not available.

SOURCE as Table 2.1.

TABLE 2.3 *Innovation by kind of company and nationality (1950–78)*[a]

Year	1950–61	1962–71	1972–8
1. Major Product and Design Innovation (numbers)	14	22	15
of which percentage by			
Western Electric (i.e. Bell Labs)	25%	7%	–
US Established Electrical Companies[b]	29%	16%	15%
Non-US Semiconductor Companies	7%	2%	18%
Established US Semiconductor companies[c]	–	30%	16%
New US companies	39%	45%	51%
2. Major Process Innovations (number)	10	11	15
of which percentage by			
Western Electric (i.e. Bell Labs)	44%	50%	–
US Established Electrical Companies [b]	22%	18%	7%
Non-US Companies	11%	–	29%
Established US Semiconductor Companies[c]	–	23%	7%
New US Companies	23%	9%	36%
Materials and equipment producers	–	–	21%
3. Total Semiconductor Innovations (number)	29	34	39
of which percentage by			
Western Electric (i.e. Bell Labs)	33%	21%	–
US Established Electrical Companies	26%	16%	8%
Non-US Companies	9%	2%	24%
Established US Semiconductor Companies	–	27%	8%
New US Companies	32%	34%	48%
Materials and Equipment Producers	–	–	12%

[a] The percentages by type of company are calculated on the total of innovation whose origin is known. Those innovations which imply both a new process and a new product are double counted. When more than one firm is responsible for the same innovation, each firm is attributed the corresponding fraction of one. Magnetic Bubbles are included in the 1962–71 period, while SOS is considered in the period 1972–8.

[b] General Electric, RCA, Sylvania and Philco.

[c] This group stands for those companies which entered semiconductor manufacturing in the previous period and established themselves as major producers with significant R & D activities. In the group we included Texas Instruments, IBM, Fairchild, Motorola, for the periods 1962–71 and 1972–8.

SOURCE As Table 2.1.

TABLE 2.4   *Patents granted in the USA in semiconductors and related devices, by country and by company*

A. *Patents by country – Semiconductor-related processes and products*[a]

Year	1963–71	1972–8
Total patents (number)	18883	14172
US origin (number)	14925	9466
Foreign origin (number)	3958	4706
of which (in percentage)		
Japan	22.3%	43.3%
W. Germany	25.6%	20.7%
United Kingdom	19.4%	9.9%
Netherlands	9.0%	7.6%
France	7.7%	6.8%
Canada	4.3%	2.9%
Switzerland	3.6%	2.8%
Italy	1.2%	1.5%

B. *Patents by company*[a][b] – *Percentages of selected semiconductor-related patents*

Year	Pre-1971	1972–8
1) IBM	6.6	7.5
2) RCA	4.7	5.8
3) Western Electric	6.5	5.0
4) Texas Instruments	5.4	4.4
5) General Electric	4.5	4.3
6) Hitachi	1.6	4.1
7) Motorola	3.0	4.0
8) Philips US	3.1	3.7
9) US Military and Space Agencies (Airforce, Navy, Army, NASA)	5.6	3.7
10) Siemens	2.5	3.4
11) Westinghouse	3.8	2.2
12) Matsushita	1.2	1.6
13) Sony	0.5	1.5
14) Toshiba	0.3	1.3
15) ITT and Standard Electric	2.2	1.2
16) Hughes Aircraft	1.5	1.2
17) Nippon Electric	1.4	1.2
18) Honeywell	1.5	1.1
19) Fairchild	1.0	1.1
20) Signetics	0.3	1.0

again the example of Bell Laboratories: *vis-à-vis* an estimated cumulative expenditure (1945–64) of \$57 million, Western Electric received around \$3 million in royalty payments and \$2.6 million worth of cross-licence benefits.[63] These features of research relate to what in the literature are called 'externalities'. Fundamental research induces a 'fallout' upon the innovating industry which is not entirely appropriable by the innovator. This appears to be a relatively general feature of that kind of research which is not strictly finalised to commercial applications. In the particular case of Bell–Western Electric, the lack of appropriability was greatly increased by the Consent Decree of 1956, settling an antitrust case again AT & T: the latter was allowed to manufacture semiconductors for in-house use only and had to make available, royalty-free, all its semiconductor patents acquired before 1956 to all American firms, and post-1956 patents at moderate fees.

Throughout the history of semiconductors, an overwhelming percentage of basic research in the USA has been undertaken by Bell Laboratories and – in the sixties and seventies – by IBM (see Table 2.5).

It is clearly difficult to draw a sharp line between 'basic' and 'applied' research. In any case, that kind of research which is not directly finalised to a specific and immediate economic objective appears to create the most conducive environment for, and to increase the probability of major technological breakthroughs. This is particularly important when there are several potential technological paradigms. Its permanent role, however, should not be underestimated even when technical progress seems to follow 'normal' and defined patterns. That kind of far-reaching research provides an important source of possible major advances and/or new technologies and new technological trajectories.

In the fifties and early sixties, there certainly were in Europe institutions and companies with a scientific and technological level

---

Notes to Table 2.4

(a) It is important to note that the patents cover a wider area than the technologies actually applied in semiconductor products and processes, so that, for example, diffusion techniques are likely to be included even if they are not applied to semiconductor manufacturing, etc.

(b) The percentages cover a sample of 7,647 patents granted between 1963 and 1971 whose application occurred after 1963 and 13,643 patents in the period 1972–8.

SOURCE   *ad hoc* report prepared by the Office of Technology Assessment and Forecast (OTAF) of the US Dept. of Commerce.

TABLE 2.5   *Basic research by major contributor and total R & D, USA, 1972 (millions of dollars)*

Bell Laboratories	15
IBM	13
RCA	4
Texas Instruments	2
Others (GE, Fairchild, etc.)	2
Total Basic Research	36
Total R & D performed by the industry (Bell and IBM excluded)	136

SOURCE   Finan (1975, p. 38).

comparable with the American counterparts. Differences, however, were also considerable.

First, the companies able to undertake such uncertain and sometimes apparently unprofitable efforts were fewer in Europe than in the USA: in terms of size only Siemens and Philips could compare with the biggest American companies. Other companies, big by European standards, involved in the field were: in the UK, AEI, GEC, Marconi, Lucas, Plessey;[64] AEG and Telefunken (later merged) in Germany; Thomson–Huston, and CSF (which were to form CSF–Thomson Huston) and CGE in France; Olivetti in Italy (who entered the field later with the partly owned SGS). The number and size of the companies has a relevance, especially when the rate of technical change is high and the patterns of technological development are not yet well established. When there are several possible directions of development it seems important to pursue most of them – if a national industry wants to keep pace with innovations, or even to be a quick imitator. Other things being equal, a consistent number of big, and some very big, firms have represented a powerful structural factor which has contributed to the different technological capabilities of western industrial countries.

Second, another factor, related to firms' size, is the minimum R & D threshold[65] which allows technological innovation (and also imitation). In semiconductors, that threshold has not been historically very high in terms of fixed capital equipment, but very consistent in terms of number and qualifications of scientists, engineers, technicians and in terms of financial outlets devoted to research projects, several of which are bound not to be profitable.

Third, European countries lacked big 'coupling' institutions such as Bell Laboratories. Moreover, the 'distance' between universities or government laboratories, on the one hand, and private enterprise, on the other hand, undoubtedly provided a stumbling block for a quick transformation of scientific discovery into commercial production.

Whenever a radically new science-based technology is emerging, there are crucial mechanisms for the *selection* and *translation* of scientific knowledge into feasible technological paths of application. All the institutions mentioned above ('coupling' research laboratories such as Bell, public research laboratories, R & D departments of big companies also involved in fundamental research) contributed to the selection of the range of *possible* economic applications of pure science.

The mentioned *structural* differences between the two sides of the Atlantic help in explaining some of the different developments of the semiconductor industry in the USA and Europe (we shall discuss below also the case of Japan). Institutional differences stemming from the different roles of governments are another crucial part of the explanation. Before analysing them in detail, however, it may be helpful to provide an overall picture of the actual directions of technical progress together with the technological and economic dimensions through which that progress can be measured.

The Dimensions of Technical Progress and the Technological Frontier

From the first discovery of the transistor upto the present time, the pattern of technical change which emerged can be described in terms of some technological and economic dimensions which represent, as it were, the co-ordinates of an n–dimensional space, wherein technical change can be described as an oriented movement of a line (or more precisely a surface) through time.

The directions of progress have been:

1. *Increasing miniaturisation* – this, in the era of integrated circuits is a function of increasing *density*, i.e. increasing number of components on a single chip.
2. *Increasing speed*
3. *Increasing reliability*
4. *Decreasing costs*

One must add to these fundamental dimensions other important parameters such as heat immunity, dispersion, energy consumption, frequency range, maximum allowable power charge, and noise immunity.

Figures 2.2, 2.3 and 2.4 – taken from the already mentioned thorough analysis of technology indicators by the Futures Group (Gordon and Munson, 1981) – illustrate the pattern of progress.

Technical change along this path has always been parallel, with respect to demand, to the extension of the range of possible application of semiconductors, in terms of both substitution for existing electronic and electromechanical devices and in terms of new 'pervasiveness' (capability of finding new applications).[66]

Technical progress in semiconductors deeply affected downstream sectors which utilise them. In the computer sector in particular the dimensions of the trajectory of progress can be for a good part identified with those characterising semiconductors.[67]

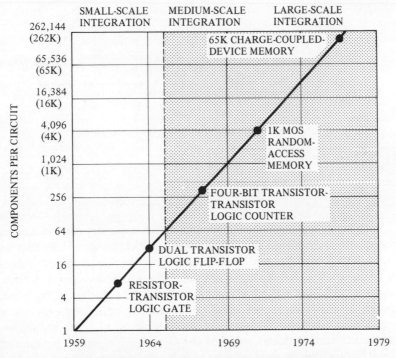

FIGURE 2.2 *The number of components per chip*

SOURCE Gordon and Munson (1981, p. 104).

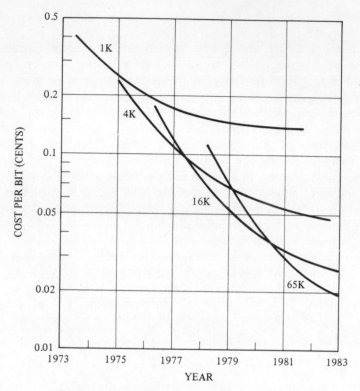

FIGURE 2.3   *Semiconductor memory cost per bit*

SOURCE   Gordon and Munson (1981, p. 106).

We already explained how a technological trajectory (or a cluster of contiguous trajectories) can define a *technological frontier*.[68] By that we mean the highest (or lowest, according to the direction of change) values of the above technological parameters achieved at any point in time, together with the highest levels of knowledge, experience, expertise, design and manufacturing capabilities. At the beginning of the history of semiconductors (and probably at the beginning of most industries, subsectors and products), most of the factors affecting the position of countries and companies *vis-à-vis* the 'frontier' is relatively disembodied from fixed equipment and embodied in 'people'[69] and organisations. This fact is quite well recognised also in 'technology gap' and product

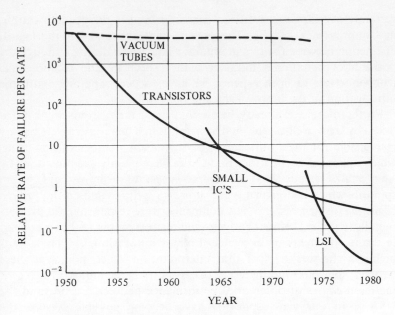

FIGURE 2.4 *Reliability of components, by technology*

SOURCE Gordon and Munson (1981, p. 107).

cycle theories of trade, and we shall come back to it below.

The process of innovation and 'technological search' in the fifties and early sixties led progressively to fairly stable patterns (trajectories) of technological development. The same process of establishment of these patterns of change was strongly connected with the establishment of the *American lead*: at the end of the process (and until the eighties) the US semiconductor industry emerged as the only one 'on the frontier'.

It is useful to analyse the factors which led to this outcome and the dynamics through which it emerged. Some initial structural differences between Europe and the USA have already been mentioned. We shall now examine other institutional factors and in particular the role of public institutions.

The Emergence of an American Lead: The Impact of Public Programmes

Let us first recall the distinction between the *introduction* of innovations and *diffusion* of the latter throughout the industry. The two processes are certainly overlapping: diffusion generally implies further innovations and improvements.[70] For the present context, however, the logical distinction between the two maintains a heuristic validity: although the position of a national industry with respect to 'the technological frontier' refers to both aspects, we have to deal separately with the introduction of the innovations and their diffusion.

Furthermore, we already know that most innovations were introduced by large, well-established firms, although newcomers were mainly responsible for their diffusion. The significant number of new firms which appeared in the fifties and sixties were mainly accounted for by 'spin-offs' of scientists and managers from established firms, or from ex-spin-offs which had grown big.[71] It is also well recognised that, *at the beginning* of their history, new companies were responsible for proportionally low R & D efforts and a low innovative output (either measured in terms of patents or in terms of major innovations).[72] These facts highlight the weakness of that interpretation which points at these frequent spin-offs (and therefore of easy entry in the industry) as one of the main *causes* of differential performance between Europe and the USA.[73] In our view, spin-offs have become possible *because* the American industry as a whole was already on the technological frontier: scientists and managers, in leaving their previous companies, were doing so in order to exploit commercially on their own the cumulated experience of previous research, successes and failures acquired in established research laboratories and institutions, or in their previous companies.[74]

We must wonder, first of all, why an overwhelming percentage of innovations has occurred in the USA. Two reasons, which are important, have already been mentioned, namely the smaller amount of high-uncertainty, far-reaching research undertaken in big European companies, due to their relative smaller size, and the absence of significant 'bridging' institutions (between pure and applied science) like Bell Laboratories. Those two factors probably accounted for fewer 'directions' of investigation and smaller advances, and a lower amount of cumulated experience and knowledge even on the directions which were investigated. There seem to be powerful additional factors, however.

First, let us consider the role of the military. As early as 1952, the US military gained interest in the possible applications of transistors as a substitute for valves, interested, as it was, in smaller size, smaller weight and increased reliability. Since then, nobody denies that the impact of the military on research and demand has been great, although there is not a comparable agreement on its ultimate affects. Table 2.6 illustrates the impact of military and, generally, public procurement policies on total demand. The percentage on total demand, either calculated in terms of direct purchases or direct and indirect ones (semiconductor inputs in purchased military equipment), reached a peak in 1959–60,[75] and then declined until 1973–4. In the second half of the 1970s it moved upward again to the same proportion as at the turn of the decade.

An exact evaluation of government contribution to R & D is much more difficult: in the early fifties total government support of R & D, products' improvements, and contributions to the expansion of productive capacity for defence purposes ranged between $4 and $8 million a year (National Science Foundation, 1963). Table 2.7 shows the total government contribution to R & D and refinement projects for the period 1955–61. To those figures one should add the amounts devolved indirectly (through other projects involving semiconductors), as well as direct expenditures by the military on semiconductor projects in their own laboratories. The quoted figures of R & D contributions, however, accounted for 25 per cent of total firm-performed R & D in 1958 and for 23 percent in 1959 (Tilton, 1971, p. 93). Exact figures for the following period, as far as we know, are not available, but the order of magnitude can be roughly reconstructed. According to the figures provided by Linvill and Lester Logan (1977), over the period 1958–74 the total government contribution to R & D has been $930 million which compares with privately funded R & D of $1200 million, i.e. an average publicly financed amount of 44 per cent. Furthermore, we know that military (and, generally, public) involvement reached a peak in the mid-sixties, related to the Minuteman II missile project and the Apollo project. On the hypothesis of an average R & D expenditure by the industry of around 10 per cent of sales[76] and a proportion of government-financed R & D of around 60 per cent, we get an estimate of around $80 million per year for the mid-sixties. Adding the financial contribution to the expansion of production facilities for military related products, we might easily get a figure well above $100 million per year. By comparison the UK total public financed R & D expenditure (both to private firms and to public laboratories and universities) in 1968 was £3.35 million, and the share directed to firms was £1.45 million.[77] In the USA, since the mid-sixties, government-financed R & D has declined, both in percentage of total R & D performed and in absolute real terms.[78] A renewed interest in military oriented R & D led in 1978–9 to a plan called VHSI (Very High Speed

TABLE 2.6   *USA: Estimates of military and direct government demand for semiconductors and integrated circuits, 1965–78, and 1979 VHSI plan*

Year	Direct public procurement % of total production by value	Federal government procurements $m.	% of total industry shipments	American military demand (direct & indirect) as % of shipments	Military demand for ICs as % of total shipments
	1	2	3	4	5
1955	38				
1956	36				
1957	36				
1958	39				
1959	45				
1960	48			50	
1961	39				
1962	39				100
1963	35	213.1	35.5		94
1964	28				85
1965	28	193.6	22.0		72
1966	27	254.4	24.1	30	53
1967	27	296.8	27.6		43
1968	25	273.9	23.0		37
1969		246.5	16.9		
1970		274.9	20.6		
1971		192.9	12.7		
1972		228.1	11.9	24	
1973		201.4	5.8		
1974		217.0			13.7
1975					15.0
1976					11.7
1977					12.3
1978		437.0	(11)		9.0

1979–84   VHSI Plan and related military projects: estimated $150–200 m subsidies and contracts

NOTES AND SOURCES

Column 1 Tilton (1971), estimated on the basis of US Department of Commerce, BDSA, *Electronic Components and Related Data*, and *Shipments of Selected Electronic Components*, various years; Electronic Industry Association, *Electronic Industry Yearbook*, 1969. (The figures include Department of Defence, Atomic Energy Commission, CIA, Federal Aviation Agency, National Aeronautical and Space Administration).

Columns 2 and 3 US Bureau of the Census, *Current Industrial Report: Shipments of Defence-Oriented Industries*, various years; except 1974 and 1978 in column 2: *Electronic Times*, 14 December 1978.

TABLE 2.7 *US Government contribution to firms for R & D and refinement projects*

	1955	1956	1957	1958	1959	1960	1961
R & D	3.2	4.1	3.8	4.0	6.3	6.8	11.0
Production refinement	4.9	14.8	.5	2.1	1.0	1.1	2.5
Total	8.1	18.9	4.3	6.1	7.3	7.9	13.5

SOURCE BDSA. *Semiconductors: US Production and Trade*, 1961, quoted in Tilton (1971).

Integration), introduced by the Pentagon in 1980 and involving around $200 million.[79]

Military Policies, Innovations, Industrial Dynamism

The long-run effect of the military sector upon technical change and patterns of growth is, generally speaking, quite controversial. We have been implicitly suggesting above that military R & D procurement policies were an important factor in enhancing US innovativeness in semiconductors. On the other hand, there is sufficient evidence that time-lags between military and civilian applications of an innovation are often extremely long.[80] Even more important, a military-based economic system may induce a process of 'ossification' of the industrial structure.[81] The apparent contradiction may find an explanation in the light of the model suggested above. The 'military trajectory' of technical change may or may not be similar to the 'civilian trajectory' (i.e. that pattern of technical change which emerges as the dominant one in the proper market sector of the industry). Only the former case may allow a positive impact of *lato sensu* military policies, upon non-military

---

NOTES AND SOURCES of Table 2.6 (*Contd.*)
Column 4 1960: Finan (1975); 1966: OECD (1968); 1972: J. P. Ferguson Associates estimates, quoted in Finan (1975). (Figures for all three years include semiconductor inputs in government purchase of military equipment.)
Column (5) See Notes and Sources for Column 1 except 1974–78: United States International Trade Commission (1979). (This source includes all government purchases.)

innovativeness. In the opposite case, a military-based economy may indeed contribute to that paralysis of industrial dynamics which has been suggested by M. Kaldor (1978).

The almost total coincidence in semiconductors, over a long period of time (at least during the fifties and the sixties), between the military pattern of technical change and the civilian pattern cannot be generalised to other industries. Bearing this in mind we may analyse the set of military–related policies.

First, it appears that the procurement policy resulted not only in increasing competitiveness, for a given flow of innovations, but it probably also contributed to *induce* and *shape* the direction of the innovative process itself.

The *selection process* between possible trajectories of technological advance was heavily influenced by military requirements. Most of the features that we attributed to the established pattern of innovation – a trend towards miniaturisation, reliability, lower energy dispersion, wider range of frequency and, later, with ICs, increased complexity of the performed functions – corresponded almost precisely with the requirements of military demand. This coincidence was missing with respect to only one 'dimension': steadily decreasing unit costs are one of the basic conditions for the expansion of non-military markets while they are much less relevant in public purchases. Two factors, however, operated in this direction too: first, interrelated product and process innovations, which allowed increased complexity, miniaturisation, reliability, etc. *at the same time* happened to lower unit costs; second, the so-called learning effect affected unit costs as the volume of production increased (see also below, Chapter 3).

Since 'yields' (the percentage of reliable devices on total output) are proportional to the cumulated volume of output, a mass military demand allowed to go further on the learning curve. Furthermore, devices which are unsatisfactory by military standards might be perfectly acceptable in other non-military applications. Military procurement contracts are generally agreed on a cost-plus basis (accounting for *total costs*); thus public procurement results in a cross-subsidisation on non-military purchases. Finally, innovations which could find military applications might have faced a shorter pay-back period on the cost of the innovation itself, given the mentioned cost-plus nature of public contracts (which include also provisions for development costs).

It should be noted that military demand involves a very high degree of *technological determinateness*, generally specifying the functions required from the products, and also the technological features of the products themselves. As we have been arguing previously this plays an important part in the troublesome emergence of new technologies.

A priori nothing can guarantee the coincidence between the military and the civilian trajectories. The former is in many respects an 'autonomous' factor, depending on political and military choices; the latter relates to the technical requirements of civilian users and depends on the existence of some – actual or potential – markets. There is no guarantee that the patterns of technical innovation defined in the two sectors will continue to coincide in the long run. There is some evidence, in fact, that a significant divergence has begun to emerge in the seventies; the military demanding almost absolute reliability, miniaturisation near the limits of semiconductor technology and immunity at rather extreme environmental conditions, and the civilian market requiring further cost decreases, extension of applications and functions.[82] These are, however, relatively recent trends after the establishment of precise directions of technical changes. In their emergence, the military had a decisive part indeed. It is important to analyse how this 'military lead' operates.

First, military procurements *guarantee a market* for any innovation which satisfies military requirements. Therefore it considerably reduces the uncertainty associated with the innovative process (*if* the latter occurs towards the required directions). It must also be noticed that both the *relative* and *absolute* sizes of military demand are important since the cost of innovating is generally less than proportional to the expected sales. Furthermore military demand is generally concentrated on the technologically most advanced products. Thus its same existence can operate as an incentive to innovate.

Second, R & D subsidies – as we saw – had been quite substantial. Their effectiveness, however, is more questionable. The evidence suggests that military R & D projects have recorded an impressive number of failures.[83] Moreover, most of the important innovations occurred in privately sponsored R & D projects. Data suggests that the R & D cost per patent received has been much higher in military sponsored projects than in company-financed ones.[84] On the other hand, in a period when uncertainty about patterns of technical change is very high, inventive and innovative activities often follow trial-and-error procedures. The positive role of failures should not be underestimated.

In many cases, the failure of military R & D projects was due to their backwardness *vis-à-vis* the 'state-of-the-art' (e.g. most of the projects on miniaturisation) or, in some other cases, to the fact that they followed viable but more expensive and less promising directions of research (as in the 'molecular electronics' project). It is also true that the entire semiconductor industry capitalised on these failures, adding to its experience and its knowledge of the potential technological trajectories (including those where a technological advance was not feasible or not profitable). To be fair, we need to mention also the successful military R & D projects, like the support given to Texas Instruments for the further development of silicon transistors and the Air Force project on ICs, again with TI (parallel to the alternative and more ambitious 'molecular electronics' project awarded to Westinghouse[85]).

Third, the military pursued a deliberate policy of expansion of productive capacity, especially in the late fifties and early sixties,[86] which probably stimulated the search for new applications and markets. (The effect of this policy on prices will be examined in Chapter 3).

To summarise, military (and space) programmes affected both the supply and the demand side of the semiconductor industry. On the supply side they provided:

1. An impetus towards precisely defined technological directions and areas in which to allocate R & D efforts. It is worth stressing the non-market nature of those 'demands'[87] and their 'determinateness'.
2. The incentive towards and the direct financial support of the exploration of possibly different alternative paths of technical change – especially when precise trajectories were not yet well defined and there was what one could call the *burden of the first comer* (together, of course, with the rewards for the first comer). This burden, caused by attempts at trying and testing a number of possible areas of advance (which is much greater than that required from imitation) has been, partly, undertaken by public institutions (military and space agencies). We are not arguing that this is the only way to promote innovations at the uncertain beginning of an industry and not even that it is the most efficient one Simply, those tasks are very important and the private business sector might often underinvest in them.
3. The speeding up of technical progress at what we could define as the 'maximum rate' compatible with the existing knowledge, technology, and experience.
4. The subsidy to expand productive capacity to certain target levels considered necessary for national defence requirements. That meant

that the industry was somehow 'forced' to find additional sources of demand for an exogenously determined productive capacity.

5. A push towards standardisation of production.[88]
6. The lowering of entry barriers for new firms which could find a market with low 'cost of access'.[89]

On the demand side, public policies resulted in:

7. A guarantee of a future market for any innovation corresponding to the required technological features. This occurred both implicitly (every firm knew that there was a market for such a device), and explicitly, through development and procurement contracts. As a consequence public-assured demand played a risk-taking role.
8. The expansion of demand, with associated powerful learning effects upon productivity and unit costs.
9. (Possibly) a subsidy element involved in public contracts which helped to cover fixed costs (such as R & D) that would otherwise have fallen upon civilian sales.

The policies of procurement, R & D financing, and explicit indication of the required direction of technological advance, together, operated as a widespread and finalised allocative mechanism of both productive and research efforts.

A Conducive Environment for Diffusion: The American Market

One of the conclusions of our argument is that public (especially military and space) policies in the fifties and early sixties operated – to put it in a somewhat extreme form – as a powerful *planning* authority which had a major role in shaping the directions of technical change and in determination of a technological frontier for the industry. In passing, we must mention that this view is not particularly popular within the industry and among the students of it. It is not very surprising: it often happens that the *context conditions* of some action or achievement are less visible than the immediate causes, even if the former are a necessary condition for the latter.

One must not underestimate the role of the US market as a very conducive environment for a swift diffusion and commercial exploitation of inventions/innovations and as a powerful incentive to further technical progress.

Our thesis, however, is that the market environment was particularly conducive *because* the American industry as a whole was establishing and reinforcing its technological lead (it being on the technological frontier). The relationship between innovative leadership and a favourable market environment produced 'virtuous circle' conditions. Among the features of a very conducive environment are: the mobility of scientists and engineers; the availability of venture capital; and the size and sophistication of the American market.[90] Some qualifications must be added, however.

First, mobility of scientists, managers, etc., other things being equal, is proportional to the quantity of advanced knowledge they embody. All this is very obvious, but it must be remembered that it makes a difference between deciding to leave, say, Bell Labs and establish a new company producing a new innovative device or, on the contrary, leaving a European company in order to produce something which is already available (probably at better quality and lower cost) from some American company. In other words, the reason why people do not rediscover the wheel and exploit their innovation through a new company rests in the fact that the wheel has already been discovered and not in the particular institutional nature of the various wheel markets.

Second, similar arguments apply to the availability of venture capital: a necessary condition for the latter (even if not a sufficient one) is a reasonably high expectation of success for the new companies. This expectation depends also on the technological level of the company concerned.

Third, an hypothesis of strict dependence of the technological levels and dynamics of a country upon the nature of its markets is highly questionable. On theoretical grounds, the above critique of demand−pull theories undermines the basic transmission mechanism between market 'signalling' and technical change. On empirical grounds, the evidence we have presented on the ways public intervention affected technical change is hardly consistent with any interpretation of the successful American innovative performance in terms of 'the magic of the market place'. Public intervention did not only affect productive capacity, size of the market and entry conditions, but − even more important − induced a huge *accumulation of knowledge*, directly aimed at technological innovation in very definite directions and influenced greatly these particular directions (the 'trajectories') where technological progress had to be pushed. In so doing, it helped to define a *technological frontier* on which, by the early 1960s, the American industry was firmly placed.

It should be clear that we do not intend to argue that this result was an effect of the *military* policies *as such* (together with the other conditions listed above, such as the existence of several big risk-taking corporations, the presence of 'bridging institutions' like Bell Labs, etc.). On the contrary, the fact that this result was achieved through military-finalised policies probably implied comparatively higher economic costs (even leaving aside any social and political judgement), and bigger difficulties and 'frictions' in diffusing the technical advances from the military to the civilian market.[91] The point is that the result (the definition of established patterns of technical change and of an ever-moving technological frontier) was partly achieved through a non-market mechanism, which pushed the accumulation of knowledge in precise directions, while making the innovative process profitable in these same chosen directions: thus, it acted as an allocative mechanism affecting R & D and investment decisions of individual firms and determining the pace of technical progress. The actual market mechanisms acted contextually as powerful forces in the diffusion of innovation, knowledge and experience throughout the industry, in further shortening the time-lag between inventions and innovations and in providing the incentive for a very high private commitment to innovation. Several successful spin-offs from established firms succeeded in transforming *very quickly* (quicker than established firms) inventions and technical experience, etc. into new marketable devices. Public policies also had a role in the process of diffusion. First, in assuring a market for the most advanced products, and also by decreasing the risk faced by new entrants (generally innovative spin-off firms). Secondly, through the requirement of *second-sourcing* (i.e. at least two companies had to produce the same device), they accelerated the diffusion of 'state-of-the-art' technology throughout the industry. Finally, the consent degree ending the anti-trust case, US Government versus AT & T, actually forced Bell Labs to disseminate their patents and technology through the entire industry.[92]

As the industry became more established, its technological features more defined, its patterns of technical change clearer, the *institutional planning role of military policies decreased*: technical change got its own momentum, while civilian markets expanded in size and in number. Once a clear trajectory of technical change had emerged, the *process of generation* of technical change became relatively more *endogenous* to the 'normal' competitive process between firms and to the interaction between semiconductor producers and components users. (We shall return to the interaction between innovation and dynamic competitive processes in the next chapter.)

At the end of the sixties, a decade after the development of Integrated Circuits, and contextual to the growth of large civilian markets (computers, professional instruments, industrial and consumer electronics), military and civilian technological trajectories began to diverge slightly. Since in ICs the design of the circuits became very important and was sometimes customised, function and performance requirements of military and commercial users did not necessarily coincide.[93] In the sixties, however, as already mentioned, innovative dynamics achieved more stable patterns. Moreover, a similar process of stabilisation of the trajectories of technical change in semiconductor-using sectors increased the technological determinateness of the relationship between producers and users of semiconductors.[94]

Before analysing the new features of the innovative process in the seventies, we must explain the differential conditions between the USA, Europe and Japan.

2.5 THE USA, EUROPE, JAPAN: EXPLAINING THE DYNAMICS OF TECHNOLOGICAL LEADS AND LAGS

What happened in the late fifties and sixties in the USA is extremely important, because that was a time when a definite technological frontier was established, assisted, as analysed above, by the co-ordinating and planning mechanism provided implicitly by public (especially military) policies. At the end of that process, a much strengthened *American technological lead* emerged. The fifties and early sixties are of central relevance also in determining the relative performance of the European semiconductor industry *vis-à-vis* the American one.

We shall assess the causes and processes which led to this result. The Japanese experience will be used continuously as a 'control case' to check the applicability of our conclusions.[95] For analytical purposes we shall maintain the differences between (a) *production* of innovation, technological advances, etc., (b) their commercial exploitation, (c) their intra-industrial *diffusion*. The process that we have been analysing with respect to the American industry was focused on the first aspect – the determination of an ever-moving technological frontier, and the correlated American technological leadership. In doing that, technology has been recognised as a complex body of knowledge ranging from pure science to manufacturing expertise, which is difficult to transfer, and which can be 'accumulated' over time through expensive efforts, trials and errors, etc. Moreover, on the American scene, through the fifties and early sixties the main identifiable subjects of this process were 'border' institutions like Bell Labs, large electrical companies, public agencies such as the military, and new very dynamic companies.[96] This interplay induced a rapid generation of technical knowledge and an outstandingly successful economic exploitation of it.

The European Scene

Some structural differences in the starting points between Europe and the USA have already been mentioned (relative size of big electrical firms, the absence of something comparable with Bell Labs, etc.). We will try now to point to some similarities and differences in the *process* of technological advance between the two sides of the Atlantic:

1. Big European companies entered the semiconductor field at different times, with different technological capabilities to begin with and devoting different financial and technical resources.[97] This aspect contributes to an explanation of the differences in the technological levels acquired by the various national industries. Some firms entered very soon: notably Philips and Siemens,[98] but there were also some British firms, for example, AEI and Ferranti (although they generally confined themselves to special applications).
2. Those companies entering the field generally focused on the 'technological directions' and applications in which they were already operating. Since most of these big companies were deeply involved in consumer electronic (Philips) and electrical engineering (Siemens, AEI, etc.), the result has been a much greater stress on technological advances fitting those applications, and a relative neglect of military and computer-related applications, where the greatest technical advances were being made.
3. The outcome (in each country and in the whole of Europe) was that fewer possible technological directions were explored and even in some of these, the progress was slower than in the USA (if we consider the industry as a whole). Nonetheless, in the selected fields a few companies managed to be very near the technological frontier (especially Philips and Siemens), in the areas of consumers' electronics applications[99] and in power devices. Taking a general overview of the European industries in the fifties and early sixties, we could say that they were generally following a pattern of *technological imitation* with a significant but not increasing time-lag *vis-à-vis* American innovations. Table 2.8 shows the average time-lag for each country.

It must be noticed that all the innovations but one refer to discrete devices and, furthermore, that the first European introduction may

TABLE 2.8 *Average lag in first commercial production, by country 1951–63*

Country		Average lag (in years)
UK	a	1.9
	b	2.2
Germany	a	2.7
	b	2.7
France	b	2.8
Italy	a	3.8
Japan	b	2.5

a. SOURCE Freeman (1974, p. 64). It covers 13 innovations first introduced over the period 1951–60 (innovations previous to transistor are excluded from the calculation).
b. SOURCE Tilton (1971, pp. 25–7). It covers 13 innovations first introduced in the period 1951–63.

NOTES
1. The sets of innovation in a. and b., although similar, do not coincide.
2. One innovation in Tilton's sample was first introduced in Japan (tunnel diode) and the American lag was one year; and one innovation in Freeman's sample was first introduced in UK (germanium rectifier). The Italian average lag refers to only 9 innovations and the German one (in Freeman's sample) to 10 innovations.
3. The original sources are: *Patterns and Problems of Technical Innovation in American Industry*, Report to National Science Foundation, US Dept. of Commerce, 1963; interviews by C. Freeman, T. Golding and J. Tilton.

have been undertaken by a European subsidiary of an American firm. There are a few innovations which are crucial in the subsequent history of semiconductor technology and which contributed to two very different developments of the industry in the USA and Europe. Among them, there appear to be silicon transistor, the integrated circuit and the MOS integrated circuit: these are precisely the fields of inquiry which were neglected in Europe, and, on the contrary, forcefully stimulated in the USA by the military innovation policies. Now, with hindsight, we recognise them as the most promising and far-reaching ones.
4. In the USA one industrial sector which benefited the most and more directly from the strive towards miniaturisation, increased speed and

greater reliability was the computer industry.[100] We can see at work there a *virtuous circle* in which exogenously stimulated technical advances found a growing commercial market which, on its side, represented the ground, the incentive and the stimuli for further innovations. In Europe, again with hindsight, we notice the origin of a somewhat vicious circle, in which one of the reasons for weakness of computer manufacturers was the European lag in components, and, conversely, the relatively small size of the computer sector failed to stimulate technical progress in semiconductors towards the most promising directions.

With the advent of ICs (which were generally silicon made, on planar technology), there is evidence that the European lag increased considerably (reaching in some cases several years). Although we cannot provide exact figures, Table 2.9 tries to give a picture of the maximum and minimum lag in first commercial production by European companies for the most recent years.

TABLE 2.9   *Lags in first commercial production in European[a] industry by class of products and technology, 1970–80*

Class of products and technologies	Lag (in years) (Estimated minimum and maximum lags)
Analog ICs	0/2
Digital ICs (other than MOS)	0/3
MOS ICs (incl MPU) and memories	2/4

[a] European stands for European-owned and it excludes also European-owned firms located in the USA.
SOURCES   Interviews

The qualitative evidence we obtained from interviews suggests that the average lag is somewhat nearer to the maximum value of the ranges shown in that Table. Furthermore, the lag is higher in the newer and fastest growing products and technologies: among them MOS integrated circuits and microprocessors.

Environment and Behaviours: Structural Constraints and Strategic Degrees of Freedom

The points we have just made hint at some wider questions which we shall discuss in the next chapter. It is worth mentioning them in order to acquire a deeper understanding of the factors which produced the relative European weakness in semiconductor technology. One may ask: Is that historically due to *wrong* choices (or wrong strategies) on the part of European companies? Or is it, on the contrary, *determined* by binding environmental constraints? The stylised facts suggested above contain a bit of both. We need, therefore, to make the interpretative model explicit. Companies (especially big companies endowed with a strong technological base and wide financial resources) enjoy some degree of freedom in the determination of their innovation and imitation strategies within constraints which do not only define the boundaries of the set of possible strategies but also tend to 'pull' companies' behaviours in defined directions (through different expected profitabilities, market perspectives, degrees of uncertainty).

Note that this is a quite different problem from that of maximisation of some objective variable which is given such an overwhelming importance in textbook microeconomics. As we shall see at greater length in the next chapter when discussing the seminal contributions by Nelson and Winter,[101] it is rather a question of regularities in the interactive strategies between companies and the external environment (in some analogy with biological evolutionary theories).[102] Maximisation criteria as such are often a *non sequitur*, since in a changing environment one does not know exactly the set of choices and the set of outcomes.[103] Behaviours on the other hand, affect the economic environment and thus the constraints and the incentives which companies will face in the future.

Let us return to the history of European semiconductors. Differential structural conditions contributed heavily to shape the strategies of European companies. By the beginning of the sixties, it was no longer simply a matter of behavioural choices of the European companies but also a *structural constraint* that the European industry had to face due to *differential technological capabilities*. Choices of pushing in certain technological directions instead of others achieved a cumulative effect and became part of the structural data that the industry and each firm had to consider. Those structural conditions, of course, can and always are changed, but it certainly requires time, resources and often a complex set of policies. In many studies on the industry this problem is overlooked and the European lag is either understood in terms of 'classical' product cycle theories (i.e. with a big emphasis on lags in demand[104]), or in terms of firms' conduct (sometimes related to competitive structure of the industry, but generally assuming that at any given time, discretionality of each firm is high and the set of possible technological options is large).[105] Of course, firms' decisions on technological strategies do matter, but their effect is cumulative: decisions of the past become constraints in the future; chosen 'patterns' of technological development condition the future innovative output of firms and of the industry.

In this sense we may use the concept of 'technological frontier' as a structural data which heavily conditions and determines the behaviour and competitive performance of American industry, as compared to the European industry. We saw, in the American case, the emergence of that frontier (more realistically a cluster of frontiers) in a complex dynamics of competing technological trajectories, whose outcome was the establishment of silicon-based technologies pushing towards an ever-increasing density, speed and complexity of the tasks performed.

The European industry remained left out of this process of definition of the new technological paths and, generally speaking, confined itself to the role of close (and fairly successful) imitator on the old technological pattern for fairly traditional applications, throughout the fifties and the sixties.

The process of innovation/improvement on the technological frontier, is often cumulative (this is why it acts as a structural constraint): the probability of advancing to the frontier is also proportional to the position already occupied with respect to it.[106] This applies to both companies and, particularly, countries.

A Comparison of Innovation Policies: The European Neglect for Semiconductors in the 1950s and 1960s

Regarding each individual company, public policies represent one of the 'environmental factors' which – as we analysed in the case of the USA – might have a powerful effect on the direction and the rate of technical progress. Let us thus consider the role of public policies in Europe (and Japan). Tables 2.10 and 2.11 provide some comparative figures on procurement policies and public R & D support in the total components industry (and semiconductors, when available). What is striking is that, at a first look, the variance between various countries is very high and does not seem to bear any relationship to the different trends in their innovative capabilities.

The UK and France share with the USA a relevant public (mainly military) demand and a high percentage of publicly financed research. Conversely, Germany, Italy and Japan had a low or negligible impact of public procurement and low or non-existent financing of R & D. In

TABLE 2.10   *Estimated size of government markets, as a percentage of the component industry's output*[a], *in the mid-sixties*

Country	Year 64	65	66
USA[b]		30%	
Japan		negligible	
UK[c]			30%
Germany		negligible	
France: Tubes		25%	
Semiconductors	12%		
Other components			30%
Italy			5%
Canada			10%
Sweden			30%

[a] Components means *active* (i.e. semiconductors and tubes, etc.) and *passive* (resistors, capacitors, etc.)
[b] Defence shipment only.
[c] Defence and civilian public procurement.
SOURCE   OECD (1968, p. 26).

other words, those figures would suggest that government policies did not matter very much in determining the industrial performance. The argument, however, must be qualified in two ways. First, the *absolute size* of both public demand and R & D financing in Europe was very different from the USA. Total British government funding of R & D (which was the highest in Europe) for 1968 was less than one-tenth of the American counterpart.[107] Second, in the USA most of the government-funded R & D was performed in industry (around 95 per cent), while in France only 45 per cent and in the UK 40 per cent[108] were.

The hypothesis we will suggest here is that policies in Europe until the late sixties had a very limited impact, (while they have been very important in Japan, as we shall see below). The technological efforts in European companies were primarily directed, in a 'spontaneous' manner, towards advances (generally through fast imitation and even with some original innovations) in the traditional fields of discrete devices for consumer electronics and electrical engineering. Government policies (either through purchases or R & D financing), when they existed, did not intervene in those areas which were already covered (despite limitations and substantial imbalance between countries) by the autonomous technological decisions of European firms. Government procurement and R & D financing were mainly concerned with military

TABLE 2.11   *State support for R & D in component industry as a percentage of total R & D (1965–8)*

Country	% of total R & D	Notes
USA[a]	$\simeq 50\%$	
Japan	0%	Until 1965
	$\simeq 10\%$	Development contracts in 1967: $1.9m.
UK (1)	30%	Around $11 m direct financing to total component industry
(2)	57%	1968; government financed research in semiconductors (either performed in industry or public institutions). The percentage of industry-performed is 35%.
Germany	Negligible	Some indirect support since the first 'data processing plan'.
France (1)	22%	1964, total components
(2)	33% (1968: 45%)	Semiconductors
Italy	0%	
Sweden	very low	

SOURCES   OECD (1968 p. 178) except for UK-(2): Golding (1971); for France-(2) (1968): Tilton (1971); USA[a]: our estimates.

applications. Remarkably, the 'technological distance' between military-finalised devices and consumers' electronics is great, much greater, for instance, than the 'technological distance' between military applications and computers' applications.

We must answer to the question whether the military market helped the innovative/imitative capability of European industry. Our reply is that even in the UK and France it had a relatively limited role. We tried to argue that the military in the USA had the function of focusing and directing the innovative efforts and helped to *plan* some of the most relevant economic and technological variables on both the demand and the supply side. What is important is not the fact that the military was involved, but the economic and technological *roles* it performed. Indeed, the fact that the military itself played this role probably involved considerable inefficiencies, strains and high costs.[109]

There seems to be a crucial *asymmetry* between the role performed by the military in the 'first coming' economy and in the 'late coming' (imitating) ones. The function of directing inventive activity is facilitated if the first-comer operates in a vacuum, while the followers face an established technological trajectory and already existing products both in the civilian and the military fields. The inevitable conclusion is that military-oriented research efforts in Europe probably had the effect of speeding up imitation *in the military field*, but lacked a general impact on innovation and fast 'civilian' imitation. In other words, each European country, facing the huge American military-oriented innovation policy had two notional choices: first, they could have decided on similar military efforts[110] to push ambitiously in various technological directions and thus undertake part of the 'burden of the first-comer'; alternatively, they could have followed (as they generally did) an imitative military-oriented strategy. In this second case, however, we would expect the 'fall-out' from the military to the civilian sector to be very limited. This fall-out effect may happen in the virgin territory of the first-comer, while imitators always find new devices already diffused from the military to the civilian sector in the leading country.

This hypothesis of a fundamental asymmetry in the impact of military demand and military-oriented research between first-comer(s) and followers is corroborated by (and in some ways is an explanation of) the very detailed evidence analysed by Sciberras (1977). In his findings, the military market in the UK produces protected 'niches' where indigenous firms can operate without facing the competition of big (American) companies on the high volume civilian market, but does not induce substantial 'spill-over' effect in the latter.

Two more points have to be made. First, it is likely that even policies of quick imitation in the military field (i.e. a policy aimed at remaining near the 'military technological frontier') might not be very successful due to the relatively limited R & D efforts devoted to it (in comparison with the USA).[111] Secondly, we must notice how the entire argument *today* favouring higher military procurement and/or military R & D funding sounds somewhat contorted and devious. The argument, in fact, states that European countries should set a goal (technical progress in military-oriented devices) to achieve another goal (technical progress in non-military devices).[112] (We analyse these policies at greater length in Dosi, 1981a.)

All through the fifties and the sixties, public intervention has been totally absent in all European countries in the non-military fields. We could say that, compared with a consistent and finalised planning of the rate and direction of innovative activity in the USA, Europe presented conditions of *free-market imitation strategies* undertaken by each individual firm.[113]

The results, as mentioned, have been:

1. A fairly short (and maybe decreasing) imitation lag in more traditional technologies (e.g. germanium discrete semiconductor), generally in the areas oriented toward consumer electronics and power
   equipment.
2. A big delay in the newer technologies (ICs, computer applications).
3. No great sign of convergence between the technological level of each
   European country, the latter being a function of choices, capabilities
   and dimensions of few national firms.

At the end of the sixties all European semiconductor industries were
relative losers[114] in the ICs race, and the distance from the USA was
especially great in digital bipolar ICs and MOS ICs. This feature was
(and is) related to the European weakness in the computer industry and
is part of the European 'vicious circle' resulting in a weakness in digital
ICs, weakness and reduced size of the European computer industry, low
incentive for each European semiconductor firm to move consistently
into digital ICs technologies, lag in the latter, etc.[115]

The High Technology Imperative: The Case of Japan

It is very revealing to compare the European scene in the fifties and
sixties with the Japanese one, with which it shares many structural
similarities and many policy differences. First, both Japan and Europe
were imitators in discrete germanium components. Europe was, at the
beginning, much better placed, with higher technological levels to begin
with, and, in certain areas, placed on the frontier itself. Japan was lagging
far behind with low scientific and technological experience in the
semiconductor fields and a much higher imitation lag. Second, both were
mainly focusing on consumer electronics applications. Europe had a
much smaller military market than the USA and Japan had none. Third,
both were characterised by big established companies entering the field
of semiconductors[116] and undertaking the process of imitation.

To observe significant differences we have to look at the industrial
policies, in a broader sense, and compare them with Europe and the
USA. Since there are major discontinuities in Japanese policies and
strategies, it is convenient to analyse the entire history of Japanese
relationship between public agencies and endogenous market trends.
One should not be misled by the figures in Tables 2.10, 2.11 and 2.12:
confining public policies to procurement and financial transfers does not
lead us very far. In the Japanese case, policies, *lato sensu*, affected the
technological outcome through direct institutional mechanisms which

TABLE 2.12   *Japan: MITI's plans for the promotion of the data-processing industry, 1972–82*
(Million Yen)

Programme for 1972–6[a]

	1972	1973	1974	1975	1976
General promotion of computer development: new machines	4,150	14,026	15,250	12,475	10,825
Peripherals	700	936	1,400	900	600
Integrated circuits		1,700	1,800	0	0
Measures for the industry generally		600	1,200	1,200	0
New generation of LSI					3,500
Loans to the NECC	2,000	1,150	3,250	4,600	4,700
Japan Development Bank grants	1,100	850	850	850	850
Information Technology Promotion Agency	37	79	100	132	123
Government guarantees to lending institutions	1,450	1,750	900	1,200	1,500
Systems development	100	205	378	1,109	1,086

VLSI Plan for 1976–9: estimated Yen 30 bn[b]

SOURCES

[a] OECD (1977).
[b] Nomura (1980). The amount refers to grants only.

did not operate by means of strictly economic incentives: this makes them more difficult to detect but certainly not less effective.

We discussed the *laissez-faire* approach in Europe upto the early 1970s.[117] In Japan, on the other hand, there appears to have been a very early determination to achieve a strong technological and commercial position in high technology industry *in general*, and thus also in semiconductors.[118] The features of this Japanese commitment are worth investigating.

European policies, even when they existed in the 1970s and only in some countries, seem to adapt to the existing structure and strategies of the industry.[119] In Japan, given certain long-term objectives, part of industrial policy was the task of removing the structural constraints which would have made those objectives unprofitable for private companies. These kinds of institutional measures included: (a) very restrictive regulations on foreign investment (formally until 1974 and informally thereafter); (b) institutional definition and public monitoring of the terms of licensing agreements, which were required to benefit not one firm but the entire industry; (c) import controls (stopped in 1974); (d) setting of technological targets (for example the recent VLSI plan) and establishment of adequate research facilities to fulfil them (for example the institution in the seventies of joint research centres between the major companies, with direct government participation).

Notably, in the 1950s and 1960s, Japan followed the same technical path as European companies. The Japanese effort, though, was much more institutionally co-ordinated and finalised, aiming at:

1. A fast decrease of the lag *vis-à-vis* the American industry. Japanese industry undoubtedly succeeded in the task. Using the average imitation lag in the introduction of the major innovations listed by Tilton (1971), this lag decreased from 3.4 years in the fifties to 1.2 years in the early sixties.
2. The avoidance of duplications in R & D efforts and the diffusion as fast as possible of the best available technology throughout all firms. This seemed to be achieved through government control of imported technology and through informal (but very effective) co-ordination between government and companies. Again it must be noticed that duplication of technological efforts has been very high in Europe, not only among countries, but inside each national industry. Furthermore, hardly any policy promoted the diffusion of 'best technologies' through the European industry: diffusion had to be reached through the painstaking effort of each national industry and each firm.[120]
3. The stimulation of internal competition among Japanese firms, to promote technological and commercial aggressiveness and to maintain the most favourable structural conditions for technical progress.
4. The guarantee of a secured market for the industry (although *not* for each firm). The task was achieved through strict non-tariff control on imports[121] and on foreign investment.[122] This second aspect in particular is very important because it recreates institutionally the same 'vacuum environment' enjoyed in its internal market by the 'first-comer'. The question will be discussed later in relation to the effect of foreign investment in Europe (Chapter 4).
5. The control over imported technology. It is noticeable that licensing agreements were allowed and strongly favoured if, and as long as,

they contributed to enhance the general Japanese technological level (making the process of imitation/improvement quicker). They were opposed if they could substitute for a Japanese-developed technology or prevent such a development (this case could not generally have happened in the fifties and sixties, but occurred in the seventies). Japanese public controls on foreign technology agreements have always been very dᴇtailed and concerned also with relatively minor technological deals.

We have already noticed that the Japanese, as far as technology is concerned, followed (in the fifties and sixties) a path fairly similar to the European one, with much greater success both on technological and commercial grounds.[123] This outcome is even more striking if judged in relation to the relative points of departure (consistently worse for Japan) and in relation to the lower Japanese R & D efforts.[124]

In the mid-sixties, Japan faced very similar problems to Europe since she was left behind in the development of the new technologies (ICs, digital applications, etc.) The realisation of the economic potential of the new technological patterns in Europe was left to the promptness and the interest in the new applications of each individual company.[125] No uniformity can be found among companies and countries in the timing and size of the 'imitative reaction', and, broadly speaking, it followed the same patterns as the described previous behaviours in the fifties. For Japan, too, the new successful technological patterns anticipated by the American industry made a great deal of its imitative efforts on the 'old' trajectories obsolete. Swiftly, Japan started a huge and co-ordinated attempt to reduce the lag in the new technological areas. The difficulties this time were much greater due to the more complex features of the integrated circuit technologies involved. By the late 1970s, however, Japanese imitative lag had shortened impressively and in some fields had disappeared altogether.

Our interpretative argument is that in Japan industrial and trade policies allowed a definition of company strategy consistent with the national objectives and not the other way round, as it has often happened in Europe.

It has been noted elsewhere[126] that Japan is also characterised by an apparent closeness between policy-makers (especially MITI) and companies, which partly explains the success of Japanese industrial policies. This closeness, however, is not uncommon to some European countries (notably France, but also Germany). What is striking in the Japanese case is the capability of policy-makers and institutions to represent the long-term interest of Japanese industry as a whole – to a certain extent forcing it upon each individual company – *making rewarding for each firm what is considered necessary for the country*. One could, in fact, say that while most other countries have considered their place in the international division of labour as given at each point in time by the international market mechanism, the Japanese have conquered it. The Japanese case is notable as the only example of success of industrial policies in nearly eliminating the technological lag *vis-à-vis* the American semiconductor industry. In our view, very consistent and comprehensive policies are an important part of the explanation of the different performance of Europe and Japan.

The choice of instruments have also been crucial: variables that in Europe had to be considered among the constraints (like foreign investment or licensing policies by American firms), in Japan could partly become instrumental variables subjected to institutional control. European policies, for their part, whenever they existed, generally emphasised just one main instrument – R & D subsidies.

On the Japanese side subsidies never played a major role until the recent four-year VLSI plan, publicly financed for $360 million of which $250 million were government loans (see Table 2.12). More importantly, Japan had non-tariff import protection, control over foreign investment and monitoring of technology transfers. On top of this came a process of building a 'corporatist' industrial consensus around technological and manufacturing targets, agreed in a detailed bargaining process between companies, the State, and the unions. In the Japanese scenario, it seems particularly difficult to assess who is the prime mover. How much of Japanese dynamism can be attributed to government policies and how much to private companies? One cannot attribute to MITI alone the general difference in performance between Japan and Europe: more correctly, the difference seems to consist in a strikingly effective relationship between institutional settings (including MITI) and an extremely competitive internal market environment (oligopolistic competition amongst the major Japanese groups).

Certainly, Japanese companies have shown a highly aggressive attitude, both in technological and market aspects, together with a high degree of far-sightedness. However, one can be very entrepreneurial in a broad set of activities, ranging from marketing very sophisticated computers to selling oranges in Naples. The fact that the Japanese followed the first route clearly depends on a set of structural and institutional factors. Government policies provided many of these. Others probably derive from the structure of Japanese society as such, and two features are worth mentioning here. First, the immobility of manpower and the system of lifetime employment, instead of being paralysing factors, probably represent a strong motivation for strategies of long-run planning and a search for growth sectors. What in Western economies, especially in the USA, is left to macroeconomic mechanisms and at micro level to the working of some kind of Schumpeterian competition (technology-based oligopolitic rivalry, emergence of new innovative companies, etc.) in Japan is internalised in the companies themselves in what appears to be both a social and economic commitment. Second, there is a more fundamental issue which relates to the fundamental 'rules of the game' and their degree of social acceptance. It is, in our view, a crucial aspect of the relation between State, firms and social groups (and the relation between planning and market mechanisms): the greater the consensus on the basic rules of the game, the greater appears also the consistency of individual (company) behaviour with a commonly accepted set of objectives. Generally, a cohesive social structure is associated with an entire set of institutions within a social hierarchy for managing shared objectives. At the same time, again not very surprisingly, planning does not need to show up in its authoritive form, but appears much more as 'natural harmony' between social groups and between individual decisions.[127] In the case of Japan, one of the 'corporatist commitments' has been the *technological imperative* of a quick upgrading of her industrial structure, well beyond any traditional short-run profitability calculation.

2.6 TECHNOLOGICAL TRENDS IN THE 1970s (AND SOME SPECULATION ON THE 1980s)

The Era of Integrated Circuits and Microprocessors

Starting from the early sixties, a transition, from the 'era of discrete components' to the 'ICs era', begins. By the turn of the decade, integrated circuits had become the dominant cluster of technologies in the industry and by far the most dynamic one. Throughout the 1970s, microprocessor-related technologies acquire an ever increasing importance. One can easily forecast a new transition to an 'era of microprocessors' for the 1980s. Let us consider the main features of the technological patterns of change and the relative position of the three Western areas (the USA, Europe and Japan) with respect to the technological frontiers that these technological trajectories define. Even if the trajectories of technical progress follow the dimension described above towards miniaturisation (i.e. increasing density of the circuits), speed, reliability and decreasing costs, a few specific aspects of the 'ICs era' (and even more so of the 'microprocessor era') must be mentioned.[128]

First, the inter-relation between manufacturing and product technology, on the one hand, and circuitry design, application and 'software', on the other hand, in the era of ICs and MPUs becomes an essential feature of technical progress. Discrete components could be assembled in several ways to obtain the required circuits related to particular applications. Increasingly, with ICs, the range of possible applications is already 'embodied' in the structure and performance of the circuit itself. Ernst (1982) argues the progressive convergence between the technology of the circuits and the technology of the systems in which they enter. In other words, the software of the final commodities becomes increasingly embodied into the hardware of the circuits. This applies particularly to microprocessors and generally to VLSI circuits (other than standard RAM memories). Since it has sometimes been suggested that, on the contrary, very large scale integration would have led to increasing standardisation of the technology,[129] the issue is worth further consideration. Increasing circuit integration means greater technological possibilities for a circuit of performing a certain range of functions. However, it also increases the cost of software applications for the users. The more a circuit is 'finalised' to a certain application, the lower is the applicative cost. In addition to this, the use of 'standard' circuits for any particular application generally implies that only parts of the full logical capability of the device are utilised. Conversely, if the cost of development of a custom circuit is spread over a short production run unit costs might be higher.[130] One can easily see how the two factors generate a trade-off between custom and standard devices both in terms of costs and in terms of applicative efforts for the users.

There is another 'dimension' to the trajectory of technical progress discussed above, namely the improvement of the trade-off between the width of the range of applications (and thus 'standardisation') of the circuits and the applicative complexity. Again, Ernst (1982) argues that the semiconductor industry is heading towards a *software bottleneck* in two senses: (a) the increasing programming complexity is not matched by comparably increasing productivity in the design of the circuits; (b) more important for the technological features of semiconductors, one of the constraints upon technical progress is defined by the capability of producing higher-level-logic programmes. Progress along this latter (software) 'dimension' improves the trade-offs related to the cost and complexity of application of the circuits. Conversely, for any given state-of-the-art in manufacturing technology and in circuit design the higher the 'synergy' between producers and users of circuits, the lower are costs and applicative difficulties for the user-sectors.

Second, we have emphasised the nature of technical progress which has historically been relatively 'disembodied' from capital equipment. While these disembodied features certainly remain, in the 1970s technical progress in manufacturing equipment has become increasingly important.[131] Product innovations themselves (e.g. ever increasing density of the circuits) are constrained by innovation in the equipment (e.g. sub-micron lithography through electron beams or X-rays). It is worth mentioning that for the first time equipment manufacturers appear as process innovators in the semiconductor industry (see Table 2.2).

On the Factors Shaping 'Normal' Technical Progress

In the early days of semiconductors, US public (military and space) policies, as we have seen, performed an important role of selection and guidance of the directions of technical progress. That role has since decreased.

We are now in the position of answering the following question: What are the factors which shape the directions of the innovative activity when powerful external factors cease to exert their 'pulling' and 'pushing' influence? We have already given part of the answer, identifying one of the factors: 'normal' technical progress maintains a momentum of its own which defines the broad orientation of the innovative activities. This in-built heuristic is particularly clear in the semiconductor case. Take, for example, the fundamental trend in the industry towards increasing density of the circuits: the doubling of the number of components per chip every year (in the late 1970s every two-three years) is almost a 'natural law' of the industry. After $1-K$ memories one progressed to $4-K$, $16-K$, $64-K$ and further increases in integration are expected. The same applies to microprocessors, from 4 to 8, 16, 32 bit devices. This *cumulative process* has an important role in the competitive process of the industry, by continuously creating asymmetries between firms and countries in their relative technological success.

A second factor stems from the relationship between innovation in semiconductors and application of these innovations in the user sectors (which are innovations as such in the latter). A mutual effect can be identified there. Technical change in semiconductors defines one of the boundaries of the set of possible technical advances in 'downstream' sectors. On the other hand, both technological problems and technological and commercial opportunities in these downstream sectors focus and lead the direction of technological advances in semiconductors.[132] We shall find the opportunity below to show that this interrelationship is not entirely represented by its 'traded' features and that an aspect, which is at least as important as market-related signals, is constituted by flows of information, various kinds of externalities, convergences and complementarities between different technologies, etc. This second factor is going to become more important, given the increasingly system-related nature of semiconductor technology.[133]

A third factor relates to the 'inducement' effect of changes in market opportunities, relative prices and distributive shares upon the directions of the innovative activities. We hardly need to stress this aspect that is the core of traditional explanations of technical progress which we criticised above. Our critique, it should be clear, was not meant to deny the existence of such a factor. To repeat, we argued, first, that this 'inducement' operates particularly with respect to 'normal' technical progress, and second, that it occurs *within the boundaries* defined by the basic technological trajectory.

Note that this third factor (market inducement) is somewhat overlapping with the other two: an implicit trend towards so-called 'factors saving' is part of the 'dimension' of the technological trajectory of progress which is quite independent of *changes* in income distribution. In other words the reduction in unit costs and the improvement in performance/price indicators actually represent permanent labour-saving and capital-saving trends which are there no matter how income distribution (wage and profit rates) behaves through time. Reactiveness to changes in income distribution, relative prices and cost structures comes on top of these long-run trends. Moreover, the inducement mechanism often affects the direction of technical change through 'untraded' producer–user inter-relationships.

As far as semiconductors are concerned one may expect that the evolution of production structures towards a higher capital intensity (see also Chapter 3) and the increasing costs of design, software, etc. will lead the trajectory of technical progress towards a much heavier emphasis on:

(a) Process innovations aimed at a diminution of the capital/output ratio (for the trends in the latter see again Chapter 3)

(b) Innovations in software and design production (computer-based automation such as Computer Aided Design – CAD – etc.).[134]

The three general factors we have mentioned (the in-built features of the technological trajectory, producer–user inter-relationships and *lato sensu* market inducements) are the *structural* forces at work in shaping the directions of 'normal' technical progress. In the next chapter we shall analyse the behavioural forces which lead the industrial system in these directions, namely the patterns of innovation-based and imitation-based oligopolistic competition. First, however, we need to describe briefly the relative technological performance of the major Western countries.

Towards a Joint American–Japanese Technological Leadership?

We have already mentioned the 'cumulative dynamics' of the American semiconductor industry which kept it in a position of unchallenged leadership until the late 1970s. On the other hand, European technological lags, have remained on average relatively high, with the partial exception of Philips in some fields within Bipolar technology, Siemens in some industrial devices and British producers, such as Ferranti, in a few areas of custom-oriented circuits. (We analyse the European semiconductor industry at greater length in Dosi, 1981a). The major change of the late seventies has been the rapid emergence of Japan as a direct threat to the US technological dominance. If we look again at Tables 2.1, 2.2, and 2.3, we notice that the increasing percentage, in the 1970s, of major innovations of non-US origin is essentially due to an increasing Japanese innovativeness. The tendency is confirmed by Table 2.4 on the distribution of patents registered in the USA, by country.

For some subsectors of semiconductors the Japanese industry has completely joined the USA in the world technological leadership (e.g. memories). At the time of the revision of this study (end of 1982) a synthetic overview of the relative position of Japan *vis-à-vis* the USA is the following: Japan can manufacture semiconductors, broadly speaking, at the same levels of density and speed as the USA, often at lower costs and higher reliability while she is still behind in terms of software capabilities (thus still showing some technological lag in highly complex microprocessors).

Our forecast is that in the 1980s:
(a) The joint USA/Japan technological leadership will become an evident phenomenon, and,

(b) the Japanese commercial exploitation of this rapid catching-up process will be increasingly felt on the international markets.

In the next chapter, among other things, we will also examine the economic consequences of the latter point.

2.7 SOME CONCLUSIONS: TECHNICAL PROGRESS AS AN ASYMMETRIC PROCESS

In analysing the basic determinants of technical progress a definition of technology has been proposed which underlines the similarities between 'science' and 'technology' and attributes to the latter some of the features which modern epistemology relates to 'science'. The following step was to discuss the relationship between 'technology', so defined, and 'economic factors'. The relationship seemed more complex than, and irreducible to, simple 'demand–pull' theories. Specifically, technological patterns appeared to be determined by the interplay between the notional possibilities provided by scientific progress, some fundamental forces in capitalist economies (like the criteria of marketability, profitability, reduction of production cost, search of new markets), together with directly institutional variables (in our empirical case the 'exogenous' requirements of the military), acting as selective mechanisms among several technological developments toward which the same body knowledge could lead.

A consequence of our argument pointed to the limitations and weaknesses of 'market forces'[135] in directing the innovative activity, at the *beginning* of an industry, when technological patterns are not yet established and potential markets are highly uncertain. Moreover, the process of the search for radically new technologies implies trial-and-error procedures: we have termed the economic and technological efforts at this stage as the *burden of the first-comer*.

As semiconductors are concerned, in the 1950s and 1960s, institutional intervention (mainly military and space agencies) performed in the USA a powerful focusing role which directed the accumulation of knowledge and expertise and helped the emergence of precise technological trajectories. The more technological patterns and markets become established, the more stimuli and incentives to technical change become endogenous to the 'proper' economic system. The country (or countries) on the frontier, enjoy a strong technological advantage *vis-à-vis* late-comers, since technical progress often appears to present cumulative features. One can easily see from the arguments how the process of technological innovation always implies asymmetries between firms and between countries.

Moreover, for the sake of clarity we made above a sharp distinction between the 'process of innovation' and the 'diffusion of innovations'. This was necessary also in order to stress the role of innovation and innovative capabilities which is often neglected in international comparative studies, thus implicitly assuming 'equal starting points' (from the technological point of view) among all major industrialised countries. We tried to show that this assumption is deeply misleading.

While maintaining the distinction between innovation and diffusion (with a logical and causal priority to the former), one can observe a strict interdependence between the two. The same existence of a 'technological frontier' on which an entire industry (eg the US semiconductor industry as a whole) is placed, points to the fact that single discoveries and innovations may contribute to produce, *in many companies*, further discoveries and innovations. This is precisely one of the mechanisms through which an industry remains 'on the frontier' and makes it advance. Here, the features pointed out by many of the frequently quoted studies on semiconductors come into play (mobility of scientists 'embodying' the best practice technology, financial conditions favouring easy entries, 'second sourcing' required by the military, etc.). One of the implications of the argument is, however, that quick diffusion is allowed also by the fact that the industry *already is* on the frontier. The 'virtuous circle' is closed and reinforced by the positive effect of quick diffusion on further advances.

Inter-firm and inter-country differences in innovative and imitative capabilities bear consequences of the utmost importance upon the competitive process, the transformation of industrial structures and the patterns of international trade and investment. The following chapter will investigate the relationship between technical change, companies' competitive behaviours and the dynamics of the main structural parameters, such as productivity, output, employment, prices, concentration and capital intensity.

NOTES AND REFERENCES

1. With respect to the discovery of the transistor, see the account by one of the inventors themselves (Shockley, 1974; 1976) and, on theoretical ground, Shockley (1950). For the history of semiconductor technology, its economic impact and implications, Golding (1971) and Braun and MacDonald (1978) provide a thorough account.

2. In this Schumpeterian distinction an '*invention*' is an idea, a sketch on a model for a new or improved device, product, process or system. Such inventions . . . 'do not necessarily lead to technical *innovations* . . . An innovation in the economic sense is accomplished only with the first *commercial* transaction involving the new product, process . . .' (Freeman, 1974, p. 22). Accepting this distinction, the borderline is that the new device or process is not only potentially *marketable* but actually *marketed*.

3. In other words, in the first definition, the 'need' to move around can be either satisfied through a horse or a space-shuttle. In the second definition, obviously the 'need' of a space-shuttle cannot emerge before the space-shuttle itself is conceived.

4. In a weak sense, it is apparent that within this approach the innovative mechanism operates in the same way as the usual mechanism of determination of prices and quantities in a general equilibrium analysis. In a stronger sense, it does not appear impossible – given several restrictive assumptions – to construct a neoclassical general equilibrium analysis which takes account of this kind of innovative activity. For the difficulties of this approach, see below.

5. Nelson and Winter (1977a). This work to which we will refer again later, is one of the first attempts to formalise a non-neoclassical model of technical progress embodying rather complex assumptions about firms' attitudes towards, and responses to the innovative activity.

6. For our purpose it is enough to mention that if we assume, at any point in time, fixed coefficient of production and constant return to scale, variations in the quantities do not effect relative prices. Therefore we are bound to lose an important part of the 'signalling' mechanism. On the other hand, a demand/supply theory of prices might be abandoned for the unavoidable difficulties of its theory of factor prices and distribution. For an account of the famous 'Cambridge Debate' on capital theory, see Harcourt (1972).

7. On this issue, see Rosenberg (1976) and Mowery and Rosenberg (1979).

8. Except in the cases in which an already existent *invention* can become a marketable *innovation*, at a certain point in time, due to changes in income distribution, or in relative prices.

9. Generally, for particular features such as limited appropriability, indivisibility, etc. see Arrow (1962) and (1962a).

10. The effort of 'endogenising' the production of knowledge, equated to the production of a commodity, accounts for the evident trend, at least in this century, towards a greater contribution to the innovative activity by institutional centres directly related to production of scientific and technological advances (and first of all by R and D facilities of big corporations). This Schumpeterian view – Schumpeter (1947) – is challenged by some scholars, for example Jewkes *et al.* (1958), who maintain that a great percentage of innovation is still attributable to private inventors. For an exhaustive discussion on this issue see Freeman (1974). The problem crucial to our discussion, however, still remains: how do technological efforts operate? Can the direction of technological advances be pushed almost frictionless in any direction? Can the lags between an assumed 'market demand' and the technological response be considered

fairly limited in time? etc. For a critical discussion of the 'black-box approach' to technology see again Rosenberg (1976) and Mowery and Rosenberg (1979).

11. A critical review of those studies is Mowery and Rosenberg (1979).

12. Ibid.

13. See Freeman (1974); Rosenberg (1976); SPRU (1971); Teubal, Arnon and Trachtenberg (1976); Teubal (1977). Some studies go as far as reconstructing some kind of 'path' leading from initial scientific advances to the final innovative product or process: see, for example, the TRACES Project (Illinois Institute of Technology, 1969). The reader can find in Freeman (1974) a thorough bibliography on the subject.

14. See also the important findings of Pavitt and Soete (1980); Soete (1982), and Pavitt and Soete (1981). Moreover, if we measure innovative output in terms of increase in productivity (as a proxy of technical progress) the impact of research efforts is significant (see, for example, Mansfield, 1968; Terleckyj, 1974).

15. As we shall discuss at length below, Nelson and Winter (1977) formalise this process and its interaction with industrial structures.

16. On scientific paradigms, see Kuhn (1963) and on scientific research programmes, Lakatos (1978). For a thorough discussion, Musgrave and Lakatos (1973). One does not aim here to argue 'what science is' or tackle the epistemological disputes on the differences between the Kuhnian approach and Lakatos' approach. For our purposes the degree of overlapping between the two approaches is great enough to borrow from them a few basic definitions of science which they have in common.

    The first to suggest independently an analogy between science and technology in 'Kuhnian' terms was Freeman (1979).

17. A very stimulating paper by Bonfiglioli (1979) defines 'science' as a 'particular technology'. Although the aims of that paper are different from ours here, there is in common the similarity and overlapping between 'science' and 'technology' and the role of institutional factors in determining the direction of both. See below.

18. 'The continuity evolves from a genuine research programme adumbrated at start. The programme consists of methodological rules: some tell us what paths of research to avoid (*negative heuristic*) and others what paths to pursue (*positive heuristic*)' Lakatos (1978, p. 47).

19. Note that here one is impressionistically using the two concepts as equivalent.

20. Kuhn (1963).

21. Nelson and Winter (1977), Rosenberg (1976).

22. They suggest two general dimensions of these 'natural trajectories', towards progressive exploitation of latent economies of scale and towards increasing mechanisation of operations, quoting as supporting evidence – among others – the studies by Hughes on electric power equipment, Levin on various petro-chemical processes and Rosenberg (1976).

23. To take obvious examples, the trade-offs between energy consumption and horsepower in internal combustion engines or that between speed and density of the circuits in semiconductors (this refers to the comparison between bipolar and MOS technologies). A definition of technical progress

in terms of multi-dimensional trade-offs is sometimes used in technological forecasting models. For a short overview, see Martino (1980). Sahal (1974 and 1978) utilises a similar definition of technology and technical progress, applied to individual industries and products. An excellent discussion of the measures of the state-of-the-art in each particular technology is in Gordon and Munson (1981).

After the first draft of this work was completed, an important article by Sahal (1981) was published. He suggests a 'system approach' to technology and technical change, seeing it as an evolutionary and continuum process. Moreover, he suggests the existence of 'technological guide-posts'. One can easily see the consistency of his thesis with what is argued here. We hope, in the present work, to throw some light also on the definition, emergence and selection of his 'technological guide-posts' and on the implications in terms of evolution of industrial structures.

24. Again one uses the term in analogy with epistemology: in our case a trajectory is more powerful the bigger the set of technologies which it excludes. For instance, it seems that the technological paths defined by nuclear or oil power-generation equipment is very powerful, meaning that many other sources of energy (many other technologies) are excluded.

25. See Rosenberg (1976) and (1979).

26. We can think of a 'frontier' as a set of points in a multi-dimensional space.

27. Nelson and Winter (1977).

28. An important attempt to define some precise criteria of 'progress' is in Sahal (1978). As it should be clear from the discussion above, a univocal criterion can easily be identified only *within* a technological paradigm (i.e. *along* a technological trajectory). Comparisons (even *ex-post*) between different trajectories might yield sometimes, although not always, to ambiguous results. In other words, it might occur that the 'new' technology is 'better' than the 'old' one in several chosen dimensions, but it might still be 'worse' in some others. One can see here a loose analogy with the epistemological discussion (whereby an 'extreme' Kuhnian approach claims strict incomparability and a Popper-like approach suggests some progressive continuity). Gordon and Munson (1981) discuss the construction of an 'index of technical progress' within each 'technology'. If one defines the latter in terms of tasks performed, then the index may be able to assess also discontinuities and to compare different technological paradigms aimed at fulfilling, broadly speaking, the same tasks.

29. For a discussion of uncertainty in R & D project evaluation, see Freeman (1974).

30. See Freeman (1974) and Walsh *et al.* (1979).

31. A convincing and thorough discussion is in Freeman (1974).

32. Nelson and Winter (1977).

33. Take the example of the oil-powered internal combustion engine. Changing oil prices put an increasing pressure towards oil substitution and energy saving. The scope for substitution, however, is limited by the technology which itself defines the range of possible technological advances.

34. Precisely as unsolved puzzles or ('falsifications') in a scientific paradigm do not imply an alternative paradigm.

35. This broadly corresponds to Teubal's concept of *market determinateness* (Teubal, 1977).
36. Von Hippel's model of innovation as determined by 'users' needs' typically applies to productive equipment. For the reasons explained above we prefer not to use the word 'need' for the ambiguities it implies. Von Hippel's 'needs' are well defined. They are actually productive requirements, attempts to overcome technological bottlenecks, pushes towards increased performances in specific industrial sectors (see von Hippel, 1976, 1977 and 1979).
37. It can be (and has been) reasonably argued that scientific developments themselves are fostered in the long run by technological and economic 'focuses' of attentions and that they are somewhat directed by the *weltanschauungen* that economic systems provide. This very wide issue concerns fields like epistemology, sociology of knowledge, etc. See Rosenberg (1981).
38. The following overview is just meant to provide a brief picture of the sector. For a clear exposition of the basic principle of solid-state physics, see, for example, Fogiel (1972) and the special issues of *Science*, 1977 and *Scientific American*, 1977, devoted to microelectronics.
39. Some of those properties have been known for a long time, although they never got a satisfactory theoretical explanation until the development of quantum physics. For instance, as early as 1833, Faraday discovered the negative temperature coefficient of resistance, differentiating semiconductors from conductors which show on the contrary a positive coefficient.
40. Those detectors were what used to be called 'cat's whisker' crystal rectifiers, employed for high frequency detection, at which valves could not operate.
41. The production of transistors did not begin until 1950.
42. Most integrated circuits are built on a single chip. These are called monolithic. Some other ICs, however, are 'hybrid', meaning that they are mounted upon an insulating substrate (e.g. ceramic) together with other components, instead of being directly manufactured in the substrate itself (in this latter case the substrate is generally silicon). Statistical data differs in that it may either include or not hybrid circuits within the 'Integrated Circuit' category. Whenever possible, we will specify whether they are included within the data we will present.
43. Inside these two fundamental technologies (bipolar and MOS ICs) there are different 'families'. Among bipolar ICs there are TTL (Transistor Transistor Logic), Schottky–TTL, ECL (Emitter–Coupled Logic), I²L (Integrated–Injection Logic), Linear. The distinctions between families is based on the patterns of design of the components on the IC, which define also the 'logic' utilised to perform a given operation on bits of information. Note that those ICs which are 'analog' in terms of type of performance are 'linear' in terms of technology.

    MOS technology includes, among others, NMOS, PMOS, CMOS (according to whether they are based on negative channels, positive channels or both, respectively), SOS (Silicon on sapphire), CCD (change-coupled device).
44. Take the example of human voice transmitted through the telephone. One

can either do so analogically, transmitting electric signals whose modulation and frequency reflect changes in the original input of the voice or, vice versa, one can transform the original signals into 'packets' of yes—no impulses which are then re-transformed into analog information at the other end of the line. (This second possibility is associated with the emerging technology of fully electronic telecommunications systems).

45. RAM memories are volatile, meaning also that whenever power is completely switched off, the bits of information disappear. Other memories such as EPROM, EAROM, etc. can be written upon through ultraviolet light and retain the information without the need of any power change. Within RAMs, one generally distinguishes between 'dynamic' and 'static' memories according to the regeneration requirements for the changes which represent stored bits of information.

46. Braun and MacDonald (1978), pp. 117—18.

47. Ibid.

48. We will always try to specify whether these devices are included in our figures. Either way will not significantly influence levels and trends of our data since they account for a relatively minor share of the total.

49. MBMs are based on magnetic materials whose domains of polarisation can be influenced by an external magnetic field.

50. This subdivision is partly adopted from Finan (1975). For the following overview we relied heavily on his brief and clear description. For a more detailed account, see Fogiel (1972), and Hittinger (1973). Here we will briefly describe the MOS process.

51. Here we do not consider the process of production of these crystals of pure silicon (which is called 'growing silicon crystals'). We will, however, discuss the technological innovations in this field, which have been very important in the development of semiconductor technology. We chose to neglect this stage of production since pure silicon crystals are generally manufactured by specialised chemical companies (in the USA, Monsanto and Wacker Chemicals), although some big semiconductor firms like Texas Instruments, Motorola, Fairchild have integrated backwards to produce their own wafers.

52. Similar researches were undertaken in the UK by some universities, the Royal Radar Establishment, GEC and British Thomson—Huston; in the rest of Europe, by Philips, Siemens, and in various research institutions in the Soviet Union. See Golding (1971); Freeman (1974); Braun and MacDonald (1978).

53. Shockley (1976); Nelson (1962).

54. Shockley (1976).

55. The 'movement' of electrons in a p—type semiconductor and of 'holes' in an n—type semiconductor: Shockley (1950 and 1976), Nelson (1962).

56. The first transistor was a 'point contact transistor', but the subsequent development occurred in junction transistors whose principles were better understood.

57. Exact figures are not available, but this trend emerges from our interviews, from Braun and MacDonald (1978) and especially from the extensive survey undertaken by MacLean for the OECD. (It is an appendix to OECD (1979)).

58. For an analysis of the history of some fundamental innovations see Mowery (1978).
59. An obvious problem is that all innovations are not of equal importance. There is a rather general agreement among experts, however, on the relevance of most of the innovations listed here.
60. In Tables 2.1 and 2.2 innovations from Bell laboratories appear under 'Western Electric', the manufacturing subsidiary of AT & T.
61. Tilton (1971) p. 62.
62. Tilton (1971) p. 57.
63. Freeman (1974), p. 139–43.
64. For a thorough analysis of UK companies, cf. Golding (1971).
65. For a discussion see Freeman *et al.*, (1965) and (1974).
66. Sciberras (1977).
67. Gordon and Munson (1981) analyse the possible measures of technical progress in computers.
68. In most of the interviews we carried out, experts and company managers, pointed out that we would express it better in terms of a 'cluster' of frontiers, each related to groups of products or technologies.
69. For the role of this particular group of people, scientists, engineers, in the diffusion of innovation, see farther. For a detailed account and an extensive analysis of the economic implications, see Golding (1971) and Tilton (1971).
70. Incidentally, note that this is one of the critical weak points in the estimation of 'diffusion curves' of innovations.
71. In the sixties we have to consider as 'well established firms' also some 'new firms' of the fifties, like Texas Instruments and Fairchild. For a mapping of the various generations of companies see Golding (1971); Sciberras (1977); Mason (1979).
72. See Golding (1971); Tilton (1971); Webbick (1977). There are few important exceptions like the introduction of silicon junction transistor by TI in 1959 a couple of years after it entered the business, and that of planar process by Fairchild in 1960. The people mainly responsible for those advances had come from Bell Laboratories and from the Shockley Laboratories, respectively.
73. The best argued case on this line is Tilton (1971). First, he points at the size and sophistication of America's market *vis-à-vis* the European one. Moreover, he identifies easy conditions of entry, availability of venture capital, mobility of scientists as the differential features between Europe and the USA. Of course, he recognises that the latter are conditions mainly related to the diffusion of innovations more than innovation as such but he seems to give a low importance to a possible 'technological gap' between the two continents. He maintains a proper 'product-cycle' approach whereby the lags in production are – at least partly – explained in terms of lags in demand. For a general discussion, see Chapter 4.
74. Any survey of the origins and background of the founders of spin-off companies confirms it.
75. Some argue that before 1955 – the first year for which data is available – the percentage of public procurement was as high as in 1960 (cf. Braun and MacDonald, 1978).

76. Tilton (1971), p. 61. The OECD estimates are lower, at around 6 per cent; cf. OECD (1968) vol. II, p. 179.
77. Golding (1971), p. 173.
78. There is a broad agreement on this trend between the results of our interview, MacLean Report—OECD (1979) and various articles in the specialised press. Furthermore, this trend is consistent with the more aggregate data – referred to the entire electrical and electronic sector – presented in OECD, *Trends in Industrial R & D in Selected OECD member Countries 1967–75*, Paris, 1978.
79. Wilson *et al.* (1980).
80. For the aeronautic industry, for example, 45 per cent of total major innovations – of which many occurred before 1945 – are not yet applied to civilian aircrafts, cf. The DOT—NASA Study quoted in Mowery (1978).
81. M. Kaldor (1978).
82. Sciberras (1977) and (1980). Evidence of this trend towards relative specialisation (which must not be exaggerated) can be found in Kleiman (1977). For a thorough discussion of companies' reactions to the mentioned Pentagon's VHSI Programme, see Wilson *et al.* (1980).
83. The Tinkeroy project (1948) sponsored by the Navy was aiming at the improvement of vacuum tube technology. After an expenditure of $4.7 million it was abandoned because it was superseded by transistor technology. The 2–D Programme by the Diamond Ordnance Fuse Laboratories of the Army (1957) tried to achieve greater miniaturisation ('microcircuits') in discrete device circuitry. It contributed to the improvement of printed circuits, thin films and incapsulation techniques. It was, however, overtaken by ICs. The same end was faced by three other military programmes: the Army Signal Corps' micromodule programme (1957, dropped in 1963 after an outlet of $26 million gone mainly to RCA); the Navy thin films researches (1958); the Air Force 'molecular electronics' project ($5 million, 1958–61; most of the financing went to Westinghouse). This last project was the most interesting from the technological point of view: despite the wrong name, the project was aimed at the exploitation of the 'bulk effect' (the possibility of exploiting bulk silicon material in order to perform in various parts of its structure the tasks of switching, amplifying and rectifying). ICs proved to be a more viable alternative. (cf. Braun and MacDonald, 1978; Kleiman, 1977).
84. Cf. Freeman *et al.* (1965). The distribution of sources of R & D and of patents for some electronic companies was as shown in table 2.13 overleaf. Although 'firms might tend to ascribe relatively few patents to the government development contracts and many of those ascribed to their own R & D might owe a good deal to knowledge acquired on government work', military supported research seems a very expensive form of stimulating inventions. Freeman *et al.* (1965 p. 73).
85. For in-depth historical accounts of military projects, see Golding (1971); Braun and MacDonald (1978); Wilson *et al.* (1980).
86. Source: A. D. Little, quoted in Freeman (1974).
87. Peck and Scherer (1962).
88. See Mowery (1978). He argues also that in the era of ICs, the strive towards

TABLE 2.13 *Government R and D and patent applications of some US firms*

Firm	Sales to governments	Government R & D contracts 51–9		$m	Privately funded R & D	Patent applications, 1951–9
	%	No.	Value $m	$m	Total no.	No. on Government work
RCA	20	566	275	324	5513	244
Raytheon	59	355	325	38	780	376
Motorola	22	425	73	54	572	31
Texas Inst.	52	40	12	18	318	19

SOURCE Freeman *et al.* (1965), quoting US Senate Proceedings, 1961 and Reports of Companies (the figures refer to *total* company activities and not only semiconductor or electronics).

standardisation has significantly decreased. We will come back to this issue below.

89. Between 1956 and 1958, for instance, 'Contracts for a total of thirty different types of germanium and silicon transistors were placed with about one dozen of the major semiconductor companies, and this helped some of these to gain a foothold in the industry', A. D. Little, quoted in Freeman (1974). A detailed account is in Golding (1971).

90. Tilton (1971) supports an explanation of the American success in terms of these variables.

91. Freeman's analysis of the pitfalls and inefficiencies of military-based innovation policies in terms of the economic system as a whole is still crucial, cf. Freeman *et al.* (1965).

92. On the diffusion processes in semiconductors, cf. Golding (1971); Tilton (1971); Finan (1975). See also Chapter 3.

93. This makes the technological fall-out from military to civilian applications less important and more difficult. This divergence between the two trajectories, which undoubtedly exists, must not be exaggerated: successful producers did not seem to find great difficulty in serving both military and civilian markets. The argument, of course, does not apply to firms – generally medium/small ones – which specialised in very customised military applications. On these issues see Sciberras (1977).

94. See Truel (1980).

95. Many times Japan is considered a 'special case' to be explained through *ad hoc* hypotheses. The Japanese semiconductor industry shows in the fifties some relevant similarities with the European one. The role of the *policies*, though, has been extremely different, and this, as we shall see, contributes to explain very different end-results. See below.

96. For our purposes here it does not matter very much whether big companies were valve producers or not. What is relevant is their size, their capability and willingness to undertake a wide range of R & D projects, and their technological level in this field. For other purposes (such as the analysis of the rate of diffusion of innovation) the category, used for example by

Tilton, of 'receiving valve producers' is important in comparing the willingness of the latter to substitute new devices (semiconductors) for old devices (valves) which they already produced (many times with high profit and big market shares). In our context, TI or Fairchild are considered in the sixties as big established firms, although they have never been valve producers.

97. This feature has been well indicated in the literature as one of the characters of the European scene, cf. OECD, (1968): 'The decision to enter a new field like semiconductors was taken essentially by the leaders of the tube industry. The decision resulted to some extent from financial possibilities and to a much larger extent from the firms' realisation that these new technologies were important ones, and that they should be pushed rapidly. In other words, the question was essentially one of judgment, both business-wise and technology-wise' (OECD, 1968, p. 97).

98. Philips is said to have manufactured the first transistor just a few weeks after Bell's announcement, owing to his significant research in this field.

99. Tilton (1971) disaggregates the innovations, with respect to the period of first introduction, between 8 innovations which occurred in the 1950s and 5 which occurred in the 1960s. The average lag (in years) between the USA and other advanced countries is the following:

	UK	France	Germany	Japan
First 8 innovations	2.6	3.0	2.4	3.4
Last 5 innovations	1.6	2.6	3.0	1.2

The data highlight that the lag did not increase, and might have even slightly decreased. Statistical analysis shows that the values for the two periods are not significantly different from each other except for Japan.

100. The relationship between technical progress in components and competitive edge in electronic capital goods has been analysed in detail by Freeman *et al.* (1965).

101. In particular, Nelson and Winter (1977, 1978, 1980). See also the very stimulating work by B. Klein (1977).

102. See below, Chapter 3.

103. Nelson and Winter (1977a); Nelson (1980).

104. For example, this is the hypothesis underpinning part of Tilton's analysis: ' . . . . in the analysis here the interest is . . . the relative contributions of different countries to this rate (of innovation). Because of the rapid and widespread dissemination of technical research through scientific journals and other media, the level of science is roughly the same in all industrially advanced countries. Consequently, demand conditions are primarily responsible for the differences among countries in introducing and diffusing new semiconductor technology'. Tilton (1971, p. 126, footnote 16). It seems to us that there is not such an easy correspondence between scientific knowledge (which is transferable through a book) and manufacturing capability. A manager of an interviewed firm was quoting the

example of the transfer *inside* the same company of certain aspects of ICs' manufacturing technology as being difficult and requiring the exchange of technicians for long periods of time. This is an extreme example pointing at the existence of wide inter-company and international technological differences.

105. It is interesting to consider the example of Philips, the biggest European semiconductor producer. As mentioned, Philips was a successful producer of germanium discrete devices, in the fifties and sixties, mainly for consumers' electronics and instruments applications. On that technological trajectory (discrete germanium devices) it was on the technological frontier, but it did not push at all in other directions (silicon, etc.). Therefore it was left far behind in (silicon-based) IC technology and did not perceive the potentials of those technologies until the mid-sixties. In the late sixties it 'decided' to enter the field; even to a firm with its financial and technological resources, it took almost ten years to shorten the lag in ICs' technology. In addition to a substantial R & D effort, that strategy involved the purchase of the fifth American producer, Signetics. Now, Philips can be considered technologically fairly strong in bipolar ICs, but it still lags behind in MOS technology, the fastest growing segment of the market and the most promising in terms of future advances. This picture (with, on the average, much darker colours) characterises all European industry.

106. Nelson and Winter (1977a) and (1978) introduce this hypothesis in their simulation models regarding the innovative output of each single firm, given a certain technological frontier for the industry.

107. Golding (1971).

108. Golding (1971); Tilton (1971).

109. Of course, this applies from the point of view of the economy as a whole, but is not necessarily so from the viewpoint of the military itself, and not even from that of each individual firm in the industry, which generally found military contracts rewarding and profitable.

110. Here, of course, the big problems of the economic capabilities of each European country, the absolute size of its military market, the minimum R & D thresholds, etc., would come into play.

111. An engineer in a European firm (involved in the military government-financed field) told us that on many occasions their design division fought to buy American-made *commercial* devices instead of the in-house custom-produced ones, for the higher reliability of the formers (this was happening as late as the beginning of the seventies).

112. It is quite understandable that pressures to increase military markets have been shared by most European firms. Feeling relatively weak *vis-à-vis* the competition from overseas, they have usually supported the expansion of a market in which the rule is generally 'to buy national' and where the government operates as risk-taker and guarantees positive returns. As we tried to argue, it is not obvious that this results in an improvement of national technological capability. It has already been mentioned that, in the seventies, even American companies have been more cautious about it. Facing the relative divergence between the military technological trajectory and the civilian technological trajectory, they have sometimes been

reluctant in accepting huge military contracts, if the latter risked cutting them off from the main stream of technical change in the (bigger and faster growing) civilian market.

113. There have been policies which indirectly affected the structure of the industry through merger and rationalisation policies (especially in France), but no explicit innovation and technology policy.

114. Here we are focusing on the technological performance of European companies. The next two chapters will analyse its effect upon commercial competitiveness.

115. The European weakness in components is not, of course, the only cause of the European relative failure in computers. It has been an important factor, though. On the relationship between semiconductor components and computers, cf. Freeman *et al.* (1965); Sciberras, Swords-Isherwood and Senker (1978); Truel (1980); Ernst (1982).

116. Hitachi, Toshiba, Matsushita, Nippon Electric, Mitsubishi Electric, Fujitsu. A partial exception was Sony, a medium firm, which first introduced transistors in Japan, and another, Kobe Kogyo, a small valve-producing firm. See Tilton (1971 pp. 136–42).

117. Public policies in Europe are analysed at much greater length in Dosi (1981a).

118. However, it is somewhat ironical that public authorities had some uncertainties in recognising the new industry at the time when Sony wanted to acquire the transistor technology at the very beginning of the fifties.

119. See again Dosi (1981a) for a discussion.

120. Of course, also in Europe, practices of licensing and cross-licensing were not uncommon. A big difference is apparent, though, between these and a provision of *automatic diffusion* of technology licensed from abroad to *all* Japanese firms. Technology licensing agreements from a foreign to a Japanese firm were not on a firm to firm basis, but on a *firm to industry* basis: a foreign company had to make its technology available to all Japanese firms. See Tilton (1970); Altman and Cohen (1977); Goode (1978).

121. To give an example, until 1974 each import above a certain quantity of ICs needed authorisation by MITI. Western companies suggest the existence of informal but strict controls implemented through the mentioned inter-relationship of government/companies. Japanese production and consumption of semiconductors was (and is) fairly concentrated and contacts with the government are rather close. Furthermore, Japanese electronic companies are vertically integrated, so that producers of semiconductors are also the biggest users. It is easy, therefore, to decide, together with the technological goals, also the import targets consistent with those goals. Tariff barriers on the contrary were relatively low.

122. On the basis of the Foreign Capital Act (1949), the government could veto any foreign investment in which foreign interests had a majority share, and prevent any foreign bid for existing Japanese companies. Tilton (1971 p. 146–7), tells the interesting story of the efforts of TI to establish in the early sixties a Japanese subsidiary, curbed by the government. TI, in response, refused to licence its ICs technology. The Japanese answer was to slow down the recognition of TI patents and to allow their imitation. A

compromise was finally reached in 1968, when the Japanese, fearing US retaliation on their electronic exports, allowed a 50–50 joint venture between TI and Sony. By that time, Japanese firms were already in the ICs business.

123. For an assessment of Japanese economic performance cf. Chapters 3 and 4.

124. OECD (1968 p. 177), gives a very low and hardly believable figure for R & D as percentage of Japanese sales in semiconductors (2% in the mid-sixties. Source: Japanese reply to OECD checklist). On the other hand, European figures are much higher. France is at 16%. From Golding's data we may estimate that in the UK (1968) it was slightly below 15% (industry-performed R & D). Even allowing a prudential figure for Europe of 10% and assuming for Japan some 5%, Japanese R & D expenditure (in absolute terms) should have fallen short of half the European one.

125. An interest, on the side of public agencies, was shown since the early sixties by the military (especially in UK and France). Furthermore, the component sector was looked at in relation to the concern for the computer industry. It did not obtain, however, an attention in its own right. cf. Dosi (1981a).

126. The Japanese institutional set-up is analysed in depth in G. C. Allen (1981).

127. One can find an illustration of the nature of the Japanese 'social bargain' between the various social actors and their *weltanschauungen* in the fascinating study by Dore (1973).

128. An excellent up-to-date and thorough analysis of the latest semiconductor development (until 1981) is in Ernst (1982). We refer to that study for all the evidence on the recent trends in technology which are discussed here in their broad features. Many of the conclusions reached independently by Ernst's study on the nature of technical change in the 1970s are very similar to ours.

129. Not surprisingly, this view leads to the argument that 'untraded relationships' between users and producers are not very relevant and that international technological imbalances in semiconductors do not affect the technological level of downstream sectors. As we shall see, this may not be the case. See also Maclean (1979); Sciberras (1980); Truel (1980); Ernst (1982).

130. This comparative analysis of 'custom' and standard circuits is drawn from Maclean (1979).

131. For a detailed account see Ernst (1982).

132. The development of the first microprocessor is an example of the interplay between trends in the technological trajectory and user–producer relationship: it emerged from the arrangement between Busicom, a Japanese consumer electronics company, and Intel, aimed at the production of a complex IC. MPU was, to some extent, a non-looked-for outcome of the technological effort in a defined technological direction.

133. One can easily see the consistency of this argument with von Hippel's hypothesis of 'user's determined' innovations; cf von Hippel (1976) and (1977). We refer essentially to industrial users and not to consumers.

134. For an in-depth discussion, cf. Ernst (1982).

135. Not only the kind of market assumed by the orthodox economic theory which, in our view, hardly exists, but also the 'real' market; the one where

consumers' preferences do not count very much, where the supply side is very important, constant or increasing returns are the rule, technical change is a fundamental variable and does not follow any well-behaved function, firms have different degrees of oligopolistic power, income distribution is socially determined, etc.

3 Technical Change and Industrial Transformation: The Patterns of Industrial Dynamics

In the previous chapter, we have been trying to assess the determinants and the patterns of innovation, suggesting the existence of quite general procedures and directions of technical progress. The model based on technological paradigms and technological trajectories helped us in interpreting these broad regularities in the innovation process. We must now look more closely at the relationship between the patterns of technical change, on the one hand, and industrial structures, on the other hand. The task has to be twofold: one must try to assess first, the conditions which, on behavioural grounds, normally induce the company sector to innovate, and, second, the effects of technical change on the evolution of industrial structures.

A rapid pace of technical change, both in terms of product and process innovations is obviously bound to bring about significant changes in the demand for the various products (old and new ones) in unit costs (for each product, each company operating in the market and the industry as a whole), in the importance of economies of scale, technological discontinuities between firms, etc. Furthermore it is likely that, given different innovative capabilities of existing firms and new entries, market shares and degree of concentration will change through time. Prices (their levels and their changes) are influenced by all the above variables (demand, costs, market structures). Moreover, the change in the structural conditions of an industry interact with changes in the pattern of behaviour of the companies.

We will follow our usual procedure of first undertaking a theoretical discussion of the relationship between technical change and structural change, followed by the analysis of the evidence from the semiconductor industry.

Two issues in particular will receive a thorough examination. The first one is the possible existence of regularities in the competitive patterns of an industry which undergoes changes in the techniques of production and in the nature of the manufactured commodities. This implies also some discussion of the 'rationality criteria' of decision-making under conditions of technical change. The second major issue concerns the relationship between the nature of technical change and the perform-ance indicators of an industry. We shall focus especially on two variables, namely trends in productivity and prices. It can easily be seen how any model of productivity changes and pricing behaviour bears important implications, not only in terms of the theory of industrial economics, but also for the macroeconomic analysis of the effects of technical change on aggregate rates of activity, employment and income distribution at which we will hint in the conclusions (Chapter 5).

3.1 OPPORTUNITIES, INCENTIVES AND CONSTRAINTS TO TECHNICAL CHANGE

Technological Opportunity, Cumulativeness and Private Appropriability

The model of technical change we have outlined in the previous chapter must now be linked to the nature of industrial dynamics and the behavioural mechanisms at work in the company sector of the economy.[1] Let us start from a very obvious but nonetheless important statement: The company sector in capitalist economies will generally undertake innovative activities if the latter involve some expectation of economic return, or if the lack of such activities involves the threat of the loss of some present economic benefits, or both. This idea clearly underpins the theoretical treatment which in industrial economics goes under the heading of 'innovation and market structure'. Different market structures are supposed to yield different incentives of innovation. Before discussing the existing models on the subject, however, let us first outline a theoretical framework aiming at a sufficient interpretative generality.

The features of technological advances suggested above will help us in relating together three concepts which are sometimes found in the literature, but are rarely given the attention they deserve,[2] namely

(a) *cumulativeness* of technical progress, (b) *technological opportunity* and, (c) *private appropriability* of the effects of technical change.[3]

We have already hinted at the non-randomness of technological advances. In a strong form, this feature of technical change, together with learning-by-doing, might lead to significant cumulative effects at the level of a company and/or of a country's industry. Of course, different technologies and different industries show different degrees of cumulativeness. A cumulative pattern of technical change implies that time profiles of innovation (and/or speed of imitation) broadly respect the initial innovative ranking (either among companies or among countries). It can be easily seen how this feature relates, in an inverse function, with the possibility of inter-company and/or international diffusion of technology.

It was suggested above that a technological paradigm also determines, together with the 'dimensions' which define progress,[4] the scope (the 'potential') of innovations and improvements[5] and the easiness in the achievement of these improvements and innovations. It is intuitive that the *technological opportunity* in electronics is much higher than in, say, clothing, but this quite obvious fact is generally neglected or ill-treated, as we shall see, when dealing with the relationship between industrial structures and innovative activities.

Most of our discussion so far has concerned the features of, and the necessary conditions which lead to, technical progress. On the other hand, the incentive which drives the business sector towards innovation and/or imitation relates to the economic benefit[6] stemming from it (or – which is basically the same – the insurance against economic losses which would be incurred if some other company, other than that in question, would appropriate the innovation). For any given perception of the technological opportunity, the economic benefits accruing to an innovator (or fast imitator) should be proportional to the degree of *private appropriability* of the innovations and of the 'externalities', which are often associated with the innovative activities (such as differential expertise, know-how, knowledge). It can be clearly seen how private appropriability is related to cumulativeness at *company level*: if innovative capabilities are serially correlated through time within each company, the economic advantages stemming from innovations are likely to be reproduced through time, too. Technological opportunity and private appropriability represent the interlinked conditions for the innovative activity in market economies. Note that the former may be considered as a *necessary* condition, but by no means a sufficient one. It is the latter which defines the degree of commitment of companies to the innovative activity, for any given level of opportunity.

Market Structure and Innovation: The state-of-the-art in industrial economics

The literature on the 'economics of innovation' that we have discussed in the previous chapter concerned mainly the *determinants* and the directions of technical change. Empirical studies focused primarily on single innovations and *why* and *how* they were brought about.

Parallel to this strand of analysis, however, a considerable stream of work has developed within industrial economics. This work has been concerned implicitly or explicitly, with the *incentives* leading to different degrees of commitment to innovative activities. This second stream of thought, both in terms of theory – following Arrow's contribution (Arrow, 1962) – and in terms of empirical analysis (see the seminal research by Mansfield[7]), developed to a large extent independently from the 'economics of innovation' questions. The empirical tests have been generally carried out through econometric analyses at industry level, in the attempt 'to explain' the cross-industries' and/or cross-companies' variance in some proxy of innovative activities (generally R & D expenditures or, less frequently, R & D employees or patents) through some structural indicator such as firms' size and industrial concentration.[8]

We will start then by trying to make a critical assessment of this formalised 'market structure and innovation' approach, beginning with the hypotheses and the foundations underlying the empirical studies. A thorough overview of the latter, surveying and discussing the major studies is in Kamien and Schwartz (1975) and (1982). A detailed critical discussion is in Momigliano (1981). Here, one will simply try to link the problems emerging from the 'market structure and innovation' approach with the interpretative suggestions of the previous chapter.

The 'firm size–market structure' approach to industrial innovation has the great merit of highlighting two crucial questions, namely (a) how firms' size affects firms' *capability* and *incentive* to innovate, and (b) what is the effect of industrial concentration upon the incentive to innovate. Implicitly, this approach assumes that the innovative activities are undertaken as a function of the economic incentive related to them and that the latter depends on some structural features of the markets. More specifically, the hypothesis that large oligopolistic firms have a relative innovative advantage *vis-à-vis* smaller size firms is sometimes referred to as the 'Schumpeterian hypothesis' (see Scherer, 1970). We shall discuss it in greater detail below.

A preliminary problem of this approach concerns the general use of R & D indicators as a proxy for companies' commitment to innovative activities. This issue is discussed at length in Soete (1980); Griliches (1980), and Momigliano (1981). It may be enough to stress that the use of such an indicator presents two major pitfalls:

(a) It is an indicator of input of resources committed to, broadly speaking, innovative and/or imitative activities which is taken to represent the *output* of technological innovations and imitation. Thus, it embodies a strong assumption of linearity in the relationship between the two. It implicitly assumes either the *irrelevance* of differences across industries in technological *opportunities*[9] or that these differences only reflect themselves in different R & D investments by firms belonging to different industries.[10]

(b) It neglects learning-by-doing and, generally, the cumulative aspects of the innovative process, which obviously are not caught by the R & D variable.[11]

One must admit, however, that availability of data may force R & D variables to be chosen. These problems add particular caution to the interpretation of the results.

Moreover, cross-industries' studies suffer from a major drawback related again to technological opportunity and private appropriability of the innovations. If one goes to test a relationship between firms' size and (possibly) industrial concentrations, on the one hand, and R & D intensities (for example R & D/sales ratios), on the other hand, on samples covering the entire manufacturing industry, one rules out *a priori* the likely effects of different innovative possibilities offered by different technologies and different degrees of private appropriability of the results of the research. The latter, to repeat, is likely to be one of the crucial variables determining the incentive to innovate.

In some ways, the same deep-rooted idea, criticised above, of *smooth* production sets (and thus of *irrelevance of the nature of the technologies*) emerges again here. Thus these testing procedures assume that the only differences in appropriability stem from size and market concentration. As far as technological opportunities are concerned, even when some proxies are introduced (sometimes in the form of pre-defined dummy variables)[12] these are quite rough indicators which – in our view – can hardly catch the inter-industrial variance in the scope of innovative possibilities.

Market Structure and Innovation: The Empirical Findings

Empirical findings on the 'market structure and innovation' question have been surveyed, as mentioned, by Kamien and Schwartz (1975), where one can find also a lengthy bibliography. In addition, Freeman (1974) provides a thorough analysis of the relationship between innovative activities and nature of the innovative units (and its change over time). We will not, therefore, attempt any summary of the discussion but only analyse some of the conclusions.

Keeping in mind the above reasons for caution related to the use of an R & D variable as a proxy for innovativeness, all studies – not surprisingly – find a strong correlation between R & D outlets and/or some other measure of innovativeness (such as number of patents or of innovations) and firms' size. An interesting question, however, concerns the nature of that relationship, whether it is linear, increasing more or less proportionally, or whether it shows a maximum. This is sometimes referred to as the 'Schumpeterian hypothesis': do big firms have a comparative edge due to the 'institutionalisation' of research in their big laboratories?[13] The question partly overlaps with the other concerning the effect of concentration upon the incentives to innovate. It can easily be seen that the answer to these two questions has implications which affect the very foundations of static microeconomic theory and general equilibrium analysis. Suppose, in fact, that the relationship of innovativeness to size and concentration shows 'increasing returns'. This is tragic indeed for a neoclassical theorist, since it would imply that the higher the divergence from static 'Pareto optimality' of the markets, the higher also their innovative dynamism. As we shall argue below this may be, partly, the case.[14]

Empirical analyses appeared to have satisfied the anxious search of economists for an 'optimal' size (or an 'optimal' market concentration) in that they appeared to support the hypothesis of the existence of a maximum in the R & D intensity (or patents' intensity) of firms in relation to their size. For a very sharp argument in favour of this thesis, supported by all the available empirical evidence, see Scherer (1965) and (1970). Moreover, the relationship between R & D and concentration (once allowance is made for firms' size effects) tended to show only a weak positive (or sometimes insignificant) effect,[15] or positive in some cluster of industries and negative in others.[16]

Several methodological theoretical and empirical problems suggest some degree of scepticism regarding these results:

1. On methodological grounds, a high multicollinearity is likely to exist between firms' size and the degree of concentration of the markets they operate in, so that whenever a test is undertaken on cross-industries analysis, it is difficult to assess what is the true influence of the 'size' and the 'concentration' variables, respectively.

2. Within highly international markets, the degrees of *international* concentration of the industry are likely to have at least as much influence as the domestic ones.

3. The crucial neglect of the 'technological opportunity' variable has been discussed above. Even when some proxy for it is introduced into the estimates, its roughness can hardly catch the effective influence of that factor which is likely to have a powerful influence upon firms' willingness to undertake innovative activities, quite independently from their size or the degree of concentration of the markets they serve.

4. As for the existence of a maximum in the correlation between firms' size and innovativeness, at the *level of each industry*, the evidence used by Scherer (1965) and (1970), is quite convincingly challenged by Soete (1977) and (1979), with estimates on more recent and more complete data. Soete finds that R & D concentration ratios are steadily higher than sales' concentration ratios, and that within the industries analysed, eleven support the hypothesis of 'increasing R & D propensities' in relation to size,[17] three suggest decreasing propensity and for the other three there appears to be no conclusive evidence.[18]

However, the empirical evidence which is used to support the verification of the wrongly named 'Schumpeterian hypothesis' may in fact be interpreted in a quite different way. Suppose that we do find an inverted U-shaped function relating, in a cross-industries examination, 'innovativeness' and firms' size (or concentration). This evidence would be traditionally used to say that innovativeness is a positive function of firms' size (or concentration) only until a certain ('optimal') level. That level would then be used also in a normative sense, to guide anti-trust policies, etc. Suppose, however, that (a) the degree of 'innovativeness' (as measured by any input or output indicator) is a negative function of the 'technological maturity'[19] of an industry; (b) that concentration is, among other things, a positive function of *past* innovativeness and of technological maturity, and (c) that for any *given* technological maturity, 'innovativeness' is a *positive* function of firms's size.[20] The interplay between these three factors could explain an inverted U-shaped cross-sectional estimate, even if – as from point (c) – the 'true' relationship between firms' size and innovativeness shows 'increasing returns'.

These problems raised by the empirical tests concerning the shape in the function relating market structure and degree of innovativeness, hint at a major issue: market structure (including in this instance firms' size and concentration) cannot be considered as an independent variable, since it is as much a function of *past* innovativeness, *past* technological opportunities and *past* degrees of appropriability of the innovations. In other words, market structure has to be fully treated as an *endogenous variable*.

3.2 THE INTERPLAY BETWEEN TECHNICAL CHANGE AND INDUSTRIAL STRUCTURES

Innovativeness and Oligopoly

Market structure is a function of the patterns of technological change at least as much as the latter is a function of the former. On historical grounds, this feature of the industrial system is quite well recognised in several taxonomies suggested in different theoretical contexts: product cycle and technology gap theories in international trade,[21] Abernathy and Utterback's theory of the development of a technology in relation to the forms of industrial organisation[22] and B. Klein's analysis of 'dynamic competition',[23] all suggest the existence of different industrial structures corresponding to different stages in the development of a technology.

The argument developed in the previous chapter appears to be of some help in analysing the nature of this relationship. The distinction, introduced earlier, between *emergence* of new technological paradigms and 'normal' progress upon *established* technological trajectories is likely to correspond to quite different structures of supply. In the first phase, the latter is likely to be quite fluid, often characterised by a high rate of birth and mortality of new 'Schumpeterian' companies, enjoying *temporary oligopolies* on clusters of innovations (e.g. the car industry between 1880s and 1920s, the electromechanical industry in the final part of the last century, the aircraft industry until the Second World War, the semiconductor industry, as we shall see, throughout the 1950s and 1960s, and quite possibly bio-engineering today).

In the second stage, whenever technological trajectories show cumulativeness and strong private appropriability, a more stable oligopolistic structure is likely to develop, production and exploitation of technical advances become much less divorced and technical change becomes itself part of the patterns of 'oligopolistic competition'.

Note that both phases are characterised by some form of oligopolistic power. In the first phase oligopolistic positions mainly relate to differences between firms in their innovative/imitative capabilities, to 'dynamic economies' associated with them (learning by doing) and to the pre-emption of the markets generally induced by major early entrants. In the second phase oligopolistic power is likely to stem also from rather stable entry barriers (cumulativeness of technological development may be one and 'static' economies of scale may be another one).

The possibility of enjoying temporary monopolistic positions (and/or long-run oligopolistic ones) on new products and processes appears to act as a powerful incentive to the innovative activity. The perspective differential advantages accruing to successful technological and market leaders, in our view, are likely to influence and stimulate the process of innovation much more than the *ex-ante* market structure as such.

The existence of big firms and high degrees of concentration appears to be positively related to a high past technological opportunity and high degrees of appropriability (i.e. high difficulty in the imitation) of the innovations (see Nelson and Winter, 1978).

On the other hand, an *a priori* expectation on the effects of concentration and market power on the patterns of innovation-based inter-oligopolistic rivalry is difficult to formulate.[24]

For any given level of technological opportunity the two variables affecting the innovative attitudes of companies may be considered the 'carrot' (appropriability) and the 'stick' (dynamic rivalry). As far as the latter is concerned it is difficult to draw precise hypotheses on the patterns of oligopolistic rivalry from the neoclassical ('maximisation') paradigm. The reader is invited to see Needham (1979) for a refined discussion of oligopolistic R & D behaviour which, however, cannot avoid rather *indeterminate* conclusions similar to those related to pricing under oligopolistic rivalry (cf. Sylos Labini, 1967). In actual fact the very existence of oligopolistic structures implies that each actor on the market has the possibility, through its actions, of affecting both the environmental conditions and the outcomes of the actions of the other actors. In our case, if one sticks to the simple maximisation paradigm, the decisions about the amount of investment in innovation and imitation are bound to take into account rival reactions. Thus, the form of the expectations about the latter are essential in determining the behaviour of each company. Very little, however, can be known *a priori* about the nature of these expectations. The question is similar to the conjectural aspect of price and quantities adjustments under rivalry. The problem is at least as old as Cournot's duopoly model: if one firm fixed an 'above-pure-competition' price, will the others adjust their quantities to keep that price? In other words: (a) are rivals' reactions adaptive or not? (b) are expectations of rivals' reactions adaptive or not? As we shall see below, only the institutional investigation of possible behavioural regularities under conditions of technical change can avoid the indeterminacy of such a world of expectations.

Let us summarise a few provisional conclusions from this brief overview of the state-of-the-art in this field:

1. Market structure and firms' size are endogenous variables, which depend also on the nature and rate of technical progress.
2. High technological opportunities and high degrees of private appropriability, other things being equal, lead to big firms' size and high degrees of concentration.[25]
3. The same considerations apply to the degree of cumulativeness of technical progress. It can easily be seen that this property is quite intuitive: a firm is likely to be big because it has been cumulatively successful in its innovative activity. If 'technological opportunities' have been high, its competitive edge over other firms will be considerable and acquire it a big market share, which in turn leads to high degrees of market concentration.
4. Market concentration and market power[26] in addition to being a result of *past* technological developments, influence *current* innovative incentives in so far as they affect, first, the appropriability of the innovations (one would expect that the latter is positively related to a firm's market share and in general to the concentration of the industry), and, second, the patterns of oligopolistic rivalry.

'Reverse Causation' between Technology and Market Structures

Let us turn to the account given in both empirical investigation and theoretical modelling to 'reverse causation' (Nelson and Winter, 1980b) or 'inverted' relations (Momigliano, 1981) between technical change and market structure (from the former to the latter).

The little attention paid in empirical literature to the question is quite surprising and might be partly explained by economists' reluctance in approaching an issue which almost certainly implies the absence of an identical production function for all firms in an industry (even more so if technical progress is cumulative at firm's level), and the existence of more or less permanent (i.e. *structural*) oligopolistic positions of some companies, whose ground lies within the same nature of technical progress. One of the few notable exceptions is the seminal work by Phillips (1971), concerning in its empirical side the aircraft industry, but with a theoretical scope which goes beyond a singular sector study.[27] The study suggests that differential advantages for first-coming firms, which are stable through time due to technological cumulativeness, yield to a strongly concentrated oligopoly.

At an empirical level one notes that only a part of the total number of innovations introduce radically new products and give rise to a completely new industry. Even in these cases (which we called above the emergence of a new technological paradigm) the new commodities are also likely to be substitutes for some existing products. Innovations often imply a powerful process of substitution between new (or improved) and old commodities. This process of 'creative destruction', in a Schumpeterian terminology, is associated with a changing relative balance between companies (and often also between industries): companies that have been successful in innovating and/or commercially exploiting the innovations grow more rapidly and increase their market shares relatively to laggard companies (the latter may eventually even die). A very similar process may be associated with process innovations: changes in the cost of production of the innovating company is likely to disrupt the basis upon which the previous distribution of produced quantities among companies was organised, putting the innovating company in a more favourable position to increase output and market shares by means of price reductions. These dynamic processes are a crucial part of the process of industrial transformation induced by technological innovations.

At a theoretical level one finds two quite different approaches to modelling. The first approach is that of some recent sophisticated and formalised attempts to make market structure endogenous within models which maintain assumptions of equilibrium and profit for maximising firms (see especially Dasgupta and Stiglitz (1980) and Futia (1980)). The study of the properties of the model is then undertaken in terms of comparative statics (in the former case) or comparing equilibrium growth paths (Futia). Dasgupta and Stiglitz show the likely non-optimality of market allocations to innovative activities. In many ways, these models push the neoclassical paradigm to its extreme limits and prove (the former in particular) that whenever some realistic features of the innovative process are introduced into the assumptions, the characters of optimality of textbook market adjustments tend to disappear. This is all the more so when the properties of these models come nearer to the sort of account of the 'stylized facts' and hypotheses outlined above. We still have some doubts, however, on their capability of describing what actually happens throughout dynamic processes of innovation and structural change: the assumptions of instantaneous adjustments in prices, quantities and number of firms might turn out to be more than simplifying (and in this respect 'neutral') devices and might prove to be essential to some of the conclusions of the models. In other words, relaxing these assumptions may yield to a quite different vision of the process of industrial adjustment under conditions of technical change.

With respect to this question, note that the innovative process implies almost by definition *disequilibrium* (including 'excess profits'). Thus it is very difficult to describe it in terms of comparative statics or equilibrium growth paths, which are based on equilibrium assumptions.[28]

A much more ambitious and, in our view, much more fruitful approach is the one recently put forward by Nelson and Winter.[29] It seeks to undertake a radical departure from traditional assumptions, and to suggest an *evolutionary model* of industrial structures under conditions of technical change which undoubtedly maintains a genuine Schumpeterian flavour. Among the features of their models one finds the following:

1. Firms undertake innovative/imitative activities as a function of their size and of their position *vis-à-vis* the companies 'on the frontier' (for any given characteristics of the technology).
2. Market structures (numbers of firms, firms' size and concentration) are *endogenous*.
3. Probabilities of innovative success for each firm are serially correlated through time. Thus, so are firms' rates of growth.[30]
4. Successful firms are allowed to enjoy 'above-normal' unit margins (and profits).
5. Concentration is a positive function of technological opportunity and of the difficulty in imitating innovations.
6. A strong exercise of market power by the leading firms tends actually *to limit* the growth in concentration.[31]

One can easily see the close correspondence between these features of Nelson and Winter's models and the 'stylized facts' we described above as being central to the double relationship between industrial structure and technical change.

As will be discussed again below, Nelson and Winter also suggest a hypothesis of firms' behaviour which implies *behavioural rules* and changes in these rules more akin to a biological evolution model than to maximisation procedures within known sets of choices and outcomes. Unfortunately, a lot of work has still to be done in order to test the model properly (see Levin (1981) for the only attempt we are aware of, and based on quite aggregate data). Nonetheless, Nelson and Winter's simulated model must be considered as embodying a powerful heuristic, which the reader is invited to keep in mind when we consider the dynamics of companies interactions and changing industrial structures.

Inter-firm Asymmetries as a Permanent Feature of Industrial Dynamics

We have already discussed in the previous chapter the permanent existence of *asymmetries* between firms (and between countries) in terms of technological capabilities, degrees of innovativeness and imitative swiftness. These asymmetries – as we have just argued – are a prime factor in changing market structures and market shares of individual firms.[32]

The importance can hardly be overestimated. First, they are fundamental variables which determine the dynamics of the system. Secondly, they bear a strict relationship with one of the basic regularities in behaviour of individual companies in market economies. Let us start from the first question.

Some kind of private appropriation of the economic benefits of innovation is, to repeat, a necessary condition which generally represents the incentive to undertake innovative activities in the company sector. Appropriation, almost by definition, implies technological and, more generally, competitive differences between firms: the latter clearly try to innovate in order to sell new or better products than their competitors, have lower production costs, or both. Moreover, time is an essential element of the process: market pre-emption is associated with different relative degrees of success in innovation imitation.

This process, which is often referred to as 'Schumpeterian competition' (see especially Schumpeter, 1919) involves an adjustment mechanism which is radically different from the process implied by neoclassical microeconomics.[33] In the latter, disequilibria in the commodity markets generate variations in prices and quantities *for given and generally uniform* technologies. In the former, imitation and technological diffusion tend to decrease inter-firm technological asymmetries (and thus decrease also the 'extra profits' of early innovators). Moreover the adjustment takes place in real time. In a 'Schumpeterian world', the crucial adjustment mechanism occurs via changes in production techniques and in products. Throughout the process changes in prices and quantities do certainly occur, but they are, in the first instance, a by-product of changing conditions of production and not a result of the fact that markets are not cleared.

As known, this image of the competitive process underpins the Schumpeterian theory of innovation and growth. That same image, however, is not very distant from the 'microfoundations' implicit in the dynamic theory of some classical economists (Smith and Ricardo) and explicit in Marx. Even if it is not possible to analyse here with any satisfactory depth the conceptions of competitive markets held through the history of economic thought, it is worth noticing that the permanent existence of inter-firm technological differences is compatible, in the tradition of classical economists,[34] with the existence of market conditions which are defined as 'free competition'. We are forced to wonder: in this context, where can we draw the line between a 'free competitive' environment which is nonetheless characterised by the permanent existence of ever-changing monopolistic/oligopolistic positions, and an unmistakable oligopolistic environment? In other words, in the dynamic perspective we are taking here, how can we define any oligopolistic market structure?

One can notionally see two opposite answers to that question. At one extreme, it could be argued that oligopolies are a permanent feature of the dynamics of the system, so that a purely 'competitive environment' is just some kind of ideal type set up by modern economic theory (with hardly any descriptive role). At the other extreme, one could argue that in a dynamic context most of the markets are 'competitive' in that any single monopolistic/oligopolistic position tends to be eroded by technological diffusion, imitation and further innovations by other companies. Part of the question is certainly a matter of definition. There is more to it than that, however, and any substantive hypothesis on the nature of the markets in the long run bears important implications for the analysis of prices, margins, profit rates (and ultimately income distribution).

What is an 'Oligopolistic Environment'?

Throughout the first part of this chapter, we based our discussion on the relationship between technical change and industrial structures on what we may call *a weak definition* of oligopolistic environments. Let us make their characteristics explicit:

1. Technological differences (asymmetries) between firms in terms of innovativeness, conditions of production or both are a crucial consequence of technical change.
2. Individual firms (and their interplay) are able to, and do continuously affect their environment through their actions. This implies also that context variables are actually determined to some degree by companies' behaviour.
3. The capability of each firm of affecting the environment differs, as a function of its position *vis-à-vis* the technological frontier, its size, market share, etc. A corollary is that only some firms may have the structural capability of being price makers.
4. Due to technological differences between firms (point 1), performance indicators and in particular productivity, profit margins and profit rates permanently vary across firms.

We maintain that these are rather general features of economic systems where technical change takes place. These sets of conditions are sufficient to rule out the existence of the 'pure competitive' environment suggested by neoclassical economics, whereby firms are reactive units to a *given* context and prices are set through an auction-like mechanism.

The same set of conditions, however, is necessary but *not* sufficient to rule out the existence of a competitive environment in what we can define the classical sense. By the latter we mean an environment whereby the *trend* prices, margins and profit rates gravitate around those determined by the *average* conditions of production,[35] so that, again as a trend, differential oligopolistic profits *for the industry* as a whole average around zero.[36] On the contrary, the existence of an oligopolistic environment, in this context, implies a long-run positive differential between the rate of profit in a particular industry and that rate of profit, uniform across industries, which would have been established in competitive conditions: we shall term this as the *strong oligopolistic hypothesis*.

On purely theoretical grounds we do not face overwhelming difficulties in defining the competitive rate of profit: it can be represented by that rate which solves a system of industrial interdependencies (*à la*

Sraffa) once given the wage rate, and whenever the input coefficients of the matrix are taken to be the average values for each industry.[37] The underlying behavioural assumption is that inter-industrial capital movements will tend to eliminate inter-industrial differentials in profit rates. In actual fact, however, we cannot make counterfactual experiments: we hardly know what the competitive rate of profit should have been and thus we do not know whether a difference between the actual and competitive rates of profit exist.[38] One is therefore forced to use more indirect means of detecting the possible existence of oligopolistic environments (in the *strong* version).

As already mentioned, oligopolistic conditions, in the *weak* sense, defined above, are necessary but not enough to generate permanently above-normal profit rates. We are going to argue that sufficient conditions often *do* exist and are closely related to the nature of technologies and technical change. Let us examine more closely the crucial property underlying the 'weak hypothesis': despite continuous inter-firm asymmetries, trend profitabilities correspond to the competitive ones. In the last resort, that hypothesis states that capital mobility and inter-firm technological diffusion outpace or at least compensate for oligopoly-creating effect of technical change. Moreover, there must not be permanent size-related technological discontinuity between firms. Whether this is the case in any industry is primarily an empirical matter. *A priori*, however, one can easily define the conditions which allow the existence of 'strong' oligopolistic environments. In particular, the greater appropriability, cumulativeness and scale economies, the greater will be the likelihood that trend oligopolistic profit rates would emerge.

Note that we can state this hypothesis without making any assumption on degrees of market power.[39] To illustrate the point the reader is invited to recall the example suggested by Sylos-Labini (1967, Chapter 2) of three sets of firms, belonging to different size classes and permanently characterised by different unit costs.[40] Conversely, as we shall discuss at greater length below, there can be one *permanently* innovative firm in an industry containing also a group of imitative firms. In both cases we can expect oligopolistic profits to emerge, independently from any hypothesis on the market power of the leading firms. The latter, jointly with demand characteristics may affect the level of such an oligopolistic profit, but not its very existence.

Appropriability and cumulativeness of technical progress and scale economies do not only affect profitabilities through *entry barriers*[41] but also — and perhaps even more so — through *mobility barriers*, to use a concept suggested by an important contribution by Caves and Porter (1977). In other words, inter-firm asymmetries are at least as important as barriers against potential new competitors in allowing 'above-normal' profits (in the sense defined above). Pushing in the opposite direction, one should not forget the diffusive/imitative processes which are always at work jointly with intra- and inter-industrial mobility of firms. The final outcome of the two opposite mechanisms depends on the pace and nature of technical progress and on related capabilities of individual firms to stabilise their asymmetric position *vis-à-vis* actual and potential competitors.

Rationality Criteria and Structural Regularities: A Re-assessment of the Relationship between Structure, Conduct and Performance

The development of our argument on the relationship between technical change and industrial structures led us quite far from the traditional focus of industrial economics. One can easily see how our choice of the variables and relationships, deemed to be important, departed substantially from the approach which is at the core of any textbook dealing with prices, quantities, costs, market equilibria, etc. We feel the need to state clearly where we stand with respect to traditional theory, since we believe that the differences are greater than the simple fact that they concern static equilibria, while we have been discussing technical change, dynamics, etc. There are indeed differences which relate to the basic assumptions about rationality criteria, companies' behaviours, relationships between environment and behaviours. These points are clearly the foundations of economic thought and would require a book on their own on the philosophy of economics. However, we decided to venture into this field partly as a thought-provoking exercise and partly because it seems necessary to spell out the assumptions which inspire and direct some of our arguments. We shall be forced to repeat also many things which are well known to philosophers of social sciences. Needless to say, we cannot aim at any satisfactory degree of thoroughness in our examination.

The basic paradigm of orthodox economic theory strongly implies some kind of *rational solipism*: a reactive decision-making takes place whereby individuals try to maximise some objective function, given an exogenous context and a known set of choices and outcomes.[42] There are three parts to these foundations of neoclassical economics, namely: (a) the decision-making mechanism is basically reactive, (b) the context is exogenous, and (c) the set of choices and outcomes is known (or probabilities can be attached to them). The first two points are clearly interlinked and relate to the hypothesis of static pure competition, while the third actually corresponds to a heuristic criterion of the kind: when considering time and change, reduce the problem to a static one, or paraphrasing Nelson, assume that man is as omniscient as God.[43] In the last resort, the problems which can be addressed are limited to *trivial* situations where the choice is *obvious*: it is simply a matter of an engineer-like exercise in which something has to be maximised under constraints.[44]

Even leaving aside the problem of dynamics, the very existence of oligopolies, challenges the first two assumptions, since (a) it makes the context partly endogenous, and (b) it prevents a one-to-one relationship between context and rational conduct. This applies also to a *static* context (a context without technical change and growth) and underlies the problem of *oligopolistic indeterminateness*: unique conducts and performances cannot generally be deduced, within this theoretical framework, from the simple knowledge of the context. On the other hand 'true' dynamics (characterised by technical change and limited knowledge about the future) undermines the third assumption of a known set of choices and outcomes,[45] *independently* from the oligopoly problem.

On the top of all this, problems related to the role of organisational structures, information costs, decision and implementation costs, etc. throw doubts on the adequacy of the assumption that an organisation such as a firm is intimately similar to a rational individual, even in a 'static' world, let alone a world characterised by technical change and continuous transformation.[46]

The 'structure–conduct–performance' approach, familiar to all students of industrial economics, is a neat framework where the relationship between features of the context, behaviours and outcomes can be analysed.[47] However, the hypotheses about the link between structure and conduct (and thus performance) stand or fall together with the rationality and decision-making assumptions this approach embodies.

Different ways out of the impasse can be conceived. The first one is a game–theoretical approach (in order to deal especially with problems of oligopoly and generally of inter-actions).[48] The field in which to play games is practically unlimited: an almost infinite series of rules and initial conditions can be notionally imagined and so also an infinite number of PhDs and academic articles. However, since we are not told *under which circumstances, which* games are played, we are left with very little interpretative power. If we are allowed a very 'unscientific' remark, it seems to us that part of the rising success of game–theoretical approaches lies in their philosophical foundation, similar to the traditional neoclassical one, whereby the basic image of the economy (and of society) is something like a *sum* of individuals or groups of individuals who are seen as both normative and constitutive of the economic system (or for that matter of society). As Nelson notes, Robinson Crusoe still lingers around (Nelson 1981).

A more detailed investigation of the relationship between micro and macro may be useful to introduce two other lines of enquiry into the (a) behavioural regularities across firms, and (b) regularities into the dynamic properties of the systems we are trying to analyse (i.e. economic and technological systems).

'Micro' and 'Macro': Regularities in Behaviours and Regularities in the Directions of Change

The idea of a difference between micro and macro relates to the idea of *systems*, and that systems are *not* (because they are *more than*) the sum of their composing parts. Even at the risk of bordering on philosophical questions, we must spend a few words on these questions because they underpin concepts such as 'structural change', 'dynamic competition', and 'evolutionary theories'.

In his thought-provoking book on dynamic economics, B. Klein (1977) warns from the beginning about the 'fallacy of composition error' which is assuming . . . 'what is true or seems to be true of the parts (micro-behaviour) . . . to be true of the whole (macro-performance) or what is true or seems to be true of the whole . . . to be true of the parts' (p. 21). The warning is necessary because – he convincingly argues – the dynamic properties of the economic system cannot be extrapolated by the micro-behaviour postulated by – in his terminology – 'classical' (i.e. neoclassical) micro-theory. In particular, the innovative process cannot be simply predicted on the basis of maximisation assumptions of behaviour. The idea of 'systems' which change through time and whose change is 'something more' than simple increases or decreases in the value of unchanged variables, may be something fairly difficult to understand if one strongly sticks to the Walrasian tradition in economics, but is necessary if one wants to construct a predictive theory (see again Klein, Chapter 1 and 5). Certainly systems change through the change of their parts, but each part is defined contextually to the system and the directions of change of the system may be different from that of each individual part.[49]

Above, we argued that the 'rational–decision' maximisation-based framework is unsuitable to describe any acceptably general regularity in the relationship between structures, conducts and performances whenever the context is partly endogenous and changing through time. This theoretical inadequacy is based essentially on two reasons. First, the approach yields indeterminate results whenever some of the economic agents maintain a degree of freedom in their actions and thus also the capability of 'changing the world' with their behaviours. This inadequacy applies even under static conditions of no technical change. The only account that the theory can provide of 'multi-exit' oligopolistic environments are complex conjectural models where basically everything can happen. In comparison, the wheels and epicycles of pre-Copernican astronomy look very simple: at least planets were not allowed to change course according to their own conjectures on where the others were going. The second fundamental inadequacy relates to the relationship between economic agents and change. Outside the Christian theology on the omniscience and omnipotence of God, it is difficult to find examples of rational choice about an intrinsically uncertain future. Thus, the behavioural regularities in the relation between structural conditions and final outcomes can hardly be found in the rationality criteria of the decision process.

Abandoning the search for regularities, however, would involve also the abandonment of the attempt to build up any theory. Fortunately the maximisation approach is not the only possible behavioural regularity for any given environment. An alternative hypothesis about competitive processes is that of *inter-acting institutions (firms) operating through a combination of routine behaviour, 'gambles' and meta-rules for adaptation to changing environments*: in conditions where the future is intrinsically uncertain, technological advances are both one of the main instruments of survival and an 'insurance' for future economic benefit (both in terms of profits and growth). This follows Nelson and Winter's *evolutionary approach* (a major evolution itself, originating from the 'behavioural theories' of the firm).[50] The regularities are in terms of routines and 'meta-rules' which characterise behaviours under conditions of 'bound rationality'. The evolutionary approach – unlike the neoclassical paradigm discussed above – is able to account for (a) the structural existence of asymmetries among firms which yield to oligopolistic positions of some of them, (b) processes of *dynamic adjustment* where time, and thus also the history of an industry are explicitly considered as one of the explanatory variables, and (c) the specific organisational nature of firms which need not look like a perfectly knowledgeable individual.

Conversely, we can also state that dynamic systems (such as those characterised by 'Schumpeterian competition') *imply* evolutionary approaches to the behaviours of competitive actors. The previously cited work by Egidi (1980) argues this point convincingly: 'since the change in the behaviours of the actors depends on the configuration of the system, in Schumpeter we have a complete inversion of the view of methodological individualism: while in Walras, once given the natural characteristics of human behaviour all the set-up of the economy becomes determined, in Schumpeter, on the contrary, economic behaviour depends on the set-up of the economy and, more in general, is locally determined'.[51] The importance of this point can hardly be overestimated. The possibility of establishing some kind of link between context and conducts cannot reside in some *unchanging* principle of rationality which informs behaviours: on the contrary the environment contributes to *define* and *select* between different bound rationalities (the routines and meta-rules) which characterise conducts, and which are more than one.[52] Evolutionary theories point in the direction of a theory of regularities in behaviours which can be easily integrated with all the extra-economic knowledge we have about the nature of social and cultural 'rules of the game' which are specific to a country, a historical period, or an industry.[53]

We have also been arguing implicitly above that the interaction of these behaviours could lead to rather stable patterns of change in the economic structure of which a few have been sketched out, such as the existence of powerful tendencies towards oligopolistic configurations of supply. Different behaviours and different patterns of interaction may lead to quite diverse trends in the economic structure and in the 'performance variables'. One can think, e.g., of the alternative possibilities of collusively conservative or, conversely, aggressive and risk-taking attitudes towards technical change. Which course of action will be actually followed depends, among other things, on the nature and stage of development in the technological trajectories (which determines technological opportunities and degrees of appropriability), the institutional nature of the firms (as Abernathy and Utterback suggest, their degree of organisational rigidity,[54] etc.) and, last but not least, on some fundamental 'rules of the game' which characterise each individual industrial structure and society. In this respect, Klein (1977) tries to develop a theory linking the nature of the behavioural routines with changes in the American innovative performance and, more generally, in its economic performance. Note that these 'rules' determine the kind of 'rationality' on which companies operate (e.g. their basic attitudes towards uncertainty, change, growth, profitability, etc.). At each moment in time, for each individual company, the external environment is given and defines the set of constraints for its behaviours. These behaviours and their interactions on their part change the external environments.

'Behaviouralist' vs 'Structural' Models: Evolutionary Models as the Microfoundation of a Theory of Structural Change

We are now in a position to ask the following question: Within the framework of 'evolutionary theories' and 'bounded and multiple rationalities', are we better equipped to establish some general relationship between the nature of the environments and performance indicators, thus avoiding the intrinsic indeterminateness associated with oligopoly and technical change in the traditional theory?

Our answer is positive, subject to some qualifications. After abandoning the strait-jacket of orthodox microeconomic assumptions, we shall argue that it is possible to establish *proximate* but sufficiently general relationships between environmental conditions and performance variables (such as, for example, prices, margins, profit rates, etc.), once we are supplemented with some information about the history of that environment and the institutional features of the actors involved. Let us make the question clearer.

We have been arguing that, in order to analyse problems of oligopoly and technical change, we must abandon the neoclassical framework because we cannot assume an exogenous and given context and many God-like actors who behave in accordance with a uniform rationality. Under conditions of changing contexts, interdependence between actions, uncertainty, etc., the actors maintain some behavioural degrees of freedom. Behavioural theories of the firm[55] stress precisely this point and try to find regularities in the institutional features of the actors. These theories, however, are not free from problems and pitfalls. In a strongly behavioural model of interaction between the environment and the economic actors and between the firms themselves, we can (a) assess the regularities in firms' rules of conduct (What is their innovative behaviour once faced with a given technological opportunity? How do they react to changing market conditions, profitabilities, etc?), and (b) establish *ex post* their performance, only after we have reconstructed the *history* of the dynamics of that environment. In other words, behavioural theories do not allow us to make predictions on performance variables such as prices and margins without first simulating the behaviour and the interaction of each firm. What we are wondering now is whether it is possible to establish some broad regularities linking 'structural variables' and 'performance variables', taking, as it were, some snapshots at some points in time, without having to reconstruct the entire 'biological history' of the industry. This second procedure is what we have adopted above in discussing the existence of permanent oligopolistic structures of supply and asking for example questions like: Is there a relationship between economies of scale and above-normal profits? We must assess the legitimacy of this procedure in the light of the present discussion.

The reader will certainly realise that the problem is quite intricate and has far-reaching implications. At the core of it is a crucial problem (possibly *the* crucial problem) common to several social sciences, namely, the relationship between context and individual actors or, which is the same, the relationship between structures and freedom. Were we to allow unconditionally a 'structuralist' view of economic dynamics, this would actually imply that, in the last instance, different institutional patterns of behaviours are irrelevant. In the opposite case, were we to accept very large degrees of freedom to individual actors, we would be incapable of having proper social sciences, since we would be in the uncomfortable position of being unable to draw any conclusions on the direction of change of the system without first seeing it moving in each single part.[56] The reader can visualise the dilemma by comparing the difference between a strictly Newtonian world where all the relations can be deterministically defined, and a strictly Darwinian world where we must wait for every minute mistake of nature before knowing where the world is heading. Both alternatives leave us unsatisfied: in the first, any degree of freedom for the actors disappears, while in the second, we just have 'unfinalised' history plus chance.[57]

This is not the place, and neither do we have the adequate instruments, to undertake anything like a general theory of system transformation. For the time being, we must be content with some approximations from two opposite directions.

First, the evolutionary theory developed by Nelson and Winter, already mentioned several times, presents a major development *vis-à-vis* the 'behavioural' approach *à la* Simon, in that (a) it selects among all the notionally possible behaviours a set of routines and meta-rules which in themselves represent a theory of firm conducts in changing environments, and (b) it provides a quite general theory of the nature of the feedbacks between a changing environment and the change in behaviours and, vice versa, between behaviours and the changes in the environment. In doing so, evolutionary theories can introduce a 'weak teleology' into behavioural models which were originally blind on the directions of change.

Secondly, the approach adopted here, which could be defined as a *weak structural model*, suggests that the joint knowledge of structural conditions and of some fundamental 'rules of behaviour' (which cannot be deduced from the former) allows the analysis of the proximate levels of the performance variables and the broad directions of change. Let us illustrate the point with another biological metaphor. Imagine a 'Lamark-like' world: knowing the environment is not enough to determine the directions of evolution; however, if we know both the environment and some fundamental adaptive rules of the species, then we could predict the broad and proximate directions of change without seeing it all happen first. In this sense, the evolutionary theory and the 'weak structural approach' (that we are going to utilise in the discussion that will follow on prices and margins under conditions of technical change) can be seen as somewhat complementary.

The complementarity between the two does not mean that it is easy to operate an univocal 'translation' of one into the other. Nelson and Winter models are behaviourally much richer and do not make it easy to define some simple 'structural' relationship between 'state' variables (such as technological lags and leads between firms, etc.) and 'perform-ance' variables (such as prices and margins, both at firm and industry levels). In order to know the latter, in Nelson–Winter models, one must also know the entire behavioural history of the industry. On the other hand a more 'structural' approach like that implied in the following discussion is bound to be only a broad approximation (since functional relationships *do* depend on the history of the industry itself), even if it is easier to link microeconomic analysis with macroeconomic indicators (such as income distribution, the 'degree of monopoly' in the economy, etc.) Loosely speaking, there is a complementarity similar to that existing between a series of pictures taken from an airplane, on the one hand, and a film of a microscope observation, on the other hand. Only the latter allows us to observe the evolution of life, while the former simply gives a rough but general picture of how the world looks. A more organic reconciliation between the two appears to be one of the major theoretical tasks which emerges in different economic fields and sometimes goes under the heading of 'microeconomic foundations of macroeconomics'. It is not the ambition of this work to provide it. We hope, however, that it will help in clarifying the basic hypotheses on the complex and bi-univocal relationships between structures, conducts, and performances whenever technical change (and generally dynamics) is taken into account and whenever the economy structurally presents oligopolistic formations. We shall have the chance of testing the heuristic capabilities of these hypotheses in the analysis of prices and margins under conditions of technical change.

More generally, the thrust of our discussion concerns both the *rules of transformation* of a complex system, characterised by technical innovations and growth, which undergoes qualitative changes and the ways in which the *directions* of change relate to the *structure* of the system at each moment in time.

It has been mentioned previously that the patterns of evolution of the system (in our case the evolution of an industry) are determined by the interaction between structural constraints (such as technological asymmetries between firms) and behavioural degrees of freedom of each economic agents. Nelson–Winter's model suggests a theory of evolution as a function of the behavioural regularities. We shall be essentially concerned with the *evolution of the structural boundaries of these degrees of behavioural freedom*. This is the meaning of what we termed a 'weak structural theory'. Whenever economic agents are able to change their environment and to choose within a limited set of alternative strategies, a strictly deterministic theory is impossible. Strategic freedom, however, is not boundless and our model will focus on the evolving relationship between the range of possible performance outcomes and the nature of structural conditions.

We had to search painstakingly for hypotheses and models in a relatively unexplored area. In the prevailing economic theory these questions cannot even be considered, since its core concerns optimal allocation within a given structure.[58]

We have been trying to argue that an *evolutionary theory* of the relationship between behaviours of the economic actors and a changing environment can prove to be a more adequate microfoundation for a theory of structural change. Having said that, it is not for us to deny that firms utilise maximising procedures *whenever it is possible*: for example, the choice between two well-defined techniques of production for a given wage rate and for given desired quantities of output will involve a straightforward maximisation of the profit rate; a scrapping investment decision, given productive techniques of the various vintages of capital equipment will similarly involve maximising procedures with respect to net revenues. The corollary of our argument above, however, is that these maximisation/minimisation exercises are *locally circumscribed*[59] and are not an adequate description of either the overall behaviours of the firms or of the outcome of their actions.[60] The complementary use of evolutionary theories based on behavioural rules, adaptation procedures to changing environments, etc., on the one hand, and 'structural' models of some fundamental regularities in the patterns of evolution of the system as a whole (or some relatively self-contained part of it) on the other hand, will prove to be – in our view – analytically more fruitful.

3.3 COSTS AND PRICES UNDER CONDITIONS OF TECHNICAL CHANGE

Pricing Procedures and Price Levels

Most empirical studies on pricing behaviour in the manufacturing industry, at very different levels of aggregation, are consistent with the thesis that prices are generally determined on some kind of cost–plus basis,[61] with generally little or no influence on short-run fluctuations in demand.

Different models have been proposed to interpret observed behaviours. They could be subdivided into three broad clusters:

1. The first tries to save the traditional microeconomic theory, together with its assumptions of maximisation and marginal pricing, by introducing in the objective function (the function to maximise) the expected rival reaction (which is supposed to account – at least partly – for 'limit pricing' procedures) and/or assuming that 'mark-up' pricing is a practical 'rule of thumb' to achieve a target, intermediate with respect to the ultimate goal (maximisation of the objective function) which remains unchanged.[62]

2. The second line of thought led to the development of more 'realistic' models of the firm, in an attempt to incorporate more 'behavioural' assumptions than those present in a traditional neoclassical model, to account for the existence of goals different from short-run profit maximisation (primarily the objectives of growth, 'target' market shares, etc.) and for a multiplicity of strategies pursuable by a firm.[63] For our purpose these models can be considered the ancestors – in a logical even if not necessarily in a chronological sense – of the evolutionary theories *à la* Nelson–Winter.[64]

3. A third approach tried to link the 'structural' conditions existing at any moment in time in each oligopolistic market with the levels and changes in the margins over average prime (variable) costs.[65]

Our discussion above should serve also as a critique of the first cluster of models mentioned here. Therefore, we shall not examine again their limitations and the 'oligopolistic indetermination' they are not able to avoid in analysing the relationship between costs, margins and prices.

The second cluster (and especially evolutionary theories) are, in our view, essential to the explanation of *how* certain performance variables (as in the case of prices, considered here) come about, through some regularities in firms' behaviour and the pattern of their interactions. They are not best suited, however, to easily answer the question about *which* proximate levels of the performance variables are likely to be associated with a certain set of technological (and more generally 'structural') conditions.[66]

In order to answer to that question we must employ some kind of 'structural' approach (in the sense explained in section beginning on p. 107). First, we shall consider the current state-of-the-art. Then, we shall attempt to provide a model of prices under conditions of rapid technical change.

Technological Discontinuities between Firms, Prices and Margins: The-State-of-the-Art

Let us briefly outline the basic assumptions of the 'structural' approach (we use this expression in this chapter as a form of shorthand to mean that stream of thought pioneered by Bain and Sylos-Labini):[67]

1. There are permanent (although changing through time) technological discontinuities between firms, related to firm size, which yield different variable and total unit costs of production.
2. There is a minimum scale of production which is technologically determined.
3. Short-run price elasticities of demand for the industry and for each firm (at least around the point of 'oligopolistic equilibrium') are well below infinity.
4. Cross elasticities of substitution between the commodity of the considered market and other commodities are relatively low (especially in the short run).
5. Productive technologies for each size–class are characterised by non-decreasing returns. (At any level of activity below full capacity).

The first two conditions define the technological *barriers to entry*. One generally adds to those structural conditions a behavioural assumption often referred to as the 'Sylos postulate': firms set the price at a level which deters entry and furthermore is expected to maintain unchanged levels of output in the case of new entries.

As is well known under these conditions, price is determined by the market leader(s) according to:

$$P \le P_m = \frac{s_0}{\pi_0} + a_0 + \frac{K_0}{x_0} + g_m \qquad\qquad 1$$

and the actual pricing procedure is to apply a mark-up to average 'normal' variable costs:

$$P = \left(\frac{s}{\pi} + a\right)(1 + q) \qquad\qquad 2$$

where P = unit price, s = labour cost, π = 'normal' labour productivity (i.e. at 'normal' levels of output), K = fixed total costs, a = other variable inputs (other than labour), g = net unit profit, x = 'normal' level of output, q = gross margins over variable costs. The suffices s_0, π_0, K_0, etc. stand for labour costs, productivity and capital stock for the potential entrant, while g_m is the minimum net unit profit corresponding to the minimum rate of profit the potential entrant is ready to accept, and P_m is the related minimum price. The price leader(s) will fix the price in relation to that minimum price.

The margin q is thus determined in relation to (a) barriers to entry, (b) elasticities of demand for industry and for firms, (c) incidence of fixed costs per unit of output. Barriers to entry are determined by technology, the absolute size of the market (through the ratio between the 'minimum efficient scale' and the total market), possible absolute cost advantages, economies of scale, and the size of the financial outlets necessary for the 'minimum scale investment' – reasonably assuming that capital markets are not perfect markets. (See Bain, 1956.) The elasticity of demand for industry is important because barriers of entry are determined by the above 'technological' conditions in relation to the form of the portion of the demand curve to the right of the oligopolistic equilibrium point.[68]

Once q and P are determined, industrial output is univocally determined. Furthermore, this pricing model allows the determination of the changes in price levels due to variations of unit variable costs which are general to industry.[69] Notably, in this kind of model, 'equilibrium' prices are determined independently from short-run fluctuations in demand (which just determines the levels of output) and, even in the long run, demand affects pricing conditions only in so far as it influences 'normal' unit costs and/or barriers to entry.

Let us turn to the limitations of the model, some of which relate to the behavioural assumptions included in it and some to the structural conditions assumed. As far as behavioural assumptions are concerned, the 'Sylos postulate' appears to be more reasonable generalisation around oligopolistic behaviour rather than a 'general law'. This implies that if large new entries occur, then 'counting has to be done again'[70] to obtain the new equilibrium values for the level of prices and mark-ups. The objective ground of the 'Sylos postulate' relies upon the existence of a 'normal' level of capacity utilisation below which fixed costs per unit of output increase and on the existence of some market share target which is often found among firms' considerations. Both elements militate against adaptive behaviours *vis-à-vis* new entries. One may consider the 'Sylos postulate' as a proxy for a firm's behaviour which has a *lower generality* than the structural relationship between barriers to entry, on the one hand, and levels of profit margins and profit rates, on the other hand.[71] The question is of importance for our following argument, and thus will require some additional investigation.

Current literature on industrial economics generally associates the contribution of what we termed the 'structural approach' (and especially that of Sylos-Labini) with the 'limit pricing hypothesis'. We will try to show that this does not do justice to these theoretical contributions and is somewhat misleading. In our interpretation the theory of oligopolistic prices and margins can be distinguished by two hypotheses:

(a) Whenever there are size-related technological discontinuities between firms, the profit margins and the profit rates of the leading firms are, *ceteris paribus*, a function of the difference between the unit costs of potential entrants and those of the leading (i.e. in this case, the lowest cost) firms. Note that this theory of the *proximate* determinants of profit margins (for given capital/output ratios) holds[72] *independently* from any hypothesis on firms' behaviour. In other words no matter what are the exact criteria of price determination, an increase in the technological discontinuities is expected to increase the profit margin of the leading firms[73] (and thus also the dispersion of profit margins and profit rates across firms within an industry[74]) and vice versa. This applies even if firms do not charge 'limit prices': it only requires that the 'pricing routines' remain unchanged.

(b) If in addition we assume limit pricing, then the theory defines the *exact* price levels and not only their proximate determinants and their direction of change in relation to changes in inter-firm technological discontinuities.

However, it is important to stress that hypothesis (a) is more general – even if less accurate – than hypothesis (b). Moreover, it provides us with all the information we need to establish the pattern of regularities in the relationship between technologies of production, profitabilities and their change through time. For that purpose a 'limit pricing' hypothesis is sufficient but not necessary.

There are three additional issues, related to the variables assumed to influence oligopolistic power, which we shall consider in turn.

First, as noted in a seminal article by Caves and Porter (1977) entry barriers are not a purely structural datum but are partly a result of firms' actions.[75] This is consistent with what we have been arguing above. In order to determine performance variables, such as prices and margins, in addition to 'structural' technological discontinuities between firms, we need to know also some basic regularities in their 'rules of behaviour'. In our case we cannot deduce them from a simple maximising criterion but we need some empirical (institutional) pieces of information. In passing, note that on very general grounds, the existence of barriers to capital mobility and of structural asymmetries between firms is *not* an 'imperfection' of the markets: on the contrary their *creation* is a fundamental 'rule of the game' in inter-firm competition.

A second issue, also discussed in Caves and Porter (1977), concerns internal *mobility barriers*: asymmetries between firms do not apply only – and not even primarily – to would-be entrants but also to the set of existing firms, which can be clustered – as Caves and Porter do – in 'subgroups'.[76] This feature of supply structures emerges clearly also from our discussion in Chapter 2 on leads and lags in innovation. The implication of this is that price/margin determination cannot depend on the single structural parameter of the costs for potential entrants, but must account also for the 'clusters' of existing firms and their relative structural differences (among other things, in terms of unit costs and, as we shall see, of innovative capabilities).[77]

Finally, a third set of issues concerns the nature of technical change. Bain-Sylos models – as they stand – fit relatively 'mature' industries particularly well: in new fast-changing industries, rapid and 'radical' technical change (both in terms of process and product innovation) continuously affects the technological conditions of the industry, preventing a fairly stable definition of entry barriers, while at the same time influencing demand for the output of that industry, substitution for other products, etc.

In their basic and most straightforward form, Bain/Sylos-Labini-type models rely heavily on size-related, cost-based discontinuities between firms. They allow technical change, but the best suited cases of the latter are 'incremental' changes and process innovations.[78] Keeping in mind also the specific problems of price determination in the semiconductor industry (which we shall analyse in the second part of this chapter) one must conclude that these models in *the present form* have a limited interpretative power for fast-innovating industries. The theoretical question of the determination of equilibrium prices and quantities, however, remains relevant, together with its role with respect to more general economic problems such as the existence and the degrees of oligopolistic power, the 'distribution of gains' from technical progress, the effects of oligopolistic competition on the dynanism of an industry, etc. The next section will try to define a model of price determination whenever inter-firm discontinuities are not related to economies of scale but to different degrees of innovativeness and to 'learning economies'.

The Impact of Product and Process Innovation on Prices and Margins

Irrespective of the theoretical framework one chooses in order to analyse pricing policies under conditions of rapid technical change, a necessary requirement is that the model has to be made explicitly dynamic. Pricing decisions of a firm are, in practice, taken in relation to a set of expectations regarding the future (related to *future* market and cost conditions, technological developments, etc.): present structural conditions as such may guide directly those decisions as long as they do not change rapidly enough to prevent any extrapolation from the present to the future. If changes are indeed of this kind, then the *path* of change in the relevant structural variables have to be described in order to define price levels and changes. Which price is actually set in practice depends, partly, on the correspondence between firms' expectations and the objective pattern of change in the relevant variables. However, since we are not interested here in the pricing behaviour of each firm but in the equilibrium price that will be set at industry level, the way how expectations are formed at the level of each firm, in a first approximation, may be overlooked. (Further in this chapter the effect of wrong forecasts on industry pricing will be briefly discussed). For the time being, we will implicitly assume that expectations of 'price-making' firms do correspond to the 'true' path of change over time in the relevant variables.[79]

It is useful to explore some hypotheses on pricing behaviour under conditions of technical change, initially assuming that the latter takes the form of product innovation alone and then allowing also process innovations into the picture. Let us introduce the following assumptions:

1. A new product is brought to the market by a firm which for a certain length of time enjoys a monopoly position on that commodity.
2. The innovative product, owing to its technological features, 'creates its own market'. In other words, the demand function for that product is defined by its technological features.
3. The time lag between the innovator and would-be imitators is again technologically defined (i.e. pricing policy of the temporary monopolist do not affect the time lag itself).
4. There are continuous learning economies in the production of that commodity, so that unit costs of production are inversely proportional to the cumulative volume of production.[80]
5. There exists a minimum scale of production (which is supposed to be fairly small, at the beginning).

One could reasonably assume also that during the 'life-cycle' of the commodity, demand is rather rigid with respect to prices at the beginning (during the initial introduction of the product), more elastic in the 'growth' phase, again fairly rigid when approaching 'maturity'.[81] The assumption, however, is not at all necessary. Moreover, one may initially introduce the following simplifying assumptions:

6. The possibility of substitution between the new product and the old one is nearly absent at the relevant range of prices.
7. There is no joint production between old and new products.

Given these conditions, the temporary monopolist faces three practical alternatives: (a) it can first charge a monopolistic price and, later, 'come down' to a 'limit pricing' at the end of the lag interval with respect to imitators; (b) conversely, it can charge a 'penetration price' below the entry deterring level in order to pre-empt the market, 'go down the learning curve', and increase the margins only later when this strategy has built-up additional entry barriers; or, (c) it can charge from the start a 'limit price'.[82] By 'limit price' we mean the price, that after a certain (technology-determined) initiation lag, will be just below the cost plus a minimum profit for the potential entrant. The reader should keep in mind that the three cases of behaviour outlined above are 'ideal types': in the real world, various combinations of these strategies are possible.

Figure 3.1 illustrates the two extreme cases of an initial monopoly pricing (P_1) or, conversely, 'penetration' pricing (P_2) (see top right

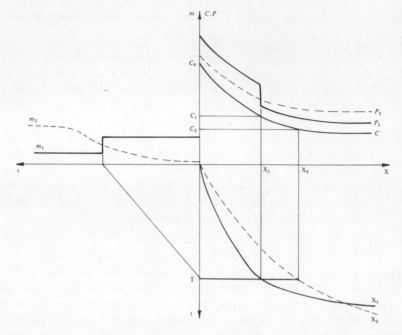

m = gross margins over variable costs, c = unit variable costs, X = cumulated production, t = time, T = time lag between the innovation and would be imitators

FIGURE 3.1   *Prices, costs and margins with 'learning effects' and imitation lags: two extreme examples*

quadrant). Unit costs (c) decrease in accordance with a technologically determined 'learning curve'. After the 'lag period', T, however, cumulative production would be lower in the monopoly pricing case than in the 'penetration' case ($x_1 < x_2$ – see bottom right quadrant), and thus also the unit cost differential between the innovator and the potential imitative entrant (the distance between C_0 and C_1 is obviously lower than the distance between C_0 and C_2).[83] The difference in unit costs between the innovative firm and potential entrants, however, contributes to determine the levels of margins thereafter, so that, in the penetration pricing case, margins can be progressively increased because barriers to entry based on 'learning' effects are higher than in the 'monopoly' pricing case (top left quadrant).[84] In other words, it is a matter of trading off present profits against future profits.[85] Which strategy a firm will actually follow cannot be decided *a priori* on the sole ground of the hypotheses and assumptions outlined above.

Any analysis starting from an 'individualistic' approach based on some function to maximise will not lead us very far. One can attempt an exercise of profit maximisation, i.e. suppose that a firm maximises the discounted cumulated profits over a certain period. In this framework we will hardly be able to go much beyond the statement that pricing strategy will crucially depend on the time horizon of the firm: the more it is 'short-sighted' the higher also the preference for a short-run profit maximising strategy. Conversely, the more 'far sighted' it is and the more similar it is to God (in terms of knowledge of the future), the higher also the preference will be for a 'penetration' strategy (provided that the life-cycle of the product is sufficiently long).[86] In actual fact, however, we know neither the time horizon of the firms nor do we have any binding *a priori* hypothesis on it. Moreover, we do not know how much a firm knows (or believes it knows) about the future and how it discounts future uncertainty. In addition to all this, if the time horizon over which the maximisation occurs is sufficiently long we are likely to find time profiles of the 'penetration' price and of the 'short-run monopoly' price which are equivalent in terms of total discounted returns. Both strategies can be profit maximising even if the time distribution of profits is different. In this context, exercises of dynamic programming can certainly help any individual firm in choosing its pricing strategy, but cannot be of a great help in understanding what actually happens to prices and margins under sufficiently general conditions.

We can try, however, to establish some broad patterns of regularity with the help of two considerations, one theoretical and the other empirical:

(1) No matter what the actual firm strategy is, the *structural parameters* (in our case, the length of the imitation interval and the slope of the learning curve) bear a univocal relationship with the levels of margins and profits. More specifically, for a *given strategy*, profit margins (and profit rates) will be a positive function of the imitation lag and of the steepness of the learning curve. This is because the cost differences (which in this case is the asymmetry underlying monopolistic/oligopolistic power) between the innovator and the potential imitator are directly related to the time it takes to imitate and to the learning advantages the innovator can achieve during the imitation period. In other words, the position of the trade-off between present and future profits, becomes more favourable, irrespective of the strategy a firm

decides to adopt. Note that, in this context, another way to express that trade-off is in terms of a trade-off between present profits and present growth (see again bottom right quadrant and compare with top-left quadrant in Fig. 3.1). The equivalence of the two expressions highlights the noticeable property that the alternative between 'profit-maximisation' and 'growth-maximisation', which is clear-cut and sharp in a static context, becomes more blurred and tends to disappear in a dynamic context:[87] in other words, high present growth is likely to mean high future profits (through learning curves, etc.).

To come back to our main issue, we can further illustrate the point at stake in the following way. Suppose innovative firms have some rough but reasonably realistic estimates of their advantage over future competitors. Irrespectively of whether they maximise profits, in the short or in the long run, or whether they apply some more routinised rule of conduct, as long as profits are one of their objectives (which it is very plausible to assume), the *longer is the imitative lag the higher is also the price they can charge* without fears of eroding (or foregoing) their cost advantage over the potential competitors.

(2) On practical grounds, the conduct of the innovative firm will have to balance two opposite objectives. On the one hand, the investment in the innovation will have to be paid back as soon as possible, since the more differred returns are, the higher the uncertainty associated with them. On the other hand, the higher the cost advantage *vis-à-vis* potential competitors, the more favourable also is the long-run competitive position of the firm. Moreover, the higher the share of 'potential demand' already pre-empted by the innovative firm, the higher the difficulty for potential entrants to join in. (This would not be true, of course, if markets were perfect, but we know they are not and market shares show some considerable 'stickiness'). These empirical considerations suggest that in actual fact firms will generally choose a strategy somewhat intermediate between the two extremes illustrated in Figure 3.1.

If we consider jointly the 'qualitative' relationship[88] between imitation lags, learning effects, margins (point 1) and the above empirical remarks (point 2) we can construct a model of the *proximate* determinants of margins and prices, *as if* the latter were determined through some limit pricing procedure. To repeat, in this context we are not so much interested in the individual pricing procedures, as in the effects of technological parameters upon the actual level of prices and margins:

individual firms will sometimes apply limit pricing criteria, while at other times they may simply balance the two opposite empirical criteria just mentioned at point (2) above (i.e. high returns in the short run *vs* building up future oligopolistic power). The theoretical limit price we are going to define will then be some kind of *notional benchmark*, which will move in the same direction as actual prices provided that the pricing strategy (no matter which one it is) does not change. As from point (1) above, actual margins (and profit rates) will move in the same direction as the structural parameters (innovation leads and learning coefficients). In a similar fashion, also a notional limit price (and the related margin) will move in the same direction. Since it is easier to deal with the limit price (and the limit margin) because it bears a straightforward relationship with these structural parameters, we can apply some kind of transitive property and state the following proposition: irrespective of firms' strategies, actual margins will move in the same direction as a notional limit margin (the one associated with the limit price) which we can define through the sole knowledge of production and demand conditions. Moreover, by virtue of the empirical argument (point 2) we can add that the actual prices and margins will not only move in the same direction as the limit counterparts but are likely to be somewhere in the neighbourhood of these notional limit price and limit margin.

The discussion above on inter-firm asymmetries provides the foundation for these properties. We have been arguing at length that the source of oligopolistic power lies in structural differences of various sorts between existing firms and potential entrants and between existing firms themselves. The competitive dynamics of industry will tend to eliminate any oligopolistic margins in excess of those structural differences (which, to make it simple, can be represented through cost differentials). A 'limit price' model, on its side, takes those inter-firm differences as the grounds of a behavioural rule. Even if this behavioural rule does not apply, however, prices will tend to that ('limit') value for the simple reason that monopolistic/oligopolistic margins in excess of those allowed by structural asymmetries will always be eliminated by the mechanisms of 'Schumpeterian competition' (imitation, new entries, etc.).

What follows is an attempt to illustrate the relationship between technological asymmetries and prices using the assumption of some behavioural rule based on limit pricing. Let us stress again, however, that the assumption is just a simplification: it is introduced in order to make the properties of the model clearer and the conclusions straightforward.

The Effects of Imitation Lags and Learning-by-Doing on Prices and Margins: A Simple Model

Let us consider the case of an innovator which enjoys a lead over potential imitators. For simplicity we assume that the time length over which a firm plans its pricing strategy is equal to the technologically determined lag between the innovators and imitators ($= T$). Prices will be:[89]

$$P_t = mc_0 X_t^\beta \qquad\qquad 3$$

and the margins

$$m = P_t/c_0 X_t^\beta$$

where P_t = price at time t, m = the level of mark-up over variable cost, c_0 = unit average variable costs for the initial production (in order to simplify, one may assume those costs to be equal to wage costs divided by initial labour productivity), X_t = the cumulative production from time zero to T, β = the 'learning coefficient'[90] (which has clearly a negative or zero value).

The demand function is

$$x_t = f(P, t) \qquad\qquad 4$$

which we may render as follows

$$x_t = A \cdot P_t^{-\alpha} \cdot e^{\lambda t} \qquad\qquad 5$$

In other words, quantities are – as usual – a function of prices but also, and more important, of time, i.e. of innovations and learning effects by users, and of income. These variables are captured by the exponential expression $e^{\lambda t}$ where t is time and λ is an exogenous parameter. Cumulative production is, by definition,

$$X_t = \int_0^T x_t \, dt \qquad\qquad 6$$

When a potential entrant will be prepared to enter the market (after time T), its unit costs will be

$$c_e = c_0 \cdot g(t) \qquad\qquad 7$$

The entrant's initial costs will be the same as the original innovator minus a certain percentage ($g(t)$) which represents a diffusion effect as a function of time: in other words there is likely to be a 'watch and learn' effect.

Thus unit costs differentials at time T between the innovator and the potential entrant will be:

$$D_T = c_0 \cdot X^\beta - c_0 \cdot g(t) \qquad\qquad 8$$

It is reasonable to assume that this difference is positive in every case the second firm does not succeed in some further innovation: the 'learning effect' is likely to be greater than the amount of that learning which leaks out to potential imitators. Our argument suggests that the actual price will be near

$$P_t^* \le m_m \cdot c_0 \cdot g(t) \qquad\qquad 9$$

provided that

$$m^* = \frac{P_t^*}{c_0 X^\beta} \ge m_i \qquad\qquad 10$$

Otherwise:

$$P_t = m_i c_0 X^\beta \qquad\qquad 11$$

Let us explain the logic of our hypothesis: prices will tend to be near a level that accounts for the differential in costs between the innovator and the potential entrant and that other things being equal, is likely to deter entrance since it would yield a margin for the entrant below that minimum (m_m) which corresponds to the lowest acceptable rate profit.[91] The price will be set around that level (P_t^*), provided it assures a margin for the innovator sufficient also to cover some pre-established part of the innovation costs (i.e. $m_i > m_m$).[92] If learning curves are sufficiently steep, this condition will always be met. Having defined the price, quantities are then determined (through equation 4). The latter determines cumulative production (X) and thus the total impact of learning-by-doing.

Therefore the actual margins m (from equation 9) take the form of a dependent variable which depends on: (a) m_m, the 'minimum' rate of profit (b) the imitation lag (T); (c) the 'learning by doing' coefficient (β) (d) technological diffusion (as expressed by $g(t)$); (e) the elasticity of demand (in so far as it affects cumulated quantities);[93] (f) the absolute size of the market (again affecting cumulated quantities and thus 'learning' effects upon costs).[94] Stating the same concept in a different way, if one interprets equation 9 as a strict equality, price is determined by entry conditions, quantities depend on the form and position of the demand function, while the level of mark-up 'adjusts' correspondingly. However, if one interprets more realistically condition 9 as a true inequality, then there might be a definite range of values for x_t and m

compatible with that condition, the choice among which will depend on more 'behavioural' aspects of firms' strategies, their attitude towards growth, their financial possibilities, etc.[95]

The relationship between 'learning economies' and prices, in a fairly 'impressionistic' form, is quite common in management literature.[96] The attempt here is to outline, in as precise a way as possible, the nature of this relationship, discuss its implications with respect to the dynamics of the considered industry, and compare the results with the traditional theories of the firm.

There are some important consequences of this process of innovation leading to an initial 'monopolistic' position of the innovative firm.

First, innovative firms entering with a new product 'find' a market, whose size is partly defined by the technological features embodied into the commodity. In relation to that, however, they *build up* their market through their pricing policy. A 'dynamic' pricing policy accounts precisely for this strategy.

Second, as a consequence, entry barriers are *built* by the innovative firm itself: a bigger market for the innovator represents also greater cost differentials with respect to possible imitators. Entry barriers will therefore depend on the 'technological nature' of the product (which contributes to determine the initial size of the market), on the learning coefficient, on the imitative lag between the first introduction of a product and the possibility for others to enter with similar ones, while they are inversely related to 'technological diffusion'.

One can see that these properties link together with our discussion on 'appropriability' as a source of inter-firm differences, and, conversely, on technological diffusion as a 'convergence mechanism' between firms.[97] To repeat, since entry barriers are partly built by the firm itself, through its pricing strategy during the period in which it is a virtual monopolist, there are in actual fact some 'degrees of freedom' for firm behaviour to 'trade off' higher growth (and greater entry barriers) for lower initial mark-ups. The greater is the growth of the innovative firm (for a given potential market), the greater are 'built-up' entry barriers against imitative firms.

We must consider at some depth the relationship between market growth and entry barriers. The prevailing view in the literature seems to be that the greater the growth of the market, the easier it is for other firms to enter. The argument relies on both the incapability of existing firms in keeping up with a fast-growing market and the incentive that the latter places on entry.

There are some special properties relative to those fast-growing markets where it is the process of innovation itself which *creates new market opportunities.* Certainly a fast-growing market performs as a 'signal' and as an incentive for other firms to enter, if they have the technological capabilities to do so (i.e. after the 'imitation lag' time). Would-be entrants can do it in three ways: with exactly 'the same' commodity, with a fairly similar, 'improved' commodity (a case which can fall to some extent into 'product differentiation'), or with a new, substantially innovative product. In the latter case (and partly in the second one) entry is allowed by a further 'creation of new markets', which will affect the original one in the long-run (i.e. accelerating the process of maturity/decline in the life-cycle of the product). An existing firm cannot prevent other firms from innovating: what it can do is to prevent, as much as possible, the others from entering its own market, and it is likely to do so by erecting cost-based entry barriers and by pre-empting as much as it can the 'potential' market opportunity on that commodity.[98] However, if a firm has exploited a great deal of the market opportunities of a certain commodity (which implies also the rapid growth of that market), it has been 'signalling' the profitability of that activity, but it is also forcing would-be entrants to innovate, if they want to enter, because the existing market is 'blockaded' by cost differentials, and 'pre-empted'.[99] These processes are right at the core of innovation-based dynamic competition.

An issue which is worth mentioning concerns the case of positive 'cross elasticities of substitution' between new and old products. This process of substitution (a) is not instantaneous, and (b) does not depend only on relative prices but also on the relative technological characters of new and old commodities. It is likely to affect primarily the relative growth rates of demand for the old and the new commodity rather than prices which are likely to be still determined by costs of production, 'dynamic' entry barriers, etc. Even if the introduction of a new product has a short-run influence on the position of the 'old product' demand curve, whenever prices are determined under some mark-up procedure, the possibility of cross-substitution should not induce any downward change in the 'old product' price, since its technological conditions of production do not change.[100]

The same applies to 'new' products. A process of 'substitution in the growth of demand' of new for old products will take place. Changes in the relative prices between the old and the new certainly affect the respective evolution of demand patterns. The reverse, however, is not generally true: the substitutability between the two does not affect relative prices. An example may illustrate the point. Suppose that we have two products, an 'old' one, say a transistor, and a 'new' one, say an IC, which is technologically equivalent to ten transistors. Suppose also that before the introduction of the IC, the price of transistors was 2, the elasticity of demand equal unity and demand growing over time at a certain positive yearly rate g. When the IC is introduced, its initial price is set, with a procedure similar to that described above, at, say, 30. Demand for the IC has a certain 'autonomous' growth (due to new applications, income growth, etc.) while the demand for the transistor continues to grow at a somewhat lower rate than it would have done otherwise, had the introduction of the IC not occurred. Later, due to the mentioned 'learning economies', etc. price for the IC can be set at, say, 15 while the price of transistors remains 2. At that price the IC will start superceding transistors and demand for transistors will stop growing or start decreasing. Nonetheless, the price of transistors will not generally change, while in the *relevant interval* the 'short-run' demand curve for transistors may well keep the same price-elasticity: it could become more price-elastic, only if the price was lowered somewhat below 1.5, but probably at that price the mark-up would be even negative.[101] In other words, the appearance of new products is likely to affect essentially the *position* of the demand function for the old ones, more than their elasticity.

Throughout the history of technologies and industries one can find plenty of products whose demand declines because they are substituted by new ones, while their relative prices rise because they undergo less technical progress and they can enjoy lower degrees of learning economies.[102]

Patterns of Demand, Elasticities and Market Shares: Some Unconventional Properties

Let us analyse the role of demand elasticities. Their effect upon profit margins[103] in our simplified model is *positive* (i.e. the greater price elasticity, the greater also the margins). This occurs through the effect that a fast expanding market has on learning economies for the first-comer: a relative small decrease in prices allows a relatively big expansion in quantities and thus substantial learning economies.[104] Figure 3.2 illustrates the mechanism.

In order to make the illustration clearer we assume that demand curves are straight lines[105] and that the flow of production, x, equals the stock, X: since the latter is a function of the former and of time, the conclusions are not substantially affected.[106] Suppose we start from a price P_0 which corresponds to unit costs C_0 and thus margins P_0/C_0. (The function $C(X)$ represents average unit variable costs). Assume two

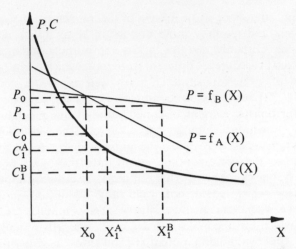

FIGURE 3.2 *Demand elasticity and profit margins in presence of learning-by-doing*

notional demand curves

$$P = f_A(x) \quad \text{and} \quad P = f_B(x)$$

whereby f_B is more price-elastic than f_A. A small decrease in the price from P_0 to P_1 will lead to an increase in quantities to X_1^B and X_1^A, respectively. In the case of the more elastic demand curve one will move further along the learning curve so that unit costs will decrease to C_1^B which compares with C_1^A in the alternative case. Unit margins will be higher in the B case: $P_1/C_1^B > P_1/C_1^A$, provided that there are some learning economics in production (i.e. provided that $C(X)$ is not a straight line parallel to $x - $axis). This is a remarkable property: *under conditions of technical change and in presence of learning effects, a high price elasticity bears a positive influence upon profit margins.* Moreover, these oligopolistic margins depend on *structural* conditions of production while they are *prima facie independent* of market power (i.e. they do not depend on the capability of the monopolist/oligopolist to restrict supply).[107] Exactly the same argument applies to 'static' economies of scale (in fact, by virtue of our simplifying assumptions the two are made identical in the formal elaboration in note 104 page 205, and figure 3.2).

One may argue against our thesis that there is, even in our case, a 'supply restriction' since the producer(s) do not necessarily push output to the point where marginal costs equal prices, and that this is the 'source' of monopolistic/oligopolistic margin of the innovator. The argument is quite subtle and requires some discussion since it has rather wide implications. Certainly, margins, prices and outputs obtained through our mark-up procedure are different from those which correspond to the definition of 'pure competition'[108] (as well as to the definition of monopoly[109]) from textbook economics. This is *not*, however, the *cause* of the oligopolistic margins obtained through our procedure. In the case of downward-sloping cost curves the criterion price–equal–marginal–cost may yield a meaningless definition of competitive output since the corresponding profit rate may well be negative. Conversely, one can easily see that our mark-up criterion applies also to those cases which could not yield any significant monopolistic solution (i.e. whenever demand elasticity is below unity).[110] The process through which an oligopolistic margin is obtained is fundamentally different from 'withholding potential production' in order to obtain a higher price, which is the basic mechanism of the 'static' monopolist/oligopolist. On the contrary, here the monopolist/oligopolist *expands* production in some kind of self-fulfilling prophecy that unit costs will come down together with prices and that this same movement will shelter him/her against future competition.

At this point the reader might wonder why production is not expanded to near infinity. Marshallian economics provides a clear supply-constraint by means of the usual U-shaped cost curves. Our argument, however, implies that cost curves are downward sloping (or flat whenever learning economies and size-related economies of scale are absent). We are bound to find some other explanation which can jointly account for three 'stylised facts' – namely (a) increasing or constant returns to scale are the rule in manufacturing industry, but, this notwithstanding, (b) production is not necessarily pushed to the point where one meets the macroeconomic constraint of full employment, and, (c) each industry does not rapidly reach conditions of 'natural monopoly'.

The apparent contradiction can be disentangled by closely examining the theory of demand.[111] In line with the 'methodological individualism' we criticised above, in traditional economics, demand functions for each industry are generally derived, by aggregation, from utility schedules of individual consumers. Within that framework not much can be said *a priori* on the patterns of demand and on price elasticities[112] since they are functions of subjective and unknown marginal rates of inter-commodity substitution, etc.

There is, however, an alternative. Our hypothesis, which corresponds quite closely to an implicit assumption of classical economic thought, is that the composition of the basket final consumption is jointly determined by the interplay between some basic anthropological needs and the evolution of social organisations, modes of consumption, patterns of use of leisure time, together with income levels and income distribution. The hypothesis will probably be understood more easily by the non-economist reader, for one can find an immediate reference in common sense: for example, no matter what is the relative price between food and a pocket calculator, the former has a strict priority in consumption; no matter what is the price of food itself, demand for it will reach saturation above a certain level, etc. The argument leads to a 'ranking of commodities in consumption' as Pasinetti (1981) does – according to 'anthropological' and social criteria. Moreover, if one considers the patterns of demand of a certain commodity in relation to income, one will generally observe a kind of Engel's curve, whereby per capita consumption after a certain point will increase at decreasing rates until it will become asymptotic to a saturation value[113] (in the real course of time it might even decrease, due to substitution by other 'superior' or new commodities, as a result of product innovations). At each point in time, for a given level of income and given income distribution we would thus expect a relatively fixed proportion between the different commodities in the consumption basket. The dynamics of relative prices and short-run changes in the 'real' price of each commodity in terms of income[114] may only accelerate or slow down some kind of 'natural' (more precisely, social and institutional) evolution of the patterns of demand. Were we able to separate a 'pure' demand curve relating only quantities and prices at a given instant, we would probably find it generally quite rigid.[115] Since we make our observations in real time, the demand elasticities we generally depict for an industry pick up also the trend changes in baskets of consumption due to income growth and social change.

A similar argument applies to intermediate and capital goods. Demand is quite rigidly fixed at any point in time by the final demand for which they represent a direct or indirect input. Through time, demand of intermediate commodities changes in relation to (i) the patterns of final demand for which they are an input, (ii) the rate and nature of innovations in the user sectors (which affect the relative intensity and the patterns of diffusion of intermediate commodities) and (iii) the rate of substitution between new and old commodities (i.e. between different kinds of material inputs and different capital goods). Certainly relative prices influence the use in production of different material inputs and varieties of equipment. However, this is by no means an instantaneous process and it generally requires changes in manufacturing techniques and products.[116] With relatively fixed baskets of consumption and techniques of production which in the short term are given (since 'bygones are bygones' and techniques are embodied also in the existing equipment), we must expect the short-term price elasticity of demand for each industry (for both final and producer goods) to be rather low.[117] The conclusion of the argument is quite clear and has far-reaching implications: since for a given level of income, and at a given time, demand for an industry is generally quite rigid to changes in prices, *any further expansion of production in advanced capitalist economics is not generally limited by supply constraints* (such as decreasing returns to scale) *but by the size of the market.* One can easily see that this represents some kind of foundation at industry level of Keynesian macroeconomics. Our argument can thus easily account for the coexistence of increasing or constant returns to scale and the general absence of full-employment production.

We have not yet explained why such productive conditions do not rapidly lead to a complete monopolisation of the industry. We can find an explanation by recalling the discussion on the sources of oligopolistic margins and by linking it to the hypothesis of unelastic 'instantaneous' demand curves. To repeat, the source of oligopolistic margins lies in structural discontinuities between firms (of both the 'static' and 'dynamic' kinds, such as economies of scale and learning economies). The demonstration which follows applies to all cases when price elasticity of demand for the industry is significantly below infinity. The argument relates to both entry and mobility barriers and can be considered a generalisation of Sylos-Labini's analysis of an industry composed of a distribution of firms *créée par hazard*, in the presence of different unit costs by firm size.[118]

We must expand our model characterised by only one innovative firm[119] and assume at least two or more firms, with different market shares. The 'leading' firm (the one characterised by the higher share and thus the lowest cost via learning curve) fixes its price at the entry-limit level. Both firms will enjoy an oligopolistic margin (even if the margin of the first firm is higher). Any attempt by the leading firm to conquer the entire market, however, would bring both prices and margins *down*, provided that the learning curve effect does not entirely compensate the decrease in prices.[120] This could only happen if demand was very elastic with respect to price. Given our remarks above on the nature of demand, this is an unlikely case.

To state the same concept in a different way, an oligopolistic firm can monopolise the market only if it gives up its oligopolistic profits and behaves, in terms of prices and margins, *as a competitive firm* or sometimes a 'hyper-competitive' firm (with margins below the competitive minimum).

The property is worth stressing: whenever demand elasticity for the industry is relatively low, the cost of upsetting an oligopolistic equilibrium based on structural asymmetries between firms is much higher than the potential benefit. Notably, the most important means of acquiring higher market shares, by changing the pattern of these inter-firm asymmetries without in the meantime paying the costs in terms of lower prices, is through technical change, either in the form of innovations or (for the firms lagging behind in terms of productivity and market shares) technological imitation.

A corollary is important as well: for *given* technological discontinuities between firms and for a *given* distribution of firms according to these discontinuities, *the levels of prices and margins will be in inverse proportion to the degree of concentration of the industry.* In other words the higher is concentration, the lower are prices and margins, provided the demand elasticity is not very high in relation to learning economies or for that matter, to size-related economies of scale.[121]

Note that here we are not making any assumption on inter-firm collusiveness, and we maintain that competitive forces will erode those profit margins[122] and those market shares which are above the levels allowed by technological asymmetries between firms.

A more detailed investigation of this property will make the mechanism clearer and will also highlight the relationship between structural variables and behavioural degrees of freedom of firms. Let us consider an industry characterised by a distribution of firms placed on different segments of the 'learning curve'. Suppose that this industrial structure is due to the fact that a small group of firms entered the industry, at the beginning, because they were all very near the 'technological frontier' and that successive entries occurred, either because of minor product innovation, etc., despite limit prices, or because the existing firms actually did charge a price above the entry-deterring level. We may reasonably assume that market shares are a function of inter-firm differentials in unit average variable costs, so that the highest cost firms enjoy the lowest market share. It can be shown that under the demand conditions outlined above, and for *given technological discontinuities*, margins are an inverse function of the market share of the leading firm. Let us attempt an exercise of comparative dynamics as above. Suppose the initial conditions correspond to prices and quantities (X_0, P_0) where P_0

is the 'entry-deterring' price. The market shares of the existing firms are $\mu_1, \mu_2, \ldots, \mu_n$ where firm 1 is the leading firm and firm n is the infra-marginal one. An increase of the market share of the leading firm through the elimination of the n–firm will imply lowering the price by an amount proportional to the difference in costs between the 'first' potential entrant and the infra-marginal firm.[123] We suppose also that price elasticity of demand for each firm is equal to that for the industry.[124]

Let us call C_1 the average unit costs at (X_0, P_0) of the leading firm, C_n the costs of the infra-marginal firm and C_e the notional costs of the potential entrant on which the limit price is based. Moreover, we suppose that in the relevant interval the market share of the i–firm is approximately linear in the difference between the unit costs of the potential entrant and its own costs:

$$\mu_i = \lambda(C_e - C_i) \qquad \qquad 17$$

The elimination of the n–firm will increase the market share of the leading firm[125] by $\Delta\mu_1 = \mu_n$. Such an increase in market share would however imply a decrease in prices by (at least)

$$-\Delta P = C_e - C_n$$

We can thus re-write equation 17 as

$$-\Delta P = \frac{1}{\lambda}\Delta\mu_1 \qquad \qquad 17.1$$

Making use of equations 13 and 16 (note 104 page 205 and note 120 page 207) we obtain

$$\Delta M = \frac{P_0 - (1/\lambda)(\Delta\mu_1)}{C_1\left[1 + \beta\cdot\alpha\cdot\dfrac{1}{P_0}(1/\lambda)(\Delta\mu_1)\right]} - \frac{P_0}{C_1} \qquad \qquad 18$$

That expression gives us the relationship between changes in margins, ΔM, and changes in market shares, $\Delta\mu$, for given technological discontinuities between firms: it will be generally negative, if the absolute values of β and α are not very big.[126]

Note that the parameter $(1/\lambda)$ which enters into the margin market share equation and defines the distribution of firms according to their relative costs, is *a historical parameter*. It depends on the past history of the industry, namely on the way technological lags and leads and pricing policies have affected the dynamics of entry and market shares in the past.

We mentioned that the model allows a useful definition of the relationship between structural conditions and firms' behavioural degrees of freedom. At each point in time firms can be ranked according to their unit costs. We may put in the ranking all the existing firms and also the 'queue' of potential entrants.[127] Pricing policies of the leading firm(s) draw the line, as it were, between the potential and the actual producers. In doing so, they affect both their market shares and their profit margins. The higher the latter, generally the lower the former, because some firms are put in the condition of entering the industry. One can fully appreciate that the limit price is a *relative concept* which can be given a definite meaning only once given the entire range of inter-firm technological asymmetries, jointly with the firms' strategies regarding the trade-offs between margins and market shares.

Note that there is no contradiction between the argument just put forward on the existence of a trade-off *for each individual firm*, at *each point in time*, between market shares and margins, on the one hand, and the hypothesis that margins are positively related to market shares in a cross-firm analysis of an industry, on the other hand. At the *level of an industry*, both margins of the leading firms and their market shares are a *positive* function, as we have been arguing, of the *structural asymmetries* between firms.[128] However, all the firms that can be price-makers through their pricing policies can trade-off higher margins against higher market shares. The trade off is a *static* one: in a dynamic context, innovation is precisely the factor which eliminates that trade-off since it tends to increase both market shares and margins, by means of building up additional technological asymmetries between firms and by means of pre-empting the markets.

The joint consideration of inter-firm technological asymmetries and the nature of demand patterns explains, as it should be clear from the above argument, the relative 'stickiness' of market shares and mobility barriers.[129] Again, technical progress is one of the major factors which continuously changes inter-firm asymmetries, therefore upsetting also the nature and pattern of mobility barriers.

In order to summarise the argument, figure 3.3 (p. 134) depicts an industry characterised by four firms. The initial price is P_0 which corresponds to X_0 quantities.[130] The market share of the leading (and minimum cost) firm is $(X_0 - X_2)/X$; C_1, C_2, C_{n-1}, C_n are the average costs of each firm depending, say, on different learning economies. If any firm wants to increase its market share it must lower its prices and margins to expel the n–firm from the market. Suppose the leading firm does it by increasing its output by $(X'_0 - X_0)$ and thus lowering the price to P'_0. We do not need to make any hypothesis on how the share of the marginal firm will be

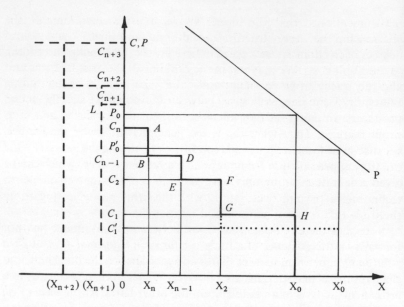

FIGURE 3.3   *Cost structure of the industry, by firm, and gross margins*

distributed. No matter how it will happen, we know that concentration will increase and margins (both for the leading firm and on the average of the industry) will decrease. The figure also helps us in illustrating the *relative nature* of entry barriers and their relation to the degrees of freedom that each firm has in choosing its pricing policy. For example, entry could be deterred only against firm $(n+2)$, if the price were high enough to allow firm $(n+1)$ into the industry. *Technological discontinuities perform as both entry barriers and mobility barriers, while firms' behaviours determine how much of these barriers are exploited in order to pre-empt markets and increase market shares.*

It is worth noticing that the behavioural degrees of freedom are themselves a function of structural discontinuities between firms. In terms of pricing behaviours for a situation defined by (P_0, X_0) the degrees of freedom of the n–firm are near zero. Conversely the leading firm(s) enjoy the highest degrees of freedom in their pricing policies and thus in 'choosing' their market shares for given technological asymmetries.

Figure 3.3 highlights also the meaning of our 'weak structural theory': the steepness of the $X_0\,HGFEDBAC_nC_{n+1}L$ . . . line is proportional to the degree of *asymmetry* of the industry and then also represents the *boundaries* of the degrees of freedom each company can enjoy. Thus, one can see that the 'pure competitive case' is that limit condition whereby the line is perfectly flat and 'everyone is equal'.

We did not mention either differentiation or market power. The model above holds for any homogeneous oligopoly: market shares are relatively stable provided that price elasticity for each firm is not much higher than price elasticity for the industry. If indeed this (unlikely) case occurs, then it will reinforce the advantage of leading firms even if it might increase the relative instability of market shares within the industry as a whole.

Patterns of product differentiation clearly interact with technology-based discontinuities. On the former we must refer to the innovative model suggested by Porter (1978), and Caves and Porter (1978), based on *strategic groups* within each industry and mobility barriers between these groups. Their model and that suggested here are broadly consistent with each other.[131] The 'strategic group' approach highlights how in a dynamic context 'strategies become structures', i.e. how patterns of behaviour in terms of differentiation, advertising, choices of market segments, etc. influence entry barriers, mobility barriers and degrees of rivalry, thus defining relatively stable 'strategic groups' within an industry. Our model focuses on the structural constraints and boundaries of the strategies and in particular on those related to *lato sensu* technological asymmetries.

Our model has so far been independent of any hypothesis about inter-firm collusion and market power. Oligopolistic margins as they have been defined here are totally independent from the discretionary power of existing firms to restrict supply and charge 'above normal' prices. For any given industrial structure, different degrees of collusiveness may indeed occur, but the model clarifies their limited scope. Consider again figure 3.3. A 'collusion' on price setting between the four firms (called 1, 2, $(n-1)$, n) allows a range of variation of prices corresponding to the difference in unit costs $(C_{n+1} - C_n)$, between the infra-marginal firm n and the first notional entrant. A higher price would be curbed by a new entrant. Only when the technological differential between the *last* firm of the industry and the set of potential entrants is very high then the possibility of collusive behaviour makes entry barriers a (relatively) common asset for the industry,[132] which can be collusively exploited.

The Dynamics of a 'Schumpeterian Industry'

In practice, product innovations are quite often associated with process innovations, either because they come together or because they stimulate each other. The cases in which a process innovation is brought about by (and linked with) a specific product innovation do not induce any major problem to the framework that has been outlined above: if the 'imitation lag' for the new product is equal to the imitation lag for the new process, nothing should change in the above formulation. In the cases when product–imitation lags and process–imitation lags are different, the formulation becomes more complicated, but conceptually the functions remain identical: an innovative lead on a process associated with a product innovation performs identically as a 'barrier to entry' which allows an asymmetric role of the leader and the imitator. The former can exploit 'learning economies' and 'pre-emptive effects' constructing in this way dynamic entry barriers. Furthermore, if the imitation lag on the process is very long, then this phenomenon performs a role similar to the 'absolute cost advantages', in Bain's terminology.[133]

Before further complicating the story with process innovations unrelated to products, etc., it is worth taking an overview of the long-run trends in prices, mark-ups and entry possibilities in our hypothetical industry characterised by (a) a fast rate of technical change which takes the form of product innovations (and process innovations strictly associated with them); (b) a creation of new market opportunities by the innovations themselves, together with an acceleration of the 'decay' of old products (although not through instantaneous substitution); and (c) significant 'learning economies' that induce decreasing average unit costs as a function of the cumulative volume of production. In addition one may now add that (d) prices are determined, through the above procedure, with a mark-up over prime costs, whose level depends on imitative lags, 'learning' coefficients, elasticity of demand, size and growth of the market (the 'actual' and the 'potential' one)[134] and degrees of technological diffusion.[135]

To simplify the picture, one may suppose that the number of firms is equal to the number of products of the industry: each new product is brought to the market by a new firm and the old products gradually disappear together with the firms that introduced them. This extreme 'Schumpeterian' process[136] is, of course, greatly unrealistic, but it helps to illustrate the point. The 'market' for the industry is actually composed by a number of 'sub-markets' equal to the number of commodities that the industry produces. Some sub-markets expand and some others shrink due to the substitution – based on technical progress – between new and old products. At the same time, new products open up new markets so that the 'total market' for the industry expands in real terms. One may assume for simplicity that each firm – which at one time has been an innovating one – has succeeded in keeping potential entrants out of its market, practising the 'limit price' described above, but not able to do anything about the introduction of new commodities by others. One may suppose that the mark-up over variable costs remains nearly stable through the growth/maturity period of the 'life-cycle' of a product (on empirical ground it could be allowed to increase somewhat in the maturity/decline phase[137]). We may define the 'price index' for the industry[138] as

$$P_t = \sum_{i=1}^{n} m_{i_t} \cdot c_{i_t} \cdot s_{i_t} \; (i = 1, \ldots, n) \qquad 19$$

where m_{i_t} is the gross margin at time t for commoditity i over average variable costs c_{i_t} and s_{i_t} is the weight for that commodity (e.g. the share of that commodity in the total output of the industry). Some long-run features of this hypothetical industry are worth mentioning.

(a) Since 'learning effects' make the cost curve slope downward, given a fairly stable margin, prices are bound to decline as a function of time and the growth of the market. However, the cost curve is related to cumulative quantities through a logarithmic function: therefore, progressively, unit costs become more and more insensitive to 'learning effects' and the curve tends to approach a straight line. The rate of decline in the price index over time is thus related to the rate of innovation and to the share of new products in the total output (those two factors are obviously correlated with each other). This is even more true if the margins tend to increase in the late part of the life-cycle of a product.[139]

(b) The 'aggregate' (i.e. average) margins for the industry will be a direct function of (i) the variables which determine asymmetries between innovators and imitators on each single product, and, if we allow margins to increase in the maturity/decline phase of the life-cycle of a product, (ii) the weighted distribution of commodities produced by the industry between old and new ones.[140]

(c) One can see from this stylised picture the process through which an industry may approach 'maturity'. If the rate of product innovations slows down (and thus also the rate at which new market opportunities are created), the 'learning effects' upon labour productivity become less important,[141] static barriers to entry increase their role, while dynamic barriers become less relevant. A mature industry will look more like a Sylos–Bain typical industry at least as far as price determination and entry barriers are concerned.

(d) A crucial feature of the hypothetical growing industry described here is the role of technology and innovation. It has been assumed that each firm (which is a monopolist upon its own commodity) practises prices low enough to prevent any entry on that market. The possibility to do so for a particular firm has been given by its asymmetric position as an early innovator *vis-à-vis* future imitators. Technological levels (i.e. innovative capabilities), thus determine dynamic entry barriers. However, existing entry barriers at each point in time are ineffective with respect to new commodities (i.e. forthcoming innovations). New firms willing to enter the industry market are *forced to create new sub-markets* through new products, and find the incentive to do so in the past experience of innovative firms making oligopoly profits[142] in new markets which they themselves created through the introduction of their innovations. Using the terminology of Chapter 2, 'dynamic barriers to entry' are very powerful with respect to any firm placed below the technological frontiers, but are extremely weak with regard to firms on the frontier itself. This is an important property, to which we shall come back when discussing international differences in industrial structures and degrees of competitiveness (Chapter 4).

(e) Something can be said on the fundamental question of the 'distribution of gains', stemming from technical progress. If this 'stylized picture' of the growth of an innovative industry is an adequate one, there is no reason to assume that productivity increases are distributed in the same sector in which they are generated. This would imply either a steady increase in the 'degree of monopoly' as measured by m, the gross unit margin, or an 'indexation' of labour costs on productivity changes in the same sector (i.e. wages rising at the same rate as sector labour productivity).[143] It can be reasonably argued that 'distribution of gains' from technical progress is mostly bargained at aggregate level (between wages and profits) while differential increases in productivity are mainly distributed through variations in relative prices.[144] Supporting this argument there are both theoretical and empirical reasons. First, on the side of profits, we know from the previous analysis that the level of margins can be considered as a dependent variable which, for any given firm strategy, is determined by technological and demand conditions. An hypothesis of rising margins must assume that, through time, technological and/or demand conditions change accordingly, to allow rising 'equilibrium' values of m. From the previous analysis this does not seem to be the general case. Second, on the side of wages, an hypothesis of wage growth equal to labour productivity growth (even when the latter is well above the aggregate average) would imply that the bargaining strength of workers is somewhat proportional to the 'degree of innovativeness' of a sector, and/or that firms operate in markets whose size is nearly fixed and whose elasticity of demand is very low, both in the short and long terms, so that they are ready to pay even high wage increases without affecting their markets and their profits.[145] The first condition seems quite unrealistic. The second one may be dismissed in the light of simple casual empiricism. There is no evidence suggesting that workers' strength is systematically correlated with the degree of innovativeness of a sector: steel and chemicals are two examples of industries historically both characterised by relatively high bargaining strength and unionisation while presenting very different degrees of innovativeness; conversely many areas of electronics and textiles have in common (especially in the USA) low degrees of unionisation and low wages, while obviously differing in terms of technical progressiveness. Moreover, the description of a 'typical' growing market given above suggests that prices – relative prices *vis-à-vis* the old commodities which the new products are going to substitute, and 'real' prices of the new commodities in terms of income – are important *in the longer term* in determining the size of the market and its degree of pre-emption by the leading firms.

A more convincing interpretation is that the rate of growth in wages is determined, to a significant extent, on aggregate level, while *differential* rates of growth in labour productivity, even in an oligopolistic condition, are passed on to prices, thus continuously modifying the structure of relative prices in the economy and allowing technical progress to affect other sectors also through changing input prices. This applies despite the basic difference between a competitive structure and an oligopolistic structure in terms of *levels* of profit margins and rates. The link between wage growth and productivity growth, which generally characterise oligopolistic contexts, accounts more for the *aggregate* manufacturing level than for each individual industry, and especially for those characterised by fast technical progress. This can be true despite the fact that all the sectors might have oligopolistic structure. Changes in relative prices and 'downward' diffusion of the effects of technical progress are dynamic features of a capitalist economy which do not seem to disappear in oligopolistic conditions.[146]

(f) It is worth looking at greater length at the role of demand in relation to prices. We tried to argue with the help of our simplified model that in a context of rapid technical progress prices are set to take into account the dynamic effects of pricing policies on the size of the market, on present and future quantities and present and future entry barriers. Since the future deeply affects pricing decisions, forecasts and expectations are obviously relevant. The previous discussion, nonetheless, has been conducted on the assumption that forecasts are always correct so that the hypothesised demand curve over which pricing decisions are taken happens to be the 'true' one. It is time to relax that assumption and investigate more realistically the effect of changes in demand. These might be distinguished between long-run (trend) changes and short-run (cyclical) changes, and, among the latter, between 'expected' and 'unexpected' ones.

With regard to long-run changes in demand, given 'dynamic' economies, an increasing production (in terms of both cumulative production and flows of production per unit of time) brings about decreasing unit cost (if the growth in wage rate does not more than compensate productivity growth). No supply-side constraint operates, so that no U-shaped long-run cost curve is likely to appear.[147] On the contrary, other things being equal, prices will decrease more (increase less) as a function of the increase in demand over time. In a similar fashion, if short-run forecasted variations in demand have any influence at all on prices, this happens through changes in cost conditions so that the greater the growth in demand, the lower are unit costs and prices. Changes in demand will generally affect prices only in so far as they affect average 'normal' production cost: the bulk of the adjustment *vis-à-vis* short-run changes in demand is taken up by quantities and not by prices. The structural reasons for this property have been implicitly given in the foregoing discussion on the nature of demand in relation to cost conditions. In 'normal' circumstances (i.e. different from Germany in 1923 or South American countries with three-digit inflation), increasing or at least constant returns in production, the general lack of scarce factors (at below-full-employment rates of activity), the indivisibility of equipment – on the supply side – and the nature of the baskets of consumption with the associated low short-term elasticities to price – on the demand side – jointly define the 'upper ceiling' of the rates of activity of the industry in terms of levels of demand rather than decreasing returns in production. Conversely, these same conditions make any adjustment in quantities based on variations of prices very costly (for the individual firms and for the industry as a whole). Whenever these structural features are associated with (a) an industrial organisation characterised by at least some price-makers (as we expect from our oligopolistic model with pronounced inter-firm asymmetries) and (b) an inter-firm distribution of productive capacity not very far from the 'equilibrium' distribution related to the pattern of asymmetries themselves (cf. equation 17, page 132), then we would expect every 'excess demand' or 'excess supply' (*vis-à-vis* trend values) to be absorbed via quantity changes leaving price levels nearly stable. There is, however, a case in which demand conditions might affect, in a more traditional way, the level of prices in the short run: this is in relation to *unforecasted* variations in demand. The relevance of this case is likely to vary a lot between sectors. A 'forecasted' variation in demand implies that, over the relevant time horizon, once firms have set their price, quantities are adjusted to meet the corresponding demand. Suppose that in some sub-markets (markets of specific products) the produced quantities are in excess *vis-à-vis* demand at that price. If the divergence is relatively low and, moreover, if the life-cycle of that product is relatively long, probably not much will happen. Let us suppose instead that the divergence is high and/or that the particular product will rapidly decline in the future. Then, if the firm keeps a stock of that commodity, the latter's value will rapidly shrink, even if one overlooks the discount rate that the firm applies to the future value of the inventory. In this case, the firm might be quite ready to undercut the prices in order to sell the excess supply. Conversely (but apparently more rarely, since firms are generally able to increase their production in a fairly short time[148]), in conditions of heavy excess demand customers might be ready to pay a premium in order to shorten delivery lags. The mechanism through which both phenomena occur are often variations in the discounts that firms generally apply on listed prices.[149] Their same existence and their role point at the status and the limitations of our proposed interpretation of price levels and changes: the argument developed in this chapter is meant to account, on a fairly general level, for the *trends* and the *gravity centres* around which prices are generally likely to set, allowing at the same time for observable recurrent divergences. However, our theoretical choice should by now be clear: we suggest that variations in prices due to costs and structural conditions of the industry are the *norm*, while wide variations due to excess supply or excess demand are, if we are correct, an exception.

(g) During the discussion of 'limit pricing' it was suggested that in practice it would have been difficult to define a precise price at which all the entries were 'blockaded'. Even when such a price is applied, it might well happen that entries nonetheless occur, due to (a) 'incremental' product improvements somehow equivalent to product differentiations, to the exploitation of new potential markets and applications, or, (b) simply to the fact that a group of firms is near enough to the technological frontier, so that none of them succeeds in gaining a big lead over the other competitors. These two factors, together with a continuous process of 'proper' innovations, account for the empirical observation that in new markets we generally find some scattering of companies and not just one innovator. The account of pricing levels (and pricing behaviours) under these circumstances does not present particular conceptual problems. In so far as the innovator(s) (which are generally also the market leader(s)) and the subsequent entrants can be considered part of the same 'market', differential unit costs between the former and the latter will operate in a manner very similar to the technological discontinuities discussed above, leaving to the market leader(s) the determination of 'equilibrium prices' in that market, whose level will be, again, defined by technological conditions, demand conditions and the technological history of that segment of the industry (imitative time lags, technological discontinuities, distribution of the firms by size, etc.). In other words *mobility barriers* will contribute to price and margin determination jointly with entry barriers.

Two aspects, however, need to be mentioned. First, it is always possible for an established firm with sufficient financial resources to enter a certain market, provided that it is ready to undertake losses (or at least profits below the 'minimum') for a significant period of time. Such a firm might well find it worth entering if it perceives the growing potential of that market. This feature clarifies the asymmetric role of small innovative (and often new) firms *vis-à-vis* big companies: as mentioned already, there is no entry barrier for a company on the innovation frontier, while there are significant barriers for imitators (i.e. for firms which are not on that frontier), which may eventually be overcome – although with significant difficulties – by big and financially powerful firms. This feature, as we shall see, helps to explain why, in semiconductors, entries by new firms occurred quite often in the USA but not in Europe and, conversely, why the European and Japanese producers are generally big established companies.

Second, if one allows a certain amount of entry to occur in practice, then the average mark-up in each sub-market (and in the aggregate) is likely to depend on the distribution of firms by size on each sub-market and the degree of concentration. The relationship between concentration/market power/profitability has been a topic of intense discussion in industrial economics. Although empirical investigations do not appear to be conclusive, there seems to be some evidence (even if not overwhelming) of a positive relationship. If our argument above is correct, however, the main relationship does not run from concentration to inter-oligopolistic collusion and market power and profitability. On the contrary it runs from inter-firm asymmetries to *both* concentration and profitability, while collusive behaviours are not necessary to our explanation, although they sometimes happen. Accordingly, in the formula for the aggregate level of prices (equation 19), the m_{i_t} (margin over cost) in each sub-market to be taken is that of the market leader, while the 'average' margin in each sub-market and for the industry as a whole will depend, other things being equal, on the distribution of market shares between 'low cost' and 'high cost' firms.[150]

(h) We may now add another variable to our interpretative framework in order to describe in more detail the relationship technical progress/productivity/prices, namely process innovations (of the capital-embodied kind), on the assumption that they are unrelated to product innovation and 'size neutral' (i.e. unrelated to economies of scale). Suppose a distribution of the capital stock according to its *vintage, à la* Salter.[151] The distribution of unit labour costs is thus a function of the distribution of the total capital stock according to its vintage. The condition for investment will be positive expected net discounted returns,[152] and the scrapping criterion will be that *operating* costs on the oldest vintage in use will have to be higher than the *total* costs (including depreciation allowances and interests) on the new investment. Notably it has been shown that the validity of the criterion does not depend on market structure (i.e. whether one is considering a 'free competitive' situation or an oligopolistic one), but simply on a cost minimising criterion, applicable in either market environment.[153] An additional step, however, has to be taken if we want to integrate our previous analysis on 'learning economies' with capital-embodied technical progress. From our definition, 'learning economies' concern the relationship between (cumulative) output and unit costs, on the grounds of an unchanged technology.[154] This implies that they affect unit labour cost *independently* from the vintage of the capital to which labour inputs are applied. Different levels of net investment, and therefore different forecasted increases in output, will thus affect also unit operative costs of the past vintages. Conversely, learning economies will also influence replacement decisions and decisions regarding the amount of net investment. Gross and net investments, prices, quantities and margins[155] have to be determined simultaneously. In formal terms one could add to the system of equations 3, 5, 6 and 9 an equation which determines investment in relation to demand conditions and scrapping criteria. The various vintages (i.e. capital embodied technical progress) define the 'maximum' labour input and (physical) capital input coefficients: learning effects represent a more efficient use of the existing capital stock and labour. Actual input coefficients, therefore, are not 'variable' because of factor substitution but due to an increasingly efficient use of them, owing to learning.

(i) There might be yet another functional relationship between investments, prices, quantities and margins, via the financial requirements for the investment. In other words, cash-flow requirements[156] may help to determine price levels. The question basically concerns the possibility of changes in prices and margin levels corresponding with changes in gross investment outlets. In this respect one should distinguish between two cases.

A first question – which does not present particular problems – concerns changes in investment outlets, for any particular product, determined by changes in the capital/output ratio: in this cases, it is very plausible that the entire structure of margins (for the innovators and for potential entrants as well as for possible infra-marginal existing producers) would tend to change correspondingly: the 'minimum' margin for the entrant would increase (decrease) according to the increase (decrease) in the capital/output ratio, in order to continue to reflect the minimum acceptable rate of profit.

A second case regards the possibility of changes in prices of a certain product as a result of an increase in the rate of investment for given capital/output ratios and given inter-firm asymmetries. Our model of the determinants of oligopoly prices would exclude that possibility as a general or permanent phenomenon. If the sources of the oligopolistic margins do not change, such a pricing policy would lead to decreasing market shares even under conditions of perfect collusion between the existing producers, since new firms would tend to enter the market.

There is a more general point here. In our view, those models which suggest a direct relationship between investment-related cash-flow requirements and profit margins, tend to underestimate the forces of competition in capitalist economies. These forces operate both in 'free competitive' and oligopolistic environments: in the longer term non-competitive rates of profits are only allowed (and limited in their size) by structural asymmetries amongst producers and between these and potential ones.[157]

(j) Let us consider the effects of capital-embodied technical progress on entry conditions.[158] Clearly, the unit costs of existing producers represent a weighted average of different input coefficients corresponding to different vintages. On the other hand, the notional unit costs for the potential entrant stem from the newest (the most efficient) vintage. These facts lead us to the following remarkable property: for given rates of product innovation, given 'physical' obsolescence of capital stock and given imitative lags (as far as products are concerned), *cost-based asymmetries between innovators and imitators are inversely related to capital-embodied technical progress.* Existing producers are, as it were, held up with old vintages while new ones can fully reap the benefit of technical progress. In actual fact, one can observe in the history of several industries that capital-embodied technical change is often associated with economies of scale and size-related entry-barriers which partly curb (or even more than compensate) the diffusive effect of the former. Leaving that aside, capital-embodied technical progress as such induces competitive dynamics and tends to reduce entry barriers. One may easily conceive an 'ideal type' of structure opposite to the oligopolistic one considered so far, whereby there is a *negative* cost differential between existing producers and entrants.[159]

The Pace of Innovation and Imitation: the Conditions for 'Classical' Competitive Environments

These aspects of technical progress have far-reaching implications. Suppose technical progress, after one product innovation, takes only the form of freely marketed capital-embodied process innovations, while learning-by-doing, 'disembodied' process innovations and new product innovations are absent. Under these conditions the original product-innovator will have a rather low incentive to practise 'penetration' or limit pricing since after the imitation lag period its advantage will completely disappear: a monopolistic strategy will be more likely. Conversely, after the imitation period, new entrants, utilising the most efficient vintages of equipment will join the market, progressively eroding the innovator's monopolistic profits and even pushing them below the competitive minimum. In a large enough industry charac-terised by several products of different ages or – which is analytically the same – in a one-product industry characterised by different vintages of equipment, one will be able to observe an inter-firm variance in profit rates. The *average* rate of profit of the industry, however, may well be near the *competitive* one. This stylised picture clearly corresponds to what we have termed above (see p. 100) as 'weak oligopolistic hypothesis'. Monopolistic and/or oligopolistic positions by individual firms always exist but they are always withered away by newly emerging competition. It can be easily seen how this process is similar to a stylised 'classical' dynamics or in several respects to an 'early Schumpeterian one' (Schumpeter, 1919).

The crucial difference with our model outlined above is that there are no grounds for *structural* asymmetries between firms, or, even if there are, such as a continuous flow of product innovations which require time to be imitated, the competitive effect brought forward by ever new vintages of capital equipment compensates for them. One of the main differences between the 'weak' and the 'strong' oligopolistic hypotheses depends on learning-by-doing[160] which, as such, drives toward cumulative inter-firm asymmetries and represents a powerful mechanism of private appropriation of technical progress. Whenever the long-run private appropriation of technical progress (in the forms of non-diffusable knowledge and productive techniques, serial correlation in the innovative capabilities, etc.) is relatively unimportant, then the 'classical' view of dynamic competition appears perfectly adequate (cf. for the most organic account, that part of Marx's works which analyses 'how things were' in nineteenth-century capitalism): technical progress is then essentially about 'the battle for cheapening the commodity'[161] and occurs mainly through capital-embodied process innovations. Our model does not imply the absence of that process. On the contrary, it is still at work and is a fundamental one: together with that, however, one has to consider the mechanisms of *internalisation* within the firm[162] of some aspects of technical progress, which – in our view – have become increasingly important in this century, due also to the increasing complexity of technologies and to the very nature of the patterns of change analysed in Chapter 2. Technical progress based on 'learning-by-doing' or, for that matter, economies of scale, is almost by definition asymmetric: it implies that someone is 'better' than someone else, because he/she produced a certain commodity first or because he/she has bigger and more efficient plants, or both. By definition, not everybody can be 'better' and, moreover, there is no reason, given a certain basic technology, why the 'better' ones of today should become 'equal' (or 'worse') tomorrow: economies of scale and learning economies tend to be self-reinforcing. Conversely, in the case of capital-embodied (and size-neutral) innovations, there is no *a priori* impediment to a diffusion of best-practice techniques throughout an industrial sector. This does not happen instantaneously, but capital investments, once undertaken, are there for their entire economic life. As Salter (1969) reminds us, 'bygones are bygones'. Fast innovators of yesterday might be 'held up' by yesterday's capital stock which is still viable (even if not the most efficient one) today. This clearly provides a general competitive mechanism which allows new firms, other things being equal, to gain an advantage over old ones. In this context oligopolistic positions can only be temporary.

We have thus reached a fairly complete picture of the opposing factors affecting both inter-firm technological asymmetries and costs structures, and the related competitive process. On the one hand, innovation and technical change continuously induce asymmetric positions of innovative and imitative firms, characterised by entry barriers and pre-emption of the potential markets for the new commodities. On the other hand, the existence of temporary monopolies on innovative commodities, and the differential advantages accruing to early-comers appear to act as a strong incentive for further innovation. Moreover, technological imitation and capital-embodied diffusion of new process technologies represent powerful competitive forces which sustain the competitive dynamism of an industry. The relative rates of these processes, together with the rate of learning-by-doing and the degree of appropriability of innovations, determine whether monopolistic/oligopolistic positions – which in themselves are a permanent feature of technical progress – lead also to permanent oligopolistic margins for the industry as a whole. In other words, *the relative pace of asymmetry-creating factors and diffusive factors discriminates between 'weak' oligopolistic conditions* (those which might still be consistent with 'classical' competitive markets and average competitive rates of profit) *and 'strong' oligopolistic conditions* (which we have analysed throughout this chapter).

The framework outlined above is meant to suggest the range of equilibrium prices and margins to which the industry is likely to tend, given certain technological and market conditions, and to intepret the basic trends in its dynamics. From the point of view of each individual firm, 'there are more things between heaven and earth' than we can account for in any economic model. On a more general level, however, this framework appears capable of selecting from the infinite variety of an ever-transforming world few fundamental trends and their determinants, thus escaping the indeterminacy of the prevailing 'individualist' methodology, while in the meantime granting some behavioural degrees of freedom to economic agents which are able to influence their environment and their future.

Throughout the process of technical change and structural transformation of an industry, disequilibrium (*vis-à-vis* some 'normal' levels of prices, quantities, profit margins and productive capacity) is likely to appear continuously and to stimulate adjustment and structural change. The description of the determination of prices and margins in the hypothetical industry analysed above does not rule out by any means the occurrence of 'disequilibrium situations', of 'price wars', etc. On the contrary, it is just meant to define, as it were, the gravity centres and boundaries of the process of adjustment in the industry.

The following section will attempt to illustrate the process of structural change and price determination in the semiconductor industry making use of the theoretical framework outlined here.

3.4 TECHNICAL CHANGE AND GROWTH: THE WORLD SEMICONDUCTOR INDUSTRY

An Overview

Commercial production of semiconductor devices started around 1950. Since then, the industry has experienced impressive growth rates: in the period 1958–76, the American industry grew in monetary terms at an average annual compound rate of 18.5 per cent and in real terms at a rate of 44 per cent (Table 3.6). These meant that semiconductor prices came down at a vertiginous rate. Similar but somewhat lower rates of growth were achieved by the European industry. Tables 3.1 to 3.3 chart the growth in markets, output and employment in the non-Communist world's semiconductor industry: this growth was particularly high in integrated circuits (including microprocessors), by far the most dynamic segment of the semiconductor market.

Despite such impressive rates of growth the size of the industry, in terms of output and employment, remains limited: estimated *world*

TABLE 3.1   *Estimates of major world semiconductor markets 1974–80ᵃ (US $ m. in current prices)*

	1974	1975	1976	1977	1978	1979	1980
US Total semi- conductors	2,345	1,801	2,904	3,253	3,937	5,061	6,360
of which ICs	1,236	938	1,909	2,223	2,694	3,684	4,876
Western Europe Total semi- conductors	1,333	1,139	1,564	1,826	2,527	2,820	3,105
of which ICs	520	471	720	885	1,336	1,566	1,788
Japan Total semi- conductors	1,171	1,126	1,866	2,008	2,331	2,714	3,044
of which ICs	593	625	862	927	1,289	1,590	1,838

NOTES
ᵃ Figures include estimated in-house market of firms which also produce for the open market but exclude consumption of firms exclusively producing for in-house use (e.g. IBM, Western Electric).

SOURCE   *Electronics.*

semiconductor output in 1978 was around $10,400 million (Table 3.2)[163] and employment around 260,000 people (Table 3.3). European output and employment can be estimated in the same year at around $1,700 million (including US-controlled production) and around 50,000 employees. Employment grew much more slowly than output; in the USA, the only country where historical data are available, total employment grew at an annual rate of 9.5 per cent over the period 1958– 78. Productivity growth has been strikingly high: we estimate for the USA (1958–76) a compound rate of around 33 per cent (Table 3.6).[164]

Despite the relatively small size of the industry, semiconductors represent a technologically vital input in a great and growing number of electronics and electronics-related industries. Table 3.7 provides a disaggregation of the major end-user sectors in the USA and Western Europe.

KEY TO TABLES

Official statistical data for semiconductors are seldom available. Many figures are therefore based on company and consulting organizations' estimates. An effort has been made whenever possible to keep the data from the various sources consistent with each other. Many discrepancies still exist, however, and one should be extremely cautious in interpreting the data as anything more than a simple indicator of the orders of magnitude. In particular:

(a) estimates of markets and market shares are often downward biased by the underestimate of in-house consumption;
(b) different countries give slightly different definitions of semiconductors, with respect to borderline products such as opto-electronic devices, magnetic bubble memories, and semi-finished parts;
(c) Japanese figures on employment and productivity are – in our view – somewhat underestimating the former and overestimating the latter, since in multi-divisional firms activities indirectly related to semiconductor production may not be accounted for (some research and marketing activity, etc.);
(d) semiconductor smuggling is a rather widespread phenomenon, at least in Europe (our estimates in the Italian case suggest it represents around one quarter of the Italian market!) This reduces the size of recorded trade flows and of internal apparent consumption.

    − : nil
    .. : negligible
    ( ) : estimated
        : a space signifies information not avail-
        able

'World' excludes the centrally planned economies.

TABLE 3.2 World production of semiconductors by region and by ownership, 1973, 1976 and 1978[a]

	All semiconductors			of which ICs		
	1973	1976	1978	1973	1976	1978
Production ($m)						
World total	(6,000)	(7,450)	(10,400)	(2,700)	(3,900)	(6,000)
By region:						
(2) US	3,640	4,470	(5,800)	2,000	2,740	(3,950)
(2a) of which estimated in-house consumption	1,200	1,400				
(3) Western Europe	1,100	1,250	1,700	280	415	(660)
(4) Japan	1,280	1,500	2,500	400	660	1,330
Shares in Production (%)						
(5) *World*	100	100	100	100	100	100
By region:						
(6) US	61	60	56	74	70	66
(6a) of which estimated in-house consumption	20	19				
(7) Western Europe	18	17	16	10	11	11
(8) Japan	19	20	24	14	16	22

By ownership:				
(9) US-owned	71	69	79	76
(10) W. European-owned	11	12	6	9
(11) Japanese-owned	18	19	13	15

NOTE

[a] This table excludes centrally planned economies, includes estimated US production for in-house consumption, and includes semi-finished parts. It excludes assembly in developing countries in rows (1) to (4), but includes the latter in (9) to (11). World production (row (1)) is thus underestimated to the extent that items assembled in developing countries are not returned to the original country. The underestimate is about 10% for all semiconductors and 15% for integrated circuits. Control of developing country assembly of semiconductors is estimated to be 78% in the hands of US firms, 15% Japanese, and 5% European.

SOURCES

Rows (1), (2) and (2a): Dataquest, corrected for US in-house production using data from US Census and Annual Survey of Manufactures and interviews.

Row (3): Mackintosh Consultants (various years), Dataquest, interviews;

Row (4): Nomura Research Institute (1980), Dataquest;

Row (9) to (11): Dataquest, Nomura Research Institute (1980), interviews.

Due to different estimates of in-house production and to the underestimate of LDCs assembly, production (Table 3.2) and markets (Table 3.6) do not necessarily match.

TABLE 3.3 *Employment in world semiconductor industry by region and ownership, 1958–78*
('000)

	1958	1963	1966	1969	1972	1973	1974	1975	1976	1977	1978
(1) *World* Total											(263.0)
By Region											
(2a) US (Department of Commerce)	23.4	56.3	82.2	98.8	97.6	120.0	133.1	96.7	102.5		
(2b) US (International Trade Commission)							106.0	84.7	102.2	112.4	131.6
(3) Western Europe						69.3					(56.7)
(4) of which UK						15.2					(12.2)
(5) Germany						21.2					(16.6)
(6) France						15.2					(13.0)
(7) Italy						8.1					5.8
(8) Japan						(33.0)	33.9	31.9	33.1	32.9	33.3
By Ownership											
(9) US-owned		58.4	90.8	165.5	173.7		202.9	150.4	175.8	185.5	210.9
(10) of which outside US		2.1	8.6	66.7	89.1		69.8	58.7	78.3	81.1	89.3
(11) Western European-owned											(54.8)
(12) of which outside Europe											(18.0)

NOTES AND SOURCES

Row (1) World estimates are obtained by the *sum* of rows (2b), (3) and (10) (estimated from Mackintosh (various years)) *plus* Far Eastern employment in European facilities (estimated at 10,000) and Japanese facilities (estimated at 15,000);

Row (2a) US Department of Commerce, Bureau of the Census, *Census of Manufactures* and *Survey of Manufactures*, various years;

Row (2b) United States International Trade Commission (1979) (data obtained through a survey covering practically the entire statistical universe in 1978, but not in 1974 and 1975; hence discrepancy in these years between rows (2a) and (2b);

Rows (3) to (7): for 1973: unpublished data from Italian consultants; for 1978 own estimates.

Row (8): United States International Trade Commission (1979);

Row (9): 1963–72: Finan (1975); 1974–8: United States International Trade Commission (1979);

Row (11): Own estimates.

TABLE 3.4   *Value of semiconductor shipments per employee for various countries, 1973 and 1978*[a]

(US $ '000 in current prices)

		1973	1978
(1)	US	30	40
(2)	Europe	17	30
(2a)	European-owned companies	15	
(3)	UK[b]	12	23
(4)	Germany[b]	16	34
(5)	France[b]	14	29
(6)	Italy[b]	11	24
(7)	Japan[c]	39	75

NOTES

[a] Figures in this table represent rough orders of magnitude only. Apart from the problem of reliability of the original data, different degrees of vertical integration and product mix, together with exchange rate fluctuations, affect comparability.

[b] European figures tend to be overstated due to American assembly in Europe (the value added of which is rather low while the final output is high). Estimates on some European companies suggest that output per employee (including overseas employees in LDCs) ranged in 1978 between US $12 and 20,000.

[c] Figures are likely to be substantially overstated because of the restrictive way that semiconductor employment in conglomerate companies is estimated. Nonetheless, for 1978 at least, this does not change Japan's ranking.

SOURCE   Calculated from Tables 3.2 and 3.3.

Production is US dominated: US companies, either directly or through foreign subsidiaries, controlled in 1976 around 69 per cent of world production, while the US market accounted for around 40 per cent of the world market for semiconductors (Tables 3.1 and 3.2). Western Europe, on the other hand, accounted for 27 per cent of world consumption and for around 17 per cent of world production (of which 13 per cent was European-controlled). After a large catching-up effort the Japanese semiconductor industry has come to account for around one-quarter of world production as well as of world consumption. Over the last decade, the share of European companies in total semiconductor output appears roughly stable. Some increase in European-controlled production occurred, however, due to the purchase, by European companies, of American firms.

The European share in world output – broadly speaking – appears to

TABLE 3.5   *World market share and geographical distribution of markets of major world semiconductor producers, 1978*[a]

(%)

	World market share	Geographical breakdown of sales			
		USA	Japan	Europe	Other
Texas Instruments	11	55	10	31	4
Motorola	8	62	5	25	8
Philips	7	24	4	63	9
Nippon Electric	7	8	77	4	11
Hitachi	5	6	80	2	12
National Semiconductors	5	65	5	19	11
Toshiba	5	6	70	4	20
Fairchild	5	63	3	18	15
Intel	4	59	3	27	11
Siemens	3	12	0	78	10
Others	40				
Total	100				

NOTE
[a] Excludes in-house production.

SOURCE   Nomura (1980).

be inversely related to the degree of complexity and innovativeness of the commodities. It is higher in discrete semiconductors, much lower in integrated circuits and very low in microprocessors. Notably, such differences in the European shares in world output are much greater than the differences in the corresponding European shares in world consumption. This is, of course, reflected in the European trade balance, and will be discussed in the next chapter.

A more disaggregate analysis of market shares broadly confirms the US market leadership and the European weakness in most semiconductor devices. Let us consider the following examples, elaborated on the basis of the authoritative *Dataquest* estimates.[165] Extreme cases are MOS integrated circuits (share of European companies, 1980: 6%; Japanese companies: around 27%, while the rest, to 100%, can be almost entirely attributed to US companies), MOS memories (European companies, 1980: 2–3%, Japanese companies: 27%, US companies 70%). The Japanese catching up is highlighted especially by memories, e.g. 64–K Dynamic RAMs (1980) (European Companies: nil; Japanese companies: 60%; US companies: 40%); 16–K Dynamic RAM (European companies; less than 2%; Japanese companies: 40%; US

TABLE 3.6   *US: indices of shipments, productivity and prices in the semiconductor industry, 1958–78*[a]
(1972 = 100)

	S_c	S_p	VA_{m-h}	P_{m-h}	I
1958	9.3	0.5	36.8	1.8	2114.0
1963	25.4	4.6	41.5	8.1	555.6
1964	26.5	6.7	45.5	12.5	392.8
1965	33.7	11.3	47.0	17.6	298.4
1966	41.5	19.6	48.4	24.5	215.4
1967	42.2	21.9	47.5	26.1	192.7
1968	48.7	31.8	51.9	35.4	152.9
1969	58.2	49.5	52.3	43.8	117.5
1970	55.5	45.1	59.2	46.6	123.0
1971	59.1	50.0	81.2	71.8	118.2
1972	100.0	100.0	100.0	100.0	100.0
1973	134.9	158.5	107.3	120.4	85.1
1974	159.2	189.9	115.3	123.0	83.8
1975	121.2	172.3	140.8	203.3	70.3
1976	165.4	249.5	161.1	235.9	66.2
1977	(196.0)				
1978	(236.0)				

S_c = Shipments at current prices
S_p = Shipments at constant prices
VA_{m-h} = Value Added per man-hour of production worker (at current prices)
P_{m-h} = Productivity per man-hour of production worker
I = Price index of semiconductor output.

NOTE
[a] The price and productivity indexes do not take into account the rapidly increasing complexity of the devices produced. Had this been possible, productivity would have shown a greater increase and prices a manifold greater decrease.

SOURCES
Calculated on the basis of data in US Department of Commerce, *Census of Manufactures*, and *Annual Survey of Manufactures*, various years. Own elaboration for the price index and value added deflator. See Appendix I.

companies 58 %). The American leadership is particularly pronounced in microprocessors and microcomputers, e.g. 4-bit microcomputers (1980) (European companies: near zero; Japanese companies: 36 %; US companies: 64 %), 8-bit microcomputers (Europe: 1 %; Japan 15 %; US: 83 %); 8-bit microprocessors (Europe: 3 %; Japan: 15 %; US: 82 %); 16-bit microprocessors (Europe: nil; Japan: 3 %; US: 97 %).[166]

The world semiconductor industry is dominated by a relatively small

TABLE 3.7   *End-users of semiconductors on US and Western European markets, 1978*
(%)

	US	Western Europe
Computers	56	20
Consumer products	9	30
Automotive	2	
Industrial	11	18
Communications	9	14
Government	13	5
Distributor	a	13
Total	100	100

NOTE
a Attributed to estimated end-users.

SOURCES
US: Arthur D. Little, Inc.
Western Europe: SGS–Ates.

number of firms, resulting in a level of concentration that is high if one takes into account the remarkable number of new entries (see Table 3.5 for the world market share of the top ten firms in 1978 and Tables 3.8, 3.10 and 3.11 for the basic data on the major activities of the largest firms of Western Europe, the USA and Japan respectively.[167]). Remarkably, the levels of concentration are particularly high in microprocessors. Estimates, based again on *Dataquest* data, suggest a *world* market share of 45 % for the leading producer of 4-bit microcomputers and 83 % for the four leading firms. The corresponding figures are 27 % and 78 % for 8-bit microcomputers, 13 % and 38 % for 8-bit microprocessors; 49 % and 93 % for 16-bit microprocessors.

Until recently, however, there has been no indication of increasing concentration for the world semiconductor industry as a whole: the 4-firms concentration ratio was 33 % in 1973 and 31 % in 1980, and the 8-firms ratio was 48 % in 1973 and 49 % in 1980.[168]

The degree of concentration reflects also the importance of pronounced dynamic economies of scale: other things being equal (includng manufacturing technologies), productivity appears to be a direct logarithmic function of the cumulative volume of production. This is the already discussed 'learning curve' effect. Increasingly, static economies of scale also appear to be relevant – that is, an increasing productivity in

TABLE 3.8 *Major Western European-owned semiconductor producers, 1978*

Firm (country of ownership)	Location of semiconductor production (* including R & D)	Company turnover ($m)			Main area of firm specialisation	
		Total	SCs	ICs	Within SCs	All firm activities
Philips[a] (Netherlands)	Netherlands*, Germany*, France*, UK*, US*, Far East	15,121 (100%)	500[b] (3.3%)	250[b] (1.7%)	ICs (linear and digital bi-polar), discrete SCs (consumer). Standard and custom (in-house use).	Consumer, telecommunications, professional, military, peripheral/terminals.
Siemens (Germany)	Germany*, (France) (Italy) Far East	13,860 (100%)	300[b] (2.2%)	120[b] (0.9%)	ICs (bipolar, MOS, MPU), discrete SCs (industrial). Standard and custom (in-house use).	Industrial, military, heavy electrical, telecommunications, office equipment, some consumer, data processing.
Thomson[c] (France)	France*, N. Africa	5,075 (100%)	160[b] (3.1%)	25–30[b] (0.5%)	ICs (mainly analog), discrete, Telecom for consumer and military.	Consumer, military, telecommunications, small data processing equipment.
SGS–Ates[d] (Italy)	Italy*, France, UK, Far East	120[e] (100%)	120 (100%)	(65) (54%)	ICs (analog standard and custom, digital bipolar), discrete	Specialisation of holding company (STET): telecommunications, military
AEG–Telefunken (Germany)	Germany*	6,000	150[b] (2.5%)	(50)[b] (0.8%)	Discrete SCs (and some ICs) consumer, military, industrial. Custom and standard	Consumer, electrical engineering, military

TABLE 3.8 (contd.)

Firm (country of ownership)	Location of semiconductor production (* including R & D)	Company turnover ($m)			Main area of firm specialisation	
		Total	SCs	ICs	Within SCs	All firm activities
GEC (UK)	UK*	4,214	30 (0.7%)		Custom SCs for military and industrial	Electrical engineering, military, consumer, industrial
Plessey (UK)	UK*	1,100[b]	20 (1.8%)	10–15	Custom SCs for military and telecommunications	Military, telecommunications
Semikron (Germany)	Germany*		40		Discrete SCs for industrial	
Ferranti (UK)	UK*		25	12	Custom ICs for military & telecommunications	Military, data processing, telecommunications

NOTES

[a] Includes Signetics (US) and all European subsidiaries

[b] Including in-house consumption

[c] Includes SESCOSEM, SILEC (70% Thomson-owned) and EFCIS (owned 50% by Thomson, 50% by Atomic Agency)

[d] Part of STET holding company

[e] For STET: $3,495 m

SOURCES Brezzi (1980), Truel (1980), company reports.

TABLE 3.9 *Western Europe: shares of major firms in major national semiconductor markets, selected years*

	All W. Europe 1978	Germany 1968	Germany 1972	Germany 1978	France 1968	France 1972	France 1978	Italy 1973	Italy 1978	UK 1962	UK 1968	UK 1973	UK 1977
Philips[a]	19	25	18	15	22	16	14	7	10	49[c]	22[c]	17	18
Texas Instruments	14	16	12	13	20	12	13	15	13	13	23	18	22
Siemens	11	22	26	21		3		6	5	2	7	13	8
ITT	8	10	8	7				7	9		6	14	11
Motorola	7	6	7	6	5	10	12	10	8				
AEG-Telefunken[b]	6	9	12	9			6		3		14	2	3
SGS-Ates[b]	5	6	3	3	7	6	6	20	19				
SESCOSEM	4				20	15	16	6	5				
Fairchild	3	{6}	{14}	{26}	{26}	{38}	{28}	13	3	{e}	{e}	4	8
Intel	3							{16}	3	{e}	{e}	{e}	
RCA	3								2	{e}	{e}	{e}	
National Semiconductors	2								4	{e}	{e}		5
Ferranti	{18}									10	5	4	1
GEC										7[d]	4	{e}	6
Other									12	19	19	28	18
Total	100	100	100	100	100	100	100	100	100	100	100	100	100
Of which US-owned firms:		36	51	43	33	55	60	n.a.	61	n.a.	53	59	64

NOTES

a Valvo in Germany, RTC in France and, from 1968 Mullard in the UK.

b SGS was originally established as a joint venture between Fairchild, Olivetti and Telettra.

c Production in ASM, a joint venture of Mullard (Philips) and GEC, entirely taken over by Mullard in 1968.

d Production in AEI, purchased by GEC in 1967.

e Included under "other".

SOURCES For UK: Golding (1971); Sciberras (1977 and 1980, for shares of US-owned firms in other countries: 1968), Finan (1975, 1978), interviews; for other figures: Tilton (1971) and interviews.

TABLE 3.10 *Major US semiconductor producers, 1978*

	Total turnover ($m) 1	Semiconductor turnover ($m) Total 2	Semiconductor turnover ($m) In-house use 3	Major areas of firm specialisation 4
Texas Instruments	2,550	1292	112	Semiconductors, consumer electronics, data processing.
IBM	21,076	(750)	(750)	Computers, office equipment, telecommunications.
Motorola	2,220	732	(40)	Semiconductors, consumer electronics, military.
Fairchild[a]	534	389	6	Semiconductors, consumer electronics.
National Semiconductors	719	364	337	Semiconductors
Intel	400	298	(30)	Semiconductors, micro-computers.
Western Electric	41,744[c]	(200)	(200)	Telecommunication utility, telecommunications equipment.
Signetics[b]	180	180	n.a.	See Philips (Table 3) of which it is a subsidiary.
ITT	15,261 (Total of the group)	170	n.a.	Telecommunications, military, consumer electronics, diversified activities.
RCA	6,601	(130)	n.a.	Consumer electronics, household appliances, military, data processing.

NOTES
[a] Taken over by Schlumberger (France) in 1979 (cf. Table 3.11).
[b] Taken over by Philips in 1975 (cf. Table 3.11).
[c] Total for ATT.

SOURCES Truel (1980, p. 269); Brezzi (1980, p. 197); company reports; estimates of US turnover for in-house consumption, based on the report *Integrated Circuit Engineering* (1979), appear only to refer to in-house production within the USA and not to the total for the firm.

TABLE 3.11 *Foreign investments in the US semiconductor industry, selected years 1969–79*

Year			Equity ownership (%)	Investment ($)
1969	Monolithic Memories	Northern Telecom Ltd	Canada	12.4	285,000
1971	Micropower	Daima Seikosha (Seiko)	Japan	77.0	3,385,000
1972	EXAR	Toyo Electronics	Japan	53.0	1,073,000
1975	Maruman	Mansei Kogyo Kabushiki-Kaishi	Japan	60.0	2,700,000
	Signetics	N. V. Philips	Netherlands	100.0	43,850,000
1976	Supertex	Hong Kong Interests	Hong Kong	n.a.	n.a.
	MOS technology	Commodore International-Ltd	Bahamas	100.0	10,000,000
1977	Frontier	Commodore International-Ltd	Bahamas	100.0	10,865,629
	Intersil	Northern Telecom Ltd	Canada	24.0	3,500,000
	Interdesign	Ferranti Ltd	United Kingdom	100.0	14,230,000
	American Micro-systems	Robert Bosch, Gmbh.	West Germany	25.0	16,200,000
	Litronix	Siemens, Gmbh.	West Germany	80.0	26,723,087
	Advanced Micro Devices	Siemens, Gmbh.	West Germany	20.0	
	Solid State Scientific	VDO	West Germany	25.0	4,500,000
	Siliconix	Lucas	United Kingdom	24.0	6,100,000
1978	Electronic Arrays	Nippon Electric Co.	Japan	100.0	8,905,000
1979	Fairchild Camera and Instrument	Schlumberger	France	100.0	363,000,000

SOURCE United States International Trade Commission (1979, p. 106), based on hearing before the Committee on Commerce, Science and Transportation, United States Senate on Governmental Policy and Innovation in the Semiconductor and Computer Industries, (95th Congress, second session). Serial No. 95–138, 1978, pp. 96–7, and elaborations.

relation to the scale of production. To the extent that static and dynamic economies of scale and degrees of process innovativeness are captured by indicators of labour productivity, the estimates of the value of shipments per employee in major producing countries in Table 3.4 show the relatively strong position of Japan and the USA (though one must keep in mind that the figures in this table are biased by the different accounting procedures). Moreover, the European figure includes American subsidiaries which push the ratio up because they generally present a lower degree of vertical integration, apart from any possible difference in productivity.

The relative stability of degrees of concentration has historically been due to successive waves of new entries into the industry in the USA. These were mainly new innovative firms which originated as spin-offs

TABLE 3.12   *Western Europe: production of integrated circuits, by country,*
1974–8[a]
(US $m)

Country	1974	1975	1976	1977	1978
European Economic Community[b]					
Belgium	8	6	3	3	3
France	74	65	78	78	84
Italy	29	15	49	55	84
Netherlands	7	16	14	20	23
United Kingdom	100	100	100	118	147
West Germany	112	115	134	191	250
Subtotal	330	317	378	465	591
Other European countries					
Austria	4	4			
Spain	2	2	4	4	4
Sweden	3	4	5	6	7
Switzerland	4	4	25	27	40
Subtotal	13	14	34	37	51
Total	343	331	412	502	642

NOTES

[a] A slight divergence between this table and row (3) of Table 3.2 is due to different accounts for semi-finished parts and European assembly of imported parts by American companies.

[b] This does not include data for Luxembourg, Ireland and Denmark.

SOURCE
United States International Trade Commission (1979, p. 119).

TABLE 3.13 Major Japanese semiconductor producers, 1978

| | Turnover ($m) | | | Major areas of firm specialisation | |
	Total group[a] 1	Total parent company 2	Semi-con-ductor 3	Within SCs 4	All firm activities 5
Nippon Electric	3,765	2,932	581	MOS, linear.	Telecommunications, computers, semiconductors.
Hitachi	12,260	7,187	450	MOS–ICs, bipolar, memories.	Consumer electronics, industrial, computers, telecommunications.
Toshiba	9,110	5,905	386	Very diversified. Linear for consumer application, MOS, automotive applications, discrete SCs.	Consumer electronics, industrial, data processing, telecommunications.
Matsushita Electric	10,218	7,614	232	Discrete SCs, linear for consumer products.	Consumer electronics.
Mitsubishi Electric	4,851	4,451	197	Very diversified. MOS, memories, discrete SCs.	Industrial electronics, consumer, data processing, telecommunications.
Tokyo Sanyo	2,634	2,520	23	Linear bipolar.	Consumer electronics.
Fujitsu		2,100	106	MOS (especially memories) digital bipolar.	Computers, telecommunications, industrial electronics, semiconductors.
Sony		1,977	11	Discrete SCs, ICs for consumer electronics.	Consumer electronics.
Sharp		1,311	37	MOS (especially for calculators, etc.)	Consumer electronics, calculators.

NOTES
[a] Consolidated.

SOURCES Nomura (1980); except column 2 figures for Tokyo Sanyo, Sony and Sharp from Brezzi (1980); columns 3 and 4 also supplemented by information from interviews.

from existing firms (at the beginning of the industry, spin-offs of scientists and technicians for Bell Laboratories and big electrical companies and later from established semiconductor companies).[169]

In the seventies the number of new entries progressively decreased and came to a halt by the end of the decade.[170] On the other hand, the quick rise of Japanese companies curbed the growth of market shares of established US companies.

A new phenomenon of the early eighties which is hardly caught by market share figures is the emergence of so-called 'silicon-foundries', companies (generally small ones) which manufacture on order semiconductor devices that are partly or entirely designed by a customer (the latter sometimes manufacture also the 'mask'[171] of the circuit).[172] Finally, 'side' entries by already established companies show an increasing trend. Those newly established productive facilities in existing companies quite often provide semiconductors for in-house use.

In Europe, no significant entry of new innovative firms occurred throughout the history of the industry. Similarly in Japan, most of the semiconductor producers are big electronic companies.

A noticeable feature of the end of the seventies and early eighties is the increase of capital/output ratios, due to the increasing complexity of the circuits and the increasing automation of production.[173]

As already mentioned, throughout the history of the industry prices have been falling over time (not only relative prices, *vis-à-vis* the price index of manufacturing output, but also absolute prices). An attempt to construct a price index for semiconductor output can be found in Table 3.6. Performance-weighted prices have been falling at a much greater rate: it is estimated that the price per logical unit of an IC (expressed in current French francs) was 10^{-1} in 1970, 17.1^{-2} in 1975, 3.10^{-3} in 1980 and is expected to go down to 5.1^{-4} in 1985.[174]

The Factors Affecting the Entry of New Companies

Making use of the framework suggested in the theoretical sections of this chapter we can now discuss some fundamental trends in the industry. In many respects, the analysis that follows may be considered a partial test of the former.

Chapter 2 dealt primarily with the generation of innovations and its determinants, while the process of commercial exploitation of the innovations themselves was largely overlooked. So, one had to stress the role of big established companies, especially in the early days of the industry, in the production of the major technological breakthroughs.

Conversely, the history of commercial successes on the new innovative commodities shows the primary role of new companies (generally spin-offs from already existing semiconductor producers). Complete descriptions of this feature of the semiconductor industry can already be found in the literature.[175] Thus we shall refer to these studies for the detailed evidence on the phenomenon. Few general points, however, need mention. One might wonder why these new entries occurred. In Chapter 2, the *necessary* conditions were discussed, namely, the fact that the American industry was placed on the technological frontier, and the features of the technology itself, which for a long time remained 'people-embodied' rather than 'equipment-embodied'. The first condition, it was also suggested, explains why several new entries occurred in the USA but not in Europe and Japan.

Those necessary conditions, however, are by no means sufficient ones. One can easily imagine, for example, a scenario where big established electrical companies were not only responsible for the technological advances but also for their full market exploitation. Some tentative hypotheses can be suggested regarding the factors allowing the successful emergence of new companies:

(a) One of the few clear cases in which the oligopolistic structure of an industry is likely to hinder a swift introduction of innovative commodities might occur when new commodities replace some other ones already produced by existing oligopolistic firms. In fact, the first semiconductors (transistors and diodes) were substitutes for thermoionic valves. Moreover, throughout the history of the industry, new vintages of products very often accelerated the decline of existing products belonging to 'old' technological vintages. Given these conditions, suppose that a certain firm, which has a significant market share on an existing product, succeeds in developing a new device, which is likely to substitute the previous one. A decision by that firm to commercialise the new commodity is very similar to an investment decision: the investment is undertaken only if the discounted returns are greater or equal to the cost of the investment itself. In this case, the decrease over time of the returns on the old product have to be considered as 'costs' for that firm, while, of course, they would not be so for any other company which is not producing the old commodity.[176] It might well be that it is not profitable for the company to invest in the new commodity, while it would be so for a new firm. In this exercise of evaluation of future returns over the new investment, the estimates regarding the degree of monopoly that the considered firm maintains upon the new technology is obviously crucial: the above calculations are correct only in so far as the firm assumes that no one else will introduce the new product, in case the 'old' firm does not. Clearly the estimates of profitability on the new commodity would be different for a group of scientists and engineers leaving that company and taking with them the 'knowledge' around the new product. We can call this the 'opportunity cost differential' between new and established firms.

(b) Even when the 'old' company is willing to invest in a new commodity, the researchers in which the new technology is 'embodied' might still retain the choice between letting their company exploit the innovation or establishing a new company by themselves. In the second alternative total returns in the wake of success are likely to be much greater: they would get, in fact, the profits which otherwise would go to the company.[177] On the other hand, one must account for the uncertainty and risk associated with the introduction of the new product. Had the researchers decided to establish a new company, they would also face the associated uncertainty. If the attitude towards risk and uncertainty turns out to be systematically different between established companies and would-be entrants, one could go as far as saying that established oligopolies objectively favour the establishment of new risk-taking firms, while being ready to buy them at a later stage, if they are successful.[178] At any rate, even if the attitude towards risk and uncertainty is identical regarding the established company and the potential enterpreneurs, the higher perspective return for the latter is likely to yield to an apparent 'risk-loving' bias on their part.[179]

(c) A significant factor, favouring the establishment of new companies, especially in the fifties and early sixties, was the Consent Decree between the US government and AT & T, in which the latter agreed to distribute its (strategic) semiconductor patents to any requesting firm and not to manufacture semiconductor devices other than for in-house use. In other words, a powerful potential oligopolist was prevented by legislative measures from exploiting its entire technological advantage.

(d) A set of more behavioural factors helps to explain the low degree of commerical swiftness of big established firms. Complex institutional structures, as firms are, routinise most of their interactions with the environment through decision rules which show the advantage of reducing the cost of decision-making but, at the same time, also hinder the promptness of any 'creative' reaction to change.[180] The argument is reinforced by our model of technological change, based on the existence of some kind of technological paradigms. These paradigms are likely to be linked to an 'organisational sociology', built on or around them, which routinises and promotes advances along a technological trajectory, while inducing relative blindness and institutional resistance with respect to radical change. It is a known fact of life that, in any social system, revolutions are generally difficult: this is due partly to the fact that each system tends to become miopic with respect to the possibility of alternative worlds, and partly to the fact that the system itself embodies rules which make its performance efficient (on the ground of its own criteria) and repress certain kinds of (more radical) change.

With these considerations in mind, one can easily appreciate the rich account of the organisational structure of semiconductor producers given by Wilson *et al.* (1980).[181] We can reinterpret their advocacy of a 'balance between decentralisation and control' as the most conducive set-up to a successful performance, in terms of a Nelson–Winter evolutionary theory: the most successful companies have been characterised by an organisational structure which was 'coupling' efficient rules of decision-making (such as costs and profit assessment jointly with hierarchical control) together with some 'meta-rule' of change (generally involving decentralised decisions and 'creative' behaviours).

It is difficult to assess precisely the relative importance of the four mentioned factors. One can only safely say that the third reason (licensing policy by Bell Labs) and the first were more important until the early sixties than at a later stage. There is evidence that existing firms learned very quickly that any monopoly position on their innovative activity was very uncertain and temporary (in relation to both competitors and their own employees who could leave the company) so that the time-lag between innovation and commercialisation has been generally reduced to a minimum.[182] In the sixties and early seventies the second factor (point b) has probably been the most important one as an incentive to the establishment of new innovative companies.

The emergence of 'Schumpeterian' companies on the American scene has actually been a powerful mechanism for *diffusion* of innovations.[183] Some of those companies were able to grow and become 'established semiconductor oligopolies' (e.g. Texas Instruments, Fairchild, National Semiconductors, Intel, etc.). Many others failed or were absorbed by larger companies.

Another kind of new entry could be defined as *side entry* i.e. already existing companies (either operating in the electrical field or elsewhere) entering the semiconductor business. This sort of entry in the first two decades of the industry has often been similar to the 'Schumpeterian entry': researchers, technicians and managers leaving an existing semiconductor company and joining the potential entrant.[184]

Throughout the history of the industry, the survival of existing companies has depended on their ability to keep pace with technical progress, not only on purely technological grounds (as one saw in Chapter 2, established companies were responsible for many technological advances) but also in the commercial arena. In this respect, the record of the big electrical companies of the early fifties is strikingly poor: among them, only RCA keeps a significant share of the market (as mentioned, AT & T is a major producer, but only for in-house use).

Among new entrants, some maintained a leading technological and market position (first of all, Texas Instruments), while others began to decline together with the products and technologies with which they

TABLE 3.14   *Market shares in US semiconductor market by major companies 1957–74*

	1957	1960	1966	1974*
Texas Instruments	20	20	17	18
Transitron	12	9	3	–
Hughes	11	5	(b)	(b)
General Electric	9	8	8	3
RCA	6	7	7	7
Western Electric	5	5	9	(c)
Raytheon	5	4	(b)	–
Sylvania	4	3	(b)	–
Philco-Ford	3	6	3	(b)
Westinghouse	2	1	3	–
Motorola	(b)	5	12	14
Fairchild	–	5	13	10
General Instruments	(b)	(b)	4	2
Delco	–	(b)	4	(b)
National Semiconductors	–	–	(b)	7
Intel	–	–	–	5
Signetics	–	–	(b)	4
AMI	–	–	–	3
Rockwell	–	–	–	2
Int. Rectifier	–	–	–	2
Mostek	–	–	–	2
AMS	–	–	–	2
Others	23	16	12	15

* N.B. in-house sales and government contracts are excluded for 1974.
(b) Negligible.
(c) Only in-house producer.

SOURCE   Truel (1980, p. 79) (his elaboration in Tilton (1971) and DAFSA (1977)).

originally entered the market (for example Transitron, or, to some extent, Fairchild).

The reasons for the total absence of new 'Schumpeterian entries' in Europe[185] and Japan[186] have already been given in Chapter 2, in terms of technological lags. As a consequence, market shares have been much more stable in Japan than in the USA (see Tables 3.14 and 3.15).

In Europe the relative instability of market shares has been due to the entry of American companies, rather than to the emergence of new indigenous firms.[187]

The different dynamics of entries, exits and market shares in the USA, Europe and Japan, support the hypothesis, suggested above, of the *asymmetric nature of entry and mobility barriers*, especially in cases when the latter essentially consist of different innovative capabilities: entry (on mobility) barriers are a direct function of the technological lag of the imitative firms.

Imitative countries, as we shall see at greater length in the next chapter, in order to enter a market characterised by high innovation-based entry barriers, are likely to require big companies characterised by

TABLE 3.15 *Shares of Japanese semiconductor market, 1959–78*

	1959 (% in volume)	1968 (% in volume)	1978 (% in value)
NEC	15	7	20
Hitachi	15	23	17
Toshiba	26	21	14
Matsushita	16	15	8
Mitsubishi	2	3	7
Kobe Kogyo	5	3 }	} 4
Fujitsu	1	2 }	
Tokyo Sanyo	2	13	4
Sony	11	2	2
Sharp			6
Oki			3
Others	5	2	3(a)
Imports	2	10	13(a)
4 biggest producers	72	66	59
8 biggest producers	93	81	77

(a) Texas Instruments accounts for around 3.5 % of the market, of which 2.5 % is produced in Japan and 1 % imported.
    Source: Truel (1980, p. 87).

SOURCES Tilton (1971); Truel (1980); Nomura (1980).

(a) a sufficient financial strength capable of financing heavy research investment and prolonged losses, and, (b) some kind of strong behavioural rule of the kind: 'You must be in the high technology, high growth areas, because this is where your markets and your profits will be in the long run, irrespective of present profitability calculations'.

Learning Effects and Market Pre-emption

Mirroring what has just been said, a crucial feature of the industry, which corresponds to the illustrative model suggested in the previous section of this chapter, concerns the *differential advantages* accruing to early comers (i.e. innovators or fast imitators). These differential advantages relate to (a) 'learning effects' and (b) 'pre-emption effects' of the potential markets.

Both elements are well established in semiconductor literature,[188] and the reader can find there an exhaustive treatment supported by case studies of individual firms.

As is known, the 'learning effect' refers to the inverse relationship between unit cost of production and cumulated volumes of output, on the basis of an *unchanged* capital-embodied technology. Most of the literature on semiconductors, however, adopts a definition of 'learning curve', generally borrowed from managerial economics, which actually includes (a) proper learning effects, (b) economies of scale, and (c) proper technical progress. The resulting concept of 'learning curve' is an impressionistic measure of the dynamic combination of these three factors.[189] On the other hand, the difficulties of an exact measurement of the proper 'learning' are overwhelming:[190] the most satisfactory attempt to measure it is in Webbick (1977), although his estimates are not exempt from the previously mentioned drawbacks.[191] The good correlation coefficients of his estimates are not at all surprising: technical progress (whenever not extremely discontinuous) is associated with time and so are cumulative volumes of production. Moreover, economies of scale (related to the rates of output per unit of time) are also associated with cumulated output.[192] In a case like this, any attempt to distinguish between the different sources of *lato sensu* technical progress becomes quite difficult and econometrics is not of great help, for multicollinearity problems are likely to arise[193] (leaving aside the lack of appropriate data). All this notwithstanding, estimates of the relationship between costs (or prices) and cumulated quantities for the whole industry or broad categories of products maintain their power as a descriptive synthesis.

Another possible attempt to measure the effect of changes in output on changes in productivity is by the estimate of the 'Verdoorn–Kaldor equation', relating percentage increases in output and percentage increases in productivity.[194] This is yet another 'synthetic measure' which summarises (a) economies of scale on existing plants, (b) different degrees of utilisation of the labour force which is often a 'quasi-fixed' factor, (c) 'short-run' dynamic economies, (d) effects on productivity of the new vintage investments. Some attempts to estimate the relationship, on time series of American data referring to the whole semiconductor industry yield very poor results:[195] the instability of the relationship suggests that in a sector where technical change is rapid, radical and only partly embodied in capital equipment, proportional changes in productivity may take place in ways independent of short-run changes in output and fixed investment.[196]

This result, if applicable also to other high technology sectors, is remarkable: it shows the importance of that part of technical change which is disembodied from capital equipment. The result *per se* is far from denying the existence of a 'Verdoorn–Kaldor' law. However, it highlights a difference between innovative sectors and more mature ones. The former are likely to constitute a rather small, although crucial part of the manufacturing sector. Conversely, with respect to the latter, the Verdoorn–Kaldor relation actually captures the diffusion of innovations embodied in equipment which is often manufactured by or indirectly related to the 'innovative' industries.

Finally, attempts to estimate proper static economies of scale by plant size, for the American industry, show rather unsatisfactory results on 1967 data, while suggesting the existence of relevant static economies of scale in 1972.[197] According to our estimates, each doubling of plant size (in the early seventies) produced an increase of 8–9 per cent in productivity per man-hours. This is in accordance with the hypothesis, confirmed by various interviews, that in the last decade also static economies of scale have become relevant (and will be even more so in the future).[198]

To summarise: the quantitative evidence available on the semiconductor industry appears to be consistent with the existence (suggested by most experts and analysts of the industry) of very pronounced learning economies. The interlinkage between 'learning economies', technical progress and proper economies of scale, does not allow a more precise quantification of the 'learning coefficient'. Even if it certainly is below the 30 per cent elasticity of the 'synthetic learning curve' which often appears in the literature, it is nonetheless significantly high. This implies that the 'dynamic entry barriers' described in the previous sections are operating powerfully, as all the qualitative studies on the industry suggest. Moreover, one must take into account the more recent (and increasing) importance of size-related economies of scale.

One also faces serious difficulties in trying to define in precise quantitative terms the 'pre-emption' effects of early comers on markets opened up by the technological potential and new possible uses of the innovative products. In order to test the hypothesis precisely, one would need a very disaggregated breakdown of the semiconductor market by products, the date of their first introduction, the companies which did it, and their market shares. Unfortunately, this detailed set of data is not generally available, so that one has to rely on more impressionistic and qualitative evidence. Few examples, however, may be quoted. On general grounds, there is sufficient evidence of the pre-emption effect on the European market induced by American companies,[199] allowed by the existence of (on average) sufficiently high technological lags between American and European companies. On a more disaggregate level, one can cite the relatively high market share of Texas Instruments in the TTL family of ICs – 41 per cent of the world market in 1970 and around 25 per cent in 1980, which is significantly higher than its rather stable world share in the total semiconductor market (around 12 per cent). TI was responsible for the first introduction of the TTL family of ICs and for several innovations inside that technology (Schottky TTL, etc.). Another example is the very high market share of Motorola in ECL circuits (a percentage of world market always well above 30 per cent in the period 1970–7).

In actual fact, it quite often happens that a small group of companies are all near the innovation frontier and introduce a new device at almost the same time. Clearly in these cases our model can easily account for their market leadership – of the group as a whole – but is not meant to explain the factors of differential success of each company belonging to the group. This will depend on the commercial strategies of each firm, the specific characteristic of each product, etc.

The picture is further complicated by the phenomenon of second sourcing: as already mentioned, it is fairly common for an innovative firm to allow other firms to manufacture a new product, often in exchange for a percentage royalty on sales. Second sourcing (a) responds to a requirement of the users, who prefer to have more than one source of supply; (b) from the point of view of the innovator, is part of a market penetration strategy, especially in the case of different competing proprietors' products which strive to become the industry standard, and

(c) sometimes, the innovator makes virtue out of necessity, since other firms might be capable of imitating the new product anyhow. Second sourcing is relatively more important for small innovative firms which start from a narrow market base rather than big firms which already have a wide foothold in the market.

With these considerations in mind, let us examine again concentration ratios. Their relatively high level and stability through time militates in favour of a market pre-emption hypothesis: the innovative companies become leaders in markets which are, at least partly, created *ex novo* by the innovations themselves, and maintain relatively high market shares thereafter. The hypothesis is also supported by the fact that concentration ratios tend to increase with the level of product disaggregation. We may consider at greater length the case of microprocessors and single-chip microcomputers. DATAQUEST, the previously cited American industry analyst, subdivides the market into four segments (very low-end, low-end, mid-range, high-end)[200] according to costs and the performance of the products (which is closely related to the length of the 'word' the microprocessor handles, i.e. 4–bit, 8–bit, 16–bit). Within each segment, concentration is high or very high (well above the semiconductor average) and bears a significant relationship with the group of companies which have been active innovators (such as Intel, Texas Instruments, Motorola, Zilog, General Instruments) or quick imitators (such as Nippon Electric). In the segment characterised by the *lowest* degrees of concentration (the mid-range market) the first four producers accounted in 1980 for around 47 per cent of world markets.[201] The leaders were three innovators (Motorola, Zilog, and Intel) and one aggressive imitator (Nippon Electric). In the other segments of the market, 4–firm world concentration ratios ranged between 80 per cent and marginally below 100 per cent. The case of Intel, in particular, is worth considering. That firm was the first to introduce the microprocessor and is still one of the market leaders in all the mentioned segments apart from the very low-end one (its overall world market share in MOS microprocessors for 1980 was estimated by DATAQUEST at round 23 per cent),[202] and this is despite the fact that a good number of firms have second-sourced Intel microprocessors.[203] A rough estimate of the total market share of microprocessors based on Intel technology is around double Intel's share.

In passing, note that Intel, a new innovative company operating to a great extent on the technological frontier and with a market leadership in several innovative products, enjoys margins and profits significantly higher than the average. The average ratio of pre-tax profits to sales during the period 1977–80 has been 19.2 per cent, which compares, for example, with a corresponding ratio of 5.7 per cent for Texas Instrument (which is itself the leading semiconductor company and a market leader in many products).

The Stability of Margins and the Role of Demand

The structural features of the semiconductor industry appear to correspond to the conditions outlined on pp. 122–42 of this chapter as possible determinants of oligopolistic prices (technological lags, learning effects, economies of scale, pre-emption of the market by 'early comers', etc.).

We must try to assess whether those structural conditions determine oligopolistic pricing behaviours. The hypothesis of stable mark-ups over variable cost (at least in the short run) will be tested against the 'competitive hypothesis' of price fluctuations (relative to costs) in relation to short-run fluctuation in demand.[204]

The theoretical status of the test requires a close scrutiny. The mark-up hypothesis actually implies the joint existence of two phenomena:

1. Firms in the industry (at least some of them) do have the oligopolistic power of fixing prices. In other words, the price is not determined through auction-like procedures but is directly fixed by some price-making firms. This broadly corresponds to what we have defined above as the 'weak oligopolistic hypothesis'.

2. The price-making criteria are such that fluctuations in demand only yield to corresponding changes in produced quantities without an effect on prices.

It is important to notice that point 2 is *sufficient but not necessary* in order for point 1 to be true. In other words, if fluctuations in demand do not affect price levels, then certainly the industry is characterised by some price-making oligopolistic power. The reverse is not necessarily true since firms with oligopolistic power might fix their price with some other criteria sensitive to demand.[205] For example, a neoclassical maximiser will change its prices in relation to demand fluctuations (if the marginal cost curve is not flat), since changes in the demand curve (for the industry and for each firm) will also change the marginal revenue curve for each firm and its intercept with marginal costs. Another possibility is a pricing criterion which tends to stabilise the *rate* of profit on the invested capital throughout the cycle, so that margins are set in an *inverse* function of demand fluctuations.[206]

Our long discussion on the structural determinants of oligopolistic margins, however, supports an empirical prediction of a *fixed* mark-up throughout the business-cycle, since we may expect the inter-firm asymmetries which lead to these margins to be stable in the short run.

Our model does not rule out *medium-term* changes in the 'normal' level of margins, but predicts that they should be independent from market conditions and should be a function of the process of technological innovation and imitation. We would expect that the lower inter-firm differences are, in terms of innovative capability and unit cost,[207] the nearer should margins be to some 'competitive' level, and vice versa. In other words, *oligopolistic margins capture the degree of private appropriability of technology and the relative balance between innovation and imitation*. There is also the corollary that we would expect a degree of long-run stability of margins higher in 'mature' sectors[208] than in new sectors characterised by a high rate of technical change and discontinuities in the innovative process. This hypothesis, with its corollary, may be considered a (modified) reformulation of the 'Schumpeterian' hypothesis on the long-run 'withering away' of innovation-based 'super-profits'. We can state it in the following way: *whenever, (a) the rate of imitation overtakes the rate of innovation, and (b) no other inter-firm discontinuity (such as size-related economies of scale) emerges, then, both inter-firm asymmetries and entry barriers will tend to decrease and, with them, also oligopolistic margins and profit rates.*[209]

One should rigorously test the model at a very disaggregate level, for each product or products group, corresponding to each relatively homogenous market. Unfortunately, the appropriate series of data is not available. One has therefore to investigate the relationship price/costs at industry level.[210] The required indices of output and prices, and the value added deflator had to be constructed by the author.[211] A certain number of relatively 'heroic' assumptions had to be made in order to derive those indices. This fact must suggest an additional degree of caution in the interpretation of the results, even if — in our view — it is not likely to undermine the main conclusions.

A mark-up pricing procedure would lead to an equation of the form:

$$P = f\left(\frac{w}{\pi}, m\right) \qquad\qquad 24$$

with p = price, w = direct labour costs, π = productivity (i.e. value added at constant prices per hour of direct labour), and m = unit cost of materials.

A 'competitive pricing' hypothesis would lead to an equation of the form:

$$P = f\left(\frac{w}{\pi}, m, d\right) \quad \text{with} \quad f'(d) > 0 \qquad\qquad 25$$

where d is some proxy of the level of demand.[212] Table 3.16 shows the results of regression analysis of prices on variable costs and demand levels.

For practical reasons, the estimates have been conducted on yearly data, without allowing for time lags, thus assuming *actual* yearly wage rates and productivity levels as the 'normal' ones. Given the fast rate of change in productivity and technology, this does not appear to be a serious drawback, for the horizon on which firms fix a certain price is rather short. Moreover, from the model defined above, one would expect 'forecasted costs' to play a role at least as great as 'present' costs (not to speak of past costs): this rules out any important direct influence of time lags. On the other hand, the way expectations are formed is extremely difficult to assess.[213] The assumption that, in general and *on the average*, the forecasts made by the firms on a limited time horizon (one year) are *nearly* correct, appears to be a good approximation.

The results of the estimates seem to be consistent with a mark-up pricing procedure. Even overlooking estimates 1 and 2 (whose extremely good correlation coefficients may be imputed to the existence of strong time trends in both the dependent and independent variables), estimate 3, formulated in $\Delta \log s$[214] shows a satisfactory correlation between levels of costs and prices ($R^2 = 0.59$). The independent variable coefficient is significant at 1 per cent level. When a proxy of demand levels is added, its coefficient appears either not significantly different from zero (estimate 5) or significant and *negative* (estimate 4).[215] Both cases, of (a) no influence of demand on prices, or, (b) an *anti-cyclical* behaviour of prices (with respect to costs), would certainly fall inside an oligopolistic determination of prices (as opposed to a 'free competitive' one). The former case would represent the mark-up hypothesis *stricto sensu*, as outlined in the previous section, while the latter would suggest that market leaders vary their mark-up in an inverse relation to the growth of output, possibly in the light of two considerations:

1. It is likely that, during slumps in demand, the incentive to enter decreases and, conversely, during booms, it increases.
2. Firms, in fixing their unit margins, might also take into account some

TABLE 3.16 Estimates of gross margin in the semiconductor industry, 1958–76

Dependent variable	Constant	Independent variable(s)	Years of estimation	R^2	DW
1. p	16.84 $(4.90)^{**}$	$+0.72\ (W/\pi)$ $(0.006)^{**}$	1958, 1963–76	0.99	0.84
2. $\log p$ =	0.67 $(0.02)^{**}$	$+1.01\ \log\left(\dfrac{W}{\pi}+m\right)$ $(0.03)^{**}$	1958, 1963–76	0.99	1.30
3. $\Delta \log p$ =	-0.07 $(0.03)^{**}$	$+0.59\ \Delta \log\left(\dfrac{W}{\pi}+m\right)$ $(0.15)^{**}$	1962–76	0.59	1.50
4. $\Delta \log p$ =	-0.004 (0.03)	$+0.51\ \Delta \log\left(\dfrac{W}{\pi}+m\right)\ -0.24\ \Delta \log D$ $(0.10)^{**}\qquad\ (0.06)^{**}$	1964–76	0.81	1.24
5. $\Delta \log p$ =	-0.07 (0.03)	$+0.52\ \Delta \log\left(\dfrac{W}{\pi}+m\right)\ -0.01\ \Delta \log\left(\dfrac{\Delta D}{D}+20\right)$ $(0.17)^{*}\qquad\ (0.04)$	1965–76	0.52	1.13

NOTES

Standard errors in parenthesis; DW = Durbin Watson statistics; * significant at 5% level; ** significant at 1% level.

P = unit prices; w = production workers hourly wages; π = productivity of direct labour per manhour; m = unit material costs; D = shipments (at constant prices).

(a) estimation in equations 3 and 4 are made on the period 1963–76, for the lack of comparable data for 1959–62.

(b) in order to estimate equation 5, in logarithmic form, we had to increase all the percentage changes in demand $\left(\dfrac{\Delta D}{D}\right)$ by 20%.

This affects both the coefficient on the independent variable and the intercept, but there is no a priori reason to expect that it should bias the significance of the variable.

SOURCE as Table 3.6 and elaborations (cf. Appendix I).

target rate of profit (on invested capital), so that they try to vary unit margins to stabilise as much as possible their rate of returns on a capital stock, which, in the short run, is fixed.[216]

On this question, our econometric tests are inconclusive: part of the good fit of the variable expressing percentage variation in shipments (with a negative sign in estimate 4) may be due to some collinearity between demand growth and costs decreases (via learning curve); however, an anti-cyclical behaviour of profit *margins* may actually be due to the attempt of stabilising as much as possible profit *rates*. Such a pricing routine is still perfectly consistent with the general model outlined in the first part of this chapter: it is simply a different behavioural procedure of exploiting the degrees of freedom allowed (and bounded) by the pattern of inter-firm asymmetries.

If variations in prices (relative to costs) are easier for market leaders than for price-taking firms, this would yield a variance in profit rates during the cycle inversely related to the size of the firms (with the exception of small innovative firms which are leaders on their 'new markets'). The scarce data on the subject would tend to confirm this hypothesis (see Table 3.20).[217]

It is interesting to notice that in all the above estimates there is no sign of the 'cut throat' price competition which is often mentioned in describing the semiconductor industry. Of course, one cannot deny the existence of a fierce competition in the industry; simply, it appears to act more through innovation, exploitation of new markets, search of new applications rather than through violent fluctuations in price/cost margins. Moreover, what has just been said does not mean that the continuous fall in prices is not felt as a major threatening factor by the producers whose average costs are above those of market leaders (e.g. by most of European producers). This price fall, however, may occur, as we tried to show above, even in an oligopolistic structure, while prices for market leaders are stable with respect to costs.[218] It might well be that on a more disaggregate level, prices would show a lower stability and would retain some signs of the 'price wars'[219] recorded in the history of the semiconductor industry. Nonetheless, it is already significant that on aggregate level there is no sign of demand/supply – induced variations in price levels: it appears extremely unlikely that the result is simply the exact statistical compensation of 'excess supply' in some sub-markets and 'excess demand' in other sub-markets.[220] It is worth noticing that the apparent inexistence of those "market clearing mechanisms" suggested by traditional microeconomic theory occurs despite very violent cyclical fluctuation in demand, much greater than those

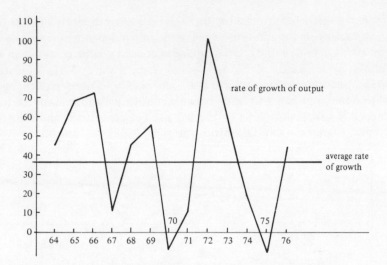

FIGURE 3.4   *Rates of growth of output (at constant prices)*

SOURCE   as Table 3.6 and elaborations

undergone by the aggregate manufacturing output (see Figure 3.4).
Certainly some reservations and a lot of caution are suggested by the
poorness of the data on which the calculations are made. So, we would
not presume to say that the estimated coefficients are the 'true' ones. We
would be very surprised, however, if the main results of the estimates
were just a 'statistical aberration', a pure effect of the way the series of
data has been constructed.

An additional corroboration of the hypothesis of the existence of
powerful sources of oligopolistic positions in the industry stems from
the existence of significant differences in profitability between big firms,
on the one hand, and small–medium firms, on the other hand: as shown
in Table 3.20, for the period 1970–5, net income as a percentage of
stockholders' equity was on average 15.2 per cent for the firms with
more than $100 million sales, 3.97 per cent for medium firms ($25–100
million sales) and 4.98 per cent for small firms (below $25 per cent
sales).

Entries, Capital Intensity and Long-run Changes in Profit Margins

The considered statistical evidence seems to rule out the 'competitive
hypothesis' which implies also a direct influence of short-run fluctuations of demand on prices. The levels of mark-ups with respect to costs

appear, nonetheless, to change through time independently of changes in variable costs (in addition to being roughly independent from short-run changes in demand). Gross margins (over variable costs) seem to follow some kind of 'long cycles' (see Figure 3.5) unrelated to short-run demand variations, but – more likely – linked with changes in technological lags and leads between innovative and imitative firms, entries of new firms, shifts in the balance between direct and indirect labour, changes in capital/output ratios.[221]

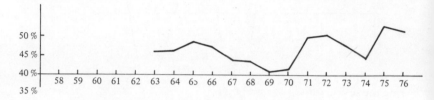

FIGURE 3.5   *Gross margins over variable costs*

SOURCE   as Table 3.6 and elaborations

Those 'long cycles' show a decline in the second half of the sixties and an increasing trend in the first half of the seventies (notably the maximum is in 1975, a year of deep depression). Trying to estimate precisely the impact of the various possible factors on the 'long-run' changes in gross and net margins, given the available data on the industry, would be like guessing the exact shape of an elephant starting from some knowledge of the form of its tail. It is possible, however, to make a few remarks about the factors which might influence them. As far as new entries are concerned, the peak was reached in the late sixties: this might be one of the causes of declining unit gross and net margins over the same period. As we tried to show in the first part of this chapter, entry barriers, 'limit prices', etc. are *relative* concepts which draw a line within a set of existing and potential producers, ranked according to their innovative capabilities and unit costs of production. Thus, entries may be considered a somewhat stochastic function of (a) the technological innovativeness of potential entrants (i.e. their distance from the technological frontier), (b) prices on existing products, (c) possibilities of finding new end-user markets (i.e. some kind of product differentiation). If there are many would-be entrants which are not very far from the frontier (as defined in Chapter 2) and many potential markets to exploit, entries are likely to occur, even if existing firms practise an 'entry-deterring price'. The number of firms 'on the frontier'

TABLE 3.17   *Number of companies in the semiconductor*
industry — USA, 1963–72

Year	Number of companies
1963	86
1967	141
1972	282

Semiconductor: SIC code 3674
SOURCE   *US Census of Manufactures*, various years.

and the distance of all other firms from that same frontier bear a clear
relevance for the margins enjoyed by the industry.

As previously noted, the rate of new entry has been bottoming out
during the seventies. On the other hand, 'side entry' by established firms
has increased. In so far as the latter develop semiconductor productive
facilities mainly for in-house use, however, the two kinds of entries
might have had quite different impacts on prices and margins: only the
former is likely to have some significant de-stabilising effects on 'normal'
profit margins. A similar argument applies to 'silicon foundries' which
operate on a very differentiated custom market.

Another possible reason for 'long-run' changes in unit margins might
have been a shifting balance between direct and indirect labour:
if firms set their prices through a cost–plus procedure on variable
costs, a relative shift in the composition of the workforce in
favour of indirect labour, should imply, other things being equal, an
increase in gross margins, to compensate the changing balance of costs.
As shown in Table 3.19, the semiconductor industry manifested a
pronounced trend towards the relative diminution of direct workers,
especially after the mid-sixties.

A third factor which may affect unit margins can be found in the state
of international competition. So far, our discussion of pricing dynamics
in the semiconductor industry has been conducted on the American
industry as if the latter were a closed economy. The American industry,
as discussed in Chapter 2, has been enjoying until recently a considerable
technological and manufacturing lead. Most of the competitive pressures which could check a certain profit level of market leaders were
likely to emerge *inside* the USA itself rather than from foreign
competitors. As will be discussed in greater detail in Chapter 4,
competition with foreign companies occurred mainly *in foreign markets*.
The existence of an increasingly unified world market affected the

TABLE 3.18 *Gross margins and net earnings after taxes as a percentage of sales,*
1964–77

| | Semiconductors | | All manufacturing |
| | (1) | (2) | (3) |
Year	Gross margins as a % of sales	Net earnings as a % of sales	Net earnings as a % of sales
1964	46.8	5.2	5.2
1965	48.5	5.9	5.6
1966	47.4	5.3	5.6
1967	43.5	3.6	5.0
1968	43.3	3.4	5.1
1969	40.6	3.2	4.8
1970	41.5	1.1	4.0
1971	49.9	2.7	4.2
1972	50.1	5.0	4.3
1973	47.5	7.4	4.7
1974	44.7	6.1	5.5
1975	52.8	3.9	4.6
1976	51.9	5.4	5.4
1977		5.1	5.3
14-year average 1964–77		4.5	5.0

(1) Margins over variable costs as a percentage of sales.
(2) Net earnings after taxes as a percentage of sales.

SOURCES US Department of Commerce (1979, p. 57) and elaborations on *US Census of Manufacturers* and *Annual Survey of Manufacturers*, various years.

structure and strategies of foreign industries much more than the American one. Recently the situation has changed: the Japanese entry into the American market, made possible by their success in the catching-up effort (both on technological and manufacturing grounds) introduces an additional variable in our analysis of prices and margins in the American market. Its effect, however, is unlikely to appear in the available series of data which stops at 1976. We shall discuss the question of American–Japanese competition below.

Finally, another possible factor, affecting the long-run variation in gross (and net) margins relates to variation in capital/output ratios. It is worth undertaking a fairly detailed analysis of this variable, for it also bears direct implications in terms of macroeconomic impact of technical

TABLE 3.19 *Employment in the US semiconductor industry, 1954–76*

Year	Total ('000s)	Production workers as a % of total
1954	4.3	58
1956	11.2	na
1958	23.4	75
1959	36.5	77
1960	52.6	68
1961	53.2	66
1962	53.1	64
1963	56.3	67
1964	55.3	69
1965	67.4	72
1966	82.2	72
1967	85.4	68
1968	87.4	69
1969	98.8	70
1970	88.5	68
1971	74.7	61
1972	97.6	60
1973	120.0	62
1974	133.1	61
1975	96.7	54
1976	102.5	56

SOURCE US Department of Commerce (1979, p. 28).

progress.[222] *Vis-à-vis* changes in the capital/output ratio, margins tend to be readjusted in order to achieve the new 'equilibrium' mark-up compatible with the existing asymmetries (as defined in the previous section). Technological asymmetries jointly with behavioural pricing rules define a vector of profit rates, corresponding to each firm in the industry. If the capital/output ratio changes, margins – we suggest – are readjusted to keep this vector of profit rates unchanged.

Note that capital/output ratios depend on both the amount of 'physical' capital required per unit of 'physical' output and on the relative price of capital goods *vis-à-vis* the produced goods. Thus, changes in the ratio are a function of:

1. *Process*- related technical progress in the production of *capital goods* which tend to lower the unit price of capital equipment.
2. *Product*-related technical progress in *capital goods* which tend to lower the amount of 'physical' capital required per unit of final output.

3. Technical progress in the equipment-using sector which tends to lower both the 'physical' capital/output ratio, and the price of the final commodity.

Unfortunately, we have neither the data on capital stocks, nor the specific deflator for the investment expenditure in the sector. Few very tentative remarks, however, can be made using a moving average of the investment/output ratio (I/Y), which one may heroically assume to move in the same direction as the capital/output ratio (K/Y).[223] Table 3.21 and Figure 3.6 show the series 1963–76 for I/Y (at current and constant prices), for the relative prices between investment and final goods, and an estimate of K/Y on the period 1969–76. During the sixties, I/Y followed a 'long-cycle' with a strong increase by the middle of the decade and a decreasing tendency thereafter. The seventies, on the contrary, show an increasing trend. Although precise data are not available after 1976, this tendency appears to have accelerated in the latest part of the decade.[224] Whether this is the upswing in another 'cycle' in the K/Y ratio or, vice versa, part of a long-run increasing trend, it is hard to say. Many experts support the latter hypothesis. In the past, however, it appears that each major technological advance involving a substantial increase in 'capital intensity' had been slowly compensated by capital-saving improvements and a 'learning process' which augmented the efficiency in the use of the equipment.[225] The net result was, roughly, the stability in the investment/output ratio (which might be taken as a proxy for the capital/output ratio). A strong and continuous decline in the relative price of semiconductors *vis-à-vis* the equipment utilised for their production (which expresses very different trends in labour productivity in the semiconductor and the capital good sector) has been more or less counterbalanced by capital-saving technical progress (both in terms of equipment-embodied advances and 'learning effects').[226] The semiconductor industry probably represents one of the clearest examples of the mechanisms at work in the economic system which (roughly) keep technical progress on a Harrod–neutral path: technical progress in both equipment–production and equipment–use, mechanization and automation of manufacturing activities, the related dynamics of relative prices, jointly explain that 'stylised fact' of modern economic growth.

It is extremely difficult to assess the relative importance of these factors upon long-run changes in the levels of gross and net margins. In our view, the two 'long cycles' noticeable in the level of gross margins over the past two decades (cf. figure 3.5) have to be explained by quite

TABLE 3.20 Net income after taxes as a percentage of stockholder's equity for selected US semiconductor companies, 1970–5

Year	Small companies with sales under $25 m		Medium companies with sales between $25 m and $100 m		Large companies with sales above $100 m		All sample		All manufacturing
	Number of companies	Net income as % of stockholders' equity	Number of companies	Net income as % of stockholders' equity	Number of companies	Net income as % of stockholders' equity	Total number of companies	Net income as % of stockholders' equity	Net income as % of stockholders' equity
1970	13	−2.9	6	−3.50	2	13.34	21	9.09	9.31
1971	17	−1.21	4	−520.00	2	6.70	23	−0.28	9.66
1972	22	7.63	6	3.43	2	12.93	30	10.93	10.60
1973	20	13.67	8	28.39	3	21.24	31	21.87	12.84
1974	17	13.59	9	18.18	6	18.27	32	17.97	14.83
1975	13	−4.40	11	−9.96	4	12.03	28	8.02	11.42
Six years average		4.98		3.97		15.20		12.60	11.60
Standard deviation		7.50		211.1		4.80		7.30	1.90

SOURCES Webbick (1977, p. 178) and elaborations.

TABLE 3.21 *Investment expenditure, output and estimated capital stock. US semiconductor industry, 1963–76. (Indices. 1972 = 100)*

	Total investment (at current prices) (1)	Output (at current prices) (2)	Investment–output ratio (2 yrs moving average (at current prices) (3)	Total investment (at constant prices) (4)	Output (at constant prices) (5)	Investment–output ratio (at constant prices) (2 yrs moving average) (6)	Relative price investment to output (7)	Estimated capital/output ratio (at current prices) (8)
1963	30.7	25.4		43.4	4.6		12.7	
1964	25.5	26.5	108.1	35.6	6.7	698.2	18.2	
1965	35.9	33.7	102.0	49.3	11.3	471.7	24.4	
1966	72.5	41.5	144.2	96.4	19.6	471.5	34.9	
1967	76.9	42.2	178.7	99.2	21.9	471.3	40.2	
1968	69.4	48.7	163.1	85.8	31.8	344.5	52.9	
1969	84.2	58.2	143.5	98.1	49.5	226.2	73.0	124.6
1970	57.7	55.5	124.6	63.7	45.1	171.0	73.7	143.4
1971	55.6	59.1	98.8	58.0	50.0	128.0	81.0	148.4
1972	100.0	100.0	97.8	100.0	100.0	105.3	100.0	100.0
1973	196.2	134.9	126.0	185.1	158.5	110.3	124.6	90.1
1974	281.1	159.2	162.2	236.0	189.9	120.9	142.1	102.9
1975	165.9	121.2	159.4	124.1	172.3	99.4	190.2	158.7
1976	212.5	165.4	132.0	151.6	249.5	65.4	211.8	129.5
(average yearly % changes)								
1963–70	+9.4	+11.8	−1.3	+5.6	+28.5	−21.5	+28.6	
1970–76	+29.8	+24.4	+5.9	+18.9	+40.8	−12.6	+19.2	

SOURCES Elaborations on *US Census of Manufactures* and *Annual Survey of Manufactures*, various years.
(3) and (6): Moving averages are expressed in terms of indices (1972 = 100). Average percentage changes refer to 63/64–70/71 and 70/71–75/76 periods, respectively.
(4): As a deflator we utilised the fixed investment deflator of the economy as a whole.
(5): For deflation procedures see Table 19 and Annex I.
(8): Capital stock has been estimated assuming an average depreciation time of *seven years* (see US Department of Commerce (1979)) and constant depreciation allowances over the life time of capital stock.

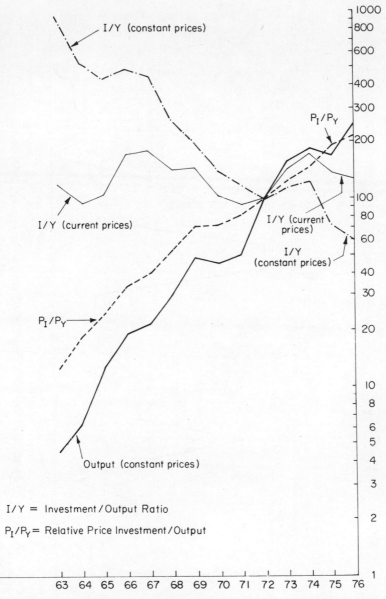

FIGURE 3.6 *Investment/output ratios (at current and constant prices), output, relative price of investment to output; indices, 1972 = 100*

SOURCE as Table 3.4

188

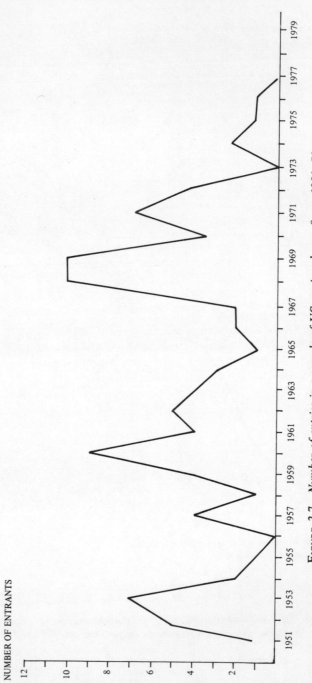

FIGURE 3.7 *Number of entries in a sample of US semiconductor firms, 1951–79*

SOURCE Elaborations by Wilson et al. (1980).

different variables. The relative increase in the mid-sixties is probably affected by:

1. The high levels of margins obtainable on the newly introduced integrated circuits.[228]
2. Possibly, the temporary increase in the capital/output ratio associated with the introduction of planar technology and generally of ICs manufacturing techniques.
3. The recovery of the industry from a situation of exogenously induced over-capacity experienced in the early part of the decade due to a government policy of building up strategic capacity in the industry.[227]

The relative decline in the margins, in the late 1960s/early 1970s, is associated with the considerable number of entries which occurred in that period in the American market, together with the relative shift of demand for the most advanced devices from the military to civilian markets.[229]

The reader is invited to compare Fig. 3.7 with Fig. 3.5. Throughout the history of the industry there is some correspondence between the sheer number of entries and changes in average gross margins. Note that historically waves of entry appear to stem from two distinct phenomena, namely, (a) a major technological breakthrough (i.e. the transistor, the planar process with the associated integrated circuit, the microprocessor), and (b) a lagged effect of a former major breakthrough, after five to ten years, associated with improvements and 'derived' innovations based on a well-established basic technology.

Finally, the increase in gross margins throughout the mid–late 1970s is probably affected by augmented 'static' barriers to entry, together with a significant increase in marginal (and average) capital/output ratios.

The Cowboy and the Samurai, or Investment in Different Institutional Contexts

In recent years (especially 1979–80) firms have put an increasing stress on cash flow and profit targets rather than 'growth' targets: they claim they are forced to do so by increasing cost of investments.[230] Many American firms suggest that over the same period (1978–80) they have been somewhat supply-constrained, because of a lack of sufficient internally generated funds to finance expansion.[231] If this happened to be a widespread phenomenon within the industry, it would also imply that firms define a rather rigid constraint on their debt/own capital ratio (and at a rather low level). Available data appears to confirm it (see Table 3.22).[232] More than a 'structural' feature of the system, however, this appears to be a behavioural regularity of American capitalism (and, before it, the English one). It is of some interest to observe the competitive interaction between the American semiconductor industry and the Japanese one, which appears to be aggressively oriented towards the maximum rate of expansion without any self-inflicted financial constraint on investments. Unfortunately, this is not the place to analyse the very complex issue of the political economy of growth in different industrial countries. We hope that the reader will nonetheless forgive us for few untested remarks and suggestions. (We shall come back in a more organic way to the structure of international markets in the following chapter).

In order to illustrate the difference between Japanese and American investment behaviours, let us imagine two national industries (say, two national semiconductor industries), characterised by the same technological levels, the same wage rates and the same rates of profit, which differ only in investment behaviours. The first industry invests on some kind of modified 'accelerator' pattern so that, at any time, the amount of net investment is a function of *both* recent changes in production and a trend value of production growth. The second industry invests as a

TABLE 3.22   *Financial structure of semiconductor and all manufacturing industry, 1969–77 (%)*

Year	Equity Semicond.	All M.	Long-term debt Semicond.	All M.	Short-term debt Semicond.	All M.
1969	70	72	29	22	1	6
1970	69	71	28	23	3	6
1971	70	71	28	24	2	5
1972	75	71	21	24	4	6
1973	80	71	18	23	2	6
1974	78	71	14	23	8	6
1975	83	72	13	24	9	4
1976	82	73	11	23	7	4
1977	85	72	10	24	5	4
9-year average	77	72	19	23	4	5

SOURCE   US Department of Commerce (1979, p. 56).

function of past and present profits.[233] Suppose also that total profits are a positive function of demand cycles and that the latter are very pronounced. The second industry will face recurrent overcapacities and capacity shortages, while the first is more likely to experience 'smooth' capacity cycles. Imagine that the first industry captures additional market shares when the second is supply-constrained and keeps them thereafter. Even without formally solving the corresponding system of finite differences equations, one can see intuitively that the first industry is slowly going to capture the entire market. The trend would obviously be accelerated if, other things being equal, the first industry accepts a 'normal' rate of profit which is lower than the second.

This is an extreme example, but it is useful to highlight one aspect of American–Japanese competition in the second half of the 1970s and in the early 1980s.[234] Why this can happen in the real world relates to the 'institutional degrees of freedom', for given structural conditions, which have been stressed many times. Institutional behaviours often relate to factors that are 'unspeakable' from a strictly economic point of view. In another work,[235] we attempt some analysis of the relationship between government and companies in Japan and of the 'growth-orientation' in Japanese companies induced by the system of lifetime employment.[236] Let us mention another factor, without any attempt to test its relevance. It might well be that, other things being equal, 'shortsightedness' in investment behaviour is a direct function of the development of financial markets.[237] In other words, the more firms rely on the stock market for their funds, the higher is their short-run profit constraint and the lower is their maximum leverage ratio. This should not be surprising, the 'Modigliani–Miller Theorem' notwithstanding.[238] Only the fantastic financial investor of the textbook knows (or believes to know) the future and accounts for his/her expectations correspondingly. In actual fact the stock markets are, loosely speaking, the economic environment which is nearest to 'instantaneous' profit-maximisation, concerned, as they are, with more or less volatile gambles on 'making money here and now'. Conversely, this environment may be compared with structured institutions (such as Japanese industrial banks, or for that matter, German banks at the turn of the century), 'whose business is financing growth'.

The behavioural difference might be even greater if we consider various ways in which the individual performance is assessed and rewarded under the two systems of relations between the financial and industrial sectors. While the archetypical stock exchange operator behaves under the pure capitalist rule of 'making money', the archetypical representative of a Japanese 'industrial–financial complex' appears, to a dilettante in sociology – as we are – to incorporate the interests of the national *gesamtkapital* as part of its fundamental rules of behaviour, criteria of assessment and power status. These observations are strictly 'unscientific': however, they should warn about the import-ance of the relations between the economic system, *stricto sensu*, and the socio–political context. The degrees of freedom which companies' behaviours maintain are filled by the institutional regularities which define the particular 'rationality' of each society, even within the broad context of the common fundamental rules of the game of capitalist systems. Moreover, the extreme archetypes suggested above – which are, as such, almost a caricature – hint at the very real possibility of conflicts and trade-offs between static efficiency and dynamic efficiency of the system, and at the weakness of short-run profitability in signalling modes of conduct which are only efficient in the long-run, in terms of growth and innovativeness.

3.5 CONCLUSIONS

Oligopoly and Economic Dynamics

In the process of growth of a new industry such as semiconductors, a crucial role is played by technical change in upsetting established oligopolistic positions, opening up new market possibilities, giving rise to new (more or less temporary) oligopolistic equilibria. In Chapter 2, we attempted to analyse the patterns of technical change defining a concept of 'technological trajectories', related to 'technological para-digms', with significant similarities to what modern epistemology defines as *scientific paradigms* or *research programmes*. There, it was stressed also that those technological trajectories are by no means 'given by the engineers' alone: we tried to show that they are the final outcome of a complex interaction between some fundamental economic factors (search for new profit opportunities and for new markets, tendencies toward cost-saving and automation, etc.) together with powerful institutional factors (the interests and structure of existing firms, the effects of government bodies, the patterns of social conflict, etc). In the light of the discussion of this chapter, some additional features of the process of interaction between technological innovative activity and the economic structure can be defined. First, as already mentioned, the more a fundamental technological pattern becomes established, the more the mechanism of generation of innovations and technological advances appears to become endogenous to the 'normal' economic mechanisms. In this respect the possibility of enjoying temporary monopolistic (and long-run oligopolistic) positions on new products and processes appears to act as a powerful incentive to the innovative activity, the development of new applications, and the improvement of existing products. The prospective differential advantages accruing to successful technological and market leaders, as we argued, are likely to influence and stimulate the process of innovation much more than the *ex ante* market structure as such. The process of innovation itself is, of course, bound to affect the industry structure and shape its transformation. In the overview of the structural evolution of the industry, one observed the emergence, especially in the first two decades of history of the industry, of 'Schumpeterian' companies, often associated with the introduction of new products. It is worth noticing that this kind of entry appears to be related to the first stages of development of new technologies (both in terms of individual products and of broad 'technological paradigms').

We have often mentioned that one of the necessary conditions for the Silicon Valley-type of entry has been the overwhelmingly 'people-embodied' nature of technology. The process of establishing a certain technological path appears to imply, broadly speaking, a trend towards the increasing *incorporation of technology into capital-equipment* and into *complex institutions* (like big firms). In the semiconductor industry one is still very far from the completion of this process. What one can already observe is the emergence of 'static' barriers to entry and the increase of the minimum scale of production, associated with increasing levels of automation of production, assembling and testing. 'Disembodied technology', however, keeps (and will keep for rather a long time) its crucial role. The present 'dual' nature of technology (both equipment–embodied and 'people–embodied') tends to hinder the emergence of new innovating firms (owing to the former feature).

This factor supports the hypothesis that, in the late seventies and early eighties, one is observing a process of *maturing of the international semiconductor oligopoly*. Probably, we are just at the beginning of this process. Even at this early stage, however, the major challenges to the stability of this international oligopolistic structure come (apart from the relative technological and manufacturing success of the various companies) from *side-entry* by already established firms either operating in related downstream sectors or trying to diversify into electronics, instead of 'innovative entries'.

The process of stabilisation of a fundamental technological pattern and the relative stabilisation of the structure of supply appear to be significantly linked with each other. Whenever technical progress tends to follow an established and widely recognised pattern, it is more likely that existing companies can capitalise on their previous technological experiences and 'internalise' the related benefits. This is not to say, of course, that from then onwards the structure of the industry becomes ossified. There continues to be more successful companies and less successful ones, side-entries, and adjustment pressures from different sources with a different impact on each company and each national industry. Moreover, there might well be new 'technological trajectories' emerging with the reshaping process starting again. It is useful, however, to draw a distinction between an early stage of emergence of a technology and an industry (or an industrial activity) and the subsequent period when the industry proceeds, at least partly, *juxta propria principia.* One could define the first phase as the proper 'Schumpeterian' one.[239] In this phase of *trials and errors,* as one tried to show above, a primary importance must be attributed to (a) the *institutions* which produce and direct the accumulation of knowledge, experience, etc., and (b) the existence of a multiplicity of risk-taking actors, ready to try different technical and commercial solutions. (The 'Schumpeterian' features properly refer to this second aspect.) In the second phase (one could call it the *oligopolistic maturity*), the production and the commercial exploitation of technical advances are much less divorced, and technical change itself becomes part of the patterns of 'oligopolistic competition'. Note that a 'competitive market', with its traditional decentralised features, with plurality of risk-takers and decision-makers, etc., appears to be crucial in capitalist economies, essentially in the first stage, and in relation to the diffusion and 'commercial testing' of technological advances. The process through which technical change becomes 'internalised' inside the company sector appears to induce also the disappearance of the fluid market structure characterised by the 'heroic entrepreneurship' often described in the literature.

Moreover, one interesting result of the analysis of this chapter concerns the relationship between this process of technological and structural change, on the one hand, and income distribution on the other hand. Even if the sources of oligopolistic positions differ structurally in the two described phases, both show some. While in the first phase (to which our data on the semiconductor industry basically refers) oligopolistic positions mainly relate to *dynamic* economies and temporary asymmetries, amongst firms and national industries, with respect to the ever-changing technological frontiers, in the stage of oligopolistic maturity, oligopolistic asymmetries tend to relate also, with greater stability, to some kind of *static* entry barriers.

In our rather impressionistic distinction between the two stages in the development of an industry, it is impossible to establish whether, in the transition from one stage to the other, the levels of margins and profits would systematically increase or decrease. Their trends are likely to depend on the variables discussed in the section beginning on p. 111 of this chapter (innovative lags and leads, learning economies, rates of technical change, static economies of scale, etc.).

The full range of transmission mechanisms of technical progress throughout the economy will be briefly considered in Chapter 5. One aspect, however, has already been discussed in this chapter. Even if technical change continuously allows more or less temporary oligopolistic positions, this same fact does not prevent permanent changes in the structure of relative prices, thus affecting the levels and rates of diffusion of the various commodities in consumption or in the user sectors.

The picture emerging from Chapters 2 and 3 suggests, not surprisingly, that oligopoly, in quite different forms, is the dominant form of economic organisation. With respect to it, the main analytical question does not appear to be whether oligopolistic market structures are more or less conducive to technical change than 'free competitive' ones, but, more importantly, *how* new would-be oligopolies, based on new technologies, are going to substitute for old ones. We hope that what we have said does not give the impression of underestimating the role of competition in capitalist economies: simply the set of incentives and constraints that the existence of oligopolistic structures places upon companies' behaviours and strategies appears to be different from the 'free competitive' picture of traditional microeconomics. The archetype of oligopolies as bare 'sleeping giants' is often a misleading one. The analysis of the semiconductor industry clearly shows how oligopolies can emerge and develop or die, together with the technological patterns which allowed their emergence. Moreover, the case of the semiconductor industry restates the obvious fact that an 'oligopoly' does not necessarily need to be very big dimensionally. The possibility of winning above-average profits is determined in relation to a technologically defined market, which could be quite small. At the same time, this possibility of achieving differential profits represents a powerful reallocative incentive inside the economy.

It has been stressed many times how market mechanisms have played a crucial role in the process of exploitation/diffusion of technological advances on the American scene. Market-determined allocation, however, is just *one* of *the possible* allocative mechanisms, even within capitalist economies. It relates crucially to a reactive process, by means of which operators adjust to external environmental conditions. These conditions, on their side, provide the incentives, the constraints and the rewards/penalties for different economic behaviours. There are other allocative mechanisms, on the contrary, which can be theoretically forced into the 'market framework' only with a lot of strain: among them, the process, considered in Chapter 2, of accumulation of scientific and technical knowledge, etc. This is not a purely reactive process: vice versa, it is a positive attempt of 'building-up the future' (in terms of new technological opportunities, new market and profit possibilities, etc.). To state the same concept in other words: in modern capitalism the process of internalisation of 'environmental conditions' inside companies and public agencies has gone rather far, so that what is left to the 'invisible hand' is less than in 'classical' capitalism. Moreover, there are certain things that the invisible hand finds hard to treat; amongst them, research, innovation, etc. Behind the process of technical change, there are, indeed, powerful economic (and political) drives, as one tried to discuss in relation to the emergence of the semiconductor industry. Not all of them, however, pass through the market. This obviously enlarges the scope of the discussion on the role of public policies, long-run strategies by the companies, etc. (we have considered these questions, regarding the semiconductor industry, at greater length in another work: Dosi, 1981).

On theoretical grounds, the interpretative framework we have presented, attempts to provide a rather general account of the relationship between structural conditions of production and 'performance variables', without relying on the indeterminateness of such concepts as 'oligopolistic interactions' and 'degrees of collusiveness'. Moreover, the model allowed us to define some proximate 'gravity centres' for prices and margins in relation to technological conditions and behavioural regularities. Finally, we tried to establish the link between inter-firm asymmetries and the behavioural degrees of freedom that each oligopolistic company enjoys in terms of margins and market shares.

In this chapter, we often talked of asymmetries amongst firms. These asymmetries are one of the necessary conditions for oligopolistic behaviours, efforts to pre-empt markets, etc. Similar asymmetries are observable on industry level, among countries. Their implications in terms of international industrial structures, trade and international investment flows will be analysed in the next chapter.

So far, the analysis allowed us to define the nature of the interaction between technical progress, changes in the economic context and regularities in corporate behaviour, under a 'closed economy' assumption. The next chapter will expand the analysis to the international arena, whereby inter-firm asymmetries are affected also by variables which are country-specific.

NOTES AND REFERENCES

1. We develop at length these topics in our contribution to the OECD Project on 'Technology, Industrial Organization and International Competitiveness'; see Dosi (1981c).
2. Important exceptions – that we shall consider at length below – are, among contemporary economists, Nelson and Winter (see for example Nelson and Winter, 1977a; 1978) and Levin (1981). In the history of economic thought, one must mention, of course, Schumpeter and, before him, Marx.
3. By 'appropriability' here and throughout the text we mean appropriability by the innovating company or country. In other words, it stands for the degree of control that the innovator has upon the economic outcomes of technical change.
4. That is, the technological and economic trade-offs of each technological trajectory.
5. In the example of the internal combustion engine, the possibility of improving the trade-offs between costs, horse power, speed, fuel consumption, etc. is constrained by the basic limits represented by the physical laws of thermodynamics.
6. We use the more generic expression 'economic benefit' instead of the more restrictive 'additional profits' so as not to be forced to discuss whether firms maximise profits, growth or some other objective function. We shall hint at the question below. Here it is enough to mention that, broadly speaking, a *positive* relationship between profits and growth does exist and that, whenever the future is uncertain, a quite good behavioural rule relates growth in sales, market shares and growth in profits.
7. A detailed exposition of his methodology and results is in Mansfield (1968).
8. The most refined tests introduce also some proxies for the 'technological opportunity' and/or for the market-product features, such as degrees of product differentiation or end-uses of the products. For this significant refinement of the tests see, among others, Comanor (1967); Scherer (1965); Schrieves (1979).
9. If these differences are important, the same amount of resources devoted to research activities would lead to different innovative outcomes.
10. This kind of mis-specification in traditional R & D testing can be avoided only through quite strong and – in our view – totally unreasonable hypotheses on the nature of R & D and the economic system in general. One may assume that (a) well-behaved production functions do exist; (b) the rate of activity of the system is limited only by scarce factors; (c) R & D is a factor of production (as well as labour and capital) whose total 'real amount' is given at each moment in time; (d) factors demand is a function of the expected marginal productivities; (e) R & D is 'demanded' in relation to its expected 'innovativeness'; (f) R & D inputs are meant to represent a factor demand schedule; (g) there is no problem in measuring either 'real capital' or 'real R & D'. If all this is true, then and only then 'technological opportunity' and 'appropriability' are implicitly taken into account through the use of R & D proxies within models based on neoclassical

frameworks. (I must thank H. Ergas for drawing my attention to this possible neoclassical explanation).

11. See Nelson (1980). Other problems concern the use of flow instead of stock variables. See Terleckyj (1980); Griliches (1980); Momigliano (1981).

12. See Scherer (1965); Schrieves (1979).

13. As a matter of fact, the 'Schumpeterian approach' is more complex and the role attributed to big corporations in the innovative activity is only a part of Schumpeter's theory of the evolution of the economic system. Taking that hypothesis alone certainly does not do justice to Schumpeter's analysis. For critical appraisals of Schumpeter's theory on the relationship innovation–size see Nelson (1980a) and Chesnais (1981).

14. See Nelson (1980a); Nelson and Winter (1980).

15. See among others, Horowitz (1962); Hamberg (1967); Scherer (1965 and 1970). Scherer finds that a strong positive correlation disappears when some proxies for the 'technological opportunity' for each industry are introduced.

16. Schrieves (1979) finds a positive sign for concentration in industries producing intermediate goods and consumer durables, and a negative and/or insignificant sign in industrial sectors producing capital equipment and consumer non-durables.

17. Both in terms of R & D expenditures and R & D employees.

18. Similar conclusions of more than proportional contributions by big firms to innovation in a good majority of industrial sectors are drawn by SPRU (1971) which analysed the origin of around a thousand innovations in the U.K. in the post war period. For an updating, which confirms the main findings see Townsend, et. al. (1981).

19. Taken as an inverse measure of technological opportunity, which – simplifying to the extreme – we assume as simply related to the 'age' of the technology.

20. Not that if the size of the market is given, the same positive function applies to industrial concentration.

21. See for example Vernon (1966); S. Hirsch (1965); Hufbauer (1966).

22. Abernathy and Utterback (1975) and (1978).

23. B. Klein (1977).

24. For thorough discussions see B. Klein (1977); Nelson (1980); Blair (1972).

25. Nelson and Winter (1977a) and (1978) describe the process in their formal models and their simulations. See also below.

26. As Dasgupta and Stiglitz (1980) point out, the two are not synonymous, although they are likely to be inter-related.

27. Katz and Phillips (1982) analyses the history of the computer industry. On the latter see also Brock (1975). MacLaurin (1949) analyses the history of the radio industry with a similar 'dynamic' approach. Few works on the semiconductor industry hint at or analyse the question with respect to the semiconductor industry (cf. Tilton, 1971; Golding, 1971; Sciberras, 1977; Truel, 1980; Ernst, 1982).

28. That the innovative process implies disequilibrium *vis-à-vis* static mechanisms of adjustment has been crucial in Schumpeter's economic theory (and in Marx).

29. See Nelson and Winter (1977a), (1978). For an excellent summary and

discussion of their approach, cf. Malerba (1981).

30. In passing, it is worth noticing that the cumulative (but still stochastic) nature of technological advances may help to explain the occurrence of some modified version of a "Gibrat Law" in the observable trends toward industrial concentration.

31. Strong exercise of market power implies high margins and therefore non-aggressive pricing and investment policies which allows nearly-marginal firms to remain in the market.

32. A thorough formalisation (perhaps with some unnecessary concessions to the traditional methodology of maximization) is in Spence (1979).

33. Schumpeter himself thought that *both* adjusting mechanisms were at work. For an original and sharp discussion, cf. Egidi (1981).

34. First and foremost in Marx, who deals extensively with the issue especially in the second and third volumes of *Das Kapital*.

35. For a detailed argument on these lines, cf. Semmler (1980).

36. Note that Schumpeter (1919) also appears to support this hypothesis. More precisely he appears to suggest a cycle in average 'oligopolistic' profits ranging between some positive value and zero.

37. cf. Sraffa (1960). In matrix notation,

$$pA(I+r) + wl = p$$

where p is the price vector; A, the matrix of inputs; l, the vector of labour inputs; w, the wage rate; r, the rate of profit and I, the unit matrix. Once given either the rate of profit or the wage rate, as known, the system can be solved in terms of a properly defined unit of measure.

38. In addition there are some serious technical problems in introducing any 'oligopoly' concept into a Sraffa-like system which cannot be dealt with here. It is enough to mention that whenever we introduce a vector of profit rates instead of a unique one, one loses some important properties of the original system, such as the invariance of its solutions with respect to the composition of demand.

39. This agrees with the argument put forward by Semmler (1980).

40. In that example, three groups of firms enjoy different levels of economies of scale and thus different unit costs. Only the smaller firms obtain 'minimum' (or 'competitive') profits. Therefore the average for the industry as a whole is permanently above that level.

41. Empirical evidence on the relationship between entry barriers and profitabilities can be found, among others, in Bain (1956); Mann (1966); Stonebraker (1976). Semmler (1980) critically reviews the literature on the subject.

42. cf. the critical analysis by Nelson and Winter (1977a). For a thorough discussion of the theory of the firm throughout modern economic thought, see Salvati (1967).

43. Nelson (1981).

44. Note that for the theory to hold, something has to be maximised but not necessarily profits.

45. Nelson and Winter (1977a), (1980), Nelson (1981).

46. A review of the problems connected with these questions is in Marris and Mueller (1980) and Nelson (1981).

47. The comprehensive and 'final' synthesis of the approach is Scherer (1970).

48. For a survey of the use of game theories in economics, cf. Schotter and Schwödiaver (1980). An alternative way out of oligopolistic indeterminacy, within the neoclassical tradition, is suggested by Baumol (1982), with his theory of 'contestable markets': such a theory, however, has to rule out *ex hypothesi* inter-firm asymmetries and differential costs of entry and exit.

49. A quite straightforward example, again from Klein, is the following: suppose an individual household doubles its saving propensity. In doing so, it certainly increases individual wealth. However, if all of them do so, they most likely induce a tremendous economic slump and also the collapse of everyone's wealth. (A Walrasian would, of course, challenge this Keynesian example and not very much can be said to convince him/her. The approaches are very different and, at the most, they can be tested in relation to which offers the best explanation of the processes of structural and technological change in modern economies).

50. Simon (1959); Cyert and March (1963); Winter (1964); Simon (1978).

51. Egidi (1981, p. 15: our translation).

52. As discussed by Egidi (1981), the behavioural alternative, generally facing a firm, between an 'innovative' conduct *vs* a 'static' behaviour of adjusting prices and quantities for given products and techniques involves two different 'rationality' criteria. *Ex post*, one could always argue that both are part of a rational maximising behaviour once risk, inter-temporal preferences, etc. are taken into account. The heuristic power of such an hypothesis, however, is practically nil.

53. Certainly we are left with a less deterministic relationship between environment and conduct than is usually hypothesised. However, it appears to use less violence in reality. In passing, note the paradox involved in the prevailing methodological individualism: while it appears to be very fond of some liberal idea of individual free choice it sets up the problem of choice itself in such a way that there is only a one-exit solution. In other words, there is generally a univocal 'right' choice which you do not choose only if you are mistaken or if you are crazy (i.e. irrational). A thorough discussion of the question is in Latzis (1976). On the other hand, for a detailed discussion of the limitations of the interpretative power of behavioural theories of the firm, cf. Salvati (1967).

54. Abernathy and Utterback (1975) and (1978).

55. In the tradition led by Simon (1959) and Cyert and March (1963).

56. A consequence of this second approach, which in economics finds its most coherent expression in 'behavioural' theories of the firms, is the importance one must attribute to 'what is in the actors' mind'. The same scientific path followed by H. Simon, ranging between artificial intelligence and economic witnesses of this theoretical link.

57. Note that the neoclassical approach produces an apparent solution to the dilemma by making change impossible and thus choice irrelevant.

58. A similar critique can be found in Pasinetti (1981), which represents an ambitious and exciting attempt to develop a theory of the dynamics of a multi-sector macroeconomic system under conditions of technical change. We shall briefly come back to it in Chapter 5.

59. This for the simple reason that under conditions of technical change and oligopolistic interaction, only God could have the amount of information

adequate to use such a criterion of decision (cf. also Nelson, 1981).
60. cf. Salvati (1967).
61. E.g., Andrews and Wilson (1951); Hitch and Hall (1939); Lanzillotti (1958); Ripley and Segal (1973); at a more aggregate level, Nield (1963); Coutts Godley and Nordhaus (1978); P. Sylos-Labini (1980).
62. With respect to the first interpretation, a very consistent discussion is in Needham (1978). For the second, see for example Baumol and Quandt (1964). The two approaches are not, of course, inconsistent with each other, but to a great extent complementary.
63. In this stream of thought, one must mention especially the works by Marris (1964); Penrose (1959); Wood (1975). This group of theories is not primarily meant to account for the determination of prices and quantities on each individual market, so as to provide a satisfactory model of firm behaviour (growth, investments, financial position, etc.) Although it is difficult to see a systematic linkage with 'structural' non-neoclassical theory of price determination (those defined at point 3 below) they appear compatible with the latter. A balanced critical appraisal of the theoretical limitations of this stream of thought is in Salvati (1967).
64. The reader is invited to compare, for example, Penrose (1959) with Nelson and Winter (1977a) and (1978). The latter can account for most of the basic behaviours analysed by the former, while being more general and avoiding rather dubious assumptions on 'alternative' maximisation procedures.
65. Following the seminal work by Andrews (1949), a 'mark-up' determination of prices (together with an explanation of the levels of the mark-ups themselves) has been provided in the theoretical models proposed by Bain (1956) and Sylos-Labini (1967). (The latter is the second edition of a work published a decade earlier). For an original formalisation of the Bain/Sylos-Labini model which tries its best to bring it within a 'maximising' hortodox framework, see Modigliani (1958). See also Wenders (1967). More recently, an ambitious attempt to link variations in the mark-ups with the investment decisions and the financial position of the firm is that of Eichner (1976); cf., with similar aims, also, Harcourt and Kenyon (1976).
66. Take the example of Wood's very comprehensive model: it is assumed that growth is the objective of the firm, that a trade-off exists between sales and net profits (due to advertisement expenses, etc.), that growth is financially constrained by a certain maximum leverage ratio (given cash-flows coming from retained profits and given a certain dividend policy). Depending on the behavioural parameters there will be a determined value for sales, profits, investments (assuming fixed coefficients of production or a defined set of technical choices). Actually, it is easier to link this model with a 'Cambridge-flavoured' macroeconomic growth model (see again Wood, 1975) rather than with a disaggregate model providing defined values for prices and quantities on each market: in actual fact price levels (as opposed to their changes) are not determined, nor are gross margins. One faces somewhat similar problems in a Nelson and Winter-type model.
67. In the first instance, one is considering here the case of 'homogeneous oligopoly' (as opposed to a 'differentiated oligopoly').
68. In the interpretation of Modigliani (1958) if demand is unelastic, the

market leader(s) can fix the price *above* P_m (from equation 1) because, provided that existing firms maintain an unchanged level of output facing a new entry, the price would in case of entry fall *below* P_m. Thus, one could rewrite equation 1 as:

$$P = f(P_m) \qquad\qquad 3$$

where the function accounts for different price elasticities of demand in the neighbourhood P_m.

69. As already mentioned, in some recent models, price changes are related also to the investment decisions of firms (Eichner 1976; Harcourt and Kenyon, 1976). This extension of the model seems in principle compatible with the original Bain/Sylos model: a greater role, however, must then be played by the 'conditions' listed above referring to the elasticities of demand and elasticity of substitution with other commodities, since one must be able to change prices in relation to investment decisions, without affecting the firm's short-run demand for the products on which the firm decided to change price levels. Moreover, it requires quite strict hypotheses on inter-firm collusion (cf. below).

70. Balconi (1977, p. 156). Chapter 5 of that work contains an interesting discussion of the applicability of the various theories of the firm to the case of the alluminium industry, characterised by fairly frequent entries and ruptures of the 'oligopolistic equilibrium'.

71. It can also be shown that, in some cases, obeying to the "Sylos postulate" may be "irrational" from the point of view of traditional profit maximizing criteria (cf. Scherer, 1970, pp. 219–30). It is hard, however, to decide to what degree this shows the limited generalizability of limit pricing or, on the contrary, the limited realism of marginal pricing theories.

72. See below for a more detailed illustration.

73. See, for indirect evidence, the empirical results of the works quoted in note 41 page 199.

74. For a corroboration of this hypothesis, see the tests by MacEnally (1976).

75. 'Barriers are not only structural and exogenous, but partly endogenous and the resource commitments that enlarge them yield a private return in excess of their social "productivity".' (Caves and Porter, 1977, p. 249). These authors identify four 'strategies' affecting entry barriers, namely, excess capacity, product differentiation, actions affecting cost differentials, and vertical integration.

76. As cost structures are concerned, one can find a similar analysis in Sylos-Labini (1967). The numerical examples in Chapter 2 of Sylos's work concern precisely price determination as a function of *both* entry and mobility barriers.

77. Inter-group mobility clearly leads to the question of the stability of market shares and their relationship with the rates of return. On these issues see Caves and Porter (1978); Gale (1972); Buzzell, Gale and Sultan (1975).

78. As far as process innovations are concerned they can most easily be treated whenever they occur across the industry (i.e. they are 'size-neutral') or are just limited to a firm or a group of firms (due to size constraints on the applicability of the innovations themselves). Sylos tends to suggest that generally process innovations are 'size-biased' (i.e. they occur more frequently in large size firms).

79. In practice, the initial simplifying assumption is equivalent to saying that, regardless of the degree of success of each individual forecast, the 'true' equilibrium prices (a) are the values around which actual prices tend *grosso modo* to adjust (i.e. there is no cumulative disequilibria), (b) even if there is a continuous divergence between actual and 'equilibrium' prices, the levels and changes in the latter can be taken as a good approximation to the former. Notably the notion of 'equilibrium' here does not embody any element of optimality: it might be defined as the level of the relevant variables which, given a set of 'structural conditions', could maintain itself, if those conditions did not change. Here, as well as in a model like Sylos-Labini's, given the size of the market, demand elasticities, and the nature of technological discontinuities, there may well be more than one equilibrium value, depending on the past history of the industry, the distribution of firms according to their size, etc. (cf. the numerical examples in Sylos-Labini, 1967, chapter 2).

80. This hypothesis has been well tested in various industrial sectors and appears to have a quite substantial importance in the semiconductor industry. Here one means proper learning economies, i.e. the decrease in average unit costs which are *independent* from changes in technology and from 'static' economies of scale.

81. These assumptions are fairly common in business economics. They are implicit, for example, in the Boston Consulting Group's 'product matrices' and their approach to the 'learning curve'. See Boston Consulting Group (1973); Hedley (1977).

82. The first two alternatives, in the case of semiconductor industry, are illustrated with reference to cases of specific firms by Sciberras (1977) and Truel (1980).

83. We assume that the potential entrant will initially have unit costs which are equal to the original costs of the innovator at the beginning of its 'learning curve'.

84. At time T, in the 'monopoly' case prices will have to be dropped – under our assumptions – to that level which would yield less than a normal profit to a potential entrant. Note that the curve of unit margins (top left quadrant) becomes flat because after time T, the potential entrant can, to some extent, 'watch and learn'. Otherwise margins could continuously grow over time.

85. For the scope of this illustration we assume that capital/output ratios do not change over time so that the analysis conducted in terms of profit margins is equivalent to that in terms of profit rates.

86. The few models of 'dynamic pricing' (including 'dynamic limit pricing') assume a time horizon from here to eternity. The assumption is obviously useful for mathematical purposes, but might be strongly misleading on interpretative grounds. For dynamic models based on maximising procedures, see Pashigian (1967) and Gaskins (1971). When the first draft of this research was already completed we became aware of an important contribution by Spence (1981). He considers a similar problem to ours: the effects of learning-curve induced inter-firm asymmetries upon prices and structural dynamics. The adopted approach is different and the model starts from profit-maximising firms operating in dynamic environments. The model is quite complex and the results of the simulations depend on a

number of assumptions on the competitive patterns between firms and on the nature of 'learning'. It is impossible to discuss them here and to compare them with the results of our model. We shall just make a few remarks. The model (which is one of the best expression of a whole new kind) is more precise than ours in that whenever one knows exactly what firms want and do, it is able to define precisely the performance and the structural outcomes. Conversely, in conditions of limited information (for the analyst) it allows very limited generalisation even on the signs of the functional relationships, which depend on unknown behavioural parameters (are equilibria open-loop or closed loop?, how do firms discount the future? etc.).

87. This appears to be corroborated by cross-firm empirical evidence: cf. Barna (1962), who shows the absence of any significant trade-off between observed profitabilities and growth rates.

88. In the sense that we know only the mathematical sign of that relationship but not its exact functional form.

89. In an extreme simplification we assume that prices are set once and for all over the entire time interval T. The assumption makes our argument much easier. Relaxing it, however, would not substantially affect the conclusions.

90. The formulation of equation 3 is practically identical to the learning curve equations; see Boston Consulting Group (1973); Webbick (1977). Here, we must stress that the coefficient m is explicitly a mark-up and not only an intercept to be estimated ex-post from a regression analysis of the equation in the logarithmic form.

91. Sylos-Labini suggests that it could be the rate of interest.

92. We thus implicitly assume that the minimum acceptable margin for the innovator is higher than that for the imitator, since we reasonably assume that innovation costs are higher than imitation costs.

93. From equation 5 the parameter α represents the price elasticity of demand.

94. The size of the market can be approximated by the parameter A, multiplied by the 'natural' growth of the market ($e^{\lambda t}$).

95. Given demand and cost curves, one may therefore establish the 'notional' range in which x_t can vary, satisfying both conditions 9 and 10.

96. See, for example, Boston Consulting Group (1973).

97. See also below Chapters 4 and 5.

98. On a more detailed and "micro" level those "asymmetries" between "first comer" and "later-comer" are described by some recent models of "oligopolistic interaction" (see Spence (1979) who considers the "strategic interaction . . . exploiting competitive asymmetries by preempting the market to some degree. The role of the firms . . . are determined by the constraints on growth and the history of the industry" (p. 14)).

99. This process of innovation-based dynamics is at the core of Downie's view of the competitive process (cf. Downie, 1958).

100. If anything, a rise in the level of the mark-up could occur since 'barriers to entry' are generally higher in declining products which may be used as 'cash-cows'.

   On the relationship between cash-flows necessary for new investments in new products and margins on the old ones see Eichner (1976).

101. 1.5 is the price at which ten transistors have the same price as the ten transistors' equivalent IC. The effect of the new product on the old

product's demand curve could be represented, for the relevant price interval, by writing *the intercepts* of the demand curve as a function of time and of relative prices, instead of the more usual procedure of writing the demand function itself as dependent on relative prices.

102. See below the discussion on the semiconductor industry.
103. The reader is reminded again that we assume unchanged capital/output ratios, so that profit rates are a monotonic function of profit margins.
104. This can be seen through solving equations 3, 5, 6, and 9 (taken as an equality). The four equations are sufficient to determine the four unknowns (P, x, X, m). Let P_0 and x_0 be the corresponding solutions of the system for prices and quantities at a certain given time. Moreover, let us call C_0 the value of the unit cost function, $C = c_0 X^\beta$. The margin is $M_0 = P_0/C_0$. Suppose the price changes by ΔP (say it decreases due to technological diffusion to potential entrants which lowered the notional 'limit' price). A comparative exercise will allow the assessment of the effect of different values for the demand elasticity coefficient. For simplicity we assume that the stock of cumulated production equals the flow ($x = X$). The change in the margin following ΔP is:

$$\Delta M = \frac{P_0 + \Delta P}{C_0 + \Delta C} - \frac{P_0}{C_0} \qquad 12$$

In order to study the changes in ΔM in relation to different values of demand elasticity ($= \alpha$) it will be enough to study the behaviour of ΔC. Consider the set of demand curves of the form $X = Ap^{-\alpha}$ passing through the point (x_0, P_0). Differentiating demand with respect to the price, we obtain:

$$\Delta x = -\alpha \cdot \frac{x_0}{P_0} (\Delta P)$$

and by substitution into

$$\Delta C = \beta c_0 x_0^{(\beta - 1)} (\Delta x)$$

we finally get

$$\Delta C = -c_0 \beta x_0^\beta \cdot \alpha \frac{1}{P_0} (\Delta P) \qquad 13$$

It can be seen that ΔC (which is negative when ΔP is negative, remembering that $\beta < 0$) increases with α in its absolute value.

A similar conclusion (although in a different context) comes from Pashigian's 'dynamic limit pricing' model (Pashigian, 1968). His argument relates the elasticity of demand and 'final' market shares, after the transition from a monopoly to an oligopoly structure of the market. The determining mechanisms are quite different: here, we are considering the effects of demand elasticity on margins via learning curves, while Pashigian analyses the optimal timing of the switch from a monopoly price to a 'limit' price. Conclusions similar to ours can be drawn from a short but important contribution by Smiley and Ravid (1983), published at the time of proof reading of this book. Remarkably, the properties of the industrial system discussed here, stemming from the joint account of asymmetries and real-time processes, hold irrespectively of the behavioural routines one assumes, as shown by their model which utilizes more traditional maximising procedures.

105. Please note that straight demand curves are just shown in Figure 3 in order to better visualise the properties of the model. The formal analysis is, however, still undertaken in terms of a constant elasticity demand curve as from equation 5.

106. One must also reasonably assume that there are *increasing* returns to scale, holding time fixed. We do not have any difficulty in making this assumption even if it conflicts with the traditionally U-shaped cost curve: learning occurs *both* through time and within each time unit. The reader might question the possibility of generalising from our simplified model where flows are assumed to equal stocks to the more general one. A complete account of the latter would change the values of the solutions but not the signs of the functional relationships, which is where our interest lies. The cost of a heavier mathematical treatment, therefore, does not appear to be matched by greater analytical advantages.

107. The relationship between restriction on the supply and margins in a static context involves, as known, a *negative* relationship between margins and demand elasticity: if demand is inelastic a small decrease in quantity leads to a high increase in prices and margins (if the slope of the cost curve is greater than that of the demand curve). By way of illustration, Figure 3.2 depicts the opposite extreme case: one may conceive the notional possibility of prices fixed at a level *below* the 'limit price' which yields *higher* margins than the latter because demand is very elastic (suppose, for example, that P_0 is the limit price and that the demand curve is $f_B(x)$: thus P_1/C_1^B is also greater than P_0/C_0).

108. As known, the general criterion is that output will be obtained through to equalisation of marginal costs to prices.

109. The definition relates to output restrictions in order to obtain the equality between marginal revenues and marginal costs.

110. Under monopolistic conditions, profit maximisation is obtained when the marginal revenue (MR) equals marginal costs. The former is $P \cdot (1 - \frac{1}{\eta})$ where η is the demand elasticity. Clearly for $\eta \leq 1$ there is no economic solution, in this framework, to the monopolistic maximisation problem.

111. The following argument has many points in common with the theory of demand of Pasinetti (1981) and the reader is referred to that work for an exhaustive discussion.

112. This indeterminacy is quite independent from the impossibility of univocally defining patterns of consumer preferences (cf. Arrow, 1963).

113. Engel (1857). Cf. again Pasinetti (1981) for a thorough discussion. Note that this idea is quite familiar to business economists who are more directly concerned with an operational concept of demand and do not find much use in playing with vague and obscure concepts such as 'utility functions.'

114. In this context these are equivalent to the change in real personal income induced by a change in the price of a commodity, other prices being equal.

115. Except for the cases when processes of substitution between new and old commodities are at work, such as the substitution between colour and black and white TVs. This, in our view, occurs only within relatively homogeneous product groups (similar to those identified by Lancaster (1971)).

116. Balconi (1977) analyses a process of long-run substitution between aluminium and copper also based on the dynamics of relative prices. This does not affect, however, short-run elasticity of demand to prices.

117. We may note that the absence of strong cross-substitutability, as implied in our argument, is sufficient to undermine the equilibrium and stability properties of neoclassical general equilibrium models.

118. Cf. Sylos–Labini (1967, chapter 2).

119. It should be clear that our discussion so far (and the discussion which will follow in the next section), based on the hypothesis of only one innovative firm for each market, is a simplifying device to highlight some 'stylised' facts and properties. Remarkably, relaxing that hypothesis renders the model more complex but does not alter its basic properties.

120. We can apply the same procedure as in note 104 page 205. The two firms (1 and 2) enjoy a market share μ_1 and μ_2, respectively. Assume that the leading firm sets a price P_0. We will thus obtain a solution for the margins of the two companies.

$$m_1 = \frac{P_0}{c_0(\mu_1 X_0)^\beta} \qquad 14$$

and

$$m_2 = \frac{P_0}{c_0(\mu_2 X_0)^\beta} \qquad 15$$

The leading firm will be able to monopolise the market only if it sets a price below (or near) the variable costs of the other firm, i.e. $c_0(\mu_2 X_0)^\beta$. The resulting change in the margin of the leading firm will be

$$\Delta M_1 = \frac{P_0 + P}{C_1 + \Delta C_1} - \frac{P_0}{C_1} \qquad 16$$

where C_1 is the average unit cost of firm 1 corresponding to P_0. Making use of the results of the exercise of note 104, page 205, we know that ΔC is a direct function of elasticity. Moreover, ΔP will have to be higher, the lower is the cost differential between firm 1 and 2. In other words the cost of 'kicking out' a firm will be proportional (under our learning curve hypothesis) to the market share of the latter. If price elasticity of demand is not very high (as well as learning economies) the resulting profit margins of the leading firm will be lower under a monopoly rather than under the original 'duopoly'. Note that these properties can be easily generalised to the case of 'static' economies of scale.

121. This phenomenon is practically identical to the result of Nelson–Winter's model of a *negative* relationship between concentration and mark-ups of the leading firms (Nelson and Winter, 1978). A similar property was already noted by Sylos-Labini (1967) ch. 2.

122. The reader is reminded again that, given our assumptions on capital/output ratios, profit margins and profit rates move in the same direction.

123. In actual fact, 'kicking out' a firm would imply lowering the price more than that, below the infra-marginal firm variable costs. In order to make the exercise easier we may suppose that the latter firm, in the medium term, will leave the industry if it earns a profit below the minimum.

124. The hypothesis makes the model simpler. It has, however, an economic significance since it is equivalent to saying that rivals' reactions to price changes are non-adaptive, so that an increase in quantities through price changes cannot be gained from the other firms if all remain on the market, but only from an expansion of the market itself.

125. The assumption that the increase in market shares was evenly distributed among the remaining firms would not affect our conclusions.

126. For the sake of simplicity we assume that the increase in the size of the total market due to the price decrease is distributed among all firms according to their market shares, and we neglect, in the cost function, the decrease in costs due to the related increase in quantities for the leading firm. A more complicated formula would not change the results. Equation 18 is finally obtained linearising around the point (X_0, P_0) and remembering that $c_1 = c_0 X^\beta$. Solving equation 18, one can see that margins will increase with an increasing market share only if the product of demand elasticity (α) and the learning coefficient (β) has an absolute value greater than one.

127. A similar concept is in Caves and Porter (1977).

128. This explains why in a cross-sector analysis, one generally finds a positive correlation between concentration and profitability.

129. Note that this argument is independent from product differentiation, etc. Obviously the latter may be an additional reason for the 'stickiness' of market shares. For a thorough discussion of several possible factors affecting the stability of market shares, cf. Caves and Porter (1978).

130. Note that here we depict flat cost curves for each firm, for the sake of simplicity of the illustration. Our argument applies *a fortiori* to the case of downward-sloping curves.

131. Whenever technology is not very important and diversification is, a few properties of our model do not apply, such as the relationship between lowest costs and highest market shares, etc.

132. In passing, note that the archetypal case of 'market power' in textbooks is defined by a group of existing producers which are equal to each other and very different from potential entrants. If our model is correct this case is extremely unlikely.

133. Bain (1956).

134. In our formulation this is captured by the constant and the function of time in equation 5.

135. As expressed by the function $g(t)$ in equation 9.

136. This process is 'Schumpeterian' in all but one respect: differential profits for the innovators do not wither away as a result of competitive imitations (cf. Schumpeter, 1919). For a discussion see below.

137. This seems reasonable since a slowly shrinking market does not provide a great incentive to entry anyhow. Another reason can be that, if the innovative firm has succeeded in pre-empting the market and in 'building up' its own entry barriers, it may thereafter gradually increase its margins. A third reason, allowing firms – outside this example – to be diversified in more than one product, is that they may finance their growth in new markets with increasing prices on the old commodities. This hypothesis (see Eichner, 1976) implies growing entry barriers and decreasing entry incentives in declining markets.

138. This could be considered the price of a composite commodity made

of all the products of the industry, taken in proportion to their share in the total output.

139. An additional feature is that 'new products' embodying technical progress can be described as being 'a multiplication' upon (i.e. 'as performing more tasks' than) the old ones.

So, if one describes unit prices per homogeneous performance (e.g. in the semiconductor case, per logical unit) technical progress generally induces a decrease in such performance-weighted price. An effort to catch this effect has been made through 'hedonic price indices' or 'performance-weighted' price indices. The trends described in the text would *a fortiori* apply if a 'hedonic' price index were used.

140. One has, of course, to maintain the assumption of 'other things being equal', regarding process innovations, capital/output ratios, firms producing just one product, etc.

141. Although they do not entirely disappear. Cf., for the case of mature industry like steel, Lundberg (1961).

142. We call them 'oligopoly profits', instead of 'monopoly profits' even if, for our assumptions, each firm is alone on its own sub-market due to the fact that the pricing behaviour is nonetheless 'oligopolistic' (while in an 'absolute monopoly' situation, price could perhaps be set, as traditional theory teaches, equalising marginal revenue and marginal cost).

143. Simplifying the problem and neglecting unit cost of materials, mark-up prices are $P = m(\frac{w}{\pi})$, with π = labour productivity and w = wage rate. In terms of percentage increases:

$$\dot{P}/P = \dot{m}/m + \dot{w}/w - \dot{\pi}/\pi \qquad 20$$

A 'no-distribution of gain' hypothesis is that which implies *unchanged relative prices* between the sector and the rest of the economy, despite different growth rates in productivity, i.e.:

$$\dot{P}_s/P_s - \dot{P}_e/P_e = \dot{m}_s/m_s - \dot{m}_e/m_e + \dot{w}_s/w_s - \dot{w}_e/w_e + \dot{\pi}_e/\pi_e - \dot{\pi}_s/\pi_s \qquad 21$$

in which the suffices s and e stand for the sector and the rest of the economy, respectively.

144. This conclusion is not consistent with Sylos's hypothesis that generally in oligopolistic sectors 'gains' tend to be directly distributed to wages and profits (cf. Sylos-Labini (1967), second part, chapters I to III). Sylos's argument is based on various points:

(a) The model is primarily concerned with process innovations in relatively mature industry. Furthermore those innovations are supposed to be 'large-scale biased'. This implies that technical progress tends to increase entry barriers through time, and therefore also the levels of oligopoly margins.

(b) Workers must be strong enough to obtain in each sector at least part of the differential increase in productivity as a differential increase in wages (as compared to the rest of the manufacturing sectors).

(c) To some extent, there is a convenience for oligopolies themselves to allow these wage increases, because, given the level of the mark-up (which is a percentage), net profits can increase in proportion (given a total transferability of costs on prices).

For a comment on these two latter points, see below.

145. One is implicitly talking here of a closed economy. *A fortiori* it applies to an open economy.

146. This contributes to the explanation of why there are not necessarily 'stagnationist' trends as strong as those implicit in Sylos's approach, where relative prices are to some extent 'fossilized'. Cf. Sylos-Labini (1967) and (1981). See also the classic works by Steindl (1952) and Baran and Sweezy (1966). For a discussion of the macroeconomic implication of Sylos's and Steindl's models, see Salvati (1971).

147. A similar picture of long-run trends in an economy characterised by continuous technical progress is given by Young (1928). See also Kaldor (1960) on the implications for the traditional economic theory.

148. For some interesting examples from semiconductors see below.

149. This is common also to various sectors other than semiconductors; for example, on aluminium, see Balconi (1977). In semiconductors, discounts are important and generally quite substantial, directly proportional to the size of purchases (the discount can sometimes be as high as 50%). All the arguments above about 'normal' pricing behaviour, however, is referred to *actual* prices and not listed prices. I must thank Mr Benda from Mullard Ltd for clarifying this aspect of semiconductor pricing policy.

150. Assuming differential average unit costs between the first-comer and possible entrants, the 'average' mark-up is an average of the margins of each single firm, weighted with the respective market share. The greater the share of the leader (which should also enjoy the lowest average cost), the greater should be also the average margin. Under the assumption of similar capital/output ratios between firms, the levels of the margin can be taken as proxy for the rates of profit. The reader should notice that there is no contradiction between the foregoing statement, on the positive relationship between average margins and market share(s) of the leading firm(s), and our discussion above on the trade-off between the two variables. Above we considered the *behavioural trade-off* for *given* technological asymmetries between firms. Conversely, here we are implicitly making an exercise of comparative statics: for *given behavioural routines*. The degrees of inter-firm asymmetries bear a positive relation with the market share(s) of the leading firm(s), with their margins, and by implication, with the average margin of the industry.

    For some empirical analysis regarding semiconductors, see below. On the controversial question of the relationship concentration/profitability, see among others Bain (1951 and 1956); Gale (1972); Brozen (1971); Demsetz (1973). A comprehensive critical review is in Semmler (1980), while a thorough discussion within the framework of neoclassical economics is in Scherer (1970).

151. Salter (1969). For a thorough discussion, cf. Salvati (1971),

152. The condition for investment is the inequality

$$\int_{t=0}^{t=l} (R - V)e^{-rt}\, dt \geq I \qquad\qquad 22$$

and, as in Salter (1969, p. 68), expressing it in terms of unit of output and assuming all the operating costs as labour costs

$$\int_{t=0}^{t=l} (P - L_n w)e^{-rt}dt \geq C_n \cdot P_c \qquad 23$$

where l = expected economic life of the investment, P = unit price, L_n = unit labour input on the new equipment, r = rate of discount, w = wage rate, R = revenue, V = operating costs, C_n = 'real' unit capital input, P_c = price of capital goods, I = investment. See also Terbourgh (1958).

153. Salter (1969); Salvati (1971).
154. In business economies the concept of 'learning economy' or 'learning curve' is much more impressionistic and includes also proper technical progress (of the embodied kind). Although that broader sense is likely to have a strong operational meaning, it is analytically unsatisfactory because it does not distinguish between the causes of decreasing unit costs.
155. In this case margins will be determined in relation to unit costs which represent a weighted average of the various vintages.
156. Cf. Eichner (1976) and Harcourt and Kenyon (1976).
157. *Prima facie*, 'investment–profit' models are appealing because they seem to provide a plausible microeconomic foundation to the 'Cambridge' macroeconomic theory of income distribution (which – as known – relates the rate of profit to the rate of growth). However, they would strictly apply only if the manufacturing industry were composed of only one firm, i.e. if the 'micro' were identical to the 'macro'!
158. The argument which follows applies *in toto* to capital-equipment which is freely available on the market and to different extents to capital-embodied process innovations which can be imitated by new entrants.
159. One is likely to find several examples throughout the history of nineteenth-century capitalism, and even today in all sectors where the rate of product innovation is relatively low, as well as economies of scale, and where learning-by-doing is not very pronounced, such as, some metal products, non-fashion clothing and leather products, simple wood manufactures, etc.
160. The implications of this form of technical progress in terms of economic theory are discussed, as already mentioned, by Nelson (1980).
161. Marx, quoted also in Semmler (1980).
162. See also Chapter 5.
163. We define the 'World' as all non-centrally planned economies.
164. Productivity is defined as value added at constant prices per hour of direct labour. The estimates are bound to be imprecise because of the lack of a complete set of relevant data and the unavoidable difficulty of a changing product mix. It must be noticed that the above figure does *not* take into account the superior performance of new products *vis-à-vis* old (e.g. the fact that an integrated circuit accounts for several thousands of transistors).
165. The estimates exclude captive markets and thus companies such as IBM and Western Electric. Note that the European share includes European-owned American companies such as Signetics.
166. The shares are in terms of number of units.

167. Table 3.5 excludes US firms producing only for in-house consumption, an estimated 30–40 % of total US output. If the largest such producers (IBM and Western Electric) were ranked by size of semiconductor output (Table 3.10) they would appear among the world's top five.
168. These figures exclude captive producers.
169. Table 3.14, however, shows a high instability of individual market shares between the late fifties and the mid seventies in the USA. For a 'mapping' of the pattern of new entries, their origin and their history, cf. Truel (1980) and Mason (1979).
170. For a discussion see Ernst (1982).
171. See above, chapter 2, for an explanation of the manufacturing techniques.
172. The US market for these 'silicon foundries' is estimated in 1981 at around $135m (source: Ernst, 1982).
173. See *Business Week*, 10 September 1979. Some company-based estimates suggest an increase of marginal capital/output ratios, throughout the seventies, from 0.25 to around one (Source: *Business Week*, 10 Sept. 1979). Data on investment/sales ratios for a group of American and Japanese companies do not appear to support the claim of an increase of that order of magnitude although it supports the existence of a trend in that direction. According to Rosen Research Inc. (cf. *Rosen Research Letter*, 17 July 1981), the ratio of capital spending to sales in a sample of 17 American companies rose from 10.5 % in 1973 to 13.8 % in 1980. As regards specifically their semiconductor operations, the ratio increased from 13.1 % in 1978 to 17.5 % in 1980.
174. Source: DAFSA (1981).
175. See Golding (1971); Tilton (1971); Finan (1975); Sciberras (1977); Mason (1979); Truel (1980).
176. A discussion of a similar case is in Salvati (1971).
177. The taxation system is likely to make the choice of establishing a new company even more favourable: even if the existing company decides to distribute some of the additional profits to the successful researchers in the form of increased salaries, the latter are taxed at progressive rates. Part of the profits of the hypothetical new company would be, on the contrary, capitalised.
178. For an argued case in support of this thesis, cf. Baran and Sweezy (1966).
179. This comes down again to an opportunity–cost problem. For an established firm different levels of risk and uncertainty are weighted against the expected returns of different possible investments. For a potential enterpreneur, on the contrary, the choice is simply between a salary and the investment in one's own technical expertise.
180. We cannot go beyond these few hints without undertaking a major discussion on the sociology of firms which is not possible here. The reader is again referred to Nelson (1981) and (1981a) which scrutinise the 'frontier' reached in this line of investigation and suggest also a wide territory still to be explored.
181. They argue that one of the factors behind the relative commercial failure of big established companies such as General Electric, Philco–Ford and Westinghouse was excessive centralisation. On the other hand, they

suggest that the relatively poor performance of Fairchild in the seventies has been due to organisational 'looseness'.

182. For a detailed account on a micro level, see Sciberras (1977) and Truel (1980).

183. By 'diffusion' one means here diffusion in production, as opposed to diffusion in consumption (i.e. expansion of the market for the innovative commodities). The two are obviously interlinked.

184. Strictly speaking, Texas Instruments, too, should belong to this category: TI was in fact a small company involved in geographical surveys.

185. Even new firms like SGS, in Italy, or EFCIS, in France, were directly established by big companies: Olivetti and Fairchild in the first case; Thomson and the Atomic Agency in the second.

186. The only case resembling a 'Schumpeterian entry' in Japan is Sony.

187. This statement is supported by qualitative evidence from interviews, even if precise figures of market shares in Europe for the fifties and early sixties, to our knowledge, are not available. For more recent data, see Table 3.9.

188. See Golding (1971); Sciberras (1977); Webbick (1977); Truel (1980).

189. The 'learning coefficient' (percentage decrease in unit costs to a doubling of volumes) of 28–30%, which is often mentioned by the experts has to be understood as a 'synthetic' measure of these three factors.

190. One would actually need company data on unit costs disaggregated by individual products.

191. Regression analysis (on log-linear equations) is conducted on nine groups of products. 'Learning coefficients' range between 25% and 47%. In the regressions, the dependent variables are average unit prices, as a proxy for unit costs. Notably that assumption is not only consistent with the hypothesis suggested here of mark-up pricing, but must implicitly introduce the stronger hypothesis of stability of the mark-ups themselves and of market shares. The coefficients on the dependent variable are all significant at 1% level and the correlation coefficients are very high (around or above .90). Durbin–Watson Tests often show cyclical serial correlation. We must mention, as it will be argued below, that serial correlation does not appear to be due to price fluctuations as a function of fluctuation in demand, but, on the contrary, to fluctuation in unit costs around the trend as an *inverse* function of the rate of growth of demand.

192. The latter is simply the sum of the flows per unit of time.

193. In the mentioned study, when the rate of output is added as an independent variable, it appears insignificant at 5% level in half of the equations. The value of the coefficients, in log-linear estimates, is always less than one and in four out of nine cases is negative (which would suggest declining or even negative marginal costs). When time also is introduced as an independent variable, the 'learning coefficients' (the coefficient on the cumulative volumes) assume unrealistic values (some are below -1.00 which again implies negative marginal costs (cf. Webbick, 1977). Certainly multicollinearity contributes to increase the uncertainty in the estimates.

194. A relationship of the form

$$\dot{\pi}/\pi = \alpha + \beta(\dot{Y}/Y)$$

where π stands for productivity and Y for output, and the expression $\dot{\pi}/\pi$ and $\dot{Y}/Y$ represent the percentage changes per unit of time. On the 'Verdoorn–Kaldor Law', see Kaldor (1966) and (1975) and, for an exciting extension to a more complete macroeconomic framework, Boyer et Petit (1980) and (1980a). We discuss the topics in detail in Dosi (1982a).

195. Our estimates, made on the 1963–76 period for the relationship between percentage change in productivity per man hour of direct labour and percentage change in output yield the following results:

$$\dot{\pi}/\pi = 30.08 + 0.02(\dot{Y}/Y) \qquad R^2 = 0.003$$
$$(0.17)$$

Even eliminating 1975 (which appears to be a quite exceptional year) we obtain

$$\dot{\pi}/\pi = 19.35 + 0.19(\dot{Y}/Y) \qquad R^2 = 0.12$$
$$(0.17)$$

(Standard errors are shown in parenthesis)

196. We must suggest particular caution in the interpretation of the results, based on rather aggregate data, instead of specific lines of products.

197. When the present study was written more recent Census data on the late seventies were not yet available.

198. Two series of estimates have been undertaken on data, by size of establishment, from the *American Census of Manufactures*. In a first estimated equation, value added per man-hour of direct worker, by size classes (π_w) has been regressed against the average size (in terms of number of direct workers) of each class size (ACS). A second equation related the same dependent variables (π_w) to the total number of direct worker in each size class (TCS). The first equation can be considered a very rough proximate of 'technical' economies of scale, while the second may be taken to represent the 'revealed' economies of scale, in so far as they are actually exploited by the firms (which would lead to a greater relative share of employment in the greater size classes). The limitations of those estimates, needless to say, are many and significant (amongst them, the facts that various establishments may produce different commodities, the degree of vertical integration in each establishment may be different and different stages of production may show different value added per direct workers, etc.). The estimated equations are:

1.1 $\log \pi_w$ (1967) $= 2.69 + 0.06 \log$ ACS (1967) $R^2 = 0.22$
$$(0.04)$$
1.2 $\log \pi_w$ (1972) $= 3.36 + 0.08 \log$ ACS (1972) $R^2 = 0.81$
$$(0.01)$$
2.1 $\log \pi_w$ (1967) $= 2.50 + 0.06 \log$ TCS (1967) $R^2 = 0.25$
$$(0.04)$$
2.2 $\log \pi_w$ (1972) $= 3.03 + 0.09 \log$ TCS (1972) $R^2 = 0.76$
$$(0.02)$$

(Standard errors in parenthesis.) Taking the two pairs of equations for each estimated year, it is encouraging to notice their similarity. In the seventies, economies of scale appear to have gained importance. In equations 1.2 and 2.2 the coefficients on the independent variable are significant at 1 per cent level.

199. See Sciberras (1977).
200. Dataquest, *Research Newsletter*, various issues.
201. Ibid; the figures are in volume terms (i.e. number of units).
202. Ibid; the datum is in value terms.
203. Ibid.
204. This same procedure has been followed by most of the studies in the field. See Nield (1963); Coutts, Godley and Nordhaus (1978); Sylos-Labini (1980).
205. To repeat, oligopolistic power, according to our model, stems from structural asymmetries between firms and does not imply any hypothesis on collusion.
206. This hypothesis is suggested by Weintraub (1958).
207. Differences both within the existing group of firms and between the latter and potential entrants.
208. We strictly refer to closed economies. The entry of new countries is a question that we shall discuss in the next chapter.
209. We believe this represents a rather general formulation of the hypothesis, suggested by Schumpeter in relation to individual entrepreneurs. For a discussion, see Chesnais (1981); Freeman (1981); and Freeman, Clark and Soete (1982).
210. To our knowledge, this is also what all other empirical tests on pricing behaviours have done.
211. For the procedures, see Appendix I.
212. The level of utilisation of capacity is often used for the purpose (see, for example, Coutts, Godley and Nordhaus (1978)). In the semiconductor industry that indicator is not available. The possibility of using the difference between trend value of output and actual output must be dismissed, since the long-run trend is made up of significantly different trend values in each demand cycle. The most satisfactory proxy appears to be the *change* in the rate of growth of demand *vis-à-vis* the previous year.
213. Firms necessarily have to consider forecasts of future technological changes, the shape of their own 'learning curve', etc.
214. This form of the estimate is, as it were, 'more demanding' than a simple log-linear regression, since it reduces the possible effect of time trends in the variables.
215. The coefficient on the 'demand variable' as approximated by the Δ log of the *change* in the rate of growth in output is not significantly different from zero. On the other hand, if demand is simply approximated by the Δ log of the output index, it becomes *negative* (significant at 1 per cent level).
216. Among those two factors, some authors suggest that the first is the most important or, at least, a crucial necessary condition (for example, Sylos-Labini (1967)). For a discussion of the second factor, cf. also Eckstein (1964); Eckstein and Wyss (1972).
217. The evidence strictly supports the hypothesis only as far as the comparison between 'large' and 'medium' firms is concerned, although it does not in a comparison between 'medium' and 'small' firms. An explanation could be

that very small firms are specialised in particular products or phases of production so that they can be to some extent 'price-makers'.

218. Note that all the econometric estimations have been conducted on American data. As we shall argue in the next chapter, the situation might have been different in Europe.

219. E.g. the sharp decline in TTL ICs, induced by an aggressive pricing policy by Texas Instruments in the years 1970–1.

220. Note that the utilised price index represents *actual* prices and not listed prices, since it has been obtained from unit value of shipment by product category (value divided by quantities).

221. Durbin Watson tests (which reveal serial correlation in the residuals) on the estimated equations do not rule out that possibility of long-term fluctuations.

222. As is well known, variations in capital/output ratios may be taken as a proxy of the existence of relative capital-saving or labour-saving biases in technical progress (if one accepts Harrod's definition of 'neutral' technical progress).

223. The relation between the two ratios is rather complex. By definition, total investment at time $t(=I_t)$ is equal to the net addition to productive capacity plus substitution for scrapped equipment:

$$I_t = \Delta K_t + aK_t \qquad\qquad 26$$

where a is a function of the rate of obsolescence. Net investment is some function of the growth of output and of technical progress, while scrapping is a function of some 'natural' obsolescence and of technical progress. Taking all this into account, and dividing both sides of eq. 26 by Y_t (output at time t), one obtains:

$$I_t/Y_t = [\lambda_1(g) + \lambda_2(a)] (K_t/Y_t) \qquad\qquad 27$$

where g is the rate of growth of output and λ_1 and λ_2 express the effect of technical progress on the new required equipment and on scrapping. If the long-run rate of growth does not change substantially, I/Y and K/Y should, broadly speaking, follow similar trends (although I/Y obviously reacts more swiftly than K/Y to any capital-saving or capital-using bias in technical progress).

224. See, above, the overview of the industry (p. 147); USITC (1979); Ernst (1982).

225. The 'learning effects' described above tend both to increase labour productivity and to decrease the 'physical' capital/output ratio.

226. It is worth mentioning that the process described here is quite different from either a process of factor substitution on a traditional production function or movement of the production function itself. Here one is describing a process whereby:

1. The relative price of capital inputs and final outputs are crucially determined by the respective trends in labour productivity.
2. Product-innovation in capital goods is by its nature capital-saving.
3. Factor substitution is intrinsically linked to cost-reducing technical progress.

The question of the existence of a production function does not even arise. For a stringent discussion of these problems see Pasinetti (1959), and, in the same issue of the *Review of Economics and Statistics*, Solow's comments and Pasinetti's reply. See also Pasinetti (1981).

227. With the slump of 1962–3, a substantial over-capacity emerged. For a brief description of public policies in this respect, see Freeman (1974). A similar situation was experienced by other industries. See, for example, on aluminium, Balconi (1977).

228. Military procurement, which, at that time, accounted for most of ICs demand, guaranteed a very substantial level of margins, at least partly protected from any worry about other competitive firms. Suppose that a firm enjoys a technological advantage in a certain product. A government contract for its purchase will generally be made on a cost-plus base. The contract will assure the demand for a certain quantity, independently of any expectation of future entry by other firms.

229. Strictly speaking, our considerations on pricing procedures, outlined in the previous section, apply to 'open' (non-procurement) markets. On military markets, a firm which enjoys a *present monopoly* may well behave as a monopolist, while we are suggesting that on 'open' markets, a *present* monopolist is likely to behave like an *oligopolist*, because he/she is not only thinking of the present but also of the future.

230. See *Electronics Times*, 7 January 1980.

231. Cf. USITC (1979).

232. *Prima facie*, this would support Eichner's view on the relationship between growth and levels of margins, through the cash-flow variable and the debt/equity constraint; cf. Eichner (1976). Note, however, that the causal relation seems to run from cash flows, as a constraint, to growth, and not vice versa.

233. A pattern *à la* Kalecki (1971).

234. An implication of this pattern is that the second industry (which is clearly a metaphor for the US one) must rely much more on being technologically ahead: if the two industries are technologically equal, the first tends to win. This is, we believe, the major difficulty facing the US industry at the beginning of the 1980s. (For a slightly different point of view, cf. Ernst (1982)).

235. Dosi (1981).

236. It is intuitively clear that if firms undergo a very high productivity growth while they are committed to lifetime employment of their workforce, they are bound to look for the highest possible growth rates.

237. In another context, this thesis is held by Odagiri (1981). See Marris and Mueller (1980) for a critical survey.

238. The theorem states that perfect markets account for capitalised profits so that the leverage ratio is irrelevant, cf. Modigliani and Miller (1958).

239. *A la* 'first' Schumpeter (1919).

4 Technical Change in the International Environment: The Dynamics of. Trade and Investment

In the previous chapter we analysed the effect of technical change upon industrial structures in relation to some fundamental variables (inter-firm technological lags and leads, productivity, prices, margins), under the assumption of a closed economy. We shall try now to extend the discussion to industries belonging to different countries and charac-terised by different capabilities to innovate and/or imitate.

By successive approximations, we will consider how technology gap theories of international trade and investment relate to the model of industrial structures and dynamics outlined above. The first section (4.1) approaches the problem considering some separate elements such as international prices and tries to define a few 'stylised facts'. Section 4.2 develops a more complete model of trade and international investment based on technological asymmetries between firms and countries. Two other important variables will be introduced in our framework, namely (a) international differences in wages, and (b) what we name 'specificity of each national market' which relates to a broad cluster of factors ranging from user–producer relationships to formal and informal trade protection.

Finally, the model will allow us to define the conditions for international convergence or divergence in terms of technological and income levels.

The second part of this chapter will analyse the case of the world semiconductor industry. International trade and direct foreign invest-ment progressively brought about the emergence of a world semiconductor market. The implications for the international structure of the industry will then be discussed.

4.1 TECHNOLOGY, TRADE FLOWS AND INTERNATIONAL INVESTMENT: AN INTRODUCTORY VIEW

Technology Gaps and Industrial Structures: Trade and Prices

Chapter 3 discussed the emergence of asymmetries among firms originated by different capabilities in producing and commercialising innovations. These asymmetries were likely to produce temporary oligopolies, a tendency towards the pre-emption of the market by the first-coming firms, and cost advantages due to dynamic economies of scale ('learning effects'). We are now in the position to generalise the model, in order to account also for foreign markets and international trade.

Let us first consider the cases whereby technology and relative technological levels of the various countries are crucial variables in determining trade flows. It seems therefore appropriate to start our discussion with a technology-based model of international trade (*à la* Posner[1]). As is well known in such a model, (a) trade flows are originated, in the first part of the life of a new product, by the existence of a positive difference between lags in consumption and lags in production in the imitating countries, as compared with the innovative one; (b) the rate of one-way trade between the innovative country and the 'rest of the world' is a function, other things being equal, of the former's rate of innovation.[2] One can easily see the intuitive consistency between the discussion undertaken above, in relation to firms in the first-coming market, and this account of foreign trade. One interesting problem concerns the effects that such trade flows have on the international structure of supply. To illustrate the point, we shall utilise Posner's model[3] with some relatively minor modifications, in order to link it more easily with our previous discussion.

Suppose the total lag between the initial introduction of a new product by a firm in country A and the first imitation by a firm in country B is equal to L, and the lag in demand is equal to λ. Obviously, the one-way trade that will occur over the period $(L-\lambda)$ and thereafter will be also a function of the *rates* of diffusion of the innovation, both in production and in consumption, in both countries. In the discussion in Chapter 3, we defined the implications of a technology lag, T, between first-coming firm(s) and imitative firms. Considerations of the same nature apply to would-be entrants from other countries. If, for simplicity, we neglect transport costs, tariffs or the possibility of discriminatory pricing in different markets, the 'barriers to entry' and the mobility barriers for foreign competitors are — in their nature — identical to those of domestic firms lagging behind (in country A), while the two possible significant advantages for a foreign company (a company from country B) could be (a) lower labour costs, and (b) a greater adaptability to the conditions of its own markets (what in the next section we will define as 'specificity-of-the-markets' effects). Let us neglect for the moment the possibility of direct investment in foreign countries and just focus on trade flows. An innovative company from country A which starts to export to country B after the demand lag (λ) is faced, in its pricing policy, with structural conditions of the same nature as discussed in the previous chapter. However, if we allow for price discrimination (but still overlooking transport costs and tariffs), the first-coming A firm might charge a price which accounts for entry barriers, mobility barriers and demand elasticity in each foreign market. Note that the innovative firm from country A has to consider the same cost function as in the previous chapter, while the demand function as well as the cost functions of would-be entrants from country B are generally different from A would-be entrants. Pricing policies in B markets will be approximately determined by the same factors outlined in the previous chapter: oligopolistic margins of the first-coming A-firms in B-markets will be a function of imitative lags (of both A-firms and B-firms[4]), learning effects, unit cost differentials between countries A and B (net of 'learnings effects'), differential 'market' advantages of B-firms, and demand elasticities.

Some properties of this simplified model are the following:

1. For any given elasticity of demand in market B, the differential, if there is any, between the price charged at any given time (after λ) in markets B and A is a *positive* function of the production lag in country B (i.e. the technologically determined lag after which the first firm from B is technically able to enter the market), a *negative* function of cost differentials between the two countries (to simplify, let us define them as differentials in wage rates)[5] whenever the latter are lower in country B, and are a *positive* function of labour productivity differentials (which is higher in country A, due to 'learning effects', etc.).

2. There is an *absolute advantage* for potential entrants belonging to

country *B* determined by such things as proximity to their own markets, untraded technological interdependences with domestic user industries, captive markets, etc. The degree of entry by country *B* firms, despite an entry-deterring pricing strategy by exporting firms from *A* is somewhat proportional to the importance of these factors.

One must stress again that what has been described as a fixed mark-up strategy must be considered merely as a yardstick for, and general approximation to, individual pricing behaviours. It is enough to recall that, in foreign markets (as well as in domestic ones), firms have two other national 'extreme' alternatives. First, they could charge 'monopoly prices' until either some firms from country *B* enter the market or other *A*-firms start exporting to *B*.[6] Second, the exporting firm from *A* could charge from the beginning a 'penetration price', well below the entry deterring one on market *B*.

Any price level in *B*-markets above the *A*-level, wherever *A*-firms are more than one, does require a certain amount of collusion between *A*-firms[7] and exercise of 'market power'. The more similar the industry is to the 'pure Schumpeterian' model of one (or a small group of) innovator(s) for each product-market (as described on pp. 135–8, the more likely is the possibility of oligopolistic price discrimination, according to the technological conditions of each country (i.e. the technological lags of *B*-firms).

Conversely, if there is no price discrimination, as one would expect if the industry is sufficiently integrated on an international level, then the *international price will be a function of the structural conditions of production in country A, the 'leading' country*. This may well yield to a price which is well below the notional 'limit price' corresponding to the conditions of production in country-*B*.

Finally, a particular case of an industry which is very integrated on an international level is that where the international price (in both countries *A* and *B*) and the margins of each company (both *A*-and *B*-companies) are a function of the relative technological differences (for given wages and exchange rates) between international firms operating in a world market.

We shall come back to these three cases and suggest that they correspond to three stages of a development of an industry, namely (a) the 'national oligopolies' stage, (b) the 'unification-of-the-world-markets' stage, and (c) the 'international oligopoly' stage.

It is of some interest to compare this simple illustration with technology–gap and product–cycle accounts of international trade. All the properties outlined above are clearly consistent with 'technological' theories of trade, to which one has only added some 'micro' considerations on price and market strategies by individual firms. Furthermore, trade flows are explained here by means of differences in the production structure amongst countries, in relation to their capability to innovate/imitate as in 'technology-gap' models.[8] Unlike strict product–cycle theories,[9] we do not identify the *deus ex machina* of trade patterns in differences in the nature of the markets and in income levels among countries. Another difference with product–cycle models is that we suppose that supply of an innovative commodity and its domestic demand may not be independent of each other. On the contrary, we suggest, a strong interdependence is likely, so that leads and lags in the introduction of an innovation favour/hinder their diffusion in consumption. The differential advantage of the innovative country rests upon a differential technological capability. This asymmetry among countries is – as it were – 'carried on' over time through the dynamic economies associated with an early production, and with the size and nature of the domestic market in the innovating country. The latter, however, is not simply a 'datum' but is partly built by the innovation itself.

On the other hand, domestic firms in the imitating countries have an absolute advantage in the interrelation with their domestic market[10] and might have another one in differential wage rates. Suppose that (a) the life-cycle of a product is sufficiently long; (b) its production technology reaches a relative stability, and (c) after some time, production technology becomes relatively standardised and internationally available. Under these circumstances the dynamic economies of scale, which represented, together with the innovative lead, the differential advantage of country A, increasingly bottom out.[11] There must come a point when the 'domestic market effect' and/or differential wage rates will completely offset the relative advantage of country A. All this might occur *despite* any possible behavioural assumption about export and pricing policies of A-firms: the latter may well try to keep their leadership in market B for as long as possible, but – if technology stabilises – they will not be able to maintain it indefinitely, since, after a certain time, this would imply charging a price in B below the price charged in A, or even below production costs. This case is rather similar to the product–cycle model. Production starts to flow down to 'second-coming' countries and then to 'third-coming' countries, etc. The argument implies that some entries in B do occur after the lag period L despite possible entry deterring pricing on exports to B, due to proximity-to-the-domestic-markets effects, captive markets, or big *B*-firms ready and capable to enter despite prolonged losses, etc. So, 'there is some game': *B*-firms start with a disadvantage but, at the end, the cost advantage associated with the late-coming countries, i.e. lower wages, becomes increasingly effective. This classical product–cycle approach actually represents a strong 'diffusionist' point of view. Everyone has a place in the international division of labour. It is a 'diffusionist' hypothesis because it allows late-coming countries to catch-up in relatively 'mature' technologies: moreover, if the growth of production and income has a long-run effect on the technological lags, the long-run trend is likely to head towards *convergence* among countries which start from different technological income levels.

Conversely, it is possible to describe the conditions under which asymmetries among countries are cumulative or, at least, stable.

Suppose that (a) the life-cycle of a product is rather short, since new products quickly substitute for the old ones; (b) the rate of technical change both in product and process technology is rather high, and (c) technical innovations are not the result of a random process, but have a cumulative nature so that, other things being equal, the innovative country of today has the greatest likelihood of being also the innovative country of tomorrow. Under these conditions, it is easy to see how production does *not* flow down to second-coming countries, but the relative advantage of *A* is kept through time by means of a rather stable flow of innovations in *A* which prevent any easy catching-up by *B*. Even if there are *B*-firms able to enter the *B*-market after the lag time *L*, they will not have time to overcome their relative disadvantage, and in the next round (the next 'vintage' of products) they will find themselves again lagging behind. Countries which did not succeed in entering the 'present round' are not likely to enter the next one either.

Asymmetries among countries will remain stable, increase or slowly decrease, depending on the rate of technical change, the technological lag and leads among countries, the degree of cumulativeness of technical progress, its appropriability and the rate of substitution between old and new products. These are the factors which determine whether a product–cycle/diffusionist case or a cumulative technology-gap one is likely to occur.

The discussion so far provides us with a few 'stylised facts' and a framework for the interpretation of the trends in trade flows and international investments. We must now attempt to provide a more organic account of the relationship between international technological asymmetries, international oligopolistic structures and trade flows.

Before undertaking this task, however, we must introduce an additional feature of technology and technical change, namely the possibility of appropriation and internalisation within companies of the 'untraded' aspect of technical change.

At least since Arrow's article (Arrow, 1962), 'knowledge' is recognised to be a particular kind of 'commodity' (or asset) with few special features which make it different from ordinary commodities. In particular, its specific characteristics, related to divisibility, tradeability and appropriability, retain some features – to use the traditional language – of a 'public good'[12] and of an 'externality'. Certainly there are important *traded* aspects of technical change and innovation, as it is embodied in tradeable commodities or traded in the form of patent licensing, know-how transfers, etc. At the other extreme, part of technical knowledge takes the form of a pure 'public good' in so far as scientific and technical articles and papers are freely available to everyone. Between these two extremes, however, there are important aspects of technical change which are *untraded* as such, but, under certain conditions, are *privately appropriable*. A clear example, whenever technology maintains some cumulative features, is learning-by-doing.

The existence, noted above, of phenomena of interlinked technological trajectories and of varying patterns of interaction between major technological systems or paradigms must also be taken into account. In some instances, technical change may represent an 'externality' to each individual company (sometimes defined as a 'conducive environment' to innovation); in others, it may be *internalised* within companies and thus becomes a differential asset. The latter may then represent a powerful oligopolistic asset. A long-forgotten article by Coase (1937) suggested this to be an important factor leading to vertical integration. Hymer (1976) and Buckley and Casson (1976) argue the role of internalisation as a determinant of the development of multinational enterprises and international oligopolies. As we shall see at more length below, when discussing Dunning's 'eclectic theory' of international investment and trade, these technology-related factors correspond to the *ownership–specific* and *internalisation–specific* advantages which multinational enterprises are likely to enjoy (Dunning, 1977 and 1979). In our view, it would be misleading to consider internalisation simply as an effect of and a reaction to some kind of 'market imperfection'.[13] It is probably more accurate to consider it as one of the inner trends (and one of the 'rules of the game') in oligopolistic rivalry towards the transformation of the untraded features of technical change into proprietor assets which, as such, also represent entry barriers and differential advantages *vis-à-vis* other competitors.

4.2 INTERNATIONAL TECHNOLOGICAL ASYMMETRIES, OLIGOPOLY AND WAGE RATES: AN ATTEMPT AT A SYNTHESIS

As many authors have stressed in recent literature on the subject (see Chesnais and Michon-Savarit, 1980; Momigliano, 1981), there is need, more than ever before, for some kind of synthesis between explanations of trade and investments. That 'synthesis' also implies the establishment of some kind of relation between regularities in company behaviour, on the one hand, and regularities in the structural features of the patterns of trade and investment of each country, on the other hand.

Dunning's *eclectic theory* provides a methodological starting point in this direction, since it begins to bridge theories of industrial organisation and theories of international location and trade (Dunning 1977, 1979, 1981). In his work, Dunning distinguishes between *company–specific* and *country–specific* relative advantages. If the former and the latter can be proved to have some dynamic relationship with each other, one is then provided with the beginning of a linkage between the micro-level (i.e. inter-firm asymmetries) and the macro-level (patterns and changes in the international division of labour and patterns of international competitiveness of each country).

It may be worth briefly recalling the questions that a combined theory of trade and investment is required to answer:[14]

1. What are the factors which explain overall *'foreign involvement'* (cf. Lall, 1980), in the form of both exports and direct investment, of companies belonging to a certain country in a given sector? In other words, where do the advantages of a certain group of companies *vis-à-vis* others of other 'nationality' and/or location come from?
2. What is the exact nature of the relations between country–specific and company–specific advantages?
3. What are the determinants of and the regularities in the choice between the two main alternative forms of foreign involvement, namely, exports and direct foreign investments?[15]

It is impossible here to discuss at length those results which are relatively established in the literature with respect to these questions. All we can do is to point out a few hypotheses which have, in our view, the most general relevance.

The International Oligopoly

The readers will have certainly noticed that the discussion of the former section is based on the same variables which underpinned the model of inter-firm asymmetries and oligopoly in a closed economy. The point must be stressed: *the same structural elements which yield to permanent (even if changing through time) differences between firms, in terms of innovative lags and leads, different costs of production, market pre-emption, etc., are also the explanatory variables of international differences in specialisation and competitiveness.*

We have identified four main sources of oligopolistic asymmetries between companies, namely:

1. Size-related technological discontinuities (associated with economies of scale).
2. Leads and lags in innovative and imitative capabilities (in both products and processes) associated with pre-emption of the markets by first-comers and different techniques and costs of production.
3. Whenever unit costs are also a function of cumulated production, through *learning curves*, leads and lags manifest themselves also through cost differentials, even holding the basic product and process technology constant.
4. Internalisation of technological interdependences, experience of management of technological systems, etc. may become a differential asset of some firms *vis-à-vis* other competitors.

Whenever these factors are at work, both within each economy and in the international arena, we may expect the development of some kind of international oligopoly. More precisely, from an historical point of view, we suggest the existence of three stages in the development of industrial organisations, associated with the emergence of a new technology and its establishment:[16]

1. A phase of *national oligopolies* (initially quite fluid, *à la* 'first' Schumpeter (1919)) and national markets.
2. A phase of *unification of world markets*, of which important aspects are international investments and a tendency towards (more or less) unique international prices.

3. A phase of *international oligopolistic stabilisation*, whereby most of the companies competing in the international markets are international companies, few new entries occurring, with the exception of 'side' entries by big conglomerates and/or ventures backed by national governments.

How far one may generalise this pattern is, of course, an empirical matter. *A priori*, however, one would expect that it is likely to suit whenever at least some of the following conditions hold:

1. The rate of technical change remains high.
2. The degree of appropriability of innovations is high.
3. Technical progress is cumulative.
4. At least some untraded aspects of technological development can be internalised within companies.
5. Technology is quite complex (sometimes related to technological *systems*), so that there might be an organisational entry-barrier related to the capability of managing such systems.
6. Unit costs are also a function of learning curves.
7. There are static entry-barriers related to size and to economies of scale.

Not all of these conditions, of course, must apply in order to achieve an international oligopoly: in some respects, industries can be placed on a continuum, ranging from, say, computers or semiconductors where most of these conditions appear to hold, down to non-fashion clothing or wood products where none of these factors are likely to be very powerful.

To put it in a provocative way, we could reverse the implicit assumption of a good part of current economics that oligopolies are 'limit cases' of a 'free competitive norm', into the opposite statement: free competitive markets are a limit case of economic conditions which 'normally' tend to oligopolistic structures of supply. We hope that our analysis, which traces the origin of this trend to the asymmetric characteristics of technology and to the processes of appropriation of innovations, has been convincing. However, the reader is also free to resort to some simple casual empiricism, and inquire whether the 'typical' contemporary industrial structure is more akin to that of the computer industry or to that, say, of handmade paper flowers.

One of the implications of the argument is the following: given other context conditions such as national wage rates and exchange rates, *technology* – in the broader meaning of international asymmetries in innovative capabilities, productivity differences, etc. *– is the crucial variable in determining total foreign involvement*.[17]

We have been suggesting that there are powerful forces driving towards oligopolistic stability. Stability, however, does not mean fossilisation. Let us recall a few quite general factors which impress dynamism on the system and affect change, both under conditions of a closed economy and in the international arena.

First, technical change, even of the most 'normal' (as defined in Chapter 2) and cumulative nature, is still a stochastic process. This implies, among other things, that even under stable oligopoly conditions a big firm, which has been very innovative in the past, is very likely, but is *not certain*, to be so in the future. In more general terms: given the stochastic nature of many technical advances, which are parts of the patterns of oligopolistic rivalry, changes in firms' relative position *vis-à-vis* each other are continuously occurring, even if the probability of disruption of the overall structure of supply is very low.

Second, we have already mentioned how the emergence of new – radically different – technologies disrupts entrenched oligopolistic positions. In our view this is one of the main mechanisms of long-run change in supply structures.

Finally, there often exist 'external' environmental factors which produce instability, at varying degrees, in both national and international oligopolistic structures. These sources of instability (whose effect may range between relatively minor changes in short-run pricing policies and major 'oligopolistic wars') stem from a wide set of factors, including political–institutional ones, major drops in demand, long-run macroeconomic divergence in productivity and growth between countries, unexpected overcapacities, etc. Historically, one of the most important factors of disruption of the international structure of supply have been wars and political changes.

In the following analysis we shall consider, step by step, the variables leading to the formation of international oligopolistic structures and those affecting their inner dynamics. The discussion above provides us with a powerful starting point: under the simplifying assumption of no international investment, inter-country asymmetries exactly mirror the inter-firm asymmetries which we analysed in a closed economy context. Loosely speaking, these asymmetries are of two kinds. First, there are commodities which some countries (companies) are capable of producing and others are not. Second, for each commodity that a certain group of countries (companies) are able to produce, some countries (companies) can manufacture them at lower cost than others. The more complex case is this second one and the discussion that follows will focus on it.

Technical progress, both in the form of *process* innovation and *product* innovations, can be regarded as an asymmetry-creating factor, which tends to induce *divergence* between firms, and between countries, in terms of international specialisation.[18] Conversely, there are factors which tend to induce *convergence* and *international diffusion* of technology.[19] Among them there are: (a) free international diffusion of scientific and technological knowledge (e.g. publications, etc.); (b) traded transfers of technology (licencing, transfer of know-how, etc.); (c) processes of technological imitation by late-coming companies and countries (both 'spontaneous' and government-induced imitation).

Multinational investment overlaps with the latter two factors and may be considered, to different degrees, a vehicle of international diffusion of technology, which does not obviously bring about convergence between companies but may do so between countries.

There are two powerful and general driving forces which, in our view, set in motion both autonomous 'catching-up' processes by domestic firms in countries lagging behind and international investment by companies from the countries 'on the technological frontiers'. They are: (a) international differences in unit variable costs and primarily *international differences in wage rates*, and (b) the 'specificity' of local markets, including everything which in traditional economics goes under the heading of 'market imperfections': the advantage enjoyed by local manufacturing due to a 'proximity-to-the-market' effect, and – in addition – various forms of government intervention, tariff and non-tariff barriers, transport costs, etc.

Wages and Costs

One can easily see the role of wages, by contrast, making use of the model developed in Chapter 3. There (e.g. especially pp. 131–5) each firm clearly had to pay the same wage rates irrespective of whether it was a leader or a follower. In the international context one must abandon that assumption. Companies belonging to late-coming countries might have wages low enough, at current exchange rates, to compensate (or more than compensate) for differences in productivity with respect to the leading companies (countries). In theory, one can always conceive of a notional wage which is low enough to match productivity differentials (of course, in practice, this wage might be below the subsistence level, or, after allowing for 'external diseconomies', might well be negative).

Capital equipment and material inputs are commodities, like any other manufactured goods, which have (approximately) unique prices on the international markets. International differentials in *total* unit costs will thus be determined by labour productivity and wage rates,[20] at any given exchange rate. The analysis from Chapter 3 on inter-firm technological asymmetries explains also international differences in productivity in terms of technological lags and leads, learning curves, economies of scale, etc.

On the other hand, wage rates – in terms of an international currency – are determined by *macroeconomic* factors.[21] Finally, the actual and the minimum acceptable[22] rates of profit in each economy are also determined on macroeconomic grounds. In this chapter we must confine the analysis to the level of any one individual sector. However, we may already advance the hypothesis that international differentials in profit rates cannot be high enough to compensate for international productivity differences.[23] Thus, we suggest the following proposition: labour productivity and wage rates are, jointly, the proximate determinants of both international differences in variable unit costs and the competitive position of each country (i.e. of the companies belonging to each country),[24] *for any given relative technological level.* (For a more rigorous analysis, cf. Appendix II.)

The point can be illustrated by redrawing Figure 3.3 from Chapter 3. Suppose there are three firms (named *1*, *2*, and *3*), corresponding to three countries. Company *1* enjoys a higher labour productivity than Company *2*, whose productivity in turn is higher than Company *3*. C_1^*, C_2^*, C_3^* represent unit labour costs[25] *if* every country had the same wage rates as country *1*. Under these conditions, company *3* could not profitably produce at the price level P (expressed in an international currency).

However, suppose that wage differences between the three companies (countries) more than compensate for productivity differentials, so that the actual unit labour costs for countries *2* and *3* are C_2 and C_3 respectively. The figure depicts a case of *competitiveness reversal* due to wage rate differentials. One can easily imagine the notional case of the *most efficient country* expelled from the market: in Figure 4.1, if the international price falls below C_1 the technologically leading country is immediately forced out of the market.[26]

The effects of wages upon inter-country (inter-firm) asymmetries will depend on technology and on the patterns of technical change *in each industry*.[27] One would clearly expect these effects to have a lower importance in high technology industries. First, as we already mentioned, there are commodities which only the technological leader(s) are

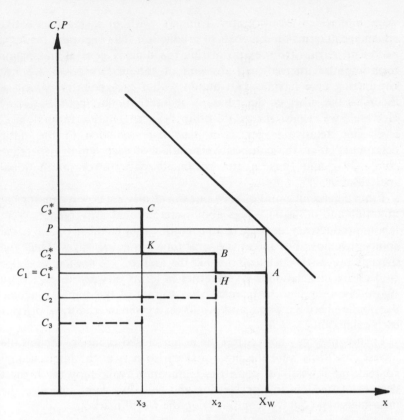

FIGURE 4.1   *Unit costs and international differences in wage rates*

capable of producing. Under these circumstances, the relative levels of
wage rates are obviously irrelevant to the international competitiveness
of each country. Second, even in the case of a group of countries which
do know how to produce a certain commodity, our discussion in
Chapter 3 suggests that the ranking of labour productivities for different
countries (companies) will show a very steep profile as a function of the
technological lags. In other words, in Figure 4.1, the line
AHBKC . . . will be very steep upwards and differential wage rates will
not substantially effect inter-country (inter-company) technological
asymmetries.

At any point in time (i.e. from a static perspective) there is a clear
relationship between relative technological capabilities and relative
wages (expressed in an international currency). In other words,
the higher the technological level of a country, the higher also the

wage rate which that country 'can pay' without losing its relative advantage in terms of unit costs of production. The impatient reader is invited to refrain from extrapolating too quickly general statements regarding the international division of labour, since we are not considering here income distribution within each country, which in theory is the other co-determinant of international specialisation.[28] However, we regard the relationship between relative technological levels and relative wages as a *good approximation* to the static determination of the competitive position of each country for each commodity, and thus of the proximate patterns of international specialisation.[29]

From a dynamic point of view one can clearly see how technological imitation and diffusion brings about international convergence. Were labour productivity identical in all countries, they could all obtain equal competitive positions and at the same time pay equal wages. Thus, the dynamic processes which tend to make the *AHBKC* . . . line flat, tend also to decrease international asymmetries in terms of wage rates. (More rigorously, they tend to increase the 'degrees of freedom' of income distribution between wages and profits for a given international price of each commodity.)

Finally, one may notice that, as in our closed economy model, the lowest cost firms were the price makers, so it is in the international context: the lowest cost countries (companies) will enjoy the highest degrees of freedom in price-setting and will thus determine also the infra-marginal country (company) on the world market.

The 'Specificity' of each Market as a Diffusive Factor

The second variable we mentioned as a convergence factor between countries characterised by different technological capabilities was the 'specificity' of each market. By that we mean, broadly speaking, some special right of access to a market segment by a group of firms, *despite* their being technologically late. This special right may be straightforward and politically induced: this is the case of import tariff and quotas. Other features of the economic system, however, perform the same function, to different degrees.

First different features of demand in each country can perform that role. Imagine the existence of an unchallenged American technological leader in the toothpaste industry. However, the Americans prefer a peppermint flavour, while, say, the Italians love a subtle spaghetti taste. Italian firms are thus somehow sheltered and can enter the market despite their technological lags, if they have a special knowledge of the 'Italian taste'.

Second, and much more important, in our view, are the patterns of user–producer relationship which often require geographical and economic proximity and induce a strong 'buy local' bias.

Transport costs are yet another factor which shelters each market from the others.

In the last resort, most of these very different factors come under the textbook headings of 'imperfect markets' and 'imperfect information'. In our framework, contrary to being a simple 'distortion' of the economic system, they are an essential feature of it and foster technological diffusion preventing the first-coming countries (companies) from higher levels of market pre-emption.

In actual fact, these cases of 'market imperfection' highlight complex and relatively unexplored trade-offs between 'static' and 'dynamic' efficiency. From a static point of view, a 'perfect market' is likely to induce the most efficient allocation of production in a 'Ricardian' fashion, based on the comparative advantage of each country in one or some productions. On the other hand, from a dynamic point of view, market imperfection – and thus some static inefficiencies – is one of the factors which allows growth and technological catching-up by countries which are not on the technological frontier.[30] Incidentally, this is also the reason why historically technological winners have always cried out in favour of unconditional *laissez-faire* and the elimination of all obstacles to trade. Extrapolating from present trends, it is very easy to forecast that in, say, ten years time, one of the items of revealed comparative advantage, in US trade towards Japan, will be economics textbooks on general equilibrium and factor proportions in the theory of trade.

Both the two considered convergence factors (differential wage rates and 'specificity' of the markets) are *country–specific* variables, and tend to favour late-coming countries and the corresponding companies *despite* their relative technological backwardness.

Multinational investment is precisely the attempt to dissociate these country–specific advantages from the corresponding domestic companies and exploit them on the part of some companies which enjoy company–specific (*lato sensu* technological) advantages.

Let us follow this interpretation of Dunning's seminal model and study the interplay between (a) technology-based inter-firm and international asymmetries, (b) different national wage rates, and (c) the 'specificity' of each market which, in terms of demand, makes imports to be only an imperfect substitute for domestic production.

Technology, Markets and Wages: The Determinants of Direct Foreign Investment

The existence of inter-firm technological asymmetries (which Dunning (1977) calls ownership–specific and internalisation–specific advantages) represents the *necessary* condition for international investment to emerge. These asymmetries are the same ones which lead to oligopolistic positions, market pre-emption by the technological leaders, etc. in a closed economy context. They are not sufficient, however, to explain direct foreign investment. In other words, given these inter-firm and international asymmetries one could easily imagine all foreign markets serviced via exports.

The model of choice between exports and investments that we are going to present follows similar attempts by S. Hirsch (1976) and Buckley and Casson (1981), but will focus on partly different variables and functional relationships.[31]

Let us consider a technologically leading firm which belongs to country A and manufactures a new product that can either be exported to market B or manufactured in B. To repeat, the company faces this choice because of its technological advantage. Direct investment, however, does not automatically follow from the latter.

Our model will focus on three factors affecting the choice (and, as we shall see, the possible mix) of exports and direct investment, namely:

1. Unit labour costs. For a given capital–embodied technique of production, unit labour costs differ in relation to international differentials in wage rates and, quite often, also to non-transferable learning-by-doing, expertise disembodied from capital equipment, etc.
2. The relationship between local investment and market shares. We can name this as the 'proximity-to-the-market' effect on market shares. This factor is implied in our discussion above on the 'specificity' of each market and the imperfect substitutability between imports and local production. Moreover, a crucial parameter entering the evaluation of the importance of foreign market shares is clearly their absolute size and their rates of growth.
3. 'External' economies and diseconomies which characterise the economic and technological environments A and B. (These economies and diseconomies often relate to technological relationships with suppliers, available skills, training costs, etc.)

What follows is an illustration of the interplay between these factors.[32] The model is based on the following hypotheses:

1. There are fixed and given coefficients of production in A and B: l_A and l_B, $k_A = k_B$ are the respective unit labour and capital coefficients (in physical terms). The technique employed in A and B is the same, but labour productivity differs due to non-transferable learning-by-doing, etc. (Thus: $l_B > l_A$).

2. There is a minimum threshold below which direct investment will not be undertaken (let us call that threshold K_m). It is clearly related to the size of the foreign market M_B and to the share of the considered company in it (s).

3. There are additional costs in investing in B related, say, to locational diseconomies (we assume that they are represented by a fixed cost, C, so that their impact upon unit costs is an inverse proportion of the production capacity built abroad).

4. Future market shares are positively associated with the size of direct investment K. Suppose, for example, that if $K = 0$, the market share will progressively tend to zero, through a certain period τ, whose length is jointly determined by (a) the degree of appropriability of the innovation which the new product embodies, (b) the imitation lag of B-firms, and, (c) the 'specificity' of market B which can shelter the imitative efforts of B-companies and give them an advantage on the local market. For the sake of simplicity, we assume here that the imitation lag time for B-companies has already elapsed, so that the latter may begin their appearance on the local market. The levels of market shares after the period τ are a function of the present direct investment and will be stable thereafter.

5. Countries A and B have different wage rates ($W_A > W_B$) but equal cost of capital (i.e. of 'machines'), P_k. We assume an exchange rate equal to one and an identical international price of the considered commodity.

From a static point of view the criterion of investment is quite straightforward and involves only the comparison of the rates of profits related to the two different locations (r_A and r_B):

$$w_A l_A + p_k \cdot k \, (1 + r_A) = p \qquad\qquad 28$$

$$w_B l_B + \left(p_k \cdot k + \frac{C}{X_B} \right)(1 + r_B) = p \qquad\qquad 29$$

where X_B is the output from the investment located in country B and p is the unit price of the commodity.

One may distinguish between two cases:

$r_A > r_B$

$r_B > r_A$

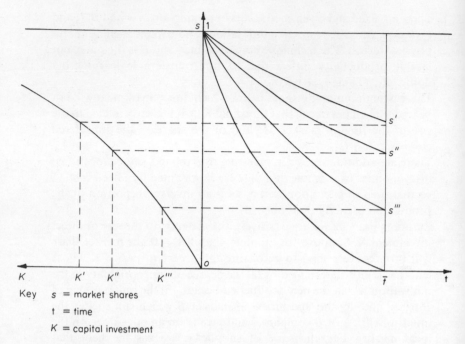

Key   s = market shares
       t = time
       K = capital investment

FIGURE 4.2   *Foreign investment and foreign market shares: an illustration*

for some $X_B \leqslant M_B/p$

where M_B is the total size of market B in value terms.

Whenever the rate of profit in B is higher than in A for some acceptable X_B, no trade-off between static profitability and long-run market shares will emerge. If anything, the question will concern how big a share of the A market will be served from the B-location, without losing market shares in A to other possible A-based competitors. This case illustrates a clear *diffusive effect of differential wage rates despite locational diseconomies and lower productivity in the country lagging behind.*

The case whereby $r_A > r_B$ for every acceptable X_B is more complex. A static criterion based on the simple comparison of profit rates would suggest a location in A. On the other hand, this choice would lead to a market share for the considered firm in market B which will progressively shrink.

For simplicity, we assume that at the beginning B-market is entirely supplied by the considered firm, so that its market share, $s_0 = 1$. Assume that market shares will take some time to adjust to the investment decisions taken at $t = 0$. The total imitation time for B-firms, which depends, among other things, on their relative technological backwardness, is equal to T. Figure 4.2 provides an illustration of the possible relationship between foreign investment and 'final' market shares in B. The 'final' market share (s_T) of the A-firm is a function of the direct investment undertaken at time zero.[33]

$$s_T = f(K_B) \qquad\qquad 30$$

The time path of market shares between 0 and T can be illustrated, for example, by a steady percentage change as a function of the initial investment

$$\begin{aligned} \Delta s/s &= f(X_B) \\ &= F(K_B) \end{aligned} \quad \text{in the interval } [0, T] \qquad 31$$

which yields to

$$s_T(K_B) = s_0 e^{\lambda T} \qquad\qquad 32$$

where $\lambda = F(K_B)$, with $F'(K_B) > 0$, $F''(K_B) < 0$

The interesting case concerns the possibility of direct investment which does not stem from 'static' profitability criteria. Firms 'thinking ahead' might still choose to undertake it, even if the present rate of profit (and for that matter, the *present* total profits) are lower with foreign manufacturing facilities than without them. If a firm is 'growth-maximising' the choice is rather obvious: an investment will be undertaken under the constraints that (a) the overall rate of profit for the firm[34] must be above a certain minimum, and, possibly, (b) the amount of productive capacity in B must not be in excess of the corresponding market share in market B at time T. Suppose that the resulting investment is K' and the corresponding 'final' market share, s', in Figure 4.2.

In actual fact, firms are likely to present less straightforward rules of investments, which, in the literature, sometimes go under the heading of 'long-run profit maximisation'. As we have already discussed, the definition is somewhat vague because we know neither how long the long-run is nor what will be the time profile of variable costs and prices.[35] All this notwithstanding, an exercise of long-run profit maximisation appears to be useful in order to highlight the parameters involved in the choice regarding the forms of foreign involvement. The calculation of the present value of future gross profits under different possible amounts of foreign investments (PV_I),[36] and its comparison with the present value of future profits under the 'export-only' scenario (PV_x), leads to the determination of some 'optimal' amount of foreign investment.[37]

Whenever $PV_I > PV_x$

for some $H_0 \leqslant M_0$

(where H is the productive capacity, in physical terms, associated with a certain amount of investment and M_0 is the size of the host market, again in physical terms), then:

$$\max\,(PV_I) \qquad\qquad 33$$

jointly with
$$\lambda = F(K)$$
$$H = \theta(K)$$

will determine the 'optimal' value of K.

We are particularly interested in the variations of foreign investments in relation to variations in the parameters. We can state the following properties, which are quite important for our discussion:

1. One of the parameters is the time length over which revenues are discounted (T): the more companies are 'far-sighted' the more they are likely to undertake foreign investment. Despite unfavourable 'static' profitability calculations, it is likely that a firm looking far enough ahead, will choose some combination between local manufacturing and exports. An identical argument applies to the rate at which the future is discounted: the lower uncertainty and risk-adversity, the higher is the amount of investment (if any is undertaken).
2. The amount of investment undertaken (if any) will depend negatively[38] on the difference in variable costs in the two countries (i.e. on the relative balance between differential wage rates and differential productivities).
3. The perspective growth of the foreign market, other things being equal, has a positive effect on present investment decisions.
4. We have already said that the responsiveness of the market share to direct investment is (a) a negative function of the relative technological 'backwardness' of B-firms, in the sense that if they are lagging very far behind, market shares of the A-firm will remain rather stable irrespective of their investment policies, thus making the 'adjustment time', τ, very long, and (b) a positive function of the 'specificity' of the B-market. The higher this specificity (i.e., in neoclassical terms, its 'imperfection' or degree of protection), the higher also is the incentive to invest, since otherwise market shares will shrink relatively quickly.

This illustration, for the sake of simplicity, considered just one A-firm.

This was done to explain the fundamental determinants of international investment which are quite independent from the specific patterns of intra-oligopolistic rivalry between A-firms. The latter, on their hand, are likely to explain the pattern and the timing of investment by a group of leading firms, as Knickerbocker (1973) convincingly suggests: if one of the leading firms does invest, the phenomenon is likely to trigger an imitation effect in other A-firms, which do not want to lose the B-market to the first foreign investor.

This simple model highlights how foreign investment, according to our hypotheses, is determined by the same variables which affect the process of international technological diffusion under a capital– immobility assumption: to use Dunning's terminology, it matches a *company–specific* asymmetry (the technological advantage of A-firms) and a few *country–specific* asymmetries (differential wage rates and specificity of local markets). In doing so, it represents both a vehicle of technological diffusion and a mechanism of international oligopolistic stabilisation.

At this point, the reader may wonder what is the long-run effect of this new actor (the international company) upon the long-run relative position of the host countries and the countries of origin, in terms of trade and international division of labour. Before suggesting few and tentative hypotheses on the issue, however, we must consider the implication of the existence of oligopolies with respect to trade flows.

International Trade and Investment: The Role of International Oligopolies

The analysis of the determinants of international investment provides, at any point in time, the behavioural link – on the part of the leading companies – between factors which exist quite independently from multinational investment: technological lags and leads between companies and countries, different productivities and wages, different degrees of substitutability between imports and local production. In so far as international trade remains *only* an effect of these factors, international investment does not change anything in the pattern of trade flows: only the ownership of the traded commodities obviously changes.

Several trade analyses, which neglect the international industrial structure and its patterns of ownership, embody precisely this hypothesis. In our view, such an assumption has stronger implications than is often supposed. It means, for example, that a given technological capability of a country is exploited to the same degree, independently of the particular configuration of supply in terms of market structure. In other words, one must assume that in the international markets, the 'visible hand', in Chandler's words, (Chandler, 1966), of companies' strategies and strengths performs – in terms of final results – in the same way as would the 'invisible hand' of free competitive market mechanisms.[39]

There are several theoretical and empirical reasons which challenge that assumption. Let us start by recalling some rather well-known empirical findings: (a) other things being equal, exports appear to be directly related to firms' size, for reasons which do not show a straightforward link with technological differentials;[40] (b) export performance (in the case of the USA) appears to be related to the nature of oligopolies (Pagoulatos and Sorensen, 1976); (c) the abundant evidence on intra-industry trade indirectly hints at the role of international oligopolistic competition and market structures in shaping trade patterns.[41]

On theoretical grounds, our discussion so far appears also to indicate that the *history* of technological and economic development of an industry and of each individual company bears an important influence upon the present competitive position of each company, even apart from the present relative technological capabilities and the present costs conditions. More precisely, the *history* of the technological development of a company and – in general – the history of its relative competitive success *vis-à-vis* other companies is also the history of market shares, market pre-emption, geographical diffusion and possibly diversification and differentiation of production:[42] all these variables affect *present* competitive performance, on both domestic and international markets, in ways which may be independent from *present* relative technological capabilities and *present* relative costs.[43]

The role of industrial organisation becomes even more important when we introduce international investment into the picture. Our entire discussion so far rests on the existence of powerful oligopolistic positions between companies which are unevenly distributed across countries.[44]

International oligopolies affect – in our view – trade flows in two ways. First, at any point in time, the oligopolistic advantages of the companies of each country reflect, *for a part*, present technological and cost advantages (or disadvantages), and as such can be directly expressed through them, *but not entirely so*. The evolution of industrial structures affects directly the patterns of competitiveness at each moment in time because it influences market penetration and, *lato sensu*, market power.[45] In other words, we must set aside entirely the idea that international markets work through 'auctions' and introduce instead patterns of international oligopolistic rivalry whereby, in determining the amounts sold, the strength of the seller counts as well as the nature of the commodity and its price.

Thus the patterns of international location of production affect international competitiveness in ways that might well be different from those which would have occurred without international oligopolistic formations, but in the presence of identical distributions of location–specific advantages and disadvantages. *A country's partici-pation in the international oligopoly for any given industrial sector, and the share of its production accounted for by foreign companies* have to be considered among the variables which explain that country's patterns of specialisation for *given* technological capabilities and *given* relative wage rates.

This property appears also in our model of international investment: for unchanged technological positions of the two countries (*A* and *B*) and unchanged unit costs, international investment clearly affects the pattern of trade flows (in our case it is going to have an import–substitution effect for country *B*).

From a dynamic point of view, international investment and the related international oligopolies contribute to shape the dynamics of country–specific advantages, in so far as they affect the international diffusion of technology and the international distribution of innovative capabilities.

This is a point which must be stressed: under conditions of technical change, *company–specific and country–specific technological advantages are dynamically inter-related.* If technical progress is somehow cumulat-ive, not only at company level but also at country level, the relative advantage of one country *vis-à-vis* others does not stem from any 'original endowment' but from differential technological knowledge, experience, etc. *which reproduce through time.* In other words, 'compara-tive advantages' are a *joint-production* with the production of the commodities themselves. From this, one can easily argue the possibility of 'virtuous circles' and 'vicious circles' in the patterns of international specialisation. Serial correlation in the patterns of technical change are a powerful factor which helps to explain the relative stability of national (technological and commercial) 'comparative advantages', through rather long periods of time, often despite impressive changes in a country's macroeconomic 'endowments' and in the 'factorial intensity' of the techniques of production of the commodities.

In order to clarify the dynamic inter-relationship between company–specific and country–specific advantages, let us consider the example of a company that internalises some technological advantages, which are also linked to the area of location (for example, an American electronics company from the 'Silicon-Valley' or a German mechanical engineering company in several German regions). Its technological success allows this company to become an international oligopolist with direct manufacturing in different parts of the world. Some activities (typically R & D) and some manufacturing (generally the most advanced and/or the most complex products) are, however, kept in the place of origin of the company, due to location-related advantages (easiness of informaton flows, technological interdependences with other companies located there, etc.).[46] Suppose also that many companies behave in the same way. In doing so, however, they *reproduce through time and increase the location–specific technological advantages of the country of origin.* The dynamic balance, between these cumulative factors (which tend to reproduce companies' oligopolistic advantages also in the form of *countries'* oligopolistic advantages) and the 'diffusionist' factors will clearly depend on the nature of the technologies themselves, on their cumulativeness and on the rate of technical progress.

In a synthesis, we could summarise our hypotheses in the following manner:

(a) The process of innovation and of private appropriation of technological advantages lead to inter-company and inter-country asymmetries and must be considered, other things being equal, a divergence–inducing process both in terms of patterns of specialisation and of incomes.[47]

(b) International technological diffusion, on the contrary, represents a convergence mechanism, which tends to close inter-country gaps in patterns of specialisation, productivity and incomes.

(c) International differential in variable costs, and among them primarily wage costs (and in some circumstances the cost of energy), represent powerful driving forces to international diffusion, both in terms of autonomous imitation by firms in 'late-coming' countries and through foreign investment by international firms which retain some oligopolistic advantage *vis-à-vis* their local counterparts. With respect to the process of foreign investment, another relatively general mechanism of diffusion–inducement may be the positive relationship between local manufacturing and local market penetration.

(d) The question of the strength of the 'diffusive impulse' stemming from multinational investment is relatively complex. It is certainly true that there always exists some diffusion effect.[48] On the other hand, if the 'virtuous' dynamic circularities between company–specific and country–specific advantages are essentially enjoyed by the home country (the country of origin of the company), a long-run asymmetry between countries is likely to remain, especially as far as technology-related advantages are concerned. We may, in other words, suggest the hypothesis that multinational investment by a domestic company, belonging to a certain technologically leading country is, from the point of view of such a country, a way of trading-off high but temporary trade advantages against lower – but more stable through time – advantages, both in terms of trade and technological leadership.[49]

(e) One could notionally define for each country a certain functional relations between relative technological levels, relative unit costs and the competitive position of that country. Moreover, as we have been arguing throughout this section, since industrial structures are *not neutral vis-à-vis* international competitiveness, such a relation is likely to be modified by the nature and characteristics of domestic structure of supply (e.g. is it characterised by few big companies or many small ones? Is it made by foreign multinational or domestic firms? Are national firms multinational? etc.).

The Methodology of Trade Tests: A Re-appraisal

In another study (Dosi, 1981c) we analyse at length the implications of the entire argument in terms of testing methodologies. Let us briefly recall some of the conclusions. In addition to international sectors' studies (inclusive of the historical reconstruction of the paths of development of an industry in terms of technology, market structures, international patterns of innovation and imitations, etc.) we suggest the complementary use of evolutionary models (*à la* Nelson–Winter) on an international scale, and cross-country tests on the determinants of relative trade performance at industry level. The former procedure should come as no surprise. Evolutionary models – it was argued in Chapter 3 – represent the 'microfoundation' of the dynamics of technical change, inter-firm asymmetries, etc. If this is true, there should be no doubt that the same applies to each individual open economy and to the world economy as a whole. An interesting property of this kind of strongly behavioural models is that *trade flows are determined as a 'residual'*, after firms have made their decisions in terms of prices and investments and after allowing for the adjustments in market shares. In other words, trade flows are determined simply by the difference between each company's market shares and the percentage of the latter supplied through local production. Trade flows would almost certainly be 'two-way', as a result of international oligopolistic competition. 'Comparative advantage' would be the indirect outcome of (a) technological asymmetries among firms, (b) international differences in wage rates, (c) exchange rates, in so far as all three affect companies' market shares and companies' locations of production.

Conversely, one may directly test – within the same sector, on international level – the role of technology, labour costs and some 'structure of supply' variables in shaping international competitiveness. The set of functional relations and interactions of an international evolutionary model (in the spirit of the Nelson–Winter approach)[50] represents the microfoundation of a competitive dynamics which – in non-planned economies – have private firms as the main institutional agent. On the other hand, the possibility of building a theory of international trade relies on the existence of regularities in the behaviours of these institutional agents, in relation to given structural conditions (e.g. the technological capabilities of each company or the wage rates of each country). Thus, the microbiology' of international competitiveness must be coupled with a 'synthetic' model, capable of capturing the overall results of the processes of innovation, imitation, oligopolistic rivalry, concentration, international investment, etc. whose history is analysed by a 'microscopic' evolutionary model. The reader can easily recognise the same theoretical duality, discussed in a closed economy context (pp. 107–10) between evolutionary models and what we called 'weak structural theories'.

Why there should be inter-country tests for each sector and not intersector tests for each country should be clear from the analysis of technology, degrees of appropriability of innovation, and oligopoly: all these variables are industry–specific, in addition to being country–specific.[51]

We suggest statistical tests of the form

$$X_i = f(T_i, C_i, O_i)$$ 36

where, in extreme synthesis, T_i = some proxy of each country's technological levels in a given sector; $C_i =$ relative unit labour costs at current exchange rates, and $O_i =$ some industrial organisation proxy for each country in the sector in question (we could term this variable as the degree of participation of each country to the international oligopoly[52]), while X_i is some indicator of international competitiveness in sector i.

The meaning of the model should by now be clear: international technological asymmetries, which are sector–specific in addition to being country–specific, define the boundaries of cost-based adjustments in international competitiveness stemming from different levels of wages (expressed in international currency). Moreover, the nature of the implied trade-offs is affected by the history of national industrial structures and their behavioural patterns. Putting it in a different way, the model highlights the relationship between *absolute advantages/disadvantages* (technology-wise and organisation-wise) *and cost factors in international trade*.

Repeating the test on different industrial sectors (given different degrees of technological opportunity, appropriability, international concentration, etc. between sectors) we would *a priori* expect a different relative importance of the T, C, O variables. In some sectors, one would expect an overwhelming importance of T (in high technology sectors); in some, all three variables might be at work (this is our expectation for example for the automotive sector); finally, in others, costs are likely to be crucial. Only after this kind of testing is repeated throughout all the industrial sectors, can one start discussing the patterns of specialisation of each country in relation to the sectoral characteristics defined through the tests themselves.

In passing, note that if one is able to find the correct specification for the oligopoly variable (or variables), some indirect conclusions can be drawn on the export–complementarity *vs* export–substitution effect of foreign investment, in so far as one finds a significant positive or negative effect of a foreign investment variable upon trade performance.

A final remark: this suggested procedure may help to solve the long-debated question of 'which are the technology-intensive sectors'. The answer can be: those where the technology variable is crucial in determining international competitiveness. Thus, we would not need an *a priori* (and in many ways arbitrary) choice but the selection would emerge from the tests themselves through the comparison of the coefficients on the technology variable from tests on different sectors. In practice, this is all too good to be true, since we only have very imperfect measures of the suggested variables. However, this procedure may lead a bit further in the correct direction.

Do Changes in International Specialisation follow a Product-Cycle?

It is of interest to compare the hypotheses and predictions of our interpretative framework with product–cycle models of international specialisation.

One has certainly noticed that the underlying 'philosophies' of the models are somewhat similar. Let us highlight the differences and the points whereby the interpretation above – in our view – maintains a higher level of generality.

(a) The entire discussion from Chapter 2 rules out a simple explanation of each country's relative technological capabilities in terms of market inducement for a given structure of demand (the latter being related with per-capita income) as the product–cycle theory suggests.[53] The model of technological paradigms and trajectories implies that the emergence and development of a defined pattern of technical change maintains significant degrees of freedom *vis-à-vis* market conditions. Certainly, technological capabilities and per capita incomes are bi-univocally related to each other, but it may well be that the dominant causal relationship runs, at least in the short run, from technology to income (and thus to demand structure) and not vice versa.

This hypothesis is reinforced by the non-independence between supply and demand of each commodity and particularly of innovative commodities. The diffusion in demand of an innovation is interlinked with the diffusion in production, so that, for example, it may well be that it is a shortening imitation lag *in production* (for any laggard country *B*) which *determines* a shortening lag in demand and not vice versa. This property is a corollary of the existence of powerful untraded technological interdependences between producers and users of innovations (in the case of capital and intermediate goods) and slow-changing patterns of consumption (in the case of final goods), influenced by corporate policies.

(b) As Walker (1979) convincingly shows there are several empirical cases whereby industries and individual products do not 'flow down' to 'second-coming', 'third-coming' countries, etc. as product–cycle theories would predict. We believe the model above is capable of accounting also for these cases. More precisely, in our interpretation, the patterns of international diffusion of innovations depend on the relative balance between the rate of technical change (jointly with its degree of appropriability at country–level in the form of 'externalities', learning-by-doing, non-transferable knowledge, etc.), in the 'leading' country, and technological imitation (jointly with the dynamics of relative wage rates), in the 'following' country. It is perfectly possible for a country to keep a technological advantage for a long time, without any 'cycle' at all. One can think of a rather obvious example like Swiss watches (before the microelectronics revolution) or German machine-tools, where country–specific technological advantages which reproduce through time, such as expertise, skills, learning-by-doing, etc., kept the 'comparative advantage' in the original leading country. In other cases, as we shall see below in the case of semiconductors, a very high rate of technical progress prevents products from flowing down along the product–cycle, because they are quickly substituted by new ones.

(c) Product–cycle theories embody an overall vision, according to which everyone has a place in the international division of labour according to some kind of 'pecking order', broadly linked with the degree of development of each country (approximated by per capita incomes). Our analysis suggests that it might not be necessarily so. This can be seen reconsidering equation 36 and rewriting it with respect to time:

$$X_{ijt} = f(T_{ijt}, C_{ijt}, O_{ijt}) \qquad 37$$

where the suffices i denote the sector, j the country, and t time. To repeat, X is some indicator of export performance and T, C, O are relative measures of technological capabilities, unit labour costs and degrees of participation to the international oligopoly,[54] respectively, all with regard to sector i.

In terms of changes over time:

$$\Delta X_{ij} = F(\Delta T_{ij}, \Delta C_{ij}, \Delta O_{ij}) \qquad 38$$

Corresponding product–cycle expressions could be:

$$X_{ijt} = g(t, GDP/N) \qquad 39$$

and

$$\Delta X_{ij} = G(t, \Delta(GDP/N), (GDP/N)). \qquad 40$$

In a product–cycle approach, each country's competitiveness in a given sector is a function of the 'newness' of the considered products[55] as measured by time (say, the time from its initial introduction) in relation to per capita incomes (GDP/N). In terms of variations, a country's international relative competitiveness changes as a function of time in relation to both the levels and the changes in per capita GDP.[56]

In our model (cf. equation 38) we cannot make clear predictions on the signs of all the variables, with respect to time. T is a technology–specific variable, in addition to being country–specific: it depends on the rates of technical progress, on the degrees of transferability of technologies and on the rate of imitation of each country. C is composed of a variable (labour productivity) which is quite strictly related to the technology variable (as far as production processes are concerned), and another variable (wage rates) which is essentially determined on macroeconomic level within each country.

Finally, we would actually expect O to be somewhat related to both the history of one country's competitiveness in sector i, and its levels of per capita income.[57]   •

We can see also the conditions under which equations 39 and 40 are roughly equivalent to equations 37 and 38, respectively.

Let us neglect variable O and concentrate on T and C. Suppose that the rate of imitation in 'intermediate countries' is relatively faster than the rate of innovation in 'advanced' countries, and that unit labour cost differentials for these countries are relatively greater than the 'technology gap' that these countries experience. Under these circumstances, for descriptive purposes our equations and product–cycle equations become roughly equivalent: the dominant trend is towards technological diffusion and this roughly respects the order of the relative degrees of development. The reader can recognise that these hypothetical circumstances are not very far from the prevailing conditions of post-war OECD countries, to which product–cycle theories were originally applied. A backlog of innovations from the USA – not yet adopted in Europe and Japan – low wage rates (relative to the USA) and/or relatively advanced technological infrastructures in the same countries, jointly determined an environment which *on average* fulfilled product–cycle predictions. Even in these cases, the latter model provides more a *taxonomy* than a theory of the changes in international specialisation. Even when, on average, 'product–cycle conditions' apply, this need not be true for every individual sector or product: different notional possibilities can be conceived for individual products such as a long-lasting competitive leadership of one country or, conversely, a change in specialisation which 'jumps over' one or all 'intermediate' countries, etc. It can easily be seen that the conditions which fulfil product–cycle predictions are one particular case of a wider set of possibilities allowed by the model: the dynamics of international specialisation depends on (a) the patterns and characteristics of technical change, specific to each industry, (b) the effect of technical change upon international asymmetries between firms and the way the history of the competitive dynamics affected the international structure of supply, (c) the macroeconomic evolution of wages,[58] and exchange rates.

A final observation may be required with respect to the implications of foreign investment for the model. The interpretative framework applies *also* when foreign-owned companies control, to various degrees, production and exports in the international arena: their impact is in fact captured by all the three variables T, C, O. In so far as foreign investment affects international transfer of technology this will show in T and in the denominator of C (i.e. labour productivity). As far as in-going and out-going foreign investment affect import and export propensities this is captured by the variable O.

The reader should be aware of the fact that the prime aim of the model is to provide a conceptualisation of some fundamental relations: testing and measurement problems remain formidable.[59]

What follows here is the interpretation of trade and investment flows in semiconductors, assessing the consistency between the empirical evidence and the proposed theoretical framework.

4.3 THE DEVELOPMENT OF A WORLD SEMICONDUCTOR INDUSTRY

Technology, Trade Balances, and the Dynamics of Industrial Structures for the Major Western Producers

Figures 4.3 to 4.8 provide an overview of the trends in exports, imports, production and consumption by the major six semiconductor producing countries.

As one would expect, the only country with continuous trade surpluses is the United States. The UK, Germany and Italy show continuous negative balances, while France, after significant deficits throughout the 1950s and early 1960s, reaches a more or less balanced foreign account in the 1970s (due to a surplus in discrete components). The Japanese trade balance presents two big cycles: a positive balance is reached in the late 1950s and its size increases until the turn of the decade; then the inversion of the trend yields to a 'negative cycle' which lasts from 1962 to 1976; a surplus appears again thereafter.

European trade balances (for each individual country and Europe as a whole) do not show any marked cyclicity. A rather stable negative balance[60] in the fifties and early sixties is consistent with the imitative pattern followed – broadly speaking – by the European industry throughout that period. The emergence of integrated circuit technology and a particularly high lag in the European response help to explain the increasing European deficit from the mid-1960s to the early 1970s. Imports into Europe are almost entirely US-controlled. Increasing penetration by American companies into the European markets is followed (and, partly, accompanied) by a wave of direct American investment in Europe around the turn of the decade.

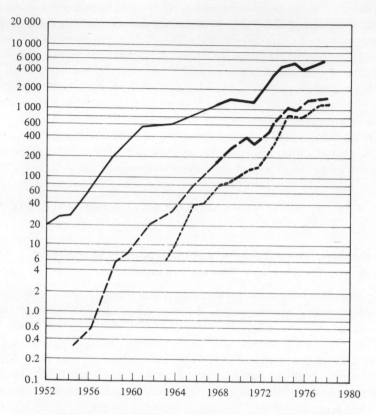

NOTE The difference between 'production plus imports' and 'imports' represents domestic production, and the difference between 'production plus imports' and 'exports' shows apparent domestic consumption.

KEY   ——————— production + imports
          – – – – – – – exports
          . . . . imports

FIGURE 4.3 *Semiconductor production, exports and imports, USA*

SOURCE Up to 1968: Tilton (1971). From 1969: own estimates based on US Department of Commerce, *US General Imports* and *US Exports*, plus sources listed in Table 4.7.

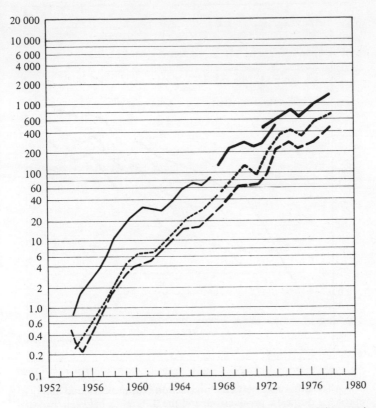

NOTE   The difference between 'production plus imports' and 'imports' represents domestic production, and the difference between 'production plus imports' and 'exports' shows apparent domestic consumption.

KEY   ——————— production + imports
        – – – – – – – exports
        . . . . imports

FIGURE 4.4   *Semiconductor production, exports and imports, Germany*

SOURCE   Up to 1968: Tilton (1971). From 1968 own estimates based as follows: for trade data: Eurostat *Analytical Tables of Foreign Trade*; for production data from 1968 to 1973: estimates based on data from Bundesministerium für Forschung und Technologie; for production data from 1972 to 1978: Mackintosh Consultants.

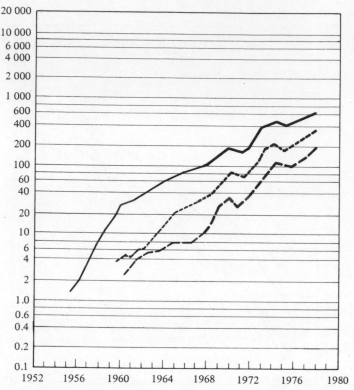

NOTE   The difference between 'production plus imports' and 'imports' represents domestic production, and the difference between 'production plus imports' and 'exports' shows apparent domestic consumption.

KEY   ——————— production + imports
       – – – – – – – exports
       . . . . imports

FIGURE 4.5   *Semiconductor production, exports and imports, UK*

SOURCE   Up to 1968: Tilton (1971). From 1968: own estimates for trade based on UK national trade statistics, company estimates, and Eurostat *Analytical Tables of Foreign Trade*; own estimates for production based on company data and Mackintosh Consultants.

In an attempt to identify significant phases of the history of the European semiconductor industry, we can define a *first phase* from the origin of the industry until the mid-1960s characterised by rather stable (or slightly decreasing) technological lags and clearly defined national

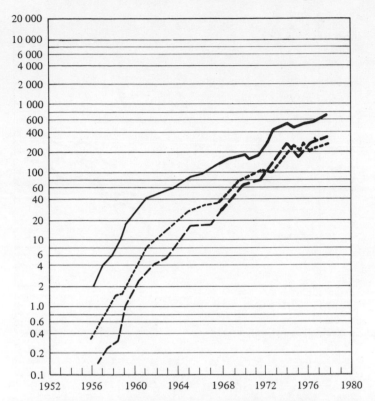

NOTE   The difference between 'production plus imports' and 'imports' represents domestic production, and the difference between 'production plus imports' and 'exports' shows apparent domestic consumption.

KEY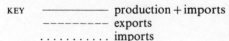

————————— production + imports
– – – – – – – exports
. . . . imports

FIGURE 4.6   *Semiconductor production, exports and imports, France*

SOURCE   Up to 1968: Tilton (1971). From 1968: own estimates for trade based on Eurostat *Analytical Tables of Foreign Trade*; for production; own estimates based on data from Ministère de l'Industrie and Mackintosh Consultants.

markets. In this phase, innovative products are first imported and, later, manufactured locally by domestic companies which are able to exploit relatively lower domestic wages and the mentioned 'proximity-to-the-market' effect. Starting from around the mid-1960s, a more aggressive

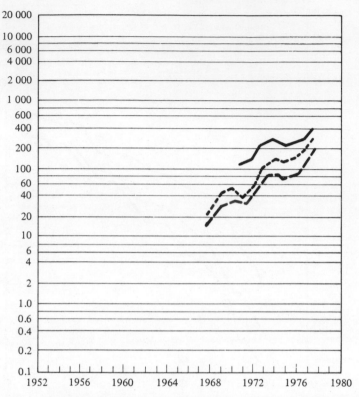

NOTE   The difference between 'production plus imports' and 'imports' represents domestic production, and the difference between 'production plus imports' and 'exports' shows apparent domestic consumption.

KEY   ———————— production + imports
            –––––––––– exports
            . . . . imports

FIGURE 4.7   *Semiconductor production, exports and imports, Italy*

SOURCE   Own estimates for trade based on Eurostat *Analytical Tables of Foreign Trade*; for production data: Ministero dell'Industria and Mackintosh Consultants.

strategy by American companies begins. Innovative companies (which are all American) tend to pre-empt European markets, exploiting their technological advantage and the high rate of substitution between new and old products.[61] Furthermore, direct investment (at least partly)

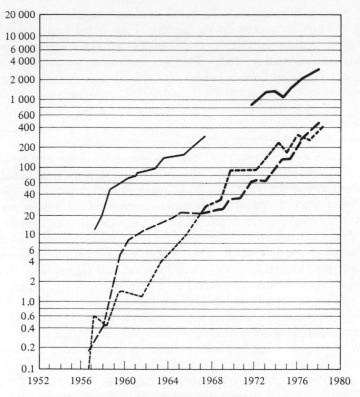

NOTE   The difference between 'production plus imports' and 'imports' represents domestic production, and the difference between 'production plus imports' and 'exports' shows apparent domestic consumption.

KEY ─────────── production + imports
─ ─ ─ ─ ─ ─ exports
. . . . imports

FIGURE 4.8   *Semiconductor production, exports and imports, Japan*

SOURCE   Up to 1968: Tilton (1971). From 1968: own estimates based on data from MITI and Nomura Research Institute.

eliminates the differential advantages of domestic companies (lower wages and the implicit protection provided by their closeness to local markets). We could call this *second phase* the *unification of world markets*. A few far-reaching consequences of this process need to be mentioned.

First, it helped partly to break the relationship between lags in production and lags in demand, which is one of the factors that allows industries and companies lagging behind to survive by exploiting a lower stage in the 'product–cycle'. This simply means that (American) companies, placed on the technological frontier, pre-empt the market of the most advanced devices which the indigenous companies cannot produce yet and, in doing so, make it more difficult for national companies to imitate at a later stage. Incidentally, it is noticeable that this phenomenon, although damaging to the local semiconductor industry, can be beneficial to the end-user industries, whose delay in the adoption of the most advanced components is likely to decrease. The evidence suggests, however, that this effect has been strong enough to jeopardise the survival of national semiconductor manufacturers, but not enough to eliminate the diffusion lag in consumption of the most advanced products.

Second, in this phase, the patterns of oligopolistic competition tend to change. In the first phase, when rather well-defined national markets exist, price discrimination in each market and significantly different international prices are more likely. Suppose, on the contrary, that several companies from the country 'on the frontier' invest in foreign markets, in order to acquire a higher market share. These companies will tend also to 'export' the patterns of competition experienced at home. In particular, according to our hypothesis, prices are set as a function of relative cost conditions and technological lag/leads (*vis-à-vis* both other competing companies and potential entrants). The higher the internationalisation of companies from the leading country, the more homogeneous are also the competitive conditions throughout the world. Prices will thus tend to equal those in the leading country. (The hypothesis rigorously applied to the set of developed countries: collusive price discrimination may still occur in developing countries, for reasons that it is not possible to discuss here.)[62] This is, in our view, what happened in the semiconductor industry between the late 1960s and early 1970s. Unfortunately, the appropriate series of data to test this hypothesis on rigorous grounds is not available. A reliable series of prices in Europe, at a sufficient level of disaggregation, did not (and does not) exist. The evidence from several interviews are, however, consistent with our suggestion.

A unified world market implies, as mentioned, a (relatively) unique price. When the latter was brutally introduced by American companies (and primarily Texas Instruments) in the middle of a slump in demand, during the so-called price war of 1970–1, all the European producers were forced out of the mass standard market, with only five exceptions: Philips, Siemens, AEG–Telefunken, SGS–Ates and Sescosem–Thomson. Other European companies which maintained their semiconductor facilities withdrew to more specialised and custom markets (GEC, Ferranti, Plessey). It is interesting to notice that there is hardly any evidence in the aggregate American semiconductor price index of cut-throat price falls in that period. It may be another sign that the 'war' has been fought mainly in Europe, allowing European prices to fall in accordance with the fall of *American costs.*[63]

Finally, one may define a *third phase* of *international oligopolistic stabilisation* (beginning with the late 1970s), whereby most of the companies competing in the world market are already international companies and few new entries occur (with the exception of 'side' entries by big conglomerates and ventures backed by national governments). In many respects this is the set-up, on international levels, mirroring what we called above 'oligopolistic maturity'. Note that the relative 'stability' refers essentially, in the semiconductor case, to the number of major producers. It does not mean that the relative positions within the oligopoly are not going to change: a factor of primary importance and likely to shake the world structure of the industry is the emergence of a Japanese challenge to the American technological and market dominance. Before discussing the Japanese case, however, it is worth analysing at greater length the trade implications of the three phases suggested above.

Innovation and Export Performance

A crucial question concerns the relationship between trade performances of the considered countries and their relative technological levels. It should be clear from the discussion above that an hypothesis relating differences in technological performances by countries and trade flows underpins our entire argument. The causal relationship should run from the former to the latter. For our hypothesis to hold one country's export performance should be a function of its capability of generating innovations, and/or fast and 'creative' imitations. We tried different tests of this hypothesis, following Pavitt and Soete's attempt to use the number of patents registered in the USA as a proxy of technological output.[64]

Econometric results are quite encouraging despite the very small number of observations available which therefore requires extreme caution in the interpretation of the results.[65]

Let us define the following symbols:

Xs = percentage share of semiconductor exports of a country in total exports of the considered countries (1977–8).

Ps = percentage share of cumulated semiconductor patents in the USA (1963–78) by a country on the total cumulated patents of the considered countries.

Xn = 1977–8 semiconductor exports by a country divided by that country's population (as a very crude proxy for the size of that country).

Pn = cumulated patents divided by a country's population.

Regression estimates yield:

$$Xs = 4.79 + 0.62 \, Ps \qquad R^2 = 0.75 \qquad\qquad 41$$
$$ (2.66) \quad (0.14)^{**}$$
$$Xn = 1.30 + 0.18 \, Pn \qquad R^2 = 0.63 \qquad\qquad 42$$
$$ (1.27) + (0.06)^{*}$$

(standard error in parenthesis)
The coefficients on the independent variables are significant at 1 per cent (**) 5 per cent (*) levels.

The hypothesis of a strong influence of technological innovation upon export capability is also supported by significant microeconomic evidence we collected through interviews: the major single factor in determining the export potential of a firm appears to be the technological level in each group of semiconductor products. This applies to both a *product* effect (technological levels, quality, reliability of the products themselves) and a *process* effect (being early innovators affects costs through learning curves; moreover, costs depend also on process innovations).

It is noticeable that econometric estimates conducted on 'specialisation' indices and on net trade balances, while still using the number of patents as independent variable, yield much poorer results.[66]

These results need not be in conflict with our proposed interpretation. On the contrary, the levels of imports (which determine, together with exports, the specialisation index and net external balances) are certainly affected by one country's technological levels, but also by the varying degree of import substitution induced by foreign direct investment, by the relative size of foreign investment itself, and by public policies related to the protection of the internal market.

Moreover, foreign investment, as we saw above, is often determined by factors which do not have any direct relationship with host countries' relative technological levels (although they affect the latter, in relation to the varying degrees of technology transfer that occurs through MNCs). Multinational investment may thus be expected to 'disrupt' the stability of the relationship between relative national technological levels as *measured by patents*[67] and trade performance. Were we able to test the full model proposed above and introduce labour costs and 'industrial organisation' as additional explanatory variables, we would capture also the entire effect of international oligopolies upon trade performance. Unfortunately, data on labour productivity (in terms of value added) is not available, and neither are consistent figures on international investment flows.

Foreign Investment and Host Industries

We have already suggested above that foreign direct investment, generally from companies belonging to a technologically leading country – in our case the USA – accelerated the international diffusion *in consumption* of the most advanced products, while at the same time jeopardising the survival of the national industry in most European countries. Tables 4.11 to 4.13 provide some estimates of American direct investment abroad, by location and by date of establishment. It is worth comparing these figures with those from Tables 4.1 to 4.4 showing import from the USA, American controlled imports, specialisation indices of the major European countries and net balances in percentage to domestic markets, respectively. The big wave of American direct investment around the turn of the decade between sixties and the seventies appears to yield a *short-run* import substitution effect (see Table 4.1). In the meantime, market shares of American companies in Europe increased (see also Table 3.19 in Chapter 3) due to a 'crowding-out' effect against domestic European companies. Direct investment, however, appears to retain a *long-run complementarity* with imports. The issue is rather controversial. The only study dealing at length with it in relation to semiconductors is Finan (1975) who suggests, despite many qualifications, a long-run declining trend in total US-controlled import penetration (direct plus indirect imports in other industrialised countries), allowing only complementarity between imports and local production in a weaker sense (imports might have declined faster without local manufacturing). In our view, what Finan observed was for a good part the short-run import substituting impact of foreign manufacturing

TABLE 4.1   *US direct export share of major foreign market consumption total semiconductors – 1967–78 – percentages*[1]

	Japan a	Japan b	UK a	UK b	Germany a	Germany b	France a	France b	Italy b	EEC[g] b
1967	11		20		21		16			
1968	10		23		32		19			
1969	13		24		30		26			
1970	19		18		28		24			
1971	15		11		21		18			
1972	6			14	18	24	29	38	20	
1973		9				20		43	26	
1974		10		24		20		41	33	27
1975		11		27		25		38	36	29
1976		11		27		22		36	33	28
1977		9		23		19		28	36	24
1978		9		25		19		29	42	26

NOTE
[1] US Exports excludes those assembled in LDCs and re-exported to other developed countries.

SOURCES   (a) Finan (1975) (b) Our elaborations on NIMEXE, MITI, Nomura Research, US Department of Commerce and Mackintosh Consultants data. Our series differs partly from Finan's, due also to the inclusion of 'parts', 'hybrid circuits', 'opto-electronic devices'.

around the beginning of the 1970s. Moreover, his figures on the decline of US penetration are somehow biased by the inclusion of Japan (whose story is rather different from Europe, as we shall see) and the exclusion of several medium-size industrialised countries.

To support a long-run complementarity hypothesis in addition to some qualitative evidence collected by Finan himself (through his interviews), one can observe that, on the *European average*, net foreign balances show rather stable values or sometimes a worsening trend (see Table 4.4, remembering that the EEC trend before 1974 can be roughly inferred from a weighted average of German, French and British data, which are the only ones available). Direct imports from the US show a decline in the 1970s, in France and to a smaller extent in Germany (Table 4.1; note that the absolute levels of our estimates are different from Finan's due to different definitions of the industry and different sources,[68] but this should not introduce any bias in the trends). On the other hand, *American-controlled* imports from countries other than the US increase

TABLE 4.2 *Trends in production, exports, imports, consumption in major industrial countries, 1968–78. (Annual compound rates of growth, at current prices, US$). Total semiconductors*

	Domestic production	Exports	Imports	Domestic market
US	16.1[a]	25.2	34.9[f]	16.3
Japan	20.8[b]	35.5	30.2	19.5[b]
Germany	18.1[c]	31.5	32.6	21.5
France	14.5[d]	29.4	24.6	13.9[d]
UK	16.3	30.0	25.8	18.3
Italy	14.0[e]	20.9	27.3	17.3[e]

NOTES
[a] For 1977–8: estimates based on US Dept. of Commerce, *Economic Outlook 1980.*
[b] 1972–8.
[c] Production for the period 1968–72: estimates based on BMFT data.
[d] 1969–78.
[e] 1972–8.
[f] Imports *unadjusted* to account for US content of devices assembled abroad and reimported.

SOURCES *US Annual Survey of Manufactures; US Exports, Commodity by Country; US Imports for Consumption, Commodity by Country;* Nomura Research; MITI; Mackintosh Consultants; NIMEXE; unpublished companies' reports on UK semiconductors.

very fast (especially from Far-Eastern LDCs).

If our interpretation is correct, the *long-run* effect of foreign (essentially US) direct investment upon net imports has been relatively low, while at the same time having strong negative influences on the market shares of domestic companies. Moreover, recent data on American controlled imports of ICs – generally speaking the most advanced cluster of semiconductor products – shows a very high import penetration into European markets (Table 4.7).

As far as net export propensities of foreign subsidiaries are concerned, the available evidence would suggest that it is indeed rather low (see Table 4.9 on integrated circuits). In the case of Texas Instruments, for example, estimates suggest that European production represents around 70–80 per cent of European sales. Texas Instruments has one of the most developed manufacturing networks in Europe. *A fortiori*, similar considerations should apply to other American companies established in

TABLE 4.3 *Specialisation indices for selected European countries. Total semiconductor and integrated circuits 1968–78[a]*

Total Semiconductors	68	69	70	71	72	73	74	75	76	77	78
Germany	−0.16	−0.25	−0.24	−0.16	−0.16	−0.22	−0.17	−0.14	−0.19	−0.24	−0.20
France	−0.16	−0.08	+0.00	+0.02	−0.04	+0.02	+0.02	−0.04	−0.01	+0.04	+0.03
UK	−0.43	−0.27	−0.35	−0.45	−0.42	−0.47	−0.37	−0.30	−0.35	−0.33	−0.29
Italy	−0.14	−0.14	−0.18	−0.03	−0.09	−0.16	−0.30	−0.33	−0.34	−0.32	−0.38
Belgium	−0.76	−0.81	−0.86	−0.80	−0.51	−0.44	−0.55	−0.48	−0.48	−0.35	−0.39
Netherlands					+0.21	+0.14	+0.06	+0.14	+0.20	−0.22	−0.17
Denmark							−0.91	−0.94	−0.94	−0.90	−0.87
Total EEC (6)	−0.25	−0.34	−0.38	−0.34	−0.26	−0.35					
Total EEC (9)							−0.35	−0.32	−0.36	−0.34	−0.30

Integrated Circuits	68	69	70	71	72	73	74	75	76	77	78
Germany	−0.54	−0.41	−0.38	−0.39	−0.36	−0.40	−0.36	−0.20	−0.28	−0.39	−0.31
France						−0.48	−0.50	−0.38	−0.52	−0.51	−0.57
UK (b)						−0.38	−0.36	−0.32	−0.36	−0.33	−0.30
(Italy) (c)						(−0.26)	(−0.36)	(−0.34)	(−0.12)	(−0.17)	(−0.24)
Belgium						−0.64	−0.57	−0.74	−0.52	−0.23	−0.29
Netherlands						−0.08	−0.27	−0.13	−0.06	−0.46	−0.38
Denmark						−0.96	−0.96	−0.96	−0.93	−0.86	−0.84
Total EEC (9)							−0.64	−0.45	−0.50	−0.53	−0.49

NOTES

There are some inconsistencies between the indices related to individual countries and those referring to EEC total. These discrepancies, due to different national accounting procedure and secrecy clauses do not affect the trends.

[a] The index is defined as $(X − M)/(X + M)$, where X = exports, M = imports.

[b] For 1968–74: estimates based on various companies elaborations on national import and export data.

[c] See note (6) in Table 4.4.

SOURCE NIMEXE

TABLE 4.4   *Net foreign balances as a percentage of domestic consumption in selected European countries. Total semiconductors and integrated circuits*
1968–78

A. *Total Semiconductors*

	68	69	70	71	72	73	74	75	76	77	78
Germany	−11	−21	−20	−16	−24	−26	−20	−20	−28	−31	−30
France		−7	+0	+3	−5	+3	+2	−6	−1	+6	+5
UK	−26	−19	−27	−28	−36	−36	−25	−27	−31	−37	−35
Italy[c]						(−13)	(−27)	(−45)	(−52)	(−55)	(−56)	(−75)
EEC[a]							−21	−21	−24	−22	−22

B. *Integrated Circuits*[b]

	68	69	70	71	72	73	74	75	76	77	78
Germany						−42	−45	−30	−41	−46	−45
France						−33	−40	−33	−55	−45	−62
UK							−33	−33	−36	−43	−40
Italy[c]						(−20)	(−43)	(−54)	(−21)	(−15)	(−22)

NOTES
One should be extremely careful in the interpretation of this data. Estimates of the domestic market are often derived from data on exports, imports and production, and pick up all the errors in the latter figures.

[a] EEC − 9

[b] It has been impossible to obtain reliable figures for the total of EEC consistent with those referring to individual countries: within NIMEXE imports and exports data on extra-EEC trade, a significant bias is produced by the exclusion of Dutch ICs figures, covered by secrecy. Figures without Philips trade policies are actually misleading.

[c] We are particularly sceptical about these Italian figures. Our estimates from interviews show that semiconductor smuggling accounts for a significant percentage of the Italian market (as high as one-quarter to one-third of the entire market). Moreover, the percentage appears to vary considerably from year to year, so that the trends shown in this table are likely to be meaningless.

SOURCES   For imports and exports: NIMEXE; for domestic consumption: 1968–73, estimates from national sources (Ministries of Industry, Business Associations, Consultancy Reports); 1973–8, Mackintosh Consultants.

Europe. Moreover, it is worth noticing that US-controlled exports from Europe and Japan are quite low.[69]

Contrary to the trends in net balance as a percentage of domestic European markets, 'specialisation' indices – defined as exports minus imports divided by exports plus imports – (Table 4.3) tend to worsen through the 1960s, but appear to improve thereafter only for some European countries (e.g. UK) whose net balances are nonetheless worsening. This result, at first sight paradoxical, is explained by the fact that both imports and exports have been growing faster than domestic production: if imports grow slower than exports but

TABLE 4.5   *Foreign subsidiaries in developed countries by ownership and location, 1974–9*[a]

Location	USA		Japan		Europe[b]	
Ownership	74	79	74	79	74	79
USA			1	2 (+1 planned)	9	15 (+1 planned)
Japan	0	4 (+3 planned)			0	1 (+2 planned)
Europe[b]	1	4	0	0	5	5

NOTES
[a] Subsidiaries with more than one plant in one country account for one. Moreover, note that the definition of 'subsidiary' here is somewhat more restrictive than that in Table 4.6. These two factors explain the considerable difference between this Table, Table 4.11, Table 4.12 and Table 4.13.
[b] European subsidiaries in Europe stand for investments in countries different from the country of origin of the company.

SOURCE   Truel (1980).

faster than domestic production, starting from a deficit situation, one may obtain at the same time worsening net balances and improving specialisation indices. The latter, in this case, show a trend towards internationalisation of production and the mutual integration of national markets (see Table 4.2 for the rates of growth of production, imports, exports, consumption in the major Western countries).[70] A particularly marked tendency has been towards the integration of regional markets (Europe, North American, Far East). This is shown also by the market policies of foreign subsidiaries: they are not generally meant to serve simply the host national markets but the entire regional markets around them.[71]

It is important to notice that the locational criteria of foreign investments are likely to induce significant imbalances between different countries within the same region. It was suggested above that important locational factors might be the size of the local host market, its 'specificity' and degree of formal and informal protection, differential wage costs and locational 'economies' or 'diseconomies'.

Within Europe, French informal protection (especially in relation to the military and telecommunication markets) and policies of discretional bargaining with would-be investors in terms of targets related to local production, imports and exports, explains the French positive trade balances during most of the 1970s. Even under these circumstances, however, the result is the sum of a surplus in discrete devices and a rather heavy deficit in ICs. Within the latter, the technologically most advanced products show a very high deficit, and microprocessors are the

TABLE 4.6   *A. US trade balances as percentage of apparent consumption, import penetration and exports as percentage of shipments*

1965–78

	1965	66	67	68	69	70	71	72	73	74	75	76	77	78
Net trade balances as % of apparent consumption	5	6	9	10	17	18	15	8	9	9	9	7	3	1
Exports as % of shipments	7	9	11	14	21	24	25	25	27	34	35	32	31	33
Imports as % of apparent consumption	2	3	3	6	7	11	14	19	21	29	29	28	29	33

NOTE
Imports *include* re-imports of devices assembled in LDCs and exports include semi-finished parts. Shipments data on which apparent consumption is calculated differ slightly in some years from those on which Table 3.6 is based, due to different sources: the latter are based on the *Annual Survey of Manufactures* and the former on the *Current Industrial Reports Series MA–36N*. Definitions and coverage are slightly different.

B. US Trade balances on ownership base as percentage of apparent consumption, import penetration from foreign companies and exports (excluding re-imported devices) as percentage of shipments

1970–7

	1970	71	72	73	74	75	76	77	78
Estimated trade balances on ownership base as % of US apparent consumption[a]		22	20	15	16	20	21	19	14
Exports, excluding re-imported devices, as percentage of US shipments[b]		20	19	19	21	26	25	23	18
Imports, except those under TSUSA items 806.30 and 807.00 as % of US apparent consumption[c]	1	2	5	7	8	7	6	5	

NOTES
[a] Trade balances exclude imports of devices exported as semi-finished parts, assembled in LDCs and re-imported and exclude the related exports. This can be taken as a rough measure of trade balances on ownership base, even if it neglects imports of finished products originated in American subsidiaries in other industrial countries (they are believed to be rather small) and European subsidiaries in the US (their impact becomes noticeable only after 1975).
[b] Exports exclude re-imported devices and parts.
[c] TSUSA items 806.30 and 807.00 allow duty free imports of the American content in products assembled overseas.

SOURCE   Elaborations on US Department of Commerce (1979, pp. 62, 68 and 59).

TABLE 4.7   *US exports' market shares and US-controlled market shares in major industrial countries: ICs, 1970–8*

		70	71	72	73	74	75	76	77	78
Germany	US X (1)				22	32	40	32	22	24
	US contr. X (2)					12	12	33	23	21
	Total (3)					44	52	64	44	45
France	US X (1)				32	37	39	b	29	29
	US contr. X (2)					16	18	b	35	33
	Total (3)					53	57		64	62
UK	US X (1)					31	34	34	17	21
	US contr. X (2)					16	11	14	18	18
	Total (3)					48	45	48	35	39
EEC (9)	US X (1)					33	26	35	22	25
	US contr. X(a) (2)					19	19	39	32	28
	Total (a) (3)					51	45	(74)b	54	54
Japan	US X (1)	25	27	11	14	18	17	16	15	14
	US contr. X (2)					4	5	5	6	4
	Total (3)					22	21	21	21	18

NOTES
(1) Market share of direct exports from US.
(2) Market share of US-controlled exports, from countries other than US.
(3) (1) plus (2).
(a) Estimates of US-controlled exports to the EEC, based on figures referring to Western Europe, on the assumptions that US share in total Western Europe is equal to the share in EEC (9) and that the latter market corresponds to 90% of total Western European market.
(b) Sometimes, imported devices are re-exported: when the amount is significant, the corresponding apparent import penetration becomes meaningless.

SOURCES   Row (1) Western European countries: elaborations on NIMEXE and Mackintosh Consultants; Japan: elaborations on Nomura Research and MITI.
Row (2) Elaborations on USITC (1979).

extreme case where imports account for nearly 100 per cent of domestic consumption.

A massive amount of American investment took place also in the UK, probably due to cost factors (relatively low wages and public incentives on capital account), in addition to less quantifiable variables (language, links between the USA and UK, etc.). There, however, the 'crowding-out' *vis-à-vis* British companies has been significant and public monitoring on production and import targets totally non-existent.

TABLE 4.8 *Japan: Net foreign balances as percentage of domestic consumption and direct exports to US as percentage of domestic production. Integrated circuits 1970–8*

A. *Net balances as percentage of domestic market*

70	71	72	73	74	75	76	77	78
−28	−32	−19	−21	−26	−18	−17	−10	−3

B. *Direct exports to US as percentage of domestic production*

		1	2	6	3	5	6

SOURCES Elaborations on Nomura Research, MITI.

TABLE 4.9 *Exports and Imports by US foreign subsidiaries located in industrial countries. Integrated circuits, 1974–78 (millions of $)*[a][b]

	74	75	76	77	78
Exports	112.53	121.12	138.10	141.78	214.68
Imports	160.59	130.52	159.28	167.40	245.51

NOTES
Exports and imports *include* trade flows *between* the considered group of countries.
[a] 'Industrial countries' include all EEC (10) except Ireland and Greece; Scandinavian countries; Canada, Japan.
[b] Note that 'imports' do *not* include parts and semi-finished products, which often represent a significant share in total foreign subsidiaries' output.

SOURCE USITC (1979, pp. 85, 94).

TABLE 4.10 *Exports by US foreign subsidiaries to selected European markets. Integrated circuits, 1974–8 ($m.)*[a]

Market	1974	1975	1976	1977	1978
France	20.0	18.37	67.80	49.97	54.29
UK	26.36	16.43	26.01	38.48	44.01
Germany	27.56	20.77	71.23	83.81	86.05
Total Europe[b]	132.07	116.72	267.00	253.82	314.69

NOTES
[a] i.e. exports to the mentioned countries by US controlled subsidiaries located outside the US.
[b] 'Europe' corresponds to all Western European countries.

SOURCE USITC (1979, pp. 85–91).

TABLE 4.11 *Date of establishment of overseas operations by American companies by type of activity, 1961–72*

	Unknown	Before 61	61	62	63	64	65	66	67	68	69	70	71	72	Total
1. Offshore assembly by US Affiliate	3				1	1	1		3	4	13	5	2	14	47
2. Offshore assembly by subcontractors	2										1	6	1	3	13
3. "Point-of-sale" assembly[a]	6		1			1		1	1	1	4	5	2	9	31
4. Complete manufacturing		5			1			1	1	1	6	1		1	17
5. Total	11	5	1		2	2	1	2	5	6	24	17	5	27	108

NOTE

[a] 'Point-of-sale' assembly stands for assembly facilities in developed countries, primarily aiming at the penetration of local markets (see the text).

NB See note (a) to Table 4.5.

SOURCE Finan (1975, p. 56).

TABLE 4.12 *Total number of LDCs' subsidiaries by area – American, Japanese, European companies, 1971–9*[a]

Area	71	74	76	79
Far East	19–21	41–43	50–51	60 (+1 planned)
Latin America	0–2	3	20	24 (+3 planned)
Mediterranean countries	0	0	4–5	5
Total	19–23	44–46	74–76	89 (+4 planned)

NOTES
[a] A subsidiary with more than one plant in a single country accounts for one. See note (a) to Table 4.5.

SOURCE Truel (1980).

In Germany, foreign investment, although significant, had a relatively lower impact on the domestic market[72] and appeared to be mainly motivated by the access to the German market (and, to a lesser extent, by the local availability of highly skilled manpower).

The incentives to a location in Italy appear to have been rather low: excluding the Fairchild joint venture in SGS,[73] the only significant and lasting foreign subsidiary is Texas Instruments. In the 1970s some *disinvestment* took place (General Instruments, Mistral-Thomson, Philips, and to a great extent Siemens, as far as semiconductors are concerned). When Italy stopped being a low-wage country, neither a big market nor an informal protection were there to compensate as incentives to foreign location.

Within the general European picture described here, possibly the only country to have made a relative gain out of MNCs' locational strategies in Europe is France (and, perhaps the UK), while – at the opposite end of the scale – Italy underwent a relative loss, for the pre-emption of European markets by American companies was not compensated by a corresponding domestic investment.

Trade Patterns for the Technological Leader: The US Case

Let us consider at greater length the trends in the American semiconductors trade. As already mentioned, American trade balances have been positive throughout the history of the industry. Big changes, however, occurred in the various phases. Until the mid-1960s trade played a rather minor part: foreign markets were relatively small (almost non-existent

TABLE 4.13 *Date of establishment of overseas operations by American firms in developed countries, 1961–72*

Country	Unknown	Before 61	61	62	63	64	65	66	67	68	69	70	71	72	Total
UK	1	3				1					4	2		1	12
France	1	1							1	1	1		1	1	7
Germany		1			1			1			1	2			6
Italy			1								2				3
Other EEC/EFTA	3										2	1			6
Total Europe	5	5	1		1	1		1	1	1	10	5	1	2	34
Japan										1	1			2	4
Canada								1							1
Grand Total	5	5	1		1	1		2	1	2	11	5	1	4	39

NOTE
See note (a) to Table 4.5.

SOURCE Finan (1975, p. 57).

for the most advanced devices like ICs) and in good part supplied by local companies. Imports were negligible (some discrete devices from Japan and some special semiconductors for industrial applications from Europe).

From the mid-1960s exports started rising very fast as an effect of (a) a much more active strategy of international penetration by American companies, (b) the fast growth of overseas semiconductor markets (note that the two factors are largely interdependent and interacting with each other), (c) the location of semiconductor assembly in low-wage countries, especially the Far East and some Latin American countries. This last factor enormously increased exports of parts and semi-finished products. Contextually, imports of devices assembled abroad and re-imported underwent a manifold increase. American net foreign balances as a percentage of the domestic market reached their maximum in 1970, being as high as 18 per cent, mainly as an effect of export penetration in other industrialised countries.

A fast downward trend emerged thereafter as a joint effort of the following variables: (a) a fast growth of LDCs sub-assembly (until the late 1970s) increased the value of imports; (b) since wafer fabrication (the high technology part of semiconductor manufacturing) had been automated earlier than assembly, the American content in re-imported devices kept decreasing from 56.4 per cent in 1970 to 45.7 per cent in 1976, increasing again in 1977 to 55 per cent), due to productivity growth in the former which was faster than in the latter operations, and (c) the short-run import–substituting effect of direct foreign investment in other developed countries started affecting American exports. Note that, although there might be – as we argued – a long-run complementarity between foreign manufacturing and exports, the long-run net export propensity associated with international manufacturing operations is likely to settle at levels lower than the pre-foreign investment one. Moreover, foreign industrial markets were increasingly served through LDCs' assembly facilities so that the impact on American exports was correspondingly lowered. Finally, the import-substituting and export-promoting efforts of Japan started affecting American trade balances by the mid-1970s.

It is worth introducing the distinction between trade balances on a *geographical base* (which we considered until this point) and those on an *ownership base*.[74] The difference between the two shows companies' relative advantage *vis-à-vis* their foreign competitors in so far as those advantages are distinguished from those of the country they belong to. This distinction is particularly relevant for the USA. The most important factor affecting this difference has been the location of labour-intensive, low-technology stages of production in low-wage countries. This has an obvious negative effect on the trade balances of the country of origin (in this case the USA) but at the same time, being part of a pattern of international oligopolistic competition, helps to maintain the competitiveness of American companies in foreign markets. For a comparison between trade balances based on the two criteria, see part *A* and part *B* of Table 4.6.

Whilst one could argue from geographical trade flows that the USA has been losing its relative commercial advantage very fast, throughout the 1970s, balances based on ownership provide a strikingly different picture: geographical net balances in 1977 were a mere 3 per cent of US apparent consumption while the corresponding figure for those based on ownership was 14 per cent. The latter, too, underwent a significant decline in the early seventies, affected by the variables mentioned above short-term substitution for American exports induced by foreign investment, assembly in LDCs of products exported to other industrial markets, etc.). Since then, however, despite a marked variance, it does not show any evident trend.[75]

It is worth noticing that, as recently as the late seventies (1974–8) direct imports in the USA of ICs from foreign companies were negligible.[76] Imports from Japan, however, appeared to grow very fast: in 1979 and 1980 Japanese imports reached a significant market share in a few ICs products. For example, they were said to be in 1980 as high as 40 per cent in 16–K RAM memories. The estimated Japanese market share in the total American semiconductor consumption in one year increased from around 3 per cent (1978) to around 5 per cent (1979) and to an estimated 7 per cent in 1980.

The Japanese tendency towards import substitution and massive export growth is likely to be a major factor affecting American foreign balances both on geographical and ownership bases throughout the 1980s.

The Drive towards a 'Comparative Advantage': The Case of Japan

Japanese trade balances, as mentioned, have presented two big cycles, with a positive peak around the turn of the decade between the 1950s and 1960s, a fast decline and a new upward trend in the 1970s which yielded positive balances again from 1976. At a first look, Japanese foreign trade is reminiscent of product–cycle accounts of international trade: after the emergence of the semiconductor industry and allowing for an imitative lag, domestic production increasingly substituted for imports; finally, Japan became a net exporter of discrete devices (mainly transistors). With the appearance, first, of silicon-based (instead of germanium-based) semiconductors and then, more important, of ICs technologies, Japanese imports of the most advanced components grew rapidly, thus worsening trade balances. After a longer imitation lag (due to greater complexity of the technology and to the fast pace of technical change within ICs), Japanese industry increasingly caught up with American leadership: by the turn of the decade between the 1970s and the 1980s, in several fields, the Japanese industry shared the world lead with the USA (e.g. in memories, where Japanese costs and prices are said to be lower than the American ones, within an equivalent product technology) or had only limited lags (e.g. in microprocessors). In the late seventies, Japanese export propensity increased rapidly, and so did exports to the USA (ICs exports to the USA were 0.6 per cent of domestic production in 1973 and 6.2 per cent in 1978), while a slow substitution for American imports took place (American-controlled import penetration in ICs was 22 per cent in 1974 and 18 per cent in 1978; cf. Table 4.7). Trade balances sharply improved also in ICs (see Table 4.8) and in 1980 achieved a significant surplus.

The growth of Japanese exports to Europe is equally impressive: starting from a very low level, Japanese companies reached, in 1979, a market share of 5 per cent in digital bipolar ICs, 7 per cent in analog ICs and 16 per cent in MOS ICs.[77]

In our view, it is misleading to interpret these product–cycle features simply as the effect of endogenous mechanisms within international markets. A comparison between the Japanese and the European cases is particularly revealing: the strong cycles of imports followed by imitation and then import substitution and exports, which are very clear in Japan, do not appear in Europe. On the contrary, there are many features of the industry which would suggest a *truncated product cycle*, where a fast rate of product and process substitution and the patterns of international oligopolistic competition prevent products from smoothly flowing down to second-coming, third-coming, etc. countries and companies. Our hypothesis is that, in the Japanese case, product cycle patterns were *allowed and induced by a rather complex set of policies and institutional factors*: among them, control of foreign investment, trade policies, and monitoring of the technology transfers from US to Japanese companies. As we discuss at greater length in the Dosi (1981) and (1981a), Japanese policies appear to have radically altered those 'neutral trends' which would have emerged by a market-led international diffusion of technology and of production. In the European case, on the contrary, the emergence of an international semiconductor oligopoly, reflecting in its structure the original imbalances between countries in terms of technological leads and lags, somewhat *stabilised* also relative imbalances in trade flows. This occurred despite the variables which, as we discussed above, tend to favour international transfer of technology and production, i.e. differential variable costs and the 'specificity' of host markets which both offer incentives to re-location of production in the host countries and, through that, affect trade flows.

We have been arguing that in a pure *laissez-faire* international framework each country's position within the international division of labour (and thus its relative trade specialisation) is determined by the interplay, to use Dunning's terminology, between *country–specific* and *company–specific* variables. In the long run, the two are not independent from each other: in particular, the technological levels of a country are both the cause and effect of innovation and location policies of its domestic companies and local foreign subsidiaries. Policies like those implemented by Japan are likely to affect both country–specific and company–specific advantages.

Therefore, in a comparison between a *laissez-faire* international oligopolistic framework and a framework characterised by active (and 'structural') industrial policies, not only the time profile of changes in international production and trade are likely to be different, but also the final long-run outcomes in terms of international specialisation of each country might differ significantly. In other words, technological and trade advantages (and disadvantages) may either be accepted as a result of the endogenous market mechanisms, or, conversely, be consciously 'conquered' by institutional and political means.

A final comment on Japanese foreign investment policies is required. Japanese companies, until recently,[78] have been rather reluctant to invest abroad. This can be interpreted in the light of the model of investment decision illustrated in the first part of this chapter. One property of the model is that, other things being equal, the amount of investment is a negative function of unit labour cost differentials (whenever the latter are higher in the host country). This appears to be particularly the case of Japan, not only in semiconductors but in a wide range of sectors. Given product technology, the relation between wage rates and labour productivity appears to be very favourable, due also to non-transferable social conditions related to the pattern of industrial relations,[79] and more generally to the Japanese institutional context. As a matter of fact, an increased

Japanese enthusiasm to invest abroad could be induced only by the other major factor identified above under the broad heading of 'specificity of local markets', in this case, a straightforward threat of protection against Japanese exports.

The 1980s will probably see a wave of foreign investment by the Japanese companies, pushed by market penetration criteria and by threats of American and European protection, and allowed by the position of technological leadership conquered by the Japanese industry. This – as we tried to show in the US case – will not reverse the patterns of export and imports, but – more likely – stabilise them within the framework of a developing world oligopoly.

4.4 CONCLUSIONS

Companies and Countries: The Role of National Economies

We started the analysis by introducing international trade and investment into the model of inter-firm asymmetries developed for a closed economy context. From the point of view of the fundamental features of industrial dynamics, nothing needed to be added to the framework outlined in Chapter 3. The constraints and opportunities which technical change places in front of each company do not have any nationality, as far as individual actors are concerned. In this respect, an evolutionary model of oligopolistic interaction applies to a closed economy as well as to the international arena. At behavioural level, the nationality of technological lags and leads, as well as of trade and investment flows, are only a statistical label which we attach to them *ex post*, but do not appear among the *direct* determining factors which affect investment or sales decisions. At a more structural level of analysis, however, the existence of different national economies *does* count because it affects context conditions in relation to which companies operate. We found three such factors, affecting the structural conditions which are specific to the existence of individual countries namely:

1. Country–specific technological capabilities including user–producer technological relationships, available skills and knowledge, location–related externalities, etc., which are all hardly transferable or, even when they are, transferable at an economic cost.
2. Wage rates, which are determined, in a first approximation, at national (and macroeconomic) level.
3. The 'specificity' of each national market, which is a broad definition including many of the heterogeneous factors defined by traditional

economies as 'market imperfections' together with different patterns of demand and, sometimes, import protection.

To these three factors, one should add also the institutional context and the pattern of industrial relations, which are extremely important, although it was not possible to analyse them here.

These factors affect structural conditions in which companies operate. Even leaving aside public policies and, in general, governmental action, these country–specific variables are intrinsically related to one general phenomenon: national economies are comprised of integrated economic systems held together by a complex thread of interlinkages which are not only input–output ones, but also technological inter-dependences together with a body of knowledge, experience and procedures (i.e. a specific 'history') which, in some respects, constitute a 'public good' of the system as a whole and differentiate it from other national systems.

Our foregoing analysis has tried to account for the interplay between inter-firm technological asymmetries and some country-related vari-ables, at the level of each single sector. The task was twofold. First, we analysed, in behavioural terms, how national characteristics affect export decisions and foreign investment of individual companies. Then we constructed a 'structural' model whereby the international com-petitiveness of a country, in any given sector and at any given time, was explained by three variables: its relative technological levels, its relative unit labour costs and its industrial structure.

Dynamically, of course, the three are interrelated: improving tech-nological levels increases the levels of wages (expressed in international currency) consistent with a given level of international competitiveness, while at the same time changing patterns of technological lags/leads modify the international industrial structure (along the lines discussed, in the closed economy case, in Chapter 3). The investigation of the semi-conductor industry has appeared to support the basic theoretical framework and, hopefully, helped to illustrate the dynamics over time of all the variables at work.

We are ready now for the final step of our analysis and will try to link the model, developed so far at the level of one sector, to the macroeconomic context.

An organic attempt to do so would certainly require a book of its own. The most we can try to achieve is to show where the linkages are. Without any claims to be exhaustive, we shall make some suggestions on the general mechanisms of adjustment and change which technical changes induce in the economic system.

NOTES AND REFERENCES

1. See Posner (1961). The discussion here is explicitly referring to the analytical framework from that seminal article. On 'technological' theories of international trade, see also Freeman (1963); Hufbauer (1966).
2. Among the things that one must hold equal there are, of course, the length of the lags, the size of the market for each new commodity, the rate of diffusion in consumption and production of the innovation in each country, etc.
3. Posner (1961).
4. With regard to pricing policies in B markets, imitative lags of other A firms matter in so far as they might be able to export to these markets.
5. One implicitly assumes here that the process technology of the first entrant in country *B* would be the same as the first imitative firm in country *A*. Under these conditions, barriers to entry are of a dynamic nature ('learning effects', etc.). Obviously, differences in process technology would affect costs' functions of foreign entrants and thus price levels.
6. A strategy analytically equivalent to that described by Pashigian (1968) for a closed economy context.
7. There is some evidence for, such a behaviour in the case of the heavy electromechanics oligopoly with respect to Less Developed Countries: cf. Newfarmer (1979). See also below.
8. See again Posner (1961). For a thorough discussion cf. Soete (1982).
9. See Vernon (1966) and Wells (1972). For a thorough critical analysis cf. Walker (1979).
10. Note that here one is still explicitly ruling out the possibility of direct foreign investment.
11. If dynamic economies have the shape of the familiar 'learning curve', they tend asymptotically to a straight line.
12. All the attempts to calculate the 'private' *vs* 'public' rates of returns on innovation show the latter much higher than the former. See Mansfield (1977).
13. Rugman (1980), among others, appears to hold this view.
14. One can see a close resemblance with the problems defined as central by Dunning (1977).
15. For sake of simplicity we neglect here both licencing and all the 'new forms' of foreign investments discussed by Oman (1980) and Balcet (1981) (i.e. joint-ventures, turn-key projects, etc.).
16. Chesnais (1981) quotes Cotta (1978) who suggests a similar view.
17. For cross-industry tests on the USA which account also for other structure-related variables (e.g. the capability of differentiating the products, advertising capability, etc.), see Lall (1980).
18. As we shall briefly see below, innovation, other things being equal, tends to induce divergence also in real wages and incomes. For a more detailed discussion, see Dosi (1982b).
19. A thorough discussion of the convergence/divergence issues is in Pavitt (1979) and (1980). See also below.
20. Another item of costs which might show a significant international variance is energy. For sake of simplicity we neglect it here. Its treatment, however, does not present any additional theoretical problem.
21. See Dosi (1982b) for a more complete discussion. The reader might have

already noticed the similarity of this argument with Pasinetti (1981, chapter XI).

22. As we saw in Chapter 3, the two are different whenever there are structural factors determining oligopolistic positions.

23. See Appendix II.

24. Note that here we rule out *ex hypothesi* the possibility of international investment. This will be brought into the picture in the next section.

25. We assume that capital/output ratios are identical in the three countries.

26. The economist reader might object that we are neglecting here all possible macroeconomic mechanisms of adjustment which may prevent this from happening. It is impossible to discuss them at length here (cf. Dosi, 1982b). It should be enough to mention that macroeconomic changes in exchange rates and levels of domestic activity affect and are affected by the *average* competitive conditions of each economy. In other words, they relate to *average* levels of technological lags/leads, *average* levels of productivity and wages. Thus, even after allowing macroeconomic adjustments the notional outcome described in the text might occur. The reader should not be surprised: a similar outcome is implicit in the classical Ricardian example of Portugal and England trading in wine and cloth. At the end of the day, Portugal loses her specialisation in cloth, even if it enjoys a higher absolute productivity than England.

27. Parboni (1980) contains an important and thought provoking analysis of the patterns of international investment in the post-war period based on the dynamics of wages and exchange rates.

28. For a rigorous treatment, see Steedman (1980).

29. See Appendix II for a discussion of the conditions under which our model strictly applies.

30. This argument, *mutatis mutandis*, applies also to companies lagging behind in a closed economy context. In our model of oligopolistic markets, characterised by more than one firm, in Chapter 3, we assume the price elasticity of demand for each firm to be rather low, equal to the price elasticity for the industry. In actual fact, relatively low elasticities are not only due to product differentiations, but also to information costs, institutional user–producer relationships, etc. Were these latter factors absent, undifferentiated industries would present even higher tendencies toward concentration, since the lowest cost producers would be able to conquer the market at a relatively low cost in terms of prices. In a static perspective, this would be more efficient, because the average production costs for the industry would be lower and so would prices. From a dynamic point of view the question is less clear. If technical progress is 'normal' and cumulative, there is no 'conservative collusion' between the big oligopolies aimed at slowing down innovation, innovative activities present non-decreasing returns to scale, etc., then a more concentrated set-up is also dynamically progressive. Conversely, if the opposite circumstances occur, a trade-off between static and dynamic efficiency may emerge. A discussion of similar trade-offs is in Nelson and Winter (1980a).

31. Hirsch (1976) defines the conditions of the choice through a cost-based exercise of comparative statics. Buckley and Casson (1981) present a

dynamic model which determines also the timing of the switch from exports to direct investments, given different profiles of fixed and variable costs and an exogenously determined rate of growth of the foreign market.

32. In many ways the 'flavour' of this illustration recalls Hirsch (1976).

33. The amount of foreign direct investment bears a direct relationship with the physical amount of foreign production, via the capital/output ratio (V):
$$K_B = VPX_B$$

34. That is to say, the rate of profit on activities in both A and B.

35. In this case, for simplicity, we assume that prices are identical in A and B and that neither prices nor costs change over time.

36. In addition to the hypotheses made above, let us suppose also that whatever investment one chooses to undertake at $t = 0$, in order to keep an unchanged market share, one must expand each year at the same rate as the growth of market B (set at g). In other words the local installed capacity must be in constant proportion to the local market in order to keep a constant market share after time τ. Let r be the rate of discount. Remembering that part of the share in the B-market might still be supplied with A-exports, in the case of positive investments, the present value of gross profits will be:

$$PV_I = \int_0^\tau \{M_0 s_0 e^{\lambda t}(p - c_A) + H_0(c_A - c_B)\} \cdot e^{(g-r)t}\, dt +$$

$$+ \int_\tau^T [M_0 s_\tau(p - c_A) + H_0(c_A - c_B)] e^{(g-r)t}\, dt - C \qquad 34$$

The first integral represents present values of gross margins during the period of market shares' adjustment, the second covers the values between t and T, while C accounts for the additional costs involved in any investment in B (due to 'external diseconomies'). The variables c_A and c_B are unit costs in A and B, which we assume, for simplicity, to remain constant over time. M_0 is the initial size of the market B (in physical terms) and s_0 the initial market share in it, while 'T' is the time horizon of the firm. The parameter λ is the adjustment coefficient of market shares as from eq. 32.

37. In the case of 'export-only' the equivalent expression in the present value of future profits will be:

$$PV_x = \int_0^\tau M_0 \cdot s_0 \cdot e^{(g-r+\lambda_x)t}\, dt \qquad 35$$

where λ_x is that coefficient which leads the market share down to approximately zero at time t.

38. Note that here we are considering the case of a cost advantage of the leading country.

39. This assumption may be held quite independently from any resort to neoclassical market adjustment mechanisms. Take for example Soete's tests of technology-gap explanations of trade (Soete, 1980) which do not assume any neoclassical adjustment based on general equilibrium hypotheses, but, on the contrary, put inter-country differentials in the monopolistic power over technology at the core of the explanation of different trade performances. Even in this case, however, industrial structures do not enter

directly into the picture: it is as if they were simply the *vehicle* through which differential technological capabilities of each country express themselves; no more, no less.

40. See Auquier (1980); Glejer, Jacquemin and Petit (1980). Auquier quotes also Rapp (1976).

41. See Helleiner (1981) and Caves (1981) where one can find also a selected bibliography. Aquino (1980) provides a thorough analysis of the patterns of intra-industry trade.

42. Size of the firms, and market shares (together with more obvious features like service and distribution networks abroad, brand loyalties, established user–producer relationships, etc.), are going to affect export performance quite independently from either technological or cost conditions:

   1. On the basis of assumptions of profit-maximising firms it can be proved that the ratio of exports to sales is positively related to firms size (Hirsch and Adar, 1974). All this *independently* from different degrees of market power that might be associated with increasing size. It seems plausible that a similar relationship can be proved to hold after abandoning assumptions of U-shaped cost curves and equalisation between marginal revenue and marginal costs.

   2. *A fortiori*, if size and market power are correlated and if we do not rule out the possibility of discriminatory pricing between different markets, we would expect a significant influence of the international market structures and firms' sizes upon export performances (although we cannot predict *a priori* the sign of that relationship, which might be negative whenever one country's oligopolistic companies make a big use of this market power on international markets, in analogy with what we argued in Chapter 3 on the leading firms in the domestic context).

   3. Again, the case of intra-industry trade in *identical* commodities exemplifies in the extreme how oligopolistic interaction may determine trade patterns independently from structural conditions. Brander (1981) shows – again under the assumption of profit maximising firms – how oligopolistic competition leads to two-way trade in the same commodity, even when that is 'inefficient', i.e. when economies of scale would make a solution of specialisation preferable.

43. Some recent important studies have started analysing the structure of international trade from the standpoint of international organisation variables. See Caves, Porter and Spence (1980) and the contributions to the special issue of *The Journal of Industrial Economics*, 1980, devoted to these topics.

44. The role of oligopolistic positions, which we have defined above as the necessary (although not sufficient) condition for foreign investment, is the focus of the analysis of that interpretative approach, building on Hymer's model, which has related foreign investment to the pattern of industrial structures prevailing in the home country (cf. Hymer, 1976; Kindelberger, 1969; Caves, 1971; Horst, 1972; Lall, 1980).

45. Note that in this context, we utilise a rather loose definition of market power, which does not stand so much for the traditional capability of setting 'higher' prices as for the possibility of exploiting all the 'market specificities', defined above.

46. For one of the few studies on the patterns of R & D location by US multinational see Mansfield, Teece and Romeo (1979). Even if there appears to be a relatively greater decentralisation of R & D location during the post-war decades, there seems to be no reversal in a pattern which still gives the overwhelming priority to locations in the USA.

47. See also Dosi (1982b).

48. Vernon (1979) provides convincing evidence on the acceleration of international diffusion of new products and processes within multinational firms, at least as far as industrialised countries are concerned.

49. In order to illustrate this proposition, let us consider two 'ideal types' concerning the dynamics of specialisation between two countries, A – the technological leader – and B – the 'backward' country. In the first scenario, let us suppose that there is no international investment and A enjoys, for some time, a monopolistic control over a new technology. Suppose also that, after a certain time lag, B-companies 'learn' the new technology and, exploiting the advantages stemming from the interrelation with the local market and from lower labour costs, enter the new market. By so doing, they acquire for their country the technological expertise (the 'technological specialisation') which takes B nearer to the technological frontier. Let us compare this 'ideal type' with a second one, whereby A-firms rapidly invest in B, leaving, however, their R & D and the most complex productions in A. This has a few important consequences: (a) international investment accelerates technological diffusion toward B, but – at the same time – makes the emerge of autonomous B-companies more difficult; (b) the technology-gap and the trade disadvantage of B decrease more rapidly than in the previous scenario; however, (c) if the innovative activities are kept in A, it may well be that country B never reaches the technological frontier, because – in the long term – the strategies of international investment reproduce through time the location–specific advantages of A and B (respectively, technological advantages in A and lower labour costs in B).

50. An attempt to outline these functional relations in an international context is to be found in Dosi (1981c).

51. Cross-industry tests show many limitations which parallel those discussed above with respect to the 'innovation-market structure' question and related to the specific features of each technology and industry. Those limitations appear especially serious when testing explanations for particular patterns of revealed comparative advantage (see Soete, 1980; or – on the neoclassical side – Leamer, 1974).

52. The empirical problems of correctly specifying the variable and obtaining adequate data clearly cannot be analysed here.

53. cf. Vernon (1966). For a critique see also Pavitt and Soete (1981).

54. In Dosi (1981c) we argue that this variable could be approximated by one country's share in total foreign direct investments in each i-sector.

55. For simplicity suppose that a sector corresponds to only one product, but suppose also that this product undergoes technical change, after its initial introduction, by means of product and process improvements.

56. Let us consider the *levels* of per capita GDP. Even if relative per capita GDP's do not change, the 'most developed' country will show over time a steady worsening of its competitive position, starting from a very favourable one; 'intermediate' countries will show a U-shaped profile and 'backward'

countries will present a steady improvement, starting from a very unfavourable position.

57. See Dunning (1981) on the long-term patterns of foreign direct investment.
58. For a more precise account of the relationship between average technological asymmetries (for the tradable sector as a whole) and wage rates, see Dosi (1982b).
59. The innovative methodology introduced by Pavitt and Soete (1980) and Soete (1982), who use US patent data to estimate the sectoral innovative capability of each country, can be considered an important step in the direction of a test of the model. At the time of final revision of this work, some further research by the author and L. Soete on tests including both a technology and a cost variable is in progress. See also below, for some tests on the semiconductor industry.
60. Here and in the following pages we will refer to trade balances in percentage of internal market, if not otherwise specified.
61. For a detailed analysis, see Sciberras (1977).
62. This is particularly likely when foreign investment is sheltered from international competition through import tariffs and quotas. We have some evidence on this phenomenon in the case of Brazil.
63. Most US prices did decrease around the turn of the decade (as they did for almost every year since the industry was born). The point is that they did *not* decrease relatively to variable costs. In other words, American unit margins remained relatively stable.
64. Cf. Pavitt and Soete (1980), Soete (1980) and (1982). US patents have been provided in an *ad hoc Special Report* by the Office of Technological Assessment and Forecast (OTAF) of the US Department of Commerce. We want to thank OTAF, and in particular Dr D. Kelly, for the kind and valuable help.
65. One was able to obtain comparable data on exports only for EEC countries and Japan. The USA was excluded, in order to avoid the bias induced by the fact that, using US patents data, American patenting in the USA is likely to overestimate American technological output (see Pavitt and Soete, 1980). Moreover, note that the number of semiconductor-producing countries is rather small.
66. Let us define net external balances in percentage of the domestic market as NBM (1977–8); cumulated patents divided by the average 1977–8 size of domestic market as Pd, and a specialisation index (export minus imports divided by exports plus imports) as SI. We obtained:

$$NMB = -73.04 + 18.71\,Pd \qquad\qquad R^2 = 0.26 \qquad 43$$
$$(25.12)\ (13.03)$$
$$SI = -0.46 + 01\,Pn \qquad\qquad R^2 = 0.23 \qquad 44$$
$$(0.17)\ (0.008)$$
$$NBM = -64.67 + 1.32\,Pn \qquad\qquad R^2 = 0.28 \qquad 45$$
$$(19.23)\ (0.86)$$

The signs of the coefficients on the independent variables are the expected ones but the coefficients themselves are not significantly different from zero and the correlation coefficients are rather low.

67. If intra-MNC technology transfer occurs, this obviously influences the host country's technological levels but need not show in the patenting activity of the foreign subsidiary of the MNC.
68. Finan's sources are mainly estimates from American companies, while our data is based on trade statistics. In addition, Finan's data should be F.O.B. American exports, while we use C.i.F. European imports. Finally, we include in semiconductors some special devices and parts apparently excluded from Finan's data.
69. Cf. Ernst (1982).
70. Moreover, note that in some countries imports by foreign subsidiaries are for re-export. This phenomenon is particularly pronounced, within Europe, in UK and France.
71. This can be seen also from the disaggregation of ICs sales by American foreign subsidiaries (USITC, 1979, pp. 83 and 85). On the period 1974–8, shipments to local host markets grow at only 3.3 % per annum, while exports increase at 21.9 %.
72. Moreover, the biggest foreign subsidiary, Intermetal–ITT can be considered a 'quasi-German' company.
73. Fairchild pulled out of the joint venture in the early 1970s.
74. A detailed discussion of this distinction in relation to semiconductors is in Finan (1975).
    Balances on ownership base equal those on geographical base minus trade flows to and from the US controlled by US companies.
75. Ownership-based balances, in our calculations, tend to be underestimated in so far as they do not account for the part of US imports originated in American foreign subsidiaries located in other developed countries. On the other hand, one considers as 'American' those companies taken over by European and Japanese firms (their impact is significant only after 1975). The two factors should roughly cancel each other out.
76. Estimates based on the values of imports from unrelated parties (from USITC, 1979, p. 93) and apparent consumption elaborated from US Dept of Commerce data suggest values for the mid-seventies, below 1 %: to this one must add imports by US subsidiaries of foreign companies. Even allowing for this, foreign companies' market share in ICs should have been very low until the Japanese started entering massively the memory market.
77. DAFSA (1981).
78. At the beginning of the 1980s, most of the major Japanese semiconductor producers started or planned to invest in both the USA and Europe.
79. See the illuminating comparison between British and Japanese industrial relations in Dore (1973).

5 Some Conclusions on Technical Change and Technological Diffusion as an Introduction to Macroeconomic Transformation

The effects of technical change are not confined within any single industrial sector. The dynamics of each industry influences and is influenced by the patterns of change in the other industries by means of inter-industrial diffusion of innovations, changes in relative prices and relative profitabilities, and derived patterns of demand for the output of each industry sector which feature as an input in other industries' techniques of production. Furthermore, there are a few directly macroeconomic dimensions related to the inter-sectoral adjustment mechanisms based on capital movements and to the relationship between technical change, on the one hand, and effective aggregate demand, foreign balances and international specialisation, on the other.

The reader will realise that a thorough treatment of these issues is a very lengthy task which cannot be undertaken here. However, if one believes, as we do, that sound microeconomic theory must be compatible and theoretically linked with macroeconomics, then there is a need to indicate the macroeconomic hypotheses which the foregoing discussion suggests. In these conclusions we will try to define briefly the implications of our analysis in terms of the patterns of transformation of the macroeconomic system.

5.1 THE DIFFUSION OF INNOVATIONS AND THE TRANSMISSION MECHANISMS OF TECHNICAL CHANGE

Differential innovative capabilities by each company on the domestic and international markets might lead, as it was shown in Chapter 3, to an oligopolistic structure of industry. The possibility of the emergence and evolution through time of this oligopoly depends on the nature of technical progress itself (whether it is more or less cumulative, and whether it yields to stable company–specific technological advantages) and, linked to that, on the relative capability of each firm to innovate and/or quickly imitate through time. An important implication of our discussion above is that the structure of the industry itself is an endogenous variable precisely as described by the often cited Nelson–Winter models. More precisely, technological lags and leads (in terms of both products and processes), industrial concentration, differential cost structures, prices, margins and market shares are themselves the *result* of patterns of oligopolistic competition, whereby innovative/imitative activities are a crucial behavioural feature of the evolution of each firm and its growth, survival or disappearance.

Diffusion as an Innovative Process

In a truly dynamic account, technological imitation within an industry is coupled most of the time with further technological innovation (either by the same firms or by other firms of the industry), along what we called, in Chapter 2, a trajectory of technical change. Within this framework one can easily define both the questions of the *inter-firm diffusion* of innovations (i.e. diffusion in production) and *diffusion in demand*. Although it is obviously simpler for the analysis to consider the patterns of diffusion of an innovation as if the latter were a once-for-all phenomenon, this might be misleading, since any major innovation is likely to yield to a series of incremental changes and improvements[1], which change the potential number of adopters and the profitability of the adoption itself. It is not possible here either to undertake a detailed discussion of models of diffusion or to provide satisfying tests with respect to the semiconductor industry. We must thus limit ourselves to a few comments and a few empirical remarks.

In the literature, the prevailing interpretations of the diffusion patterns of innovation pioneered by Mansfield (1961) and (1977) and Griliches (1957) essentially consist of the estimate of a diffusion curve, which is often found to be S-shaped.[2] At a second stage, inter-innovation and/or inter-industry differences in the coefficients of the diffusion curves are explained through various independent variables. The three which found the greatest econometric corroboration are the differential profitability of the innovation, the scale of the required investment and firm's size (the former and the latter being positively correlated with the speed of diffusion).

In our view, the 'logistic curves' approaches to technological diffusion represent a major achievement in that they establish a rather general 'stylised fact' of the process. However, they do not explain it. They provide an ex-post rationalisation on the conditioned probability of a non-adopter to become an adopter of an innovation. In that, they show exactly the same descriptive usefulness as well as the limitations of the epidemic curves (or, for that matter, probability models) to which they are formally similar: they show the pattern of diffusion of, say, cholera, and they can also relate it to some broad environmental factors, such as the conditions of hygiene of a town, the reproduction time of bacteria, etc., but they cannot explain *why* some people get it and other do not, which relates to the immunological mechanisms of human bodies, the precise ways bacteria are transmitted, and so on.

Moreover, these models present three major points of weakness. First, as already mentioned, they assume a once-for-all innovation without allowing, prima facie, incremental improvements on the supply side as well as innovative processes on the side of the adopters (whenever the considered innovation is a capital or intermediate good). Secondly, they neglect price changes of the innovation itself which may affect, through time, the profitability of the adoption of the innovation. Thirdly, they do not consider the process of diffusion in production of the innovation (i.e. the patterns of imitation in the supplying industry).

All three points are stressed by Metcalfe,[3] who develops a very stimulating model of diffusion jointly determined by the supply of an innovative commodity, whose price changes through time, and a demand for it, which depends also on its price and the profitability of adoption.[4] As we discussed in Chapter 3, the prices of any given innovative commodity change through time due to learning effects and process innovations. Thus, as Metcalfe shows, we have an *envelope* of notional diffusion curves associated with each price, while the actual diffusion path represents both diffusion along a curve and movements of the curve itself due to price changes. Two points must be stressed, namely:

1. The process of diffusion in production, i.e. both the expansion of the

innovative firms and imitations by other firms, is intimately associated with additional innovations and improvements. This is not only a corollary of 'natural' learning processes, it is also implied in the very dynamics of inter-firm asymmetries based on innovative lags and leads. As argued in Chapter 3, asymmetric innovative capabilities associated with some limit-price *force* potential entrants to introduce further innovations in order to enter the market. This same process tends to improve the performance characteristics of the innovative commodities and to widen the universe of potential adopters.

2. The process of diffusion in demand, in the case of producer goods, is hardly a simple purchasing decision. On the contrary, it almost always involves minor or major innovations on the part of the adopters who must change, to different degrees, their production processes or their products. If producer–user inter-relationships are important in stimulating further innovation[5] then we can see there a clear 'dynamic circle' of positive feedbacks.

Both these points highlight, from an economic point of view, the relationship between endogenous and exogenous technical change which was considered in Chapter 2. We will not repeat here the reasons why the original innovation (especially if it was a radical one) might not have been endogenously induced. Conversely, we see here how continuous progress *along a defined technological trajectory* is triggered and pulled by the endogenous mechanisms of oligopolistic ('Schumpeterian') competition, the 'problem-solving' activities related to the adoption of innovations,[6] the complementarities between different technologies and industries jointly with straightforward economic signals, such as changing relative prices, relative profitabilities and distributive shares.

The Importance of Technological Interdependence Between Sectors

The diffusion of the products which are not final goods brings about product and process innovation in user industries. The hypotheses we suggest here are the following:

1. For any given set of macroeconomic conditions, e.g. for a given 'level of development' of a country, the rate of diffusion among user firms will be higher, the higher are the rates of innovation and the rate of imitation in the producing industry.

2. As a consequence, diffusion in production and diffusion in demand are strongly interdependent: the rates of innovation/imitation in user industries are often dynamically linked with the technological levels of that domestic industry where the innovations come from. The opposite holds true as well: the technological levels, the size and the competitive patterns in user industries provide a more or less conducive environment for technological innovation and/or imitation in the industry which is 'upstream', i.e. the industry originating the innovations. Which one is the 'dominant' relationship depends on which one is the 'dominant' technology, on the appropriability of technical change and its nature. We would expect, for example, that in the early phases of establishment of a new technological paradigm, an overwhelming 'innovation–push' upon 'downstream' industries. Conversely, we would expect the role of the latter to be greater whenever technical progress occurs along a defined technological trajectory and, correspondingly, the patterns of change are relatively more endogenous to the 'inducement mechanisms' of the economic system.

This hypothesis of technological inter-relatedness between sectors is consistent with the existence of industrial *filières*, as the French call it. [7]

The concept of industrial *filière* (in English, 'web' or 'cluster'), despite being fairly impressionistic, helps to highlight a system of interdependence based, on the traded side, on input–output relations, and, even more importantly, on the untraded side, on technological interdependences, which are likely to be country–specific, or even region–specific and company–specific. In this context, 'chains' of innovations in different interlinked sectors might tend to be reinforcing in 'virtuous circles' affecting both sectoral technological levels and their rates of growth.

If this is the way technical change in one particular sector affects changes throughout the economy, some far-reaching implications are worth noting.

The emergence and establishment of new technological paradigms is likely to be correlated with a substantial body of untraded knowledge and experience. In this respect, the discussion in Chapter 2 shows how these untraded aspects are an essential part of the nature of technologies and technological advances. Much of this knowledge, although untraded, might, however, be appropriable. It has already been mentioned that it may often be embodied in individual people. In our case study, the history of technological diffusion and further innovation throughout the first two decades of the US semiconductor industry is strongly associated with a high mobility of scientists, technicians and managers.[8]

In some cases these untraded technological advantages might be an asset to the entire industry of a country (i.e. a 'dynamic endowment' of a country's industry). Moreover, we suggested in Chapter 3 that the final establishment of a technological paradigm is likely to be associated with an 'oligopolistic maturity' of the industry, whenever technical progress retains cumulative and highly appropriable features. An implication of it is that the formation of a stable oligopolistic structure of supply is likely to be associated with cumulative technological learning which is appropriable at company level, in addition to being an 'externality' enjoyed by a national industry.[9]

In many ways, the history of the development of an oligopolistic structure can be interpreted as the trend towards *internalisation of the untraded aspects of technological change.* Furthermore, whenever there are interlinked technologies and/or a dominant technology – as in our semiconductor case – this process of internalisation and private appropriation of untraded technological interdependences among sectors, is likely to result in a slow process of vertical integration. The *filière*, whenever it is characterised by strong technological interlinkages and whenever the latter are appropriable and transformable into a company asset, is likely to embody a significant tendency towards oligopolistic integration within clusters of industries. This is clearly in line with the 'internalisation' theories of vertical integration and international investment, as already mentioned above (Chapter 4). It is worth stressing again that it is misleading to consider this internalisation process as the exceptional result of some 'market failure', related to some special feature of the 'market of knowledge and information'. Rather, it can be considered as one of the essential features of development and change in capitalist societies. Technical progress keeps producing untraded technological interdependences, while changing industrial organisations keep trying to internalise and appropriate this 'knowledge' as a corporate asset. These considerations apply both within a domestic context, as a drive towards vertical integration, and on an international level, as a drive towards the international exploitation of these company–specific assets and the formation of an international oligopoly.

An interesting corollary is that technological interdependencies are an important driving force behind the patterns of companies' diversification, not only 'upstream' and 'downstream' but also 'horizontally', towards other sectors which are neither sellers to nor buyers from the industry in question but share with the latter similar process or product technology.[10]

Moreover, the discussion above suggests the existence of a relationship, within the same industry or the same cluster of industries, between country–specific and company–specific untraded advantages, the latter being to some extent the internalisation of the former. If this is so, this should be an additional reason to suggest some long-run complementarity between participation by a country's companies in the international oligopoly and its trade performance. Even if intra-firm international diffusion is rapid, as long as country–specific advantages reproduce themselves through time, the country of origin is likely to maintain a relatively favourable trade position. In many ways, it was argued above, technological interdependencies induce a relative stability through time of 'comparative advantages'.

International investment may be considered, at least as far as intra-developed countries' investment is concerned, as a powerful form of international diffusion of technology.[11] Our discussion in the previous chapter on trade and international investment supports this statement. A crucial point, however, which we have stressed in Chapter 4, is that international investment is *not* likely to reverse the pattern of country–specific relative technological advantages (and even less so those company–specific ones generally associated with the former). In this respect, international diffusion through multinational enterprises can be considered, from a normative point of view of host countries, as a second best alternative.[12] Conversely, we suggested in Chapter 4 that from the investing country's point of view, international investment might imply trading-off higher short-run against longer-run, although smaller, trade advantages.

The analysis of the nature of technical change suggested the existence of regularities in its patterns and directions (in the form of technological paradigms and trajectories). The following step was to study the impact of technical innovation and imitation on the structure and performance variables of the affected industry. One of the implications of the argument was that, in general, despite the continuous emergence of oligopolistic positions, prices tend to move in accordance with costs. Moreover, we suggested that the patterns of demand are shaped by long-term changes in the baskets of consumption and by the innovative processes in user industries. Changes in the real price of the commodities (in terms of income) and the relative price of substitutable commodities are intertwined with the former and accelerate/slow down these long-term rates of change in demand, even if, as we tried to show, price elasticities and inter-commodity substitutability in the short term are generally rather low. Finally, we have been hinting at the fact that processes of inter-industrial diffusion of innovation are, in their nature, induced innovative processes. A joint account of these properties of the economic system represents, as it were, the technological background of input—output tables of the economy and their change through time. In a way, one may consider our discussion as the analysis of the technological and economic variables which lead to a particular input—output configuration and keep it changing in relatively ordered ways. Conversely, input—output analysis is the 'medium term' which allows a link between our microeconomic level of investigation with macroeconomic trends. Individual changes in prices and quantities, in a highly interdependent system, lead to remarkable aggregate effects on productivity, demand and levels of macroeconomic activity.[13] It is not possible to discuss them here. However, we hope, the study has contributed to illuminate the features of technologies and industries which explain the trends in input coefficients, prices and different patterns of demand for individual commodities.

An interesting implication of the analysis of technical change, related to its 'oriented nature' along defined technological trajectories, concerns the evolution of techniques over time: the general case, we suggest, is that there are univocally superior and inferior techniques irrespective of income distribution (cf. also Appendix II). This is not to say that changes in income distribution do not affect the rate and directions of technical change (within the boundaries of a given paradigm). Clearly they do. The point is that 'new' techniques are generally such that they would have been adopted, if they existed, even at the 'old' income distribution.[14] This introduces powerful *irreversibility properties* into the economic system. At the same time, the view of technology presented here is a radical alternative to the assumption of 'production possibility sets', a concept essential to the neoclassical theory of income distribution introduced without the slightest reference to the empirical evidence on technology and technical change. Technological trajectories, on the supply side, and slowly evolving Engel-like baskets of consumption, on the demand side, define an economic system whose threads, *at any given point in time*, are consistent with an input—output description (including nearly fixed coefficients of production) and fundamentally different from the world of timeless *tâtonnements* of general equilibrium: for once, the burden should rest upon those who are so fond of the traditional theory of relative prices and income distribution to demonstrate either that production and consumption possibility sets do empirically exist or, conversely, that the properties of their models resist the exposure to technological asymmetries, time and irreversibility.[15]

5.2 CONCLUSIONS: TECHNICAL CHANGE AND SYSTEM TRANSFORMATION

We have been trying to reconstruct the patterns of generation of technical change and the ways in which it becomes a crucial factor of transformation of industrial structures. Even if the economic system represents a powerful directing mechanism on the rate and direction of technical progress, the patterns of change cannot be considered entirely endogenous. The innovative process presents a dynamics and rules of its own, which – we suggested – bear meaningful similarities with the procedures and patterns of change in scientific activities. The metaphor of technological paradigms and technological trajectories helps in clarifying the relationship between ruptures and continuity in technical change. That distinction mirrors the distinction between exogenous and endogenous technical innovation. Economic dynamics is capable of shaping the patterns of 'normal' technical change along defined technological trajectories, within the boundaries defined by the latter. On the other hand, the emergence of radically new technological paradigms cannot be simply explained by economic drives: more correctly, it stems from the complex interplay – that we tried to analyse also with reference to the semiconductor case – between advances in science, institutional factors and economic mechanisms. The former provide the universe of the possible new directions of technological development, while the latter two operate as 'focussing and selecting devices', in Rosenberg's terminology. We are far from claiming any exogenous nature of scientific advances: simply the impact of economic factors upon scientific changes pertains to a different timescale, to a looser functional relationship and to different transmission mechanisms.

Clearly it has not been possible to analyse this loop at any satisfactory depth, concerning as it does the fields of epistemology and sociology of knowledge. It is nontheless important to remark the different patterns of interaction characterising the relationship running from the emergence of new technological paradigms to the economic mechanisms, on the one hand, and from the economic environment to major technological breakthroughs, on the other hand. This is another way of saying that technical change is not entirely endogenous: any image of a completely homeostatic system which adjusts internally to changes via induced technical progress is, in our view, misleading. The virtuous circle between 'technology' and 'economics' is not entirely calibrated and leaves room for some degrees of freedom to autonomous technological advances and to the specific rules technical change follows.

In turn, the analysis of the economic environment under conditions of technical change shows how in capitalist societies *private appropriation* of the benefits from technical progress represents both the main incentive to innovation and one of the basic rules of the game of companies' behaviour. This quite evident property allowed us to develop some far-reaching implications in terms of industrial dynamics. We put at the centre of our analysis the concept of *asymmetry*, instead of those, more familiar in traditional microeconomics, of identity (between firms) and equilibrium. Asymmetries exist because the process of technological innovation and its private appropriation continuously create them. They are a structural feature of the industrial system and, at the same time, correspond to a fundamental behavioural rule of the economic actors, aimed at creating *lato sensu* technological imbalances in their own favour and eliminating those which act against them. In its essence, this is the process of *dynamic competition*. Evolutionary models of industrial interaction, as suggested by the seminal works of Nelson and Winter, provide us with the microfoundations of the theory of change in industrial structure, in that they define the rules and meta-rules of behaviours and adaptation of firms in changing environments characterised by technical change.

A further step was needed in order to build a bridge between a theory of 'what the actors do' with a theory of the directions of change of the system under conditions of technical change. One had to answer to the question: are there regularities in the relationship between structural indicators, such as the nature of inter-firm technological asymmetries, and performance indicators (such as costs, prices, margins, industrial concentration, etc.)? In Chapter 3, we considered precisely this issue. Technical change continuously produces new processes and new products, and, jointly, lags and leads in the innovative capabilities of individual firms. These asymmetries, often in conjunction with other size-related advantages, already analysed in the literature by Bain and Sylos–Labini, are capable of explaining the level or, more correctly, a definite notional range of margins, profit rates, concentration, etc. The result is important because it allows the joining together of the statics and the dynamics of the system.

It should be clear that technical progress is one of the main dynamic factors. At the same time, we want to know also what are the forces at work for a *given* and *unchanged* state of the technology. In the real world, forces of change and transformation, on the one hand, and force of adjustment and equilibrium, on the other hand, operate together; this is why we are able to observe relatively ordinated configurations of the economic system, at each point in time, and relatively regular patterns of change, over time. The analysis of Chapter 3 on prices and margins can be reinterpreted in the following way: holding innovation constant, the expansion of innovative firms (i.e. those firms which embody best practice techniques of production and manufacture innovative products), together with the process of technological imitation, tend to diffuse 'on-the-frontier' technology throughout the economy. The mechanisms of diffusion are the counterpart on the technological side of inter-firm and inter-sector capital mobility, directed towards minimum cost/maximum profit allocation of productive activities.

A system without structural asymmetries between firms (related to appropriated technologies or to economies of scale), in the absence of further innovations, would yield to a unique rate of profit and to prices in line with the costs of production. Conversely, we considered the case when exclusive appropriation of technology prevents this from occurring. The same mechanisms based on capital mobility and relative diffusion of the 'best' techniques and products are still at work, but they find a limit in asymmetries which are either permanent or reproduce through time even in absence of further innovation. Learning effects and market pre-emptions are asymmetries of this kind: by definition, if a firm arrived first and if costs are related to cumulative production, then late-comers will not be able to achieve identical costs of production, even if the innovative process stops. We hope to have shown convincingly that the difference between the 'competitive' rate of profit[16] and the equilibrium oligopolistic rates of profit is a function of inter-firm structural asymmetries. In this sense, one can see that the competitive equilibrium analysed in classical economics[17] is that limit case, whenever inter-firm asymmetries tend to disappear and average techniques of production are identical with best practice techniques, or when 'below-average' techniques compensate 'best-practice' techniques in a way that the average rate of profit for the industry is equal to the 'competitive' one. The importance of the competitive mechanism should not be overlooked for it represents a *crucial homeostatic mechanism* which guarantees (varying degrees of) 'static' efficiency of the system. Minimum cost techniques and 'better' products diffuse throughout the economy, while the price is not allowed to remain higher than what is implied by the costs of production (after allowing for possible inter-firm technology-based asymmetries).

Having focused our analysis on technological differences between firms, instead of their uniformity, we can observe an easy link between statics and dynamics. While technological diffusion tends to wither away inter-firm asymmetries, the process of innovation keeps creating new ones. Loosely speaking, we can consider the former as the 'entropic tendency' of the system (its tendency towards uniformity) and the latter as the development tendency which brings about growth, transformation and complexity. Through time both mechanisms are at work and allow an increasing complexity to be associated with (varying degrees of) inner stability and allocative efficiency.

Our investigation fell short of the macroeconomic analysis of the patterns of change in the system as a whole. However, the analysis of the nature of technical advances and of sectoral dynamics hopefully set some sound bases for this task. We have identified the *dual nature* and the *dual dynamics* of technical progress. On the one hand, it increases the efficiency of the system, by means of increasing labour productivity. On the other hand, it creates new markets, expands existing ones and, jointly, stimulates new investment opportunities. The static and dynamic mechanisms we found at sectoral level reflect themselves also in the adjustment mechanisms and growth processes of the system as a whole. At macroeconomic level, the economic system (as well as – we believe – other changing systems) embodies three fundamental forces. First, there are *laws of inner adjustment*, which, holding best-practice technology constant, tend to increase the efficiency of the system and lower prices of production. We have already mentioned them: in capitalist economies, competition, technological diffusion and capital mobility are the driving force of static adjustment, which is described in its competitive 'ideal type' by classical (we could say 'Ricardian') equilibrium models. Secondly, there are *laws of quantitative expansion* (or contraction) of the system. In economies, like the advanced Western variety, which are normally *demand–constrained* and *demand–pulled* as regards the rates of macroeconomic activity, the autonomous items of demand (investments, exports, public expenditures) determine the rates of growth of output and the rates of utilisation of the workforce. The process is the familiar one of Keynesian macroeconomics, both in the short-run version of Keynesian multipliers and its long-term version of 'Cambridge' growth models.[18] In this respect, the analysis of the sectoral patterns of growth highlights the role of 'autonomous' investment associated with the emergence of new products and new markets. Thirdly, there are *laws of transformation*, related to long-run changes in techniques of production, demand patterns, relative sizes of each sector, and industrial structures.

The foregoing analysis shows how technical change is intimately related to all three fundamental forces of the system and is a major 'engine' of all of them.[19] The aim of the present work has been to investigate some aspects of the 'microbiology' of technical change, its determinants and its impact on the structure of each sector at both national and international levels, in ways which appear to us consistent with the macroeconomic analysis of the long-run trends of growth and transformation. In many respects, our work ends where Pasinetti's (1981) begins. Although it is by no means easy to link our discussion with Pasinetti's model,[20] we can say that the latter provides the 'macro-co-ordinates' in which the process of technical change takes place, and the conditions of dynamic equilibrium which fulfil its dual nature in terms of changing demand and changing conditions of production: our analysis has aimed to discover what actually happens within each sector, while Pasinetti's model concerns what must happen at macroeconomic level owing to the patterns of interdependence between sectors and to the trends in income distribution. The properties of technical change which we analysed at the level of an individual industry are broadly consistent with the macroeconomic features of an economic system whereby there is a limited homeostasis between the mentioned dual impacts of technical advances. Two implications, in particular, are worth stressing. First, our industry model tried to show how technical change affects costs and prices. The latter exert an important influence on the rate of diffusion of innovations and thus on the dynamics of demand. However, there is nothing in the microeconomic patterns of technical change which necessarily guarantees that the baskets of demand and the relative prices, so determined, are those which will yield full employment of the labour supply. Second, our investigation supported the hypothesis that constant, or more often, increasing returns are the norm, both for individual industries and individual firms. Production is generally limited by the size of the market. These two properties, taken together, are clearly consistent with the "Keynesian spirit" of Pasinetti's model whereby a) the levels of activity of the system are limited by aggregate demand and b) price-related mechanisms of adjustment are not sufficient to guarantee full employment of the available resources.

The adjustment and transformation mechanisms operating within each economy find their counterparts in the international arena. In particular, we have analysed the determinants of international competitiveness, for given international technological asymmetries, and the resulting dynamics of international specialisation. As in the closed economy context, we had to abandon the misleading idea that technology is a free good. It is not, and even if it were, the 'fundamental rule of appropriation' of capitalist economies would tend to transform it into an asymmetric asset of some companies (and, often, as a consequence, of some countries).

The behavioural rules of 'static' adjustment based on the search for minimum-cost conditions of production (holding best-practice technology constant) are, in their nature, identical to those which operate between firms and between sectors within each economy. In this respect capital is truly internationalist. Some context conditions, however, are country–specific, and the patterns of international specialisation stem from the interplay between international technological asymmetries and international differential in wage rates. Again, the model allows a link between statics and dynamics. In a world characterised by technical change and innovation, the dynamics of international specialisation can be represented by moving trade-offs, affected by (a) technological diffusion, which, as such, is a *convergence mechanism* between countries; (b) technological innovation, representing, *ceteris paribus*, a *divergence mechanism*, and (c) the relative trends in wage rates. The macroeconomic interdependence between national economic systems operates on the grounds of these basic trends in international technological asymmetries, differential wage rates and patterns of sectoral specialisations. In this respect, the aggregate levels of exports and the import propensities of each country find their microeconomic explanation (both at each point in time and in terms of changes) through the evolving relationship between 'technology gaps' and cost differentials. In this sense, 'Ricardian' adjustment processes are the 'static' counterpart of a dynamics based on technology gaps.

A particularly intricate question we had to tackle was the role of industrial organisations. Since we put inter-firm asymmetries, associated with more or less temporary oligopolistic positions, at the centre of our analysis, we could not maintain the handy, although – in our view – misleading, hypothesis of atomistic and purely reactive firms. On the contrary, the analysis implied a view of firms as complex institutions, facing an uncertain future and capable of some (even if not infinite) degrees of freedom in shaping their own future and environment. The accounts of the question we generally find in the established economic literature are strikingly weak and unconvincing. Traditional (neoclassical) microeconomics in particular give us a totally indeterminate 'theory'; it is not actually possible to know what any oligopolistic firm will do without knowing what they think about what everyone else thinks. A different kind of indetermination is implied in what are generally called managerial theories of the firm. These theories try to find regularities in the objectives and patterns of behaviour of oligopolistic actors. In that, they open up the fruitful field of investigation into the nature of firms as institutions with an inner structure and possibly different goals. However, they appear to be unsuitable to analyse the regularities in the relationship between structural (including technological) conditions and configurations of the system (i.e. the performance variables). In this task classical economics cannot be of much help either. We could say, using again the example from physics, set forth in the introduction to this book, that classical economics tried to establish the principles of thermodynamics (i.e. the broad laws of motion of the system) without being too much concerned with Brownian motions (i.e. the behavioural microfoundations of these laws). A complete theory, in this respect, has still to come.

We approached the problem utilising what we consider to be two complementary models. First, as mentioned, Nelson and Winter's evolutionary models represent a theory of regularities in institutional behaviours which embodies also powerful predictions on the patterns of interaction between firms and environment. In the thermodynamic metaphor, it is a seminal attempt at a theory of the Brownian motion. Secondly, we suggested an approach that we called, for want of a better name, 'a weak structural model'. The sense of it is the following. Structural conditions, including – of paramount importance – technological asymmetries, define the degrees of freedom firms have in their actions. Within these degrees of freedom they behave *à la* Nelson–Winter. The weak structural theory indicates a definite range of possible configurations of the system associated with a given set of structural conditions. So, for example, if we call a certain structural state, x, we can predict that, say, profit margins will be between y_1 and y_2. We are also able to make dynamic predictions of the following kind: if structural asymmetries (x) increase, for unchanged behavioural regularities, margins (y) will also increase and vice versa. Moreover, the outcomes of the behaviours of yesterday (say, in terms of the choice of a level of margins, and associated market shares, within the range between y_1 and y_2) become part of today's structural data. In other words, *through time, history becomes structure*, while *at each point in time structures shape history*. Putting together the evolutionary model of behavioural regularities in changing environments and the 'weak structural model' of the relationship between structural states and possible configurations of the system, we can move a step forward linking, in our thermodynamic analogy, Brownian motions and thermodynamic macrostates.

Analytical problems in social sciences are often complicated by the fact that they embody a particular relationship between what we could call structures and freedom.[21] If micro behaviours are not entirely constrained and are capable of affecting their own environment and the future, strict determinism is bound to neglect the existence of a *range* of possible worlds which can emerge, holding structural constraints fixed. Conversely, behaviours and rationalities which inform them are not unbound. Moreover, the degrees of freedom of the actors are asymmetrical and somewhat hierarchical. We saw that, for example, in relation to innovative activities and pricing behaviours, innovators and minimum-cost firms could enjoy a wide range of behavioural options, as compared to technological laggards and 'marginal firms'. Competitive processes, in the form of innovative/imitative activities, capital mobility and entries/exits, variations in prices and quantities (i.e. both 'dynamic' and 'static' competition), prevent the asymmetries from exploding, often curb the exclusive advantages of the most successful actors and do not allow prices to move too far away from the 'centre of gravity' represented by the cost of productions. Over time, the structural boundaries to the actions of the agents change and, with that, also behaviours and overall performance outcomes. In some ways the complementarity between Nelson–Winter evolutionary models and our 'weak structural model' can be described in that the former consider the system *sub specie libertatis*, starting from what the actors plausibly do and how they interact, while the latter considers it *sub specie necessitatis*, focusing on the *boundaries* which constrain the microeconomic degrees of freedom and their effect on the shape of the boundaries of the possible performance outcomes. A lot more could have been formalised. We hope, however, that our discussion, for a good part of a qualitative nature, has helped to suggest an outlook and a methodology. The results of the application of that outlook to our case study appear to be encouraging.

On empirical grounds, we studied the case of the semiconductor industry. In many respects, semiconductors are an 'ideal type' of a radically new industry emerging out of new scientific principles and shaped by the joint effect of institutional intervention and 'Schumpeterian' competition. We had the possibility of observing the process by which a new technological paradigm becomes dominant and determines a 'trajectory' of technical change. Contextually, different innovative capabilities yielded powerful asymmetries between firms, and associated oligopolistic positions, upset only by further vintages of innovative products. An interesting empirical result that we obtained in this respect concerned prices and margin determination. We know that the semiconductor industry is characterised by fierce competition. However, our tests on the American industry show that this does not induce demand-related fluctuations in prices with respect to costs. In other words, inter-firm oligopolistic asymmetries allow a relative stability of mark-ups on variable costs. Prices in the industry have shown an impressive fall in monetary terms and, even more so, in real terms. The determinants of this fall are proper technical change and 'learning-by-doing' which produced a striking fall in unit variable costs and a striking growth in labour productivity. The analysis allowed us to give a precise meaning to what is often referred to as 'non-price' competition: the dynamics of innovative leads and lags, market pre-emption and ever-changing inter-firm asymmetries represent the crucial competitive engine of the industry, even if an auction-like determination of prices is absent.

The semiconductor industry highlights also the impact of appropriable technologies on international trade flows and international investment. Inter-firm technological asymmetries reflect themselves in international technological differences. Whenever there is a virtuous (or vicious) circle between company–specific and country–specific technological advantages (or disadvantages), we are then able to explain the relative specialisations of the various countries in term of processes of cumulative causation; seen through time, comparative advantage is, as it were, a 'joint production' associated with the process of manufacturing itself.

The emergence of radically new technologies represents a major factor allowing the disruption of entrenched oligopolistic positions and the emergence of new companies and new countries as major producers. We can observe this process in the case of semiconductors and, more generally, electronics, with respect to Japan. A complex set of variables allowed a very rapid successful catching-up effort and established Japan as a major world producer. There is no 'natural' inevitability why this should have occurred: institutional and policy variables played a crucial role in the process, which – on the contrary – did not happen in the case of Europe.

We have not discussed the question of policies at any length, apart from their effect on the direction of technical progress and on the technological capabilities of the major Western producers. We deal with the question in another work (cf. Dosi, 1981a). Let us mention, however, one important implication of our analysis. Varying degrees of appropriability and cumulativeness of technical progress, at both company and country levels, correlated with inter-firm and inter-country technological asymmetries, determine highly variable degrees of dynamic efficiency of the market mechanism. Whenever a technological paradigm is established, it is likely that endogenous market mechanisms operate satisfactorily in fostering further innovations within the first-coming country(ies). This might not be so in the case of other countries which are not on the technological frontier. If technological advances are somewhat cumulative and if there is some dynamic relationship between company–specific and country–specific technological advances, market allocative mechanisms alone might be 'perverse' in the sense that they might not induce any technological convergence between countries.

It was not possible to analyse the impact of the semiconductor upon the sectors which directly or indirectly use them. Our few notes on the transmission mechanisms of technical progress throughout the economy can be considered as scattered introductory remarks to the wider question of the 'microelectronics revolution'. In this respect, the present analysis of the semiconductor industry only refers to the generating core of the process which affects (and, even more so, is going to affect) the entire economy.

Throughout the history of the capitalist economy, major macroeconomic and social changes have often been linked also with technological revolutions, such as steam power, electricity, and the internal combustion engine. Microelectronics is likely to have a similar impact on economic trends and social structures. We hope that this book has helped to analyse the process by which technical progress emerges and is incorporated within economic structures, and the dynamic linkages which transform microeconomic impulses and behavioural constraints into broad trends and patterns of transformation.

NOTES AND REFERENCES

1. This point is made by Freeman (1974) and Rosenberg (1976).
2. Mansfield's estimates are based on a logistic similar to those used in representing epidemic diffusion. A through and critical survey of diffusion curves is in Davies (1979), who provides also different estimates of, and a theoretical backing for, cumulative log-normal curves, based on a PROBIT model of stochastic diffusion. For a critical discussion of the limitations in current approaches to the diffusion of innovations, see Gold (1981). For an analysis of several case studies on international level, cf. Nabseth and Ray (1974).
3. Cf. Metcalfe (1981) and, for an expanded model, Metcalfe (1982).

4. We have some reservations on the way that model describes the diffusion on the supply side, which is assumed to be restricted by productive capacity and an upward-shaped cost curve for the innovative producers. We cannot go through a detailed critique of the model. Let us just remember that we find no reason to believe the generalised existence of 'Marshallian' upward-sloping supply curves, neither in the short term nor in the long term. This stems from our argument in Chapter 3 on the trends in costs and prices under conditions of technical change. We believe, however, that the basic properties of the model hold even under conditions of non-increasing unit costs of capacity expansion.

5. This is thoroughly analysed by Rosenberg (1974) and by Von Hippel (1979).

6. Strictly speaking, this second factor does not apply to consumer goods. In this latter case, however, improving market-penetration techniques, learning market preferences, improving product performances, inventing new 'needs', and, more importantly, adapting to a changing social context play a role similar to the 'problem-solving' stemming from user–producer interdependences.

7. See, in the French literature, Perroux (1973); Lafay, Brender et Chevallier (1977); Toledano (1978). A thorough analysis of the *filère électronique* is in Truel (1980) and Lorenzi, Gaveau et Truel (1980). See also Pastrè et Tolendano (1975). We refer to the last three studies for the empirical evidence surrounding many of the hypotheses we suggest in the text. In English, see the important analysis by Rosenberg (1979).

8. See, among others, Tilton (1971); Golding (1971); Finan (1978).

9. Note that this property of technical progress at both industry and company levels is consistent with Nelson and Winter's representation of it whereby one defines (i) a 'potential' rate of technical progress at industry level (related to technological opportunity), (ii) an *actual* rate determined by the past and present innovative efforts of *all* companies within the industry, and (iii) a rate of technical progress at company level which holds a stochastic relationship with the R & D efforts of each company and is related to the position that each company already occupies *vis-à-vis* the 'potential' frontier.

10. The author is presently involved in research on this subject at the Science Policy Research University of the University of Sussex. For some preliminary findings, see Pisano and Soete (1982).

11. Some evidence on the acceleration of the process of international diffusion within multinational firms throughout the post-war period is in Vernon (1975). See also Mansfield and Romeo (1980).

12. We have already hinted (cf. Chapter 4) at the question of the technological impact of MNCs on the technological levels of host countries. For a thorough survey see Parker (1974) and the bibliography quoted there. Although there is sufficient evidence on their favourable effect on technological diffusion, they are not likely to induce a reversal in some kind of technological ranking among countries. An indirect indicator of their dynamic impact on 'country–specific' technological levels is the amount of R & D they perform abroad. This varies across sectors and across companies, but the overall picture indirectly suggests that their amount of R

& D in host countries is less than that which would have been undertaken by an hypothetical domestic-owned MNC with identical size and characteristics. For an econometric analysis of the propensity to invest in R & D activities abroad by American MNC's, see Lall (1979).

13. The reader is referred to the classic works by Leontieff (1951); Barna (1952); A. Carter (1970).

14. For some evidence, making use of inter-temporal comparisons of American input/output tables, cf. the thorough analysis by Carter (1970).

15. There is a common misunderstanding which we must warn against. It is sometimes claimed that variable coefficients, production possibility sets, etc., are the general case, which includes as a special case the fixed-coefficient one. This is epistemologically wrong and theoretically untenable. On epistemological grounds, it runs precisely against the Popperian criterion of 'power' of scientific models: the greater the possible states of the world a theory *excludes*, the higher its 'power'. Conversely, a theory which allows many such states is not more 'powerful' or 'general', but simply approaches tautology. It would be like saying that the Copernican theory is a particular case of an astronomical theory which states that 'the sun turns around the earth or vice versa'. On theoretical grounds, it is untenable because reversibility and variable coefficients, on the one hand, and irreversibility and fixed coefficients, on the other, yield radically different properties of the object of inquiry.

16. We undertook our analysis in terms of margins, but our assumptions on constant capital/output ratios, made margins and profit rates univocally linked.

17. Say, in a Ricardo–Sraffa framework.

18. Cf. Harrod (1948); Kalecki (1971); J. Robinson (1956); Kaldor (1960); Pasinetti (1974).

19. 'Innovation as the engine of growth' is the title of an important contribution by Freeman (cf. Freeman (1981)).

20. We discuss this at some greater length in Dosi (1982b).

21. However, this is not a problem unique to social sciences. For a fascinating discussion of somewhat similar questions in relation to thermodynamics and biology, cf. Prigogine (1979).

Appendix I: A Methodological Note on the Estimates of Semiconductor Prices

No published series of prices and value added deflators for the semiconductor industry are presently available. They have been constructed by the author for the period 1958–76 (with a four-year gap between 1959 and 1962) relative to the US semiconductor industry. The estimates are based on data from the US Department of Commerce, *Shipments of Selected Electronic Components Annual Survey of Manufactures* and *Census of Manufactures*, various years. What follows is a brief description of the procedures.

1. *Unit price indices for product groups.* They are obtained by dividing values of shipment by quantities, in terms of number, for groups of products. In the most recent period, we could obtain the index for eleven groups (signal transistors, power transistors, signal diodes, power diodes, Zener Diodes, Tyristors, Analog ICs, TTL ICs, DTL ICs, ECL ICs, MOS ICs).
2. *Aggregate price index.* It is constructed by weighting each unit price index through the three-year moving average of the share, in value terms, of each product group in the total semiconductor value of shipments. Since the level of disaggregation between product groups changes over time, we constructed aggregate price indices for each period characterised by different levels of disaggregation, 'linking' them by means of at least one year that they have in common with the neighbouring period.
3. *Value added deflator.* The nearest we could get to a 'double deflation' procedure was based on the assumption that the *physical* inputs of materials per unit of output did not change over time.

   Let us call X the physical quantities of output, P_x the unit price of output, VA the 'physical' Value Added (as mysterious as it sounds), P_{va} the value added deflator, S the physical inputs of materials, energy, etc., P_s the price index of materials, etc. By definition we have:

$$P_x X = P_{va} VA + P_s S \qquad\qquad 1$$

We can define also

$$P_s S / P_x X = K \qquad\qquad 2$$

Substituting expression 2 into 1 and rearranging, we obtain

$$P_{va} = \frac{1}{(VA/X)} \cdot (1 - K) P_x$$

If the physical inputs of materials, etc., per unit of output are constant (which mirrors the hypothesis of constant 'physical' value added per unit of output (VA/X), but it is a bit more intelligible[1]), then the deflator of value added moves in the same way as the output price index multiplied by one minus the ratio of the *value* of material inputs to the *value* of shipments $(1 - K)$. We have the latter and thus we can obtain a proxy for the value added deflator.

4. *Materials and energy unit inputs index.* Again under the same assumption as above, the index can be obtained by dividing the index of total material and energy expenditures at *current* prices by the index of output at *constant* prices.

5. In order to fit the estimated equations of the form $P = f(w/\pi + a)$, where w is the hourly wage rate of a direct worker per man-hour, π is labour productivity and a represents materials and energy inputs, we obtained π as deflated value added per direct man-hour. For the practical estimation of the function, we constructed an index of variable input costs as a weighted average of w/π and a, using the respective shares in variable costs in the base year, 1972.

A few explanatory notes:

a) Owing to the way the price index has been constructed, it accounts for *actual* prices and not list prices. This is an important advantage.

b) One of the limitations of the output index is that it is approximated by shipments, thus neglecting changes in the inventories. This biases somewhat the estimates of both the value added deflator and the material cost index. However, this is not likely to have any major effect on our regression estimates.

c) We are aware of the fact that there is quite a big difference in the trend between our price index and the unpublished index utilised by the US Department of Labour and corresponding to semiconductors and other electronic components (SIC 3674, 75, 76, 77, 78, 79). As a result, output growth at constant prices, in our estimates, is more than three times as high as in the BLS (Bureau of Labor Statistics) index. In our view, the difference is due to two main reasons:

1. First and foremost, the BLS index includes product categories whose productivity growth cannot be expected to be very far from the US manufacturing average (which has been well below the semiconductor rates). These products account, on average, in that index for more than half of the total weights.

2. The established procedure of BLS of using *fixed* weights for averaging 7-digit product groups (those which roughly correspond to our 'unit price indices for product groups') into 5-digit industries may underestimate, in the semiconductors case, the price fall which is highest in new products (for the reasons discussed in the text)[2].

NOTES AND REFERENCES

1. Note, however, that this is very near the convention that value added at constant prices approximates some kind of unchanging physical product.
2. BLS utilises moving weights (shares in value terms) in order to obtain the aggregation from 5- to 4-digit industries.

I am very grateful to Dr Jerome A. Mark from the US Bureau of Labor Statistics, for his kind help with data and valuable clarifications.

Appendix II: Patterns of Technical Change, Relative Costs and International Specialisation: Some Properties of Absolute and Comparative Advantages

In the text we define an equation of the form

$$X_i = f(T_i, C_i, O_i) \qquad \text{1B}$$

Let us neglect for the time being the industrial organisation variable (O_i) and focus on technology (T_i) and unit variable costs (C_i) as determinants of international trade performance (X_i) in sector i. We suggest that this relationship captures the *proximate* determinants of international competitiveness and specialisation even if it neglects income distribution between wages and profits. We must justify the hypothesis by means of some theoretical considerations on the patterns of technical change and a few 'stylised facts'.

The international technological asymmetries determine the patterns of *absolute advantages*. In this respect the innovative tests undertaken by Pavitt and Soete (1980), Soete (1980) and (1982), of equations of the form

$$X_i = f(T_i) \qquad \text{2B}$$

show the crucial importance of these absolute advantages in a good number of sectors. In the text we suggest that international technological asymmetries (i.e. absolute advantages) define the *boundaries of the universe* within which cost-based (and, *in primis*, wage-based) adjustments take place. In this simplified form, the model rigorously holds when labour is the only variable input and – more important – there is no capital input. If capital inputs exist, then one must take into account income distribution and the effects of different profit rates on the choice of techniques and patterns of specialisation. However, we are going to argue, the model remains a good approximation to the real world, even under these circumstances.

Let us recall some properties of a model characterised by reproducible capital goods and non-decreasing returns in production:[1]

1. The choice of techniques is *not* influenced by variations in the wage rate as long as the rate of profit does not change.
2. International differences in wage rates do *not* influence the choice of techniques, if (a) each country has access to the same techniques for the 'vertically integrated sector' directly and indirectly activated by the production of a certain commodity,[2] and, (b) every country is characterised by an identical rate of profit.

In conjunction with these theoretical properties, we may consider the following 'stylised facts':

3. International differences in profit rates are relatively limited, so that an hypothesis of an internationally identical rate of profit is not any big violence to reality.
4. One of the fundamental characteristics of the technological trajectories of progress (as analysed in Chapter 2) is the trend towards mechanisation/automation of production and the substitution of 'machines' for labour.
5. The same process occurs in the manufacturing of the 'machines' themselves. Moreover, product innovations in the 'machine' sector continuously tend to increase their productive capacity in physical terms.

The joint consideration of these five points provides a ground for the following hypotheses:

a) The nature of technical progress and the patterns of income distribution are such that, in general, *capital/output ratios are roughly constant both over time and across country.*[3]
b) Technological trajectories are such that there are likely to be *inferior* and *superior* techniques, for *every income distribution.*

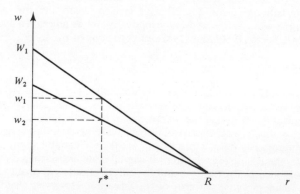

FIGURE A.1   *Wage–profit frontiers defined by each technique*

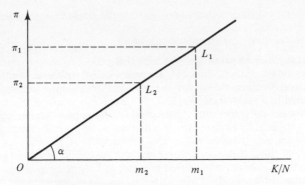

W = wage rates
r = profit rates
π = labour productivity
K = capital
N = employment
Y = output

FIGURE A.2 *Labour productivity and mechanisation/automation of production*

These hypotheses are illustrated in Figures A.1 and A.2. Harrod's neutrality of technical progress implies that an increasing mechanisation of production (as expressed by increasing capital/labour ratios, in Figure A.2) correspond to proportional increases in labour productivity, so that the capital/output ratio remains unchanged.[4] Moreover, 'new' techniques are unequivocally superior to 'old' ones.[5] Suppose technical progress produced a new (more mechanised) technique $(m_1 > m_2)$ yielding a higher labour productivity $(\pi_1 > \pi_2)$. New techniques will also define wage–profit frontiers (e.g. $W_2 R_1$ in Figure A.1) which are superior to old ones (e.g. $W_2 R$), irrespective of income distribution: in our illustration, for any given profit rate (r^*), the new technique determines a higher wage rate $(w_1 > w_2)$, and vice versa.

Conversely, suppose the two techniques belong to two different countries, at any given time: for an identical profit rate, the less developed country has an 'inferior' technique, characterised by lower mechanisation, lower labour productivity, lower wage rates and an identical capital/output ratio. The 'stylised facts' recalled above make us believe that this is actually the *general case* in modern economic growth. The process of development and catching-up acquires – in this framework – an unequivocal meaning: it is the process of diffusion of strictly superior techniques.[6]

As regards the implications for international specialisation, note that the 'backward' country may well find a 'comparative advantage' in the commodity to which the two techniques refer, whenever wage rate differentials more than compensate the absolute technological advantage of the 'advanced' country: in our case if the actual wage rate is below w_2 (Figure A.1).

It is essentially a 'comparative advantage' because, as we argued at greater length in Dosi (1982b), wage rates, expressed in international currency, bear a rather close relationship with the *average* technological gap/lead of the tradable sector as a whole.

The model has three important consequences:

1. The nature of technical progress is such that processes of factor substitution, at a *given* state of the techniques, are analytically *irrelevant*. In other words, production functions do not help us in understanding international specialisation even in a static framework.
2. International differences in labour productivity express technology gaps in relation to techniques that can generally be unequivocally ranked.
3. The relationship between wages and productivity is generally an adequate measure of those factors of competitiveness related to costs and prices and, thus, to the 'Ricardian' adjustment processes taking place in relation to given international technological asymmetries.

If our argument is correct, in relation to (a) the proximate international equality in profit rates, (b) Harrod neutrality of technical progress, and (c) unequivocal inferiority/superiority of techniques, then the model presented in the text rigorously applies also to economies characterised by capital inputs and positive profit rates. The discussion on the nature of technical progress suggests this to be generally the case.

Needless to say, no factor–price equalisation may take place for a given state of the techniques available in each country. Wage rates may only converge, in a dynamic context, if the rate of diffusion of the 'best' techniques is higher than the rate of innovation in the 'advanced' country.[7]

A final remark is required in relation to the nature of the 'Ricardian' adjustment process. If (a) the productivity coefficients appearing at the denominator of the labour unit cost variable were identical across all the firms of a country's industry, and (b) the adjustment processes were instantaneous, for given technological asymmetries, then the cost-based adjustment could lead to absolute specialisations.[8] However, it should be clear from the discussion of Chapter 3 that technological asymmetries (in terms of product technology and labour productivities) characterise also the universe of firms within each national industry, so that the T and C coefficients for each country are *averages of a distribution*. Thus, they explain average levels of competitiveness. There may always be at least a 'tail' of the distribution of domestic firms which shows a relatively high level of competitiveness. Moreover, processes adjustment are by no means instantaneous: in real time, cost-based adjustment processes for a given state of the technology (i.e. 'static' adjustments) are intertwined with dynamic processes of technical innovation and imitation, so that the static 'equilibrium points' may well never be reached.

NOTES AND REFERENCES

1. The points which follow are thoroughly discussed by Pasinetti (1981).
2. cf. Ibid. pp. 195–7. Note that by 'identical techniques' one means also the import content associated with each of them and the related terms of trade.
3. A possible exception, if any, is that less developed countries might show, for

identical techniques, a *higher* capital/output ratio due to a lower impact of wages on the total value of output. On the issue, cf., again, Pasinetti (1981).

4. The capital/output ratio (K/Y) in Figure A.2 is expressed by the angle formed by the L 0 line and the x-axis.

5. For a discussion of all notional possibilities in the choice and change in techniques, see Schefold (1976) and (1979).

6. The argument is perfectly consistent with the seminal model by Nelson (1968).

7. We discuss the issue at greater length in Dosi (1982b).

8. As in the original Ricardian model or in Steedman (1980). Under the two just mentioned conditions, absolute specialisation would be likely to take place irrespective of whether the pre-trade and post-trade profit rates have a unique value throughout the economy (as under 'competitive conditions') or are a vector of rates (as under oligopolistic conditions). The rigorous conditions for the choice of techniques under competition and monopoly in a general 'Sraffian' framework are discussed by Parrinello (1982).

Bibliography

GENERAL BIBLIOGRAPHY

W. J. Abernathy and J. M. Utterback (1975) 'A Dynamic Model of Product and Process Innovation', *Omega*.

W. J. Abernathy and J. M. Utterback (1976) 'Innovation and the Evolution of the Firm', mimeo (Cambridge, Mass.: Harvard University).

W. J. Abernathy and J. M. Utterback (1978) 'Patterns of Industrial Innovation', *Technology Review*.

A. Alchian (1963) 'Reliability of Progress Curves in Airframe Production', *Econometrica*.

G. C. Allen (1981) *The Japanese Economy* (London: Weidenfeld & Nicolson).

D. Allison (1969) *The R & D Game* (Cambridge, Mass.: MIT Press).

P. W. S. Andrews (1949) *Manufacturing Business* (London: Macmillan).

P. W. Andrews and T. Wilson (eds) (1951) *Oxford Studies in the Price Mechanism* (Oxford: Clarendon Press).

A. Aquino (1980) 'Intra-Industry Trade and Inter-Industry Specialization as Concurrent Sources of International Trade in Manufacturers', *Weltwirtschaftliches Archiv*.

H. O. Armour and D. J. Teece (1980) 'Vertical Integration and Technological Innovation', *Review of Economics and Statistics*.

K. Arrow (1962) 'Economic Welfare and Allocation of Resources for Invention', in National Bureau of Economic Research (1962).

K. Arrow (1962a) 'The Economic Implications of Learning by Doing', *Review of Economic Studies*.

K. Arrow (1963) *Social Choice and Individual Preferences* (New Haven: Yale University Press, 2nd edn).

A. A. Auquier (1980) 'Sizes of Firms, Exporting Behaviour and the Structure of French Industry', *The Journal of Industrial Economics*.

J. S. Bain (1951) 'Relation of Profit Rate of Industry Concentration: American Manufacturing, 1936–40', *Quarterly Journal of Economics*.

J. S. Bain (1956) *Barriers to New Competition* (Cambridge, Mass.: Harvard University Press).

M. J. Baker (ed.) (1979) *Industrial Innovation – Technology, Policy Diffusion* (London: MacMillan).

G. Balcet (1981) 'Nouvelles Formes d'Investissement International et Théories de la Firme Multinationale: Notes de Discussion', mimeo (Paris: OECD).

M. Balconi (1977) *La Strategia di Espansione dei Mercati: Il Caso dell' Alluminio* (Bologna: Il Mulino).

P. A. Baran and P. T. Sweezy (1966) *Monopoly Capital* (New York: Monthly Review Press; 1968, Harmondsworth: Penguin).

J. Baranson (1978) *Technology and the Multinational: corporate strategies in a Changing World Economy* (Lexington, Mass.: D.C. Heath).

T. Barna (1952) 'The Interdependence of the British Industry', *Journal of the Royal Statistical Society – Series A*.

T. Barna (1962) *Investment and Growth Policies in British Industrial Firms* (Cambridge: Cambridge University Press).

W. J. Baumol (1982) 'Contestable Markets: An Uprising in the Theory of Industry Structure', *American Economic Review*.

W. J. Baumol and R. E. Quandt (1964) 'Rules of Thumb and Optimally Imperfect Decisions', *American Economic Review*.

J. M. Blair (1972) *Economic Concentration: Structure, Behaviour, Performance* (New York: Harcourt).

L. Boggio (1971) 'Progresso Tecnico e commercio internazionale: una analisi teorica ed empirica', *Rivista Internazionale de Scienze sociali*.

A. Bonfiglioli (1979) 'Universal Science, Appropriate Technology and Underdevelopment: A Reprise of the Latin-American Case', mimeo (Brighton: University of Sussex, SPRU).

Boston Consulting Group (1973) *Perspectives on Experience* (Boston: Boston Consulting Group).

R. Boyer and P. Petit (1980) *Productivité dans l'industrie et croissance à moyen term* (Paris: CEPREMAP).

R. Boyer and P. Petit (1980a) 'Emploi et productivité dans la CEE', *Economie et Statistique*.

J. A. Brander (1981) 'Intra-Industry Trade in Identical Commodities', *Journal of International Economics*.

Y. Brozen (1971) 'Bain's Concentration and Rates of Return Revisited', *Journal of Law and Economics*.

P. J. Buckley and M. Casson (1976) *The Future of the Multinational Enterprise* (London: Macmillan).

P. J. Buckley and M. Casson (1981) 'The Optimal Timing of a Foreign Direct Investment', *Economic Journal*.

R. D. Buzzell, B. T. Gale and R. G. M. Sultan (1975) 'Market Share – A Key to Profitability', *Harvard Business Review*.

A. Carter (1970) *Structural Change in the American Economy* (Cambridge, Mass.: Harvard University Press).

R. E. Caves (1971) 'International Corporations: The Industrial Economics of Foreign Investment', *Economica*.

R. E. Caves and M. E. Porter (1977) 'From entry barrier to mobility barriers: Conjectural decisions and contrived deterrence to new competition', *Quarterly journal of Economics*.

R. E. Caves and M. E. Porter (1978) 'Market Structure, Oligopoly and Stability of Market Shares', *Journal of Industrial Economics*.

R. E. Caves (1980) 'International Trade and Industrial Organisation. Introduction', *The Journal of Industrial Economics*.

R. E. Caves, M. E. Porter and A. M. Spence (1980) *Competition in the Open Economy: A Model Applied to Canada* (Cambridge, Mass.: Harvard University Press).

R. E. Caves (1981) 'Intra-industry Trade and Market Structure in the Industrial Countries', *Oxford Economic Papers*.

CEPII (1980) 'La spécialisation industrielle en Europe', *Futuribles*.

A. D. Chandler (1966) *Strategy and Structure* (New York: Anchor Books).

F. Chesnais and C. Michon-Savarit (1980) 'Some Observations on Alternative Approaches to the Analysis of International Competitiveness and the Role of the Technology Factor', *OECD Science and Technology Indicators Conference* (Paris: OECD).

F. Chesnais (1981) 'Schumpeterian Recovery and the Schumpeterian Perspective – Some Unsettled Issues and Alternative Interpretations', paper given at the Kiel conference on Emerging Technologies, mimeo (Kiel, June) published in Giersch (1982).

J. A. Clifton (1977) 'Competition and the evolution of the capitalist mode of production', *Cambridge Journal of Economics*.

R. H. Coase (1937) 'The Nature of the Firm', *Economica*.

W. S. Comanor (1967) 'Market Structure, Product Differentiation and Industrial Research', *Quarterly Journal of Economics*.

J. Cornwall (1977) *Modern Capitalism: Its Growth and Transformation* (London: Martin Robertson).

A. Cotta (1978) *La France et l'imperative mondial* (Paris) quoted in Chesnais and Michon-Savarit (1980).

K. Coutts, W. Godley and W. Nordhaus (1978) *Industrial Pricing in the United Kingdom* (Cambridge: Cambridge University Press).

R. M. Cyert and J. G. March (1963) *A Behavioural Theory of the Firm*, (Englewood Cliffs, New Jersey: Prentice Hall).

P. Dasgupta and J. Stiglitz (1980) 'Industrial Structure and the Nature of Innovative Activity', *Economic Journal*.

P. A. David (1975) *Technical Choice, Innovation and Economic Growth* (Cambridge: Cambridge University Press).

W. Davidson (1979) 'Factor Endowment, Innovation and International Trade Theory', *Kyklos*.

S. Davies (1980) *The Diffusion of Process Innovations* (Cambridge: Cambridge University Press).

H. Demsetz (1969) 'Information and Efficiency: Another Viewpoint', *Journal of Law and Economics*.

H. Demsetz (1973) 'Industry Structure, Market Rivalry and Public Policy', *Journal of Law and Economics*.

E. F. Denison (1967) *Why Growth Rates Differ?* (Washington: Brookings Institution).

R. Dore (1973) *British Factory – Japanese Factory* (London: Allen & Unwin).

G. Dosi (1981) 'Trade, International Adjustment, Technical Innovations', mimeo (Brighton: University of Sussex, SERC).

G. Dosi (1981c) *Technology, Industrial Organisation and International Economic Performance* (Paris: OECD).

G. Dosi (1982) 'Technological Paradigms and Technological Trajectories. A suggested interpretation of the determinants and directions of technical change', *Research Policy*.

G. Dosi (1982a) 'La circolarità tra progresso tecnico e crescita: alcune osservazioni sulla "Legge di Verdoorn–Kaldor"', *L'Industria*.

G. Dosi (1982b) 'On Engines, Thermostats, Bicycles and Tandems, or moving some steps towards economic dynamics', mimeo (Brighton: University of Sussex, SPRU).

J. Downie (1958) *The Competitive Process* (London: Duckworth).

J. H. Dunning (1973) 'The determinants of international production', *Oxford Economic Papers*.

J. H. Dunning (1977) 'Trade, Location of Economic Activity and Multinational Enterprises: A search for an eclectic approach', in B. Ohlin *et al.* (eds) *The International Allocation of Economic Activity* (London: Macmillan).

J. H. Dunning (1979) 'Explaining changing patterns of international production: in defence of the eclectic theory', *Oxford Bulletin of Economics and Statistics*.

J. H. Dunning (1981) 'Explaining the International Direct Investment Position by Countries: Toward a Dynamic or Developmental Approach', *Weltwirtschaftliches Archiv*.

O. Eckstein (1964) 'A Theory of Wage–Price Process in Modern Industry', *Review of Economic Studies*.

O. Eckstein and D. Wyss (1972) 'Industry Price Equations', in O. Eckstein (ed.) *The Econometrics of Price Determination* (Washington DC) quoted in Coutts, Godley, Nordhouse (1978).

H. R. Edwards (1955) *Manufacturing Business* (London: Macmillan).

M. Egidi (1981) 'Forme della Razionalità e macrofondamenti della microeconomia nell' 'analisi schumpeteriana', mimeo (Turin: Facoltà di Scienze Politiche).

A. Eichner (1975) 'A Theory of the Determination of the Mark-up under Oligopoly', *Economic Journal*.

A. Eichner (1976) *The Megacorp and Oligopoly* (Cambridge: Cambridge University Press).

E. Engel (1857) 'Die Productions – und Consumptionsverhältnisse des Konigreichs Sachsen', *Zeitschrift der Statistischen Bureaus Des Koniglich Sachsischen Ministerium des Inneren*.

P. K. Feyerabend (1975) *Against Method* (London: New Left Books).

C. Freeman (1963) 'The Plastic Industry: A Comparative Study of Research and Innovation', *National Institute Economic Review*.

C. Freeman (1974) *The Economics of Industrial Innovation* (Harmondsworth: Penguin; 2nd edn, London: Frances Pinter, 1982).

C. Freeman (1977) 'The Economics of Research and Development', in I. Spiegel-Rosing and D. De Solla Price (eds), *Science, Technology and Society* (London: Sage Publications).

C. Freeman (1977) *Unemployment and the Direction of Technical Change* (Paris: OECD).

C. Freeman (1979) 'The determinants of innovation', *Futures*.

C. Freeman (1981) 'Innovation as the Engine of Growth', paper prepared for the Kiel conference on 'Emerging Technologies', mimeo, June 1981 (Brighton: University of Sussex, SPRU), published in Giersch (1982).

C. Freeman, J. Clark and L. Soete (1982) *Unemployment and Technical Innovation* (London: Francis Pinter).

C. Futia (1980) 'Schumpeterian Competition', *Quarterly Journal of Economics*.

B. T. Gale, (1972) 'Market Share and Rate of Return', *Review of Economics and Statistics*.

C. Ganz (1981) 'Linkages between Knowledge Creation, Diffusion, and Utilization', in R. Rich (ed.), *The Knowledge Cycle* (Beverly Hills: Sage Publications).

D. W. Gaskins Jr (1971) 'Dynamic Limit Pricing: Optimal Pricing Under Threat of Entry', *Journal of Economic Theory*.

H. Giersch (ed.) (1982) *Emerging Technology: Consequences for Economic Growth, Structural Change and Employment in Advanced Open Economies* (Tubingen: Mohr).

B. Gille (1978) *Histoire des Techniques* (Paris: La Pleiade).

R. Gilpin *Technology, Economic Growth and International Competitiveness* (Washington DC: US Government Printing Office).

H. Glejer, A. Jacquemin and J. Petit (1980) 'Exports in an Imperfect Competition Framework: An Analysis of 1446 Small-Country Exporters', *Quarterly Journal of Economics*.

W. Godley and W. Nordhaus (1972) 'Pricing in the Trade Cycle', *Economic Journal*.

B. Gold (1964) 'Industry Growth Patterns: Theory and Empirical. Results', *Journal of Industrial Economics*.

B. Gold (1981) 'Technological Diffusion in Industry: Research Needs and Shortcomings', *Journal of Industrial Economics*.

G. Gold, D. Huettner, R. Mitchell and R. Skeddle (1968) 'Long Term Growth Patterns of Industries, Firms and Products', *Proceedings of the American Statistical Association*.

J. M. Goode (1978) *Japan's Post-War Experience with Technology Transfer* Technological Innovation Studies Program (Ottawa: Dept. of Industry, Trade and Commerce).

R. J. Gordon (1975) 'The Impact of Aggregate Demand on Prices', *Brookings Papers on Economic Activity*.

T. J. Gordon and T. R. Munson (1981) *Research into Technology Output Measures* (Glastonbury, Conn.: The Future Group).

H. P. Gray (1973) 'Two-Way International Trade in Manufactures: A Theoretical Underpinning', *Weltwirtschaftliches Archiv*.

Z. Griliches (1980) 'R & D and Productivity Slowdown', *American Economic Review Papers and Proceedings*.

W. Gruber, D. Mehta and R. Vernon (1967) 'The R & D Factors in International Trade and the International Investment of US Industry', *Journal of Political Economy*.

M. Hall and L. Weiss (1967) 'Firm Size and Profitability', *Review of Economics and Statistics*.

R. H. Hall and C. J. Hitch (1939) 'Price Theory and Business Behaviour', *Oxford Economic Papers* repr. in Andrews and Wilson (1951).

D. Hamberg (1967) 'Size of Enterprise and Technical Change', *Antitrust Law and Economics*.

P. Hanel (1980) 'Mesures d'évolution de la compétitivité technologique', *OECD Science and Technology Indicators Conference* (Paris: OECD).

P. Hanel (1980a) 'Les déterminants du commerce international', *OECD Science and Technology Indicators Conference* (Paris: OECD).

G. C. Harcourt (1972) *Some Cambridge Controversies in the Theory of Capital* (Cambridge: Cambridge University Press).

G. C. Harcourt and P. Kenyon (1976) 'Pricing and the Investment Decision', *Kyklos.*

R. Harrod (1948) *Toward a Dynamic Economics* (London: Macmillan).

T. Hatzichronoglou (1980) 'Les échanges internationaux des produits de haute intensité de recherche-developpement', *OECD Science and Technology Indicators Conference* (Paris: OECD).

B. Hedley (1977) 'Strategy and the "Business Portfolio"', *Long Range Planning.*

G. K. Helleiner (1981) *Intra-Firm Trade and the Developing Countries* (London: MacMillan).

C. T. Hill and J. R. Utterback (eds) (1979) *Technological Innovation for a Dynamic Economy* (New York: Pergamon Press).

H. H. Hines (1957) 'Effectiveness of "Entry" by Already Established Firms', *Quarterly Journal of Economies.*

E. von Hippel (1976) 'The Dominant Role of Users in the Scientific Instruments Innovation Process', *Research Policy.*

E. von Hippel (1979) 'A Customer-active Paradigm for Industrial Product Idea Generation', in Baker (1979).

S. Hirsch and Z. Adar (1974) 'Firm Size and Export Performance', *World Development.*

S. Hirsch (1976) 'An International Trade and Investment Theory of the Firm', *Oxford Economic Papers.*

I. Horowitz (1962) 'Firm Size and Research Activity', *Southern Economic Journal.*

T. Horst (1972) 'Firms and Industry Determinants of the Decision to Invest Abroad: An Empirical Study', *Review of Economics and Statistics.*

S. C. Hu (1973) 'On the Incentive to Invent: A clarificatory Note', *Journal of Law and Economics.*

G. C. Hufbauer (1966) *Synthetic Materials and the Theory of International Trade* (London: Duckworth).

A. P. Hurter and A. H. Rubenstein (1978) 'Market Penetration by New Innovations: The Technological Literature', *Technological Forecasting and Social Change.*

S. H. Hymer (1976) *The International Operations of Multinational Firms: A study of direct foreign investment* (Cambridge, Mass.: MIT Press).

Illinois Institute of Technology (1969) *Report on Project TRACES* (Washington: National Science Foundation).

J. Jewkes, D. Sawers and R. Stillerman (1958) *The Sources of Invention* (London: Macmillan).

D. T. Jones (1980) 'Industrial Development and Economic Divergence', in M. Hodges (ed.) *Economic Divergence and the European Community* (London: Allen & Unwin).

M. Kaldor (1978) *The Disintegrating West* (London: Allen Lane).

N. Kaldor (1960) 'Increasing Returns and Technical Progress – A Comment on Professor Hick's Article', *Oxford Economic Papers.*

N. Kaldor (1960a) *Essays on Economic Stability and Growth* (London: Duckworth).

N. Kaldor (1966) *Causes of the Slow Rate of Growth of the United Kingdom*

(Cambridge: Cambridge University Press).

N. Kaldor (1975) 'Economic Growth and the Verdoorn Law – a Comment on Mr. Rowthorn's Article', *Economic Journal*.

M. Kalecki (1971) *Selected Essays on the Dynamics of the Capitalist Economy, 1933–1970* (Cambridge: Cambridge University Press).

M. I. Kamien and N. Schwartz (1975) 'Market Structure and Innovation: A Survey', *Journal of Economic Literature*.

M. I. Kamien and N. Schwartz (1982) *Market Structure and Innovation* (Cambridge: Cambridge University Press).

C. P. Kindelberger (ed.) (1970) *The International Corporation* (Cambridge, Mass.: MIT Press).

F. Kindelberger (1969) *American Business Abroad* (New Haven: Yale University Press).

B. Klein (1977) *Dynamic Competition* (Cambridge, Mass.: Harvard University Press).

F. Knickerbocker (1973) *Oligopolistic Reaction and Multinational Enterprise* (Cambridge, Mass.: Harvard University Press).

I. B. Kravis (1956) 'Availability and Other Influences on the Commodity Composition of Trade', *Journal of Political Economy*.

P. Krugman (1979) 'A model of Innovation, Technology Transfer and World Distribution of Income', *Journal of Political Economy*.

T. Kuhn (1963) *The Structure of Scientific Revolutions* (Chicago: University of Chicago Press).

G. Lafay, A. Brender and A. Chevallier (1977) 'Trois experiences de la specialisation internationale: France, Allemagne Federale, Japon', *Statistique et Etudes Financieres*.

I. Lakatos (1978) *The Methodology of Scientific Research Programmes* (Cambridge: Cambridge University Press).

S. Lall (1979) 'The International Allocation of Research Activities by US Multinationals', *Oxford Bulletin of Economics and Statistics*.

S. Lall (1980) 'Monopolistic Advantages and Foreign Involvement by US Manufacturing Industry', *Oxford Economic Papers*.

K. Lancaster (1971) *Consumer Demand – A New Approach* (New York: Columbia University Press).

R. F. Lanzillotti (1958) 'Pricing Objectives in Large Companies', *American Economic Review*.

S. Latsis (ed.) (1976) *Method and Appraisal in Economics* (Cambridge: Cambridge University Press).

E. E. Leamer (1974) 'The Commodity Composition of International Trade in Manufactures: An Empirical Analysis', *Oxford Economic Papers*.

W. Leontieff (1951) *The Structure of the American Economy, 1919–1939* (New York: Oxford University Press).

R. C. Levin (1981) 'Toward an Empirical Model of Schumpeterian Competition, mimeo (New Haven: Yale University).

E. Lundberg, (1961) *Produktivitet öch Rantabilitet* (Stockholm), quoted in Arrow (1962a).

G. D. A. MacDougall (1951–2) 'British and American Exports: A Study suggested by the Theory of Comparative Advantage', *Economic Journal*, Part I: 1951, Part II: 1952.

R. W. MacEnally (1976) 'Competition and Dispersion in Rates of Return – A Note', *Journal of Industrial Economics.*

W. R. MacLaurin, (1949) *Invention and Innovation in the Radio Industry* (New York: MacMillan).

S. P. Magee (1977) 'Information and the Multinational Corporation: an appropriability theory of direct foreign investment', in J. N. Bhagwati (ed.), *The New International Economic Order. The North–South Debate* (Cambridge, Mass.: MIT Press).

F. Malerba (1981) 'La Teoria Evolutiva dell'Impresa: una rassegna dei contributi di R. Nelson e S. Winter', mimeo (New Haven: Yale University), a modified version is published in *L'Industria* (1982).

M. Mann (1966) 'Seller Concentration, Barriers to Entry and Rates of Return in Industries, 1950–60', *Review of Economics and Statistics.*

E. Mansfield (1961) 'Technical change and the rate of imitation', *Econometrica.*

E. Mansfield (1968) *Industrial Research and Technological Innovation: An Econometric Analysis* (New York: Norton).

E. Mansfield *et al.* (1971) *Research and Innovation in the Modern Corporation* (New York: Norton).

E. Mansfield *et al.* (1977) *The Production and Application of New Industrial Technology* (New York: Norton).

E. Mansfield, D. Teece and A. Romeo (1979) 'Overseas Research and Development by US-based Firms', *Economica.*

E. Mansfield, A. Romeo and S. Wagner (1979) 'Foreign Trade and US Research and Development', *Review of Economics and Statistics.*

R. Marris (1964) *The Economic Theory of 'Managerial Capitalism'* (London: MacMillan).

R. Marris and D. C. Mueller (1980) 'Corporation, Competition and the Invisible Hand', *Journal of Economic Literature.*

J. F. Martino (1980) 'Technological Forecasting – An Overview', *Management Science.*

J. S. Metcalfe (1981) 'Impulse and diffusion in Technical Change', *Futures.*

J. S. Metcalfe (1982) 'On the Diffusion of Innovation and the Evolution of Technology, mimeo (Manchester: University of Manchester).

S. Meyers and D. G. Marquis (1969) *Successful Industrial Innovation* (Washington: National Science Foundation).

C. A. Michalet (1981) *Competitivité et Internationalisation* (Paris: OECD).

J. Mistral (1981) *La diffusion inter-national inégal de l'accumulation intensive et ses crises* (Paris: CEPREMAP).

F. Modigliani (1958) 'New Developments on the Oligopoly Front', *Journal of Political Economy.*

F. Modigliani and M. H. Miller (1958) 'The Cost of Capital, Corporate Finance and the Theory of Investment', *American Economic Review.*

F. Momigliano (1975) *Economia Industriale e Teoria dell'Impresa* (Bologna: Il Mulino).

F. Momigliano (1981) *Technological Innovation, International Trade and Foreign Direct Investments: Old and New Problems for Economic Theory and Empirical Research* (Paris: OECD).

F. Momigliano and D. Siniscalco (1982) 'The Growth of Service Employment: A Reappraisal', *Banca Nazionale del Lavoro Quarterly Review.*

D. Mowery and N. Rosenberg (1979) 'The Influence of Market Demand upon Innovation: A Critical Review of Some Recent Empirical Studies', *Research Policy.*

R. A. Musgrave and I. Lakatos (eds) (1973) *Criticism and Growth of Knowledge* (Cambridge: Cambridge University Press).

L. Nabseth and G. F. Ray (1974) *The Diffusion of new industrial processes* (Cambridge: Cambridge University Press).

H. Nakayama (1979) 'Japanese Industrial Policy', mimeo (Brighton: University of Sussex, SERC).

National Bureau of Economic Research (NBER) (1962) *The Rate and Direction of Inventive Activity* (Princeton: Princeton University Press).

National Science Foundation (1963) *Patterns and Problems of Technical Innovation in American Industry* (New York: National Science Foundation).

D. Needham (1978) *The Economics of Industrial Structure Conduct and Performance* (Eastbourne: Holt Reinhart and Winston).

R. R. Nelson (1968) 'A "Diffusion" Model of International Productivity Differences in Manufacturing Industry', *American Economic Review.*

R. R. Nelson and S. Winter (1977) 'In search of a Useful Theory of Innovation', *Research Policy.*

R. R. Nelson and S. Winter (1977a) 'Dynamic Competition and Technical Progress', in B. Belassa and R. Nelson (eds) *Economic Progress, Private Values and Public Policies: Essays in Honour of W. Fellner* (Amsterdam: North Holland).

R. R. Nelson and S. Winter (1978) 'Forces Generating and Limiting Concentration under Schumpeterian Competition', *The Bell Journal of Economics.*

R. R. Nelson (1980), 'Production Sets, Technological Knowledge and R & D: Fragile and Overworked Constructs for Analysis of Productivity Growth?', *American Economic Review, Papers and Proceedings.*

R. R. Nelson (1980a) *Balancing Market Failure and Government Inadequacy: The Case of Policies toward Industrial R & D* (New Haven: Yale University, Working Paper No. 840).

R. R. Nelson (1981) 'Assessing Private Enterprise', *Bell Journal of Economics.*

R. R. Nelson (1981a), 'Research in Productivity Growth and Productivity Differences: Dead Ends and New Departures', *Journal of Economic Literature.*

R. R. Nelson and S. Winter (1982) '*The Schumpeterian Trade-Offs revisited*', mimeo (New Haven: Yale University).

(Most of the cited works by Nelson and Winter have been re-published in R. R. Nelson and S. Winter, *An Evolutionary Theory of Economic Change*, Cambridge, Mass.: The Belknap Press of Harvard University Press, 1982).

R. Newfarmer (1979) 'International Oligopoly and Uneven Development in the International Economic Order', *Nordic Symposium on Development Strategies in Latin America and the New International Economic Order* Vol. II, Lund (Sweden).

R. Nield (1963) *Pricing and Employment in the Trade Cycle* (Cambridge: Cambridge University Press).

H. Odagiri (1981) *The Theory of Growth in a Corporate Economy* (Cambridge: Cambridge University Press).

OECD (1979) *Science and Technology in a New Socio-Economic Context – Final Report* (Paris: OECD).

C. Oman (1980) 'Changing International Investment Strategies: the "New Forms" of Investment in Developing Countries', mimeo (Paris: OECD).

E. Pagoulatos and R. Sorensen (1976) 'Domestic Market Structure and International Trade: An Empirical Analysis', *Quarterly Review of Economics and Business*.

R. Parboni (1980) *Finanza e crisi internazionale* (Milan: Etas Libri).

J. E. S. Parker (1974) *The Economics of innovation* (London: Longman).

S. Parrinello (1982) 'Some Notes on Monopoly, Competition and the Choice of Techniques', *Manchester School*.

P. Pashigian (1968) 'Limit Price and the Market Share of the Leading Firm', *Journal of Industrial Economics*.

L. L. Pasinetti (1959) 'On the Concepts and Measures of Changes in Productivity', *Review of Economics and Statistics*.

L. L. Pasinetti (1974) *Growth and Income Distribution* (Cambridge: Cambridge University Press).

L. L. Pasinetti (1981) *Structural Change and Economic Growth* (Cambridge: Cambridge University Press).

H. D. Passer (1953) *The Electrical Manufacturers: 1875–1900* (Cambridge, Mass.: Harvard University Press).

H. Patrick (ed.) (1976) *Japanese Industrialization and its social consequences* (Berkeley; Berkeley University Press).

K. Pavitt and S. Wald (1971) *The Conditions for Success in Technological Innovation* (Paris: OECD).

K. Pavitt and W. Walker (1976) 'Government Policies towards Industrial Innovation: A Review', *Research Policy*.

K. Pavitt (1979) 'Technical Innovation and Industrial Development: The New Causality', *Futures*.

K. Pavitt (1980) 'Technical Innovation and Industrial Development: The Dangers of Divergence', *Futures*.

K. Pavitt (ed.) (1980a) *Technical Innovation and British Economic Performance* (London: Macmillan).

K. Pavitt and Soete, L. (1980) 'Innovative Activities and Export Shares: Some Comparisons between Industries and Countries', in K. Pavitt (1980a).

K. Pavitt and L. Soete (1982) 'International Differences in Economic Growth and the International location of Innovations', in H. Giersch (1982).

M. I. Peck and F. M. Scherer (1962) *The Weapons Acquisition Process* (Cambridge, Mass.: Harvard University Press).

E. Penrose (1959) *The Theory of the Growth of the Firm* (Oxford: Basil Blackwell).

F. Perroux (1973) 'L'effet d'entrainement: de l'analyse au reperage quantitatif', *Economic Appliquée*.

A. Phillips (1971) *Technology and Market Structure* (Lexington, Mass.: D.C. Heath).

G. Pisano and L. Soete (1982) 'Diversification of Innovation, Firm Size and R & D', mimeo (Brighton: University of Sussex, SPRU).

M. E. Porter (1980) *Competitive Strategy* (New York: Free Press).

M. V. Posner (1961) 'International Trade and Technical Change', *Oxford Economic Papers*.

M. Posner (1970) 'Technical Change, International Trade and Foreign Investment', in P. Streeten (ed.) *Unfashionable Economics* (London: Weidenfeld & Nicolson).

I. Prigogine (1979) *La nouvelle alliance* (Paris: Gallimard).

T. A. Pugel (1980) 'Foreign Trade and US Market Performance', *The Journal of Industrial Economics*.

W. P. Rapp (1976), 'Firm Size and Japan's Expert Structure: A micro-view of Japan's changing export competitiveness since Meiji', in H. Patrick (1976).

F. C. Ripley and L. Segal (1973) 'Price Determination in 395 Manufacturing Industries', *Review of Economics and Statistics*.

J. Robinson (1956) *The Accumulation of Capital* (London: Macmillan).

J. Robinson (1974) *Reflections on the theory of International Trade* (Manchester: Manchester University Press).

J. Robinson (1974) *History versus Equilibrium* (London: Thames Polytechnic, Thames Papers in Political Economy).

A. A. Romeo (1977) 'The rate of Imitation of Capital-Embodied Process Innovation', *Economica*.

N. Rosenberg (1969) 'The Direction of Technological Change: Inducement Mechanisms and Focussing Devices', *Economic Development and Cultural Change* (repr. 1976).

N. Rosenberg (1976) *Perspectives on Technology* (Cambridge: Cambridge University Press).

N. Rosenberg (1979) 'Technological Interdependence in the American Economy', *Technology and Culture*.

N. Rosenberg (1981) 'How exogenous is Science?' mimeo (Stanford: Stanford University).

P. H. Rubin (1973) 'The Expansion of Firms', *Journal of Political Economy*.

A. M. Rugman (1980) 'Internalization as a General Theory of Foreign Direct Investment: a re-appraisal of the literature', *Weltwirtschaftliches Archiv*.

D. Sahal (1974) 'On the Conception and Measurement of Trade-offs in Engineering Systems', *Technological Forecasting and Social Change*.

D. Sahal (1978) *Law-like Aspects of Technological Development* (Berlin: International Institute of Management).

D. Sahal (1979) *Recent Advances in the Theory of Technological Change*, (Berlin: International Institute of Management).

D. Sahal (1981) 'Alternative Conceptions of Technology', *Research Policy*.

W. E. G. Salter (1969) *Productivity and Technical Change* (Cambridge: Cambridge University Press, 2nd edn).

M. Salvati (1967) *Una Critica alle Teorie dell'Impresa* (Rome: Edizioni dell'Ateneo).

M. Salvati (1971) *Monopolio Sviluppo e Distribuzione* (Rome: Edizioni dell'Ateneo).

B. Schefold (1976) 'Different Forms of Technical Progress', *Economic Journal*.

B. Schefold (1979) 'Capital, Growth and Definitions of Technical Progress', *Kyklos*.

F. M. Scherer (1965) 'Firm Size, Market Structure, Opportunity and the Output of Patented Inventions', *American Economic Review*.

F. M. Scherer (1970) *Industrial Market Structure and Economic Performance* (Chicago: Rand McNally, 2nd edn 1980).

J. Schmookler (1966) *Invention and Economic Growth* (Cambridge, Mass.: Harvard University Press).

J. Schnee (1978) 'Government Programmes in the Growth of High Technology Industries', *Research Policy*.

A. Schotter and G. Schwödiaver (1980) 'Economics and the Theory of Games: A Survey', *Journal of Economic Literature*.

R. Schrieves (1979) 'Market Structure and Innovation: A New Perspective', *Journal of Industrial Economics*.

J. Schumpeter (1919) *Theorie der Wirtschaftlichen Entwicklung*, English translation: *The Theory of Economic Development*, (New York: OUP, 1961, 2nd edn).

J. Schumpeter (1947) *Capitalism, Socialism and Democracy* (New York: Harpers).

Science Policy Research Unit (SPRU) (1971) *Report on Project SAPPHO*, (Brighton: University of Sussex).

Science Policy Research Unit (SPRU) (1971) *Report on the Role of Small Firms in Innovation in the UK since 1945* (Brighton: University of Sussex).

W. Semmler (1980) 'Competition on Monopoly Power: Theories and Empirical Evidence – A Reconsideration of the Centre of Gravity Concept of the Marxian and Classical Political Economy', New York, New School for Social Research (forthcoming, New York: Colombia University Press).

H. A. Simon (1959) 'Theories of Decision Making in Economics', *American Economic Review*.

H. A. Simon (1978) 'Rationality as a Process and as a Product of Thought', *American Economic Review*.

R. H. Smiley and S. A. Ravid (1983) 'The Importance of Being First: Learning Price and Strategy', *Quarterly Journal of Economics*.

L. Soete (1977) *Size of the Firm and Inventive Activity: The Evidence Reconsidered*, mimeo (Brighton: University of Sussex, SPRU).

L. Soete (1979) 'Firm Size and Inventive Activity: The Evidence Reconsidered', *European Economic Review*.

L. Soete (1980) *The Impact of Technological Innovation on International Trade Patterns: The Evidence Reconsidered* (Paris: OECD).

L. Soete (1982) 'A general test of Technology Gap Trade Theories', *Weltwirtschaftliches Archiv*.

R. M. Solow (1957) 'Technical Change and the Aggregate Production Function', *Review of Economics and Statistics*.

A. M. Spence (1977) 'Entry, Capacity, Investment, and Oligopolistic Pricing', *The Bell Journal of Economics*.

A. M. Spence (1979) 'Investment Strategy and Growth in a New Market', *The Bell Journal of Economics*.

A. M. Spence (1981) 'The Learning Curve and Competition', *Bell Journal of Economics*.

P. Sraffa (1925) 'Sulle Relazioni tra Costo e Quantità Prodotta', *Annali di Economia*.

P. Sraffa (1926) 'The Laws of Return under Competitive Conditions', *Economic Journal*.

P. Sraffa (1960) *Production of Commodities by Means of Commodities* (Cambridge: Cambridge University Press).

I. Steedman (1980) *Trade Amongst Growing Economies* (Cambridge: Cambridge University Press).

J. Steindl (1976) *Maturity and Stagnation of American Capitalism* (New York: Monthly Review Press, 2nd edn).

R. L. Stern (ed.) (1967) *Technology and World Trade* (Washington: US Dept of Commerce).

R. J. Stonebraker (1976) 'Corporate profits and the Risk of Entry', *Review of Economics and Statistics*.

P. Sylos-Labini (1967) *Oligopoly and Technical Progress* (Cambridge, Mass.: Harvard University Press, 2nd edn).

P. Sylos-Labini (1979) 'Industrial Pricing in the United Kingdom', *Cambridge Journal of Economics*.

P. Sylos-Labini (1980) 'Prices and Income Distribution in Manufacturing Industry', *Journal of Post-Keynesian Economics*.

G. Terborgh (1958) *Business Investment Policy* (Washington: Machinery and Allied Products Institute).

N. Terleckyj (1974) *The Effects of R & D on Productivity Growth in Industry* (Washington: National Planning Association).

N. Terleckyj (1980) 'What do R & D numbers Tell us about Technological Change?', *American Economic Review, Papers and Proceedings*.

M. Teubal (1977) *On Users Needs and Need Determination: Aspects of the Theory of Technological Innovation*, Maurice Falk Institute for Economic Research in Israel, Discussion Paper no. 774.

J. Toledano (1978) 'A propos des filières industrielles', *Revue d'Economie Industrielle*.

J. Townsend *et al.* (1981) *Innovation in Britain since 1945* (Brighton: University of Sussex, SPRU).

P. J. Verdoorn (1949) 'I fattori che regolano lo sviluppo della produttività del lavoro', *L'Industria*.

R. Vernon (1966) 'International Investment and International Trade in the Product Cycle', *Quarterly Journal of Economics*.

R. Vernon (ed.) (1970) *The Technology Factor in International Trade* (New York: NBER).

R. Vernon (1979) 'The product–cycle hypothesis in a new international environment', *Oxford Bulletin of Economics and Statistics*.

W. Walker (1979) *Industrial Innovation and International Trade Performance* (Greenwich, Conn.: JAI Press).

V. M. Walsh, J. F. Townsend, J. F. Achilladelis and C. Freeman (1979) *Trends in Invention and Innovation in the Chemical Industry* Report to the SSRC (Brighton: University of Sussex, SPRU).

S. Weintraub (1958) *An Approach to the Theory of Income Distribution* (Philadelphia: Chilton).

L. T. Wells (1969) 'A Test of Product Cycle Model of International Trade: US Export of Consumer Durables', *Quarterly Journal of Economics*.

L. T. Wells (ed.) (1972) *The Product Life Cycle and International Trade* (Cambridge, Mass.: Harvard University Press).

J. T. Wenders (1967) 'Entry and Monopoly Pricing', *Journal of Political Economy*.

J. T. Wenders (1971) 'Excess Capacity as an Entry Barrier', *Journal of Industrial Economics.*

J. T. Wenders (1971a) 'Collusion and Entry', *Journal of Political Economy.*

O. E. Williamson (1968) 'Wage Rates as a Barrier to Entry', *Quarterly Journal of Economics.*

S. Winter (1964) 'Economic Natural Selection and the Theory of the Firm', *Yale Economic Essays.*

R. Wood (1975) *The Theory of Profits* (Cambridge: Cambridge University Press).

A. Young (1928) 'Increasing Returns and Economic Progress', *Economic Journal.*

SEMICONDUCTOR- AND ELECTRONICS-RELATED WORKS

L. Altman and C. L. Cohen (1977) 'The Gathering Wave of Japanese Technology', *Electronics*, 9 June.

M. Badiul (1979) 'Innovation and International trade: an industry study of the dynamics of comparative advantage', *Kyklos*, 3.

E. Bloch (1981) *Critical Factors Facing the Semiconductor Industry in Turbulent 1980s* (Cupertino, California: Semiconductor Industry Association).

E. Braun and S. MacDonald (1978) *Revolution in Miniature: The History and Impact of the Semiconductor Industry* (Cambridge: Cambridge University Press).

P. Brazzi (1980) *La Politica dell'Elettronica* (Rome: Editori Riuniti).

G. W. Brock (1975) *The US Computer Industry: A Study of Market Power* (Cambridge, Mass.: Ballinger).

DAFSA (1977) *L'Industrie Mondiale des Composants Actifs* (Paris: DAFSA).

DAFSA (1981) *L'Industrie Mondiale des Composants Actifs* (Paris: DAFSA).

Dataquest Inc. (various years) *Market Shares Estimates*, quoted also in US Senate (1978).

G. Dosi (1981a) *Technical Change and Survival: Europe's Semiconductor Industry* (Brighton: University of Sussex, Sussex European Papers).

G. Dosi (1981b) 'Institutions and Markets in High Technology Industries: Government Support for Microelectronics in Europe', in C. Carter (ed.), *Industrial Policies and Innovation* (London: Heinemann).

EDP Industry Report (1978) 'Ten Billion Yen for VLSI Development'.

Electronic Industry Association (1969) *Electronic Industry Yearbook 1969* (Electronic Industry Association).

H. Ergas (1978) *The Role of Information Goods and Services in International Trade* (Paris: OECD).

D. Ernst (1982) 'Restructuring World Industry in a period of crisis – The Role of Innovation, mimeo (Vienna: UNIDO).

W. F. Finan (1975) *The International Transfer of Semiconductor Technology through US-based Firms* (New York: NBER, Working Paper No. 118).

M. Fogiel (1972) *Modern Microelectronics: Basic Principles, Circuit Design, Fabrication Technology* (New York: Research and Education Association).

C. Freeman (1982) 'The Economic Implications of Microelectronics', in

C. D. Cohen (ed.), *Agenda for Britain – 1: Micro Policies – Choices for the 80s* (London: Philip Allen).

C. Freeman, C. J. Harlow and J. K. Fuller (1965) 'Research and Development in Electronics Capital Goods', *National Institute Economic Review*.

T. Golding (1971) 'The Semiconductor Industry in Britain and the United States: a Case Study in Innovation Growth and the Diffusion of Technology', D. Phil. thesis (Brighton: University of Sussex).

R. M. Grant and G. K. Shaw (1979) 'Structural Policies in West Germany and the United Kingdom towards the Computer Industry', mimeo (London: City University).

A. Grove (1981) *The New Industrial Revolution*, (Cupertino, California: Semiconductor Industry Association).

A. J. Harman (1971) *The International computer industry* (Cambridge, Mass.: Harvard University Press).

L. Hartmann Hoddeson (1982) 'The entry of the Quantum Theory of Solids into the Bell Telephone laboratories, 1925–40: A Case-Study of the Industrial Application of Fundamental Science', *Minerva*.

E. von Hippel (1977) 'The Dominant Role of Users in Semiconductor and Electronic Subassembly Process Innovation', *IEEE Transactions on Engineering Management*.

S. Hirsch (1965) 'The United States Electronics Industry in International Trade', *National Institute Economic Review*.

W. C. Hittinger, (1973) 'Metal-oxide Semiconductor Technology', *Scientific American*.

J. Jublin and J. M. Quatrepoint (1976) *French Ordinateur* (Paris: Alain Moreau).

B. G. Katz and A. Phillips (1982) 'Government, Technological Opportunities and the Emergence of the Computer Industry', in Giersch (1982).

H. S. Kleiman (1977) *The US Government Role in the Integrated Circuit Innovation* (Paris: OECD).

J. Linvill and C. Lester Logan (1977) 'Intellectual and Economic Fuel for the Electronics Revolution', *Science*, March 17.

J. H. Lorenzi, G. Gaveau and J. L. Truel (1980) *La filière electronique française dans l'environment international* (Paris: ADECE).

Mackintosh Consultants (1978) *A Profile of the European Semiconductor Manufacturers* (Luton: Mackintosh).

Mackintosh Consultants (various years) *Yearbook of West European Electronics Data* (Luton: Mackintosh).

M. MacLean and H. Rush (1978) *The Impact of Microelectronics on the UK: A Suggested Classification and Illustrative Case Studies* (Brighton: University of Sussex, SPRU Occasional Papers, No. 7).

M. MacLean (1979) *The Impact of the Microelectronics Industry on the Structure of the Canadian Economy* (Montreal: Institute for Research on Public Policies).

D. Mason (1979) 'Factors Affecting the successful development and marketing of innovative semiconductor devices', Ph.D. Thesis (London: Polytechnic of Central London).

D. Mowery (1978) 'The Semiconductor Industry', mimeo (Stanford: Standford University).

J. Müller (1981) 'The Telecommunication industry', mimeo (provisional title) (Brighton: University of Sussex, SERC).

R. R. Nelson (1962) 'The Link between Science and Invention: The Case of the Transistor', in National Bureau of Economic Research (1962).

Nomura Research Institute (1980) *Microchip Revolution in Japan* (Tokyo: Nomura Research Institute).

OECD (1968) *Gaps in Technology: Electronic Components* (Paris: OECD).

OECD (1977) *Impact of Multinational Enterprises on National Scientific and Technological Capabilities. Computer and Data Processing Industry* (Paris: OECD).

O. Pastré and J. Toledano (1975) *Filières d'entrainement et effets externes – Le development de la filière 'Composants Electroniques' et ses effets sur l'emploi* (Chantilly: ADEFI).

E. Sciberras (1977) *Multinational Electronics Companies and National Economic Policies* (Greenwich, Conn.: JAI Press).

E. Sciberras (1980) 'The U.K. Semiconductor Industry', in K. Pavitt (1980a).

E. Sciberras, N. Swords-Isherwood and P. Senker (1978) *Competition, Technical Change and Manpower in Electronic Capital Equipment: A Study of the UK Minicomputer Industry* (Brighton: University of Sussex, SPRU Occasional Paper No. 8).

W. Shockley (1950) *Electrons and Holes in Semiconductors* (New York: Van Nostrand).

W. Shockley (1974) *The Invention of the Transistor – An Example of Creative – Failure Methodology*, National Bureau of Standards Special Publications no. 388.

W. Shockley (1976) 'The Path of Conception of the Junction Transistor', *IEEE Transactions on Electronic Devices.*

P. Stoneman (1976) *Technological Diffusion and the Computer Revolution* (Cambridge: Cambridge University Press).

M. Teubal, N. Arnon and M. Trachtenberg (1976) 'The Performance in the Israeli Electronics Industry: A Case Study of Biomedical Instrumentation', *Research Policy.*

J. E. Tilton, (1971) *International Diffusion of Technology: The Case of Semiconductors* (Washington: Brookings Institution).

J. L. Truel (1980) 'L'Industrie Mondiale des Semi-Conducteurs', Thèse de Doctorat (Paris: Universite de Paris-Dauphine).

US Department of Commerce (1979) *Report on the Semiconductor Industry* (Washington DC: US Government Printing Office).

US International Trade Commission (USITC) (1979) *Competitive Factors Influencing World Trade in Integrated Circuits* (Washington DC: US Government Printing Office).

US Senate (1978) (Committee on Commerce, Science and Transportation) *Governmental Policy and Innovation in the Semiconductor and Computer Industries*, Ninety-fifth Congress, Second Session, 1978.

J. Utterback and A. Murray (1977) *The Influence of Defence Procurement and Sponsorship of Research and Development on the Civilian Electronics Industry* (Cambridge, Mass.: MIT, Center for Policy Alternatives).

D. Webbick (1977) *Staff Report on the Semiconductor Industry. A Survey of*

Structure, Conduct and Performance (Washington: Federal Trade Commission, US Dept. of Commerce).

R. W. Wilson, P. K. Ashton and T. P. Egan (1980) *Innovation, Competition and Government Policy in the Semiconductor Industry* (Lexington, Mass.: D.C. Heath).

Z. P. Zeman (1979) *The Impact of Computer/Communications on Employment in Canada: An Overview of Current OECD Debates* (Montreal: Institute for Research on Public Policies).

J. Zysman (1975) 'Between the Market and the State: Dilemmas of French Policy for the Electronics Industry', *Research Policy*.

Index of Authors and Companies

Index of Subjects

Note: figures in *italic* refer to tables.